The Battle
of Fair Oaks

ALSO BY ROBERT P. BROADWATER
AND FROM MCFARLAND

*Gettysburg as the Generals Remembered It:
Postwar Perspectives of Ten Commanders* (2010)

*General George H. Thomas:
A Biography of the Union's "Rock of Chickamauga"* (2009)

*Did Lincoln and the Republican Party Create the Civil War?
An Argument* (2008)

*Civil War Medal of Honor Recipients:
A Complete Illustrated Record* (2007)

*American Generals of the Revolutionary War:
A Biographical Dictionary* (2007)

*The Battle of Olustee, 1864:
The Final Union Attempt to Seize Florida* (2006)

*Chickamauga, Andersonville, Fort Sumter and Guard Duty at Home:
Four Civil War Diaries by Pennsylvania Soldiers* (edited by; 2006)

*The Battle of Perryville, 1862: Culmination of the
Failed Kentucky Campaign* (2005; softcover 2011)

The Battle of Fair Oaks

Turning Point of McClellan's Peninsula Campaign

ROBERT P. BROADWATER

McFarland & Company, Inc., Publishers
Jefferson, North Carolina, and London

LIBRARY OF CONGRESS CATALOGUING-IN-PUBLICATION DATA

Broadwater, Robert P., 1958–
The battle of Fair Oaks : turning point of McClellan's Peninsula Campaign / Robert P. Broadwater.
p.   cm.
Includes bibliographical references and index.

ISBN 978-0-7864-5878-3
softcover : 50# alkaline paper ∞

1. Fair Oaks, Battle of, Va., 1862.   I. Title.
E473.65.B76   2011   975.5'453 — dc22   2011006970

BRITISH LIBRARY CATALOGUING DATA ARE AVAILABLE

© 2011 Robert P. Broadwater. All rights reserved

No part of this book may be reproduced or transmitted in any form or by any means, electronic or mechanical, including photocopying or recording, or by any information storage and retrieval system, without permission in writing from the publisher.

On the cover: *inset* George B. McClellan, ca. 1870 (Library of Congress); *The Right Wing Falling Back*, 1862, from a sketch by Alfred R. Waud appearing in *Harper's Weekly* (August 16, 1862, p. 516)

Manufactured in the United States of America

McFarland & Company, Inc., Publishers
Box 611, Jefferson, North Carolina 28640
www.mcfarlandpub.com

Table of Contents

Preface	1
Introduction	3
One • The Promise of a New Year	7
Two • "On to Richmond" Once More	23
Three • Up the Peninsula	41
Four • To the Edge of Victory	62
Five • Counteroffensive at Fair Oaks	85
Six • Another Grim Day of Battle	114
Seven • Lee Takes the Offensive	132
Eight • Race for the James	151
Epilogue	172
Appendix 1. The Opposing Forces at Fair Oaks	179
Appendix 2. Casualties at Fair Oaks	182
Appendix 3. The Opposing Forces in the Peninsula Campaign	184
Appendix 4. Casualties of the Opposing Armies in the Peninsula Campaign	192
Appendix 5. Medal of Honor Winners at Fair Oaks	195
Appendix 6. "Kearny at Fair Oaks"	196
Chapter Notes	197
Bibliography	203
Index	209

Preface

The battle of Fair Oaks, also known as Seven Pines, was one of the most interesting and important engagements to take place in the first two years of the war. Its results (or lack thereof, depending upon one's orientation) set the stage for all that was to follow in the eastern campaigns, and had far-reaching consequences in other aspects of the war as well. For instance, a relatively unknown soldier by the name of Henry Wirz was wounded at Fair Oaks. As a result of his wound, he became unfit for further field service and was transferred to duties guarding Union prisoners. Wirz would later become infamous for his cruel administration of the Andersonville prisoner of war camp in Georgia, and would be the only Civil War soldier to be convicted and executed for war crimes.

The overwhelming effect of the battle of Fair Oaks was that it dictated that the war would continue in the East. General George B. McClellan's massive Army of the Potomac failed in its mission to capture Richmond and bring about an early cessation to the conflict. McClellan's bold strategy and innovative tactics had promised great results, but a number of factors combined to prevent those results from ever coming to fruition. The Union army would advance to within sight of Richmond, but it was not able to secure its ultimate objective and capture the Confederate capital.

This campaign witnessed the first grand assemblage of armies to operate in the Eastern Theater of the war. McClellan's army numbered over 100,000 troops, while General Joseph E. Johnston's forces totaled over 80,000. By the time Robert E. Lee launched the offensive that was to become known as the Seven Days Battles, the Confederate army also numbered more than 100,000, and would actually outnumber the Federals. Never before on the American continent had such numbers been gathered together in one place to decide the fate of the nation. In fact, no other campaign in the war would witness more than 200,000 soldiers gathered together in the same place engaged in battle. Casualties in the campaign would also be the greatest the country had yet seen, and would eclipse those from Shiloh, which had shocked and horrified the troops in the field and the people back home. Because the approximately 47,000 losses were spread out over the course of the entire campaign, however, Fair Oaks would never be viewed with the same interest as battles such as Shiloh and Antietam.

This battle was directly responsible for the change in commanders for both principal armies in the East. McClellan was removed from command due to the failure of his campaign to capture Richmond, and Johnston was ultimately replaced by Robert E. Lee because of the wound he sustained on the first day of fighting. But these changes were to be only the beginning of what became an altered command structure for both armies. For the Confederates, top-ranking officers like Gustavus Woodson Smith and John Magruder left out of protest, or because they did not have the confidence of their new commander. In the North, officers like Fitz-John Porter and William B. Franklin found themselves caught up in the whirlwind of government censure aimed against McClellan, and their careers suffered because of their close ties to him.

The campaign witnessed the largest amphibious operation in American military history up to that point. It also saw the emergence of Thaddeus Lowe and the use of hot air balloons to gather military information and intelligence. The Confederates would launch their own observation balloon from a barge, and in a very real sense would create the first aircraft carrier in military history. Machine guns would be used by both sides during the campaign, and though the weapons did not garner the enthusiastic support of either war department, they set the stage for future developments that have made the weapon an integral part of any modern fighting force. An atmospheric condition known as an acoustic shadow occurred on a handful of battlefields in the war, including Fair Oaks, adding to the strange and interesting nature of the battle. This atmospheric phenomenon caused the deflection of sound waves so that the din of fighting was impossible to hear from close proximity, but could be plainly heard miles away from the scene of conflict.

All in all, the battle of Fair Oaks and the Peninsula Campaign are among the most interesting events of the Civil War. More than merely a second failed "On to Richmond" campaign, it set the stage for much that was to follow, and served as the transition from a relatively small and controlled conflict between gentlemen officers and citizen soldiers to an all-out mobilization for total war between two determined and resolved nations. In the following pages, the reader will be introduced to this interesting and important battle that was the culmination of the Peninsula Campaign and the Union effort to capture Richmond and end the war in its first year. Where possible, events will be related through the words of those who actually participated in the fighting so as to provide the reader with a personal glimpse of the action as it unfolded. I hope that the text will give the reader a greater appreciation for this battle that has long been overshadowed by other events of the war, and underreported by historians of the period.

Introduction

In the spring of 1862, most people in the United States were still of the opinion that the Civil War would be a short and easily won contest. In the South, there were critics who felt that the Confederacy had missed a golden opportunity to end the war following the battle of Manassas, when General Joseph E. Johnston failed to pursue the defeated Union forces and capture Washington. In the Eastern Theater, it was anticipated that this missed chance would be redeemed in the next campaign, and that Johnston would make amends for his previous failure by thoroughly thrashing the new Federal army that would be sent against him in the national government's attempt to capture Richmond. In reality, Johnston's failure to follow up the Manassas victory existed only in the minds of some people in the Confederate government and with civilians on the home front. Though the Yankees had been routed from that field, the Rebel victors were also thoroughly disorganized and fought-out following the conclusion of the battle, and were in serious need of rest and refitting before Johnston could even contemplate a move against Washington. The possible end of the war was not nearly as attainable at this time, as was commonly felt by the people of the South. In the North, the prevailing sentiment was that the Federal army had been badly handled in the Manassas Campaign, and the defeat had been attributed to poor leadership. General Irvin McDowell had been replaced by Major General George B. McClellan, a charismatic young officer with a flair for organization and training who was quickly styled the "Young Napoleon" by the Northern press. McClellan revitalized the Union army, and his attention to training transformed the troops from the raw recruits that they had been in 1861 into an army of disciplined soldiers. The commander imbued the army with an élan, a fighting spirit, that would characterize it for the remainder of the war. He transformed it from an armed mob into a spit-and-polish military organization, and, in the process, earned the love and admiration of the men in the ranks, who took justifiable pride in their accomplishments as soldiers.

McClellan not only created the Northern army that would face the Confederates in the coming campaign, he also gave it its identity. McClellan named it the Army of the Potomac, a title it would retain for the duration of the war, and a name that would become immortal in the annals of military history. Indeed, much had changed in the eight short months since McDowell had marched his army out from Washington in the first "On to Richmond" campaign. Most people, in and out of the military, were not yet aware that the war had become infinitely larger, even though there had been precious little activity in the principal corridor between the opposing capital cities. As both sides prepared for the final showdown, the size of the armies swelled to proportions that would dwarf the forces that had initiated the fighting. In the Confederate Army, troop totals reached more than 80,000 men, while the

Army of the Potomac grew to over 100,000 troops. A new era of warfare was about to emerge on the American continent, one that would see battles to rival the greatest epic struggles of the Old World.

The sensibilities of the nation would be shaken in April of 1862, when the Western armies came together in the bloodbath that was Shiloh. To Americans accustomed to the relatively small-scale battles that had taken place during the Revolution, the War of 1812, and the Mexican American Wars, the battle of Manassas had been a great conflict, and the casualties suffered on that field had been felt to be extreme. Shiloh was the first truly great battle to take place in the war, the first introduction to the horrors that would come to epitomize the struggle to reunite the nation. To a civilian populace who felt that the 4,704 casualties from Manassas were severe, the 24,272 suffered at Shiloh left them dazed and numb.[1] No one, on either side, had imagined that the war could be so brutal, or that its cost could be so high. The nation was simply not prepared to view casualty reports so numerous they could fill a newspaper, and in April of 1862, Shiloh was viewed to be the great battle of the war. Few contemplated that any battle could surpass it in savagery, or that any would be as costly. It was commonly stated in the Confederacy that the South never smiled again after Shiloh. However, Shiloh was to be but the first of an ever growing list of major battles, and by the time the war was finished, a large number would eclipse it for both cost and savagery. The innocence of the nation was to be lost. Never again would the war be viewed as a great pageantry, a spectator event. Never again would civilians plan picnics to watch the fighting, as they had at Manassas. The nation was about to embark in earnest on a voyage that would visit the cruel horror of civil war upon all of its residents, but in the spring of 1862, that reality was still to be discovered. Much was to change in 1862, including the reputations of many of the officers serving in the opposing armies. George G. Meade, Winfield S. Hancock, George Armstrong Custer, John Bell Hood, A.P. Hill, and many more were still relatively unknown to the general populace, and were yet to achieve the fame that now attaches itself to their names. Robert E. Lee was considered by many in the South to be a disappointment following his failed campaign in western Virginia, and he had spent the months since its conclusion as a military advisor to Jefferson Davis, serving in a staff capacity and not leading troops in the field.

In the North, it was felt that a stunning victory in the East, following closely on the heels of the Shiloh triumph, would seal the fate of the Confederacy and end the war. Surely McClellan's mighty host could crush the Rebel army and capture Richmond in one fell swoop. The South, for its part, was reeling from the reverses of its Western army, but it was still confident that the issue would be decided in the East, where the Army of Northern Virginia had yet to be bested. A second victory, like the one at Manassas, must certainly convince the Yankees that they could not defeat the new Confederacy, that the National government could not coerce the South to return to the Union by force of arms. Both sides were sure that one more grand victory would tip the scales in their favor, and that this could still be a short and easy war.

In the spring of 1862, as McClellan transported his legions to the Virginia Peninsula, each side girded itself for the massive struggle they were sure would decide the war once and for all. It was not to be the first great campaign in the war — Shiloh already claimed that honor. It was, however, to be the first great clash of armies to take place in the East, and by the time it was over some 47,000 casualties would be sustained. The campaign would see the Union army come very close to its objective, and march to the very outskirts of Richmond before the battle of Fair Oaks reversed the Federal fortunes and turned what appeared to be a certain victory into another embarrassing defeat in the East. It would also witness a changing of the guard, and the emergence of Robert E. Lee as commander of the Army of Northern Virginia. It has been said that the shot that wounded Joseph E. Johnston was one of the most fortuitous incidents of the war for the Confederacy, as it set the stage for Lee to be appointed to army command in his stead. It is certain that Lee is the commander who became universally associated with that army, and the leader under whom it earned undying fame and glory. Northern leadership would likewise be altered as a result of Fair Oaks and the Peninsula Campaign. McClellan's failure to capture Richmond would lead to his dismissal as commander of the army he had been so instrumental in forming and training. He would be temporarily reinstated to a command position during the Antietam Campaign, to reorganize and refit the army after its demoralizing defeat at 2nd Manassas, and would be the victor of the battles fought at South Mountain and Antietam, only to be relieved a second time, and left without a command for the remainder of the war. The Confederacy had found their field commander for the principal Confederate army in the East as a result of Fair Oaks and the Peninsula Campaign. The North began a search that went from McClellan to John Pope, from Pope to Ambrose Burnsides, from Burnsides to Joseph Hooker, and from Hooker to George Meade, all in the space of little less than a year.

In the following pages, the reader will learn of this first great campaign in the East, this first meeting of giants. Much of the story will be told in the words of the participants, the Union and Confederate soldiers who were there to witness the fighting. The focus of this work will be upon the pivotal battle of Fair Oaks, or Seven Pines, the decisive engagement of campaign, but the events that led up to that battle, as well as the consequences that followed, will also be related, so that the reader may acquire an understanding of how this battle came about, and the repercussions that followed it. The Peninsula Campaign would prove to be one of the costliest in the entire war, as more soldiers fell in May and June of 1862 than had been in either army at Manassas. Even so, the Peninsula Campaign has been overshadowed in history by such battles as Gettysburg, Vicksburg, Chickamauga, Antietam, the Wilderness, and more. This is due in part to the fact that the fighting in the campaign was spread out over a period of almost two months. It can also be traced to the fact that 1862 was witness to numerous great battles in the East: 2nd Manassas, Antietam, and Fredericksburg. Whatever the reasons, the Peninsula Campaign has never attained the overall stature of some of the other large battles and campaigns of the war, and has been relegated, by history, to a second tier of importance in the story of the Civil War. The purpose of this work is an attempt to elevate the Peninsula Campaign, specifically the battle of Fair Oaks, to its proper place in the history of the war, and to pay honor to the men on both sides who made the ultimate sacrifice in writing this chapter of that great conflict. It was the wind that seeded the whirlwind to follow, the end of national innocence, and it ushered in the realization that this was to be a long and bitter struggle that was to be won only through grit, determination, sacrifice, and endurance.

Almost 50 years after the guns had fallen silent at Fair Oaks, Corporal Luther Dickey, of the 103rd Pennsylvania Infantry, voiced the opinion of many of his compatriots when he complained of the diminished status the battle had been relegated to in the history of the war. "No battle of the Civil War has been more misrepresented than the battle of (Seven Pines) ... yet, when the final word is written of the battles between the North and South, the battle which occurred May 31, 1862, will head the list of the decisive contests of the Civil War...."[2] Dickey objected to the fact that Fair Oaks, or Seven Pines, was largely viewed as a minor affair, fought by only a few thousand troops, and providing no decisive results to the outcome of the war. As a veteran of that bloody field, Dickey knew that Fair Oaks was the first significant battle between the Army of the Potomac and the Army of Northern Virginia, fought in the closest proximity to the Confederate capital of any battle of the war. He realized that the savagery of the fighting there equaled that of any other major battle fought in the war, and knew that it was possibly the most decisive campaign to take place during the national struggle, as its results dictated that the war would not end in the spring of 1862. Instead, the bloodshed would continue for three more years, and hundreds of thousands of Americans would pay with their lives for the missed opportunities of the Peninsula Campaign.

ONE

The Promise of a New Year

The year 1862 would be a witness to horror and bloodshed on a scale that would shock and numb the citizens of the nation, both North and South. Before the year was ended, both nations would come to realize that this war was to be no glorious adventure. The euphoria that had induced so many young men to rush to their local enlistment centers in the early days of the war would be replaced by grim determination as both sides came to terms with the fact that this conflict would be neither short in its duration, nor slight in its cost. Eighteen sixty-two would witness the death-knell of the world's wooden navies, the employment of aeronautical balloons and telegraph lines on the battlefield, and the introduction of several machine guns into military service. The names of Shiloh, Antietam, and Fredericksburg would come to symbolize the savagery of the struggle. Men like Robert E. Lee, Ulysses S. Grant, and J.E.B. Stuart would, through their actions, attain everlasting fame, while others like George B. McClellan, Joseph E. Johnston, and Ambrose Burnside would fall from grace. But all of this was still in the future as the new year was ushered in with hope and promise on both sides. The Confederate army in the East was encamped within a menacing proximity to Washington, D.C., and Southern leaders hoped to follow up their success at 1st Manassas the previous year, by capturing the Union capital and ending the war in the spring campaign. For the Union's part, embarrassment over the loss at Manassas had been replaced by a sense of pride and accomplishment brought about by the magnificent army that was being organized and trained in the capital city. The newly named Army of the Potomac was taking shape, and though it was yet to emblazon its name on the pages of history, even a casual observer could see that the rag-tag volunteers who had marched forth to capture Richmond the previous year were being molded into a formidable military force that would rival the finest armies of Europe, a martial instrument capable of imposing the will of the National Government upon their wayward brethren of the South.

Major General George Britton McClellan was responsible for much of the hope and confidence that had been restored to the people of the Union. Northern newspapers had proclaimed him the "Young Napoleon" of the war, and heralded his command of the Union's principal army in the East with epithets usually reserved for leaders who had already attained great victories—not for commanders who were largely untested and unproven. To be sure, McClellan was responsible for providing the North its one bright spot in the East in the summer of 1861, when his Rich Mountain Campaign enabled the Union to maintain control of the Baltimore & Ohio Railroad and most of the mountainous region of the Old Dominion State that would later become West Virginia. In reality, Rich Mountain was a minor affair, and would be viewed as only a skirmish later in the war, but the achievement brought forth hearty congratulations from his military and civilian superiors. General Winfield Scott wrote him that "the Cabinet, including the President, are charmed with your activity, valor, and consequent successes." The aging hero of the Mexican-American War offered the opinion that McClellan would sweep all the Rebels from western Virginia, but added that he did "not mean to precipitate" McClellan, "as you are fast enough."[1] A strange beginning indeed for a general who was to be later accused of dragging his feet and being unwilling to fight.

George B. McClellan was born in Philadelphia, Pennsylvania, on December 3, 1826, into an influential and affluent family. His early education included local preparatory schools and the University of Pennsylvania, before accepting an appointment to West Point in 1842. He graduated from the academy in 1846 with a ranking of second in his class of 59, and was assigned as a second lieutenant to the elite Corps of Engineers. During the Mexican-American War, he was attached to General Winfield Scott's army, where his skillful and daring accomplishment of the duties assigned to him resulted in brevet promotions to first lieutenant and captain. Following the end of the war, McClellan spent three years as an instructor at West Point. He did engineering duty at Fort Delaware and during Captain Randolph Marcy's Red River Expedition, and participated in several surveys to find a possible route for a transcontinental railroad. He was selected to be an official observer to the Crimean War, and in 1855 was appointed captain of the newly created 1st United States Cavalry Regiment. His reputation was further enhanced when he translated the French bayonet manual into English, developed a new cavalry saddle that bore his name, and designed the shelter tents that would become known as pup tents to the soldiers he would later lead in the Civil War. In 1857, McClellan resigned his commission to become chief engineer of the Illinois Central Railroad. His courtship of Ellen Marcy, daughter of his commander in the Red River exploration, was, in large part, the reason for his leaving the military. Ellen's father was well aware of the slow rate of promotion in the army, and wanted a life for his daughter that was better than could be had on a junior officer's pay. McClellan's position with the railroad would provide an income suitable for respectable existence, and would mean that the couple would be able to embark on a stable life, free from the constant transfers and hardships of army service. This stability was to be realized for only four years, however, as McClellan offered his services to the Union at the outbreak of hostilities in 1861. On April 23, 1861, William Dennison, governor of Ohio, commissioned McClellan a major general in the militia, and gave him command of all the state's forces. His abilities as an organizer and administrator quickly brought him to the attention of President Lincoln, and led to his appointment as a major general in the regular army three weeks later. The date of his commission preceded all other major generals in the army, excepting Winfield Scott, and meant that by virtue of seniority, he was second-in-command in the Union army.[2]

Major General Irvin McDowell's defeat at the battle of 1st Manassas left many people in the North clamoring for his replacement in command of the army, and in August, McClellan was summoned east to make the change. McClellan arrived in Washington five days after the disaster at Manassas (or Bull Run, as it was called in the North), and immediately set to work to bring order and discipline to the defeated and demoralized army. In November, upon the retirement of General Scott, he was appointed general-in-chief of the Union armies.[3] At 35 years of age, McClellan was young, dashing, and presented the ideal embodiment of a military professional. His skills in administration and organization bore quick results, and the program of training he instituted brought discipline and a sense of accom-

Above: General Irvin McDowell. The Confederate victory at the battle of Manassas had given heart to the South and caused the North to demand McDowell's removal from command of the principal Union army in the east. *Right:* General George B. McClellan. After a successful campaign in the mountains of western Virginia, McClellan became the most celebrated general in the Union army and was called east by President Lincoln to assume command of the Federal forces around Washington (Military History Institute, United States Army War College).

plishment to the men in the ranks, and endeared McClellan to the common soldiers under his command.

This was not accomplished by pampering or indulging the soldiers under his command. Just the opposite was true. McClellan came down hard on any and all soldiers who did not perform their duties. When the 2nd Maine Infantry refused to turn out one morning, he sent in the provost guard to deal with the situation. The ringleaders of the regiment were arrested, and 63 of them were sent to Fort Jefferson, in the Dry Tortugas, as prisoners. When the 79th New York "Highlanders" refused orders to strike tents and move to another campsite, Regular Army artillery was ordered to surround their campsite, guns loaded with canister. The members of the 79th were disarmed, and 35 of their leaders were hauled off in chains. The colors of the regiment were confiscated on the grounds that the men had disgraced them. McClellan was extremely solicitous of his men, but he demanded that they conduct themselves as soldiers. A few weeks later, when the 79th New York distinguished itself in a minor affair with the enemy, McClellan sent their flags back to them. "We cheered him heartily, feeling that Little Mac was, after all, our friend," wrote one member of the regiment.[4] The commanding general dispensed a sort of tough love that challenged the troops to achieve more than they thought themselves capable of, and once they met the challenge, they were filled with pride in themselves as solders and men. For this, they loved McClellan with the adoration a child comes to know when he realizes that his father had his best interests in mind when he was being stern and strict.

McClellan's first order of business was to reorganize McDowell's army, which he soon named the Army of the Potomac, and to put it in fighting trim to undertake its role in putting down the rebellion. Though a great number of the men who had fought at Manassas had left the service due to the expiration of their 90-day enlistments, they had been replaced by a new wave of recruits who sought to avenge the dishonor to Union arms that had taken place on that field. The influx of new enlistees brought renewed hope and confidence to those in the military, as well as the folks at home, but it also brought about the first rift between McClellan and his superiors. The Young Napoleon was already under strong pressure to mount another "On to Richmond" Campaign, with all possible dispatch, but the ever-increasing strength of the Army of the Potomac served to slow down the process rather than accelerate it. The problem was that all of the newly formed regiments arrived at Washington completely void of any proper military training or discipline. McClellan was a meticulous planner who refused to be goaded into action before the army was ready. Knowing that it was easier to defend a position than attack it, he realized that his army would have to be sufficiently trained and schooled to avoid the same sort of debacle that had befallen McDowell, and he was determined not to move until his raw troops had been converted into legitimate soldiers.

In response to the prodding he received to initiate a campaign, McClellan advised that the new recruits be used as replacements for the existing units. This would bring those units up to full strength again, and it would also facilitate a much quicker training process for the army. Recruits could be assimilated into the ranks, where their training would be speedily accomplished by the veterans who surrounded them. This mixture of veterans and new recruits would also provide stability in the ranks, and would make the army stronger from top to bottom, ensuring that there would be no totally green and untried regiments on the field when the enemy was finally joined in battle. McClellan's superiors rejected this plan, largely for political reasons. During the Civil War, the individual states were responsible for raising troops who would be turned over to the Federal government for national service. Built into this system was a great deal of political patronage when it came to appointing officers for the newly created regiments. When one considers that a great deal of the recruiting was done by local and regional individuals whose personal influence was responsible for inducing men to enlist, it can easily be seen why the government was loath to adopt McClellan's suggestion. Many of the regiments were raised by men who expected to be named commander of the newly formed units, with the subordinate officer positions going to men who had assisted them in raising the regiments. The administration was afraid that enlistments would lessen appreciably if this inducement were taken away. If the reward of rank and notoriety were stripped from them, why would prominent men invest the time, effort, and money to recruit volunteers for the army? McClellan was therefore forced to deal with a situation that provided him with numbers of men, but also ensured that the units would be perfectly green, and in need of extensive training and discipline.

The process of turning recruits into soldiers took time — time that many in the government were not willing to grant. Cries began to arise for another offensive to be mounted before 1861 came to a close, but McClellan simply ignored the clamor and continued to drill his men. By the end of October, McClellan's army had swelled to some 76,000 men—approximately double the size of the force McDowell had commanded. In a written response to the mounting pressure to march this army out in search of the foe, McClellan stated:

> The nation feels, & I share the feeling, that the Army of the Potomac holds the fate of the country in its hands. The stake is so vast, the issue so momentous, & the effect of the next battle will be so important throughout the future as well as the present, that I continue to urge, as I have ever done since I entered upon the command of this army, upon the Govt to devote its energies & its available resources towards increasing the numbers & efficiencies of the Army on which its salvation depends."[5]

Even those who were most vocal in denouncing McClellan's refusal to mount an early campaign against the Confederates were forced to admit that the job he had done in transforming the Union army into a finely tuned fighting machine had been incredible. Captain William Glazier noted the "wonderful transformation which he wrought with the disordered mass of raw recruits constituting the Army of the Potomac," stating that they "soon assumed shape under the effects of his superior discipline, and gained a reputation as a magnificent body of soldiery." In his efforts to organize and train the Army of the Potomac, Glazier felt that McClellan displayed "rare genius and great qualities as a general."[6] A Connecticut volunteer proudly noted the transformation that McClellan had brought about in turning the raw recruits into an efficient body of trained soldiers: "Troops, tents, the frequent thunder of guns practicing, lines of heavy baggage wagons, at reveille and tattoo the air filled with the near and distant roll of drums and the notes of innumerable bugles—all the indications of an immense army, and yet no crowding, no rabble."[7]

A second reason for McClellan's hesitance to bring about an early confrontation with the enemy resulted from faulty intelligence he was receiving from the network of spies and detectives that had been established to provide critical information concerning the make-up and intentions of the Confederate army. Allan Pinkerton, the most renowned detective in the country, had been appointed to direct these covert operations, many of which were being conducted by the employees of his own Pinkerton Detective Agency. McClellan was advised that the Confederate army that General Joseph E. Johnston commanded in Virginia numbered about 160,000 men, with 175 to 200 pieces of artillery, placed in strong defensive positions. Pinkerton's intelligence was faulty, however, and credited the Rebels with almost twice the number of troops Johnston could actually put in the field to contest an advance by the Federal army. Pinkerton's sources included an operative who claimed to have had dinner with Jefferson Davis, Judah P. Benjamin, and other top Confederate officials, as well as interviews with 17 black contrabands and fugitives.[8] The quality of the intelligence was at best questionable, but Pinkerton was convinced of its validity. McClellan took the numbers to heart as well, and they greatly affected his plans for the employment of the Union armies. He envisioned a concerted effort by all of the various Federal field forces, aimed at pinning down the Confederates and allowing the Union to achieve superiority of numbers in their desired theaters of operation. Naturally, McClellan viewed the Army of the Potomac to be the leading player in any strategy, and felt that its campaign would hold the key to ultimate victory. The other armies would be used to perform supporting roles that would facilitate the Army of the Potomac in accomplishing its goals. The significant feature here is that McClellan led the way in planning the strategy that would eventually be used to win the war for the North. For two years, following his dismissal from the army, the various Union generals acted independently of one another in conducting their campaigns. The

Confederates were permitted to concentrate forces in a threatened area while going on the defensive in other theaters against an idle enemy that was not yet ready to take the offensive. The advantage of interior lines, and the fact that the Union armies were not being used in conjunction with one another, allowed the Confederacy to largely offset the vast numerical superiority that the Union could have brought to bear against it. When General Ulysses S. Grant adopted his strategy for the spring campaign of 1864, he was effectively reinstating the blueprint that McClellan had developed two years earlier. Enjoying the full support of the government, Grant was able to coordinate the activities of the various armies so that the Confederates were under almost constant pressure from all sides, and were not able to shift forces to meet individual challenges, as they had in the past.

Pinkerton's estimates of Confederate strength in Virginia caused McClellan to balk at any thought of an overland movement from Washington toward the Confederate capital. He was not about to repeat the errors he judged General McDowell to have made, and fight the enemy on ground of their own choosing in a strong defensive line. The exaggeration of Joe Johnston's strength pushed McClellan to come up with a plan of operations that would, according to the faulty intelligence, enable him to campaign against a portion of the Confederate forces with numerical superiority. The resulting strategy came to be known as the Urbanna Plan, a combined operation that was to include most of the Federal forces in the nation. Operations along the Mississippi River would be launched to confuse the Confederates and keep them guessing as to what McClellan's real intentions might be. Major General Don Carlos Buell and Major General Henry W. Halleck were to pin down the enemy in Tennessee and Kentucky, and prevent any reinforcements being sent from that theater to Virginia. Major General Ambrose Burnside, in cooperation with the Navy, was to execute an amphibious landing on the coast of North Carolina, preparatory to marching inland, with his final destination being Knoxville, Tennessee. With the Confederates thus occupied, McClellan should be free to launch his main thrust, with the Army of the Potomac, against Richmond and Joseph E. Johnston's Army of Northern Virginia. McClellan hoped that his multi-pronged strategy would keep the Confederates off-balance, and would force them to guard against threats from numerous directions. If the strategy was successful, Johnston would be unable to utilize his supposed numerical superiority to its fullest capacity when the Army of the Potomac marched, and McClellan might be able to concentrate a superior force at the point of attack. At least that is the way the Union commander saw it.

In a letter to Secretary of War Edwin Stanton, dated February 3, 1862, McClellan outlined his views on the proposed campaign. He began by describing the state of affairs in Washington when he assumed command of the army, stressing that he found no army to command, only "a mere collection of regiments cowering on the banks of the Potomac, some perfectly raw, others dispirited by the recent defeat." The Federal capital virtually invited attack by the Confederates, and "nothing whatever had been undertaken to defend the avenues to the city on the northern side of the Potomac." After chronicling his efforts to organize the army and provide for the defense of Washington, he complained, "In the earliest papers I submitted to the President I asked for an effective and moveable force far exceeding the aggregate now on the banks of the Potomac. I have not the force I asked for." Once he had cited his successes and pointed out that all that had been accomplished had been done with a force far below that which he had requested, McClellan was ready to discuss future operations for the army and disclose his thoughts on the best way in which to campaign against the Confederates.

I have ever regarded our true policy as being that of fully preparing ourselves, and then seeking for the most decisive results. I do not wish to waste life in useless battles, but prefer to strike at the heart.

Two bases of operations seem to present themselves for the advance of the Army of the Potomac:

1st. That of Washington — its present position — involving a direct attack on the entrenched positions of the enemy at Centreville, Manassas, etc., or else a movement to turn one or both flanks of those positions, or a combination of the two plans.

The relative force of the two armies will not justify an attack on both flanks; an attack on his left flank alone involves a long line of wagon communication, and cannot prevent him from collecting for the decisive battle all the detachments now on his extreme right and left.

Should we attack his right flank by the line of the Occoquan and a crossing of the Potomac below that river and near his batteries, we could perhaps prevent the junction of the enemy's right with his centre (we might destroy the former); we would remove the obstructions to the navigation of the Potomac, reduce the length of wagon transportation by establishing new depots at the nearest points of the Potomac, and strike more directly his main railway communication.

The fords of the Occoquan below the mouth of the Bull Run are watched by the rebels; batteries are said to be placed on the heights in the rear (concealed by the woods), and the arrangement of his troops is such that he can oppose considerable resistance to a passage of that stream. Information has just been received to the effect that the enemy are entrenching a line of heights extending from the vicinity of Sangster's (Union Mills) towards Evansport. Early in January Sprigg's ford was occupied by General Rhodes with 3,600 men and eight (8) guns; there are strong reasons for believing that Davis's ford is occupied. These circumstances indicate or prove that the enemy anticipates the movement in question, and is prepared to resist it. Assuming for the present that this operation is determined upon, it may be well to examine briefly its probable progress. In the present state of affairs our column (for the movement of so large a force must be made in several columns, at least five or six) can reach the Accotink without danger; during the march thence to the Occoquan our right flank becomes exposed to an attack from Fairfax Station, Sangster's, and Union Mills. This danger must be met by occupying in some force either the first-named places, or, better, the point of junction of the roads leading thence to the village of Occoquan; this occupation must be continued so long as we continue to draw supplies by the roads from this city, or until a battle is won.

The crossing of the Occoquan should be made at all fords from Wolf's Run to the mouth, the points of crossing not being necessarily confined to the fords themselves. Should the enemy occupy this line in force we must, with what assistance the flotilla can be afforded, endeavor to force the passage near the mouth, thus forcing the enemy to abandon the whole line or be taken in flank himself.

Having gained the line of the Occoquan, it would be necessary to throw a column by the shortest route to Dumfries, partly to force the enemy to abandon his batteries on the Potomac, partly to cover our left flank against an attack from the direction of Acquia, and, lastly, to establish our communications with the river by the best roads, and thus give us new depots. The enemy would by this time have occupied the line of the Occoquan above Bull Run, holding Brentsville in force, and perhaps extending his lines somewhat further to the southwest.

Our next step would then be to prevent the enemy from crossing the Occoquan between Bull Run and Broad Run, to fall upon our right flank while moving on Brentsville. This might be effected by occupying Bacon Race Church and the cross-roads near the mouth of Bull Run, or still more effectually by moving to the fords themselves and preventing him from debouching on our side.

These operations would probably be resisted, and it would require some time to effect them, as, nearly at the same time as possible, we should gain the fords necessary to our purposes above Broad Run. Having secured our right flank, it would become necessary to carry Brentsville at any cost, for we could not leave it between the right flank and the main body. The final movement on the railroad must be determined by circumstances existing at the time.

This brief sketch brings out in bold relief the great advantage possessed by the enemy in the strong central position he occupies, with roads diverging in every direction, and a strong line of defence enabling him to remain on the defensive with a small force on one flank, while he concentrates everything on the other for a decisive action.

Should we place a portion of our force in front of Centreville, while the rest crosses the Occoquan, we commit the error of dividing our army by a very difficult obstacle, and by a distance too great to enable the two parts to support each other, should either be attacked by the masses of the enemy while the other is held in check.

I should perhaps have dwelt more decidedly on the fact that the force left near Sangster's must be allowed to remain somewhere on that side of the Occoquan until the decisive battle is over, so as to cover our retreat in the event of disaster, unless it should be decided to select and entrench a new base somewhere near Dumfries—a proceeding involving much time.

After the passage of the Occoquan by the main army this covering force could be drawn into a more central and less exposed position—say Brimstone Hill or nearer the Occoquan. In this latitude the weather will for a considerable period be very uncertain, and a movement commenced in force on roads in tolerably firm condition will be liable, almost certain, to be much delayed by rains and snow. It will, therefore, be next to impossible to surprise the enemy or take him at a disadvantage by rapid manoeuvres. Our slow progress will enable him to divine our purposes and take his measures accordingly. The probability is, from the best information we possess, that the enemy has improved the roads leading to his lines of defence, while we have to work as we advance.

Bearing in mind what has been said, and the present unprecedented and impassable condition of the roads, it will be evident that no precise period can be fixed upon for the movement on this line. Nor can its duration be closely calculated; it seems certain that many weeks may elapse before it is possible to commence the march. Assuming the success of this operation, and the defeat of the enemy as certain, the question at once arises as to the importance of the results gained. I think these results would be confined to the possession of the field of battle, the evacuation of the line of the upper Potomac by the enemy, and the moral effect of the victory—important results, it is true, but not decisive of the war, nor securing the destruction of the enemy's main army, for he could fall back upon other positions and fight us again and again, should the condition of his troops permit. If he is in no condition to fight us again out of the range of the entrenchments at Richmond, we would find it a very difficult and tedious matter to follow him up there, for he would destroy his railroad bridges and otherwise impede our progress through a region where the roads are as bad as they well can be, and we would probably find ourselves forced at last to change the whole theatre of war, or to seek a shorter land route to Richmond, with a smaller available force and at an expenditure of much more time, than were we to adopt the short line at once. We would also have forced the enemy to concentrate his forces and perfect his defensive measures at the very points where it is desirable to strike him when least prepared.

2d. The second base of operations available for the Army of the Potomac is that of the lower Chesapeake bay, which affords the shortest possible land route to Richmond and strikes directly at the heart of the enemy's power in the east.

The roads in that region are passable at all seasons of the year.

The country now alluded to is much more favorable for offensive operations than that in front of Washington (which is very unfavorable); much more level, more cleared land, the woods less dense, the soil more sandy, and the spring some two or three weeks earlier. A movement in force on that line obliges the enemy to abandon his entrenched position at Manassas in order to hasten to cover Richmond and Norfolk. He must do this; for should he permit us to occupy Richmond his destruction can be averted only by entirely defeating us in a battle in which he must be the assailant. This movement, if successful, gives us the capital, the communications, the supplies of the rebels; Norfolk would fall; all the waters of the Chesapeake would be ours; all Virginia would be in our power, and the enemy forced to abandon Tennessee and North Carolina. The alternative presented to the enemy would be, to beat us in a position selected by ourselves, disperse, or pass between the Caudine Forks.

Should we be beaten in a battle we have a perfectly secure retreat down the Peninsula upon Fort Monroe, with our flanks perfectly covered by the fleet.

During the whole movement our left flank is covered by the water. Our right is secure, for the reason that the enemy is too distant to reach it in time; he can only oppose us in front. We bring our fleet into full play.

After a successful battle our position would be—Burnside forming our left; Norfolk held securely; our centre connecting Burnside with Buell, both by Raleigh and Lynchburg; Buell in Eastern Tennessee and North Alabama; Halleck at Nashville and Memphis.

The next movement would be to connect Sherman on the left by reducing Wilmington and Charleston; to advance our centre into South Carolina and Georgia; to push Buell either towards Montgomery or to unite with the main army in Georgia; to throw Halleck southward to meet the naval expedition from New Orleans.

We should then be in a condition to reduce at our leisure all the Southern seaports; to occupy all the avenues of communication; to use the greatest outlet of the Mississippi; to re-establish our government and arms in Arkansas, Louisiana, and Texas; to force the slaves to labor for our subsistence instead of that of the rebels; to bid defiance to all foreign interference. Such is the object I have ever had in view; this is the general plan which I hope to accomplish.

For many months I have labored to prepare the Army of the Potomac to play its part in the programme; from the day when I was placed in command of all our armies I have exerted myself to place all the other armies in such a condition that they, too, could perform their allotted duties.

Should it be determined to operate from the lower Chesapeake, the point of landing which promises the most brilliant result is Urbanna, on the lower Rappahannock. This point is easily reached by vessels of heavy draught; it is neither occupied nor observed by the enemy; it is but one march from West Point, the key of that region, and thence but two marches to Richmond. A rapid movement from Urbanna would probably cut off Magruder in the Peninsula and enable us to occupy Richmond before it could be strongly reinforced. Should we fail in that we could, with the co-operation of the navy, cross the James and throw ourselves in rear of Richmond, thus forcing the enemy to come out and attack us, for his position would be untenable with us on the southern bank of the river.[9]

What McClellan proposed was to land his army at Urbanna, Virginia, on the Rappahannock River. This would place his expeditionary force behind Johnston's army at Centreville and Manassas, northeast of Richmond. From this point, he would march westward, forcing Johnston to give up his prepared positions to march in defense of the Confederate capital. This Confederate withdrawal would alleviate the threat on Washington, and would allow the Federals to fight the decisive battles of the campaign on ground of their choosing. The Mattapony and Pamunkey Rivers would present the only natural obstacles along the Federal's line of march, but McClellan was sure that they could easily be crossed. From Urbanna, the Federal forces would have to march only about 50 miles to reach Richmond. The reduction of distance to be covered versus the overland route was another substantial merit for adoption of the plan, as McClellan saw it.

This letter had been written in response to a directive from President Lincoln that an offensive be undertaken by the Army of the Potomac by Washington's birthday. McClellan protested that his army was not yet ready to make such a movement, but his warnings against a premature initiation were largely falling on deaf ears. Edwin Stanton had been a staunch supporter of McClellan prior to becoming secretary of war. Following his appointment to that post, he had aligned himself with the radical members of the Committee on the Conduct of the War in calling for an immediate advance of the army on Richmond. Lincoln had proven to be the general's greatest ally for most of 1861, but by the end of the year, even he had become frustrated with what he viewed to be unnecessary delays. A rift had been developing between the administration and its leading general, one that would have dire consequences in the upcoming campaign. For McClellan's part, the prodding and questioning coming from the civil sector was viewed as interference from politicians who had little or no understanding of military organization or operations. He felt as if petty political intrigue was hampering his mission of defeating the Confederate armies and restoring the Southern states to the Union. Confident in his own abilities, he was prone to showing irritation, or even disdain, for what he saw to be meddling politicians who constantly required him to explain his actions and his future plans. So far as McClellan was concerned, the nation had entrusted him with the responsibility of saving the Union, and he should be allowed to accomplish that mission unfettered by the restraints of civil authority. Though an ardent supporter of Union, he was also a lifelong Democrat, and his dealing with the incumbent administration smacked of an attitude that he had been called upon to save the nation from the calamity the Republicans had brought upon it. McClellan saw the role of the administration as being supportive in nature, not as the guiding influence of the events that were to transpire. In his mind, the government should be doing all in its power to provide the men and equipment he deemed necessary to mounting a successful campaign. These untrained and inexperienced civilians should not be dictating military strategy or interfering in the prosecution of that strategy once the army took to the field. To his mind, the present emergency had been brought to a head by the very men who were now trying to dictate military policy. To McClellan, politicians had pushed the country into a military crisis, and now they should step aside and allow military professionals to clean up the mess they had made. What resulted was the appearance of arrogance, bred from both confidence and self righteousness, that the government was not ready, or willing, to accept. The "Young Napoleon" seemed to be setting himself up as superior to the government he was attempting to save. McClellan even started to state that he was following a power greater than that of the government. He was coming to see his assignment as the military leader of the nation's forces as a sort of divine destiny, and he was viewing himself as the anointed savoir of his country.

Initially, Lincoln had endured McClellan's elitist attitude without complaint. In the wake of Manassas, the National forces had been in an alarming state of disarray, and McClellan had unquestionably brought order out of chaos, and had created an army that was not only capable of dealing with the Confederates, but was seen to be the equal of the best that Europe could offer. Lincoln was gratified by the efforts of his young general, and his expertise in organization, administration, and discipline had earned him temporary carte blanche with the government. However, as the months passed by with no indication that McClellan was preparing to commit the army he had created to combat, Lincoln's gratitude turned to impatience and irritation. The fact that Union affairs were going well in other theaters should have taken some of the heat off of McClellan, and provided validation for his command decisions as general-in-chief, but quite the opposite came to pass.

Brigadier General George H. Thomas won the first major victory in the West by defeating the Confederate forces under the command of Brigadier General George Crittenden, at the battle of Mill Springs, Kentucky, in January of 1862. Thomas's victory was soon followed by the capture of Forts Henry and Donelson, in Tennessee, by forces under the command of Brigadier General Ulysses S. Grant. The capture of Nashville, and the complete disintegration of General Albert Sidney Johnston's Confederate line of defense in Kentucky and Tennessee meant that Southern forces in that sector were reeling, and would be able to lend no assistance to any operations taking place in Virginia. Brigadier General Ambrose Burnside had mounted a successful amphibious operation against Roanoke Island, North Carolina, and had established a firm Union presence along the coast in the Tar Heel State. Brigadier General Benjamin F. Butler was sailing for New Orleans, with a military force of 15,000 men, and a navy flotilla, under the command of David G. Farragut. Indeed, the South was back on its heels, as Union victories came in rapid succession. Each new reverse brought with it an ever-increasing sense in the South that maybe this was to be a short war. The victory at Manassas seemed a long-ago memory, as most of the boast and bluster Confederates had espoused in the early months of the war were replaced by dogged determination and grim resolve. McClellan should have received a fair amount of credit for the successes of the Union armies in the field, but quite the opposite was to be the case. Instead of being heralded as the architect of the victories, he was publicly denounced for his failure to move with the Army of the Potomac while all the other Union armies were gaining ground against the enemy. It was even alleged that he had nothing whatsoever to do with the victories. When the Washington *Evening Star* suggested that McClellan's strategy was responsible for the victories Grant enjoyed at Forts Henry and Donelson, the assumption was refuted from an unexpected quarter.[10] Secretary Stanton sent a letter to the New York *Tribune*, printed on February 19, 1862, openly denying that planning or strategy had anything to do with the recent victories. Stanton attributed the successes to "the spirit of the Lord that moves our soldiers to rush into battle."[11] The war secretary even hinted publicly that the spirit of enterprise he had infused the War Department with, rather than McClellan's administration of the military, had been responsible for the recent glory to Union arms. General George Gordon Meade felt that the comments made by the secretary were unfortunate and unprofessional, and obviously objected to the pressure the government was exerting on McClellan to move before he was ready. In a letter to his wife dated February 23, 1862, he stated, "To fight is the duty and object of armies, undoubtedly, but a good general fights at the right time and place."[12] Prior to McClellan's elevation to army command, and his own appointment as secretary of war, Stanton had been one of the staunchest supporters of the Young Napoleon. McClellan viewed Stanton's actions to be a personal betrayal, but the war secretary saw the defection as a way to ingratiate himself with powerful members of the Radical wing of the Republican Party. His denunciations of McClellan soon made him the darling of influential members of the Joint Committee on the Conduct of the War like Zachariah Chandler and Benjamin Wade, who were the sworn enemies of McClellan and the party he represented.

As critical as Stanton's defection was to McClellan's cause, the loss of President Lincoln as an ally was catastrophic. During the summer of 1861, Lincoln had mirrored McClellan's own views concerning the scope and objectives of the war. The seceded states were to be forced back into the Union, but it should be done with a minimum of bloodshed and with as little destruction to the social and economic institutions of the South as possible. The radical element of the Republican Party was demanding that total war be visited upon the Confederate states; it sought the immediate end of slavery and advocated the elimination of all the Southern social and economic institutions that had made slavery possible. In short, the radicals favored the elimination and eradication of all things Southern. Thaddeus Stevens gave voice to the opinion of many radicals when he said, "If the whole country [the South] must be laid waste, and made a desert, in order to save this Union from destruction, so let it be. I would rather, sir, reduce them to a condition where their whole country is to be re-peopled by a band of freemen than to see them perpetuate the destruction of this people through our agency."[13] Statements such as these had initially alienated the radicals from the mainstream of American voters, but as the war neared the end of its first year, their resolve began to gain both credence and popularity. Benjamin Wade, leader of the Radical faction and a powerful member of the Joint Committee on the Conduct of the War, attempted to add a high morale fiber to the agenda of his compatriots when he stated, "Many seem still to be frightened by radicalism, but I believe that all who have benefited the world, from Jesus Christ to Martin Luther and George Washington, have been branded as Radicals.... I am a Radical, and I glory in it." Wade had a hatred for McClellan, and made his removal from command of the Army of the Potomac his top priority and the number one objective of the Joint Committee on the Conduct of the War. Wade had demanded that Lincoln shelve

McClellan ever since the committee had been formed, but the president had resisted the constant pressure. During one meeting, Lincoln had asked Wade who he thought would be better in army command than McClellan, receiving the caustic response, "Anybody!" The president offered the rejoinder, "Wade, anybody will do for you but I must have somebody."[14] Even McClellan's status as one of the young stars of the Old Army came into question from radicals who distrusted all professional soldiers, and graduates from West Point in particular. Wade called the United States Military Academy "the hot bed from which rebellion was hatched," and attempted to rally support from Congress to abolish West Point altogether.[15]

McClellan's inactivity was empowering the radicals and causing Lincoln to re-evaluate the support he had thus far given the charismatic young officer. As summer turned to fall, and fall gave way to winter, Lincoln became embroiled in politics, and he sought to appease the powerful radical element of his own party. His support for McClellan waned as he increasingly aligned himself with the Radicals, creating a rift between the military and civil leaders that could not be resolved short of total victory and the end of the war. McClellan objected to the agenda of the Radicals, and set himself up as the leader of the opposition to their brutal and punishing views on the execution of the war. He was so outraged by what he deemed to be the barbaric treatment they advocated for the South that he willingly overstepped his bounds as an army commander to challenge the will of the government. What he failed to realize is that he was not only the voice of the opposition, he indeed had the power to thwart all of the designs of the Radicals. As previously stated, the vast majority of mainstream Americans were not yet willing to embrace the Radical agenda as it related to the treatment of the Southern states. Most Americans were still quite willing to accept the Confederate states back into the Union with open arms, and to put this whole sordid affair behind them. If McClellan wished to restore the Union without destroying the Southern way of life, he had only to win rapid and decisive victories on the field of battle. If he restored the Union to its former status, the demands of the Radicals would fall on deaf ears, and the country would be left to solve its problems through negotiation and compromise. But swift action was needed. Each month he delayed marching the Army of the Potomac out of Washington in search of the foe brought new converts to the side of the Radicals. The winter of 1861 to 1862 had witnessed a growth in their numbers, but they still represented a small minority of American voters. The spring campaign could still prevent the Radicals from rising to power, but only if it proved to be an overwhelming success to Union arms. With Lincoln, Stanton, and the powerful Joint Committee all withholding their unqualified support, such a victory would prove to be a Herculean task.

But McClellan had not exactly been an innocent bystander in the events that were transpiring. His rise to top command had been accomplished through the displacement of the nation's foremost living military hero, General Winfield Scott. Second only to George Washington as an American military icon, Scott had served his country for over 50 years by the time the nation was torn asunder. He had become a national celebrity during the War of 1812, for meritorious service along the Canadian border. In 1841, he was appointed commander-in-chief of the United States Army. In that capacity, he was the architect of the American victory in the Mexican American War several years later. In 1852 came his emergence in the political arena, when he accepted the nomination of the Whig Party as their candidate for the presidency. Internationally famous and respected by all, Scott was nonetheless a relic of a bygone age when the Civil War broke out. In his late 70s, he found it hard to adapt to the evolving changes in strategy, organization, and weaponry that would define this first modern war. Scott desired to maintain the organization of the army as it had always been: in geographic departments. He did not see the need for field units larger than brigades, and could not conceive of the necessity of divisions, corps, or armies. His Anaconda Plan for ending the war eventually proved to be completely sound, but was ridiculed at the time of its issuance because most people still believed that the war would be quickly won, and Scott's strategy seemed to be unnecessarily time consuming. McClellan felt himself to be obstructed by Scott's supervision and sought freedom from the old general's command. In conversation with leading Radical Republicans, he had intimated that Scott was the main reason his army was not yet in the field actively campaigning. Chafing for military action, the Radicals took McClellan at his word, and exerted pressure for Scott to retire. The old general submitted to the pressure, and McClellan was appointed commander-in-chief of the Union Army in his stead. But the change in leadership brought about no immediate plans for aggressive action. Instead, McClellan continued to cite reasons why his army was not yet ready to take up the fight and even announced plans to allow the season for active campaigning to pass by, ordering the Army of the Potomac into winter quarters. Radical Republicans were outraged by what they felt to be McClellan's breach of trust. They had used their influence to place him in top command, believing he would deliver the immediate action they desired. When this did not come to pass, McClellan became the target of the full ire of the Radicals, and his removal from command became their single purpose. Amid this internal division, the Union was about to launch its great endeavor to subjugate the Confederate army and force the Southern states to submit to Federal authority. It would have been a difficult undertaking even if all of the Union leaders were working in concert. The infighting and political posturing that was taking place would all but doom the enterprise to failure, and would change an already difficult proposition into one of monumental proportions.

Senator Orville Browning of Illinois, a Republican and close personal friend of Abraham Lincoln, had recently made his first acquaintance with McClellan, and the impression made by McClellan caused him to have a decidedly different opinion of the general than many of his more radical counterparts. Browning recorded in his diary: "[Lincoln] proposed that I should go with him to call on General McClelland [sic] which I did, being my first meeting with him. I was favorably impressed — like his plain, direct straight forward way of talking and acting. He has brains — looks as if he ought to have courage, and I think, is altogether more than an ordinary man."[16] Browning's positive assessment echoed the sentiments of the men in the ranks McClellan would be leading in the coming campaign, but he was already voicing a minority opinion among the leadership of his own Republican Party.

The rift that had begun between McClellan and the radical faction of the Republican Party due to his perceived lack of aggressive activity had blossomed

General Winfield Scott. As general-in-chief of the Union army, Scott was McClellan's superior when he reported for duty at Washington. McClellan would use the influence of the powerful Joint Committee on the Conduct of the War to supplant Scott as commander of the Union armies (Military History Institute, United States Army War College).

Top: Union soldiers in one of the many defensive positions that ringed Washington. *Above:* The 2nd Rhode Island Infantry in camp at Washington. These men had fought under McDowell at Manassas and were eager to avenge that humiliating defeat. They would get their chance to prove their mettle as soldiers in the second Federal drive against Richmond (Military History Institute, United States Army War College).

into open denunciation following the debacle at Ball's Bluff on October 21, 1861. The engagement had resulted in a humiliating defeat for the Union army, with 49 killed, 158 wounded, and 714 captured. The embarrassment of the National forces brought swift action from Congress in the form of the establishment of the Joint Committee on the Conduct of the War, to investigate and report on the causes of the disaster. Congress decreed that the committee be made up of three senators and four members of the House of Representatives. Benjamin Wade of Ohio, Zachariah Chandler of Michigan, and Andrew Johnson of Tennessee comprised the Senatorial members of the tribunal. D.W. Gooch of Massachusetts, G.W. Julian of Indiana, John Covode of Pennsylvania, and Moses Odell of New York made up the remainder of the committee. This group represented the extremist element of the Radical faction of the Republican Party. They favored a harsh execution of the war, one that punished the South and destroyed all things Southern, rather than the mere reinstatement of the separated states. They also sought to decrease the influence of Northern Democrats, particularly those serving in leading positions in the army. James G. Randall, in his book *The Civil War and Reconstruction*, stated that the agenda of the radicals caused them to "resent the importance given to Democratic generals," as they "labored to promote one flank of the Republican Party."[17]

General Charles P. Stone was destined to become the scapegoat for the Ball's Bluff disaster, and the first victim of the Joint Committee on the Conduct of the War. Colonel Edward D. Baker commanded a brigade in Stone's division, and had brought about the disaster through rash behavior in engaging a superior Confederate force. Baker was solely responsible for the outcome, which had cost him his life, but the committee sought to lay the blame for the affair on another doorstep. Colonel Baker was a darling of the Radical Republicans—in perfect accord with their political goals and agenda. His immediate superior, General Stone, was quite another matter. The members of the committee felt him to be soft on slavery, and in opposition to their program of punishing the South and dismantling Southern culture and institutions. Stone became the target of an investigation that can only be called a kangaroo court. The committee held an *ex parte* investigation, meaning that Stone was not allowed an opportunity to testify or defend himself. As historian T. Harry Williams put it, Benjamin Wade "conducted the inquiry in a manner that showed he had prejudged the case." Hearsay testimony and gossip was solicited from "witnesses" who gave fabricated proof of Stone's disloyalty to the cause. Stone was accused of correspondence with known Confederates, and was painted as being a Southern sympathizer at heart. The unsubstantiated falsehoods that had been presented as testimony were recorded, but were kept a secret. Stone was not even informed of the charges being brought against him. When he demanded court martial proceedings in an effort to defend himself and protect his name, the committee flatly refused. On February 9, 1862, the committee ordered the arrest of General Stone, without ever providing an official statement of the charges, or a trial date. He was confined at Fort Lafayette, before being sent to Fort Hamilton for a period of 189 days. Stone lashed out against this treatment, and the complete lack of military justice being shown on his behalf. "This is a humiliation I had hoped I should never be subjected to. I thought there was one calumny that could not be brought against me.... This government has not a more faithful soldier; of poor capacity, it is true, but a more faithful soldier this government has not had.... If you want more faithful soldiers you must find them elsewhere. I have been as faithful as I can be." A year later, Stone was finally presented a copy of the charges, and was given the opportunity to defend himself. The subsequent inquiry proved that the government's case was groundless, and Stone was reinstated to command in the Department of the Gulf, but the damage had been done. When McClellan learned of Stone's arrest, he correctly ascertained, "They want a victim." Colonel Allen, an officer on McClellan's headquarters staff, said, "Yes, and when they have once tasted blood, got one victim, no one can tell who will be next." Allen's words would serve as a prophecy, and the committee would damage or destroy the careers and reputations of many more officers throughout the course of the war. Worse than that, it would influence the outcome of future campaigns to serve its own agenda of social and political reform. McClellan was quickly becoming the poster-boy of those opposed to the radicals, and as such, he would soon receive the full attention of the committee.[18]

The coming campaign would not only pit North against South, states' rights against the Federal government, it would also witness an internal conflict within the Union leadership that would decide how the war would be fought and who would fight it. Ideologies and visions of the future would clash between those who sought a reinstatement of the nation as it had been, and those who saw an opportunity to transform the country to fit their own idea of how things should be.

Two

"On to Richmond" Once More

By February of 1862, it had become certain that a new offensive against Richmond would soon begin. Pressure from the administration and the Joint Committee was steadily mounting, leading up to Lincoln's call for a commencement of the new campaign by February 22. McClellan's plan to transfer the seat of war to the Virginia Peninsula had gained the general some time, as Lincoln agreed to postpone the jump-off date he had set, but approval of the Urbanna Plan was still very much in doubt. Lincoln was not in favor of the proposed movement, but he vacillated when it came to offering an alternative. The reason for this was quite simple. The administration was more than willing to take credit for any successes that might come out of the offensive, but it was not about to allow itself to be tied into any reverses that may take place. In other words, plausible deniability was being put in place. Lincoln had complained to Secretary Stanton that he was against McClellan's plan, but he saw no other viable option. "We can't reject it and adopt another," he said, "without assuming all responsibility in the case of the failure of the one we adopt."[1] Clearly, McClellan's Urbanna Plan lacked unqualified support from his superiors. Instead of actively backing the enterprise, the administration was engaged in assessing blame and limiting its culpability in the campaign before the first company had ever marched out of the capital. The endeavor was doomed to failure before it began because of the bitter infighting that was taking place among the leadership of the North.

Though McClellan's plan was not favored by the administration, it had already provided a substantial boon to the Union war effort. The mere fact that it caused the postponement of the proposed February 22 offensive ordered by President Lincoln meant that the Army of the Potomac would not have to fight a campaign which it had no chance of winning. Lincoln had not only insisted on a definite date, he had also mapped out the overland route of march for McClellan's army, all of which had been

President Abraham Lincoln. Pressured by political considerations, Lincoln was anxious for McClellan to mount another drive against Richmond before 1861 came to a close. He disliked McClellan's plan to attack Richmond via the Peninsula, but offered no suitable alternative (Military History Institute, United States army War College).

23

thoroughly reported in the Northern newspapers. Confederate leaders had no need for an intelligence network so long as the Northern government was willing to openly disclose its plan of attack. Work on Southern fortifications, at key points in Virginia, had been progressing steadily, and the Army of the Potomac would have been battered uselessly in attempting to assail these strong and defiant positions. What McClellan planned was to circumvent the Confederate strongholds and fight the decisive battles for Richmond upon ground that had not already been selected and prepared by the enemy. In order to accomplish this goal, McClellan would undertake to relocate his army by means of the greatest amphibious military operation the world had ever seen. It would be a daunting task to move 100,000 men, by water, and land them in the tidewater region of Virginia. The logistics of such a maneuver were monumental. The army would have to carry with it all of the weaponry, equipment, supplies, and ammunition necessary to sustain itself in the field.

Administration and logistics would not be the only problems facing McClellan as he prepared for the coming campaign. Political intrigue, which would come to define the entire enterprise, caused the general to face fire from behind long before he faced fire from in front. On March 8, McClellan was summoned to the White House for a meeting with President Lincoln. The chief executive intimated that he had a "very ugly matter" to discuss with his top commander, which needed to be resolved in person. When McClellan met with Lincoln, he was informed that the president had obtained information, in such a manner as to believe it, that the general had developed the Urbanna Plan with the traitorous intention of removing the Army of the Potomac to the Virginia Peninsula in order to uncover Washington and make it an easy mark for Johnston's army. Lincoln ended his little speech by stating that "it did look to him much like treason." At this, McClellan lept to his feet and hotly demanded an immediate retraction and apology. Lincoln, taken aback by the abruptness of McClellan's reaction, speedily assented and asserted that such rumors were flying around the capital, but he did not believe them — this, after just categorically stating that McClellan's actions looked "much like treason" to him. The general offered to settle the matter, once and for all, by taking the unprecedented step of submitting the question to a vote by his 12 division commanders. If the majority of these generals felt the plan to be too risky, he would bow to their judgment and call off the movement. If, on the other hand, the majority of the generals approved his plan, it should serve as positive reassurance to Lincoln that the general's intentions were true, and his strategic planning correct.[2]

Accordingly, McClellan assembled his division commanders at Fairfax Courthouse, Virginia, and explained to them, in great detail, his plan of operations. By a vote of eight to four, these generals supported the general's strategy, and voiced the opinion that the transfer of the army to the peninsula was the best possible course of action. The dissenting votes all came from the four Radical Republicans in division command: Generals Irvin McDowell, Samuel P. Heintzelman, John G. Barnard, and Edwin V. Sumner. The commander had left his subordinates to come to their conclusions uninhibited, as he had removed himself from the room prior to any discussion or the vote being taken. After the division commanders had been polled, they traveled to Washington to meet with Lincoln personally. McClellan did not accompany the group, so as not to influence the proceedings. When the generals were in Washington, they met with Lincoln and Stanton, during which time the eight who had voted in favor of the plan were closely questioned. Stanton believed that the eight generals that favored the plan were, in reality, afraid to fight. He caustically asked if they were all willing to "make this suffering country wait a month longer" before initiating offensive operations against the South. Lincoln was undoubtedly still not convinced, but faced with the approval of the majority of McClellan's subordinate commanders, he decided to give the operation his blessing, and "urged us all to go in heartily for this plan."[3]

Lincoln may have felt that he had no other option than to back McClellan's plan, what with the support his subordinate commanders had voiced for it, but it is evident that he was still leary of the undertaking, and wished to hedge his bets by asserting some measure of personal control over the enterprise. Later, on the very same day he had met with the divisional commanders, the president issued orders that would have serious ramifications in the upcoming campaign. In his President's General War Order No. 2, he dictated that the Army of the Potomac be divided into four corps, to be commanded by Generals McDowell, Sumner, Heintzelman, and Keyes. All four generals were aligned with the Radical Republicans, and all but Keyes had voted against the Urbanna Plan. The majority of McClellan's division commanders had been appointed by the commanding general, and were, like him, conservatives. Lincoln sought to diminish the influence of these officers by placing them under the command of corps commanders who were more in step with the interests and desires of the administration. When he did this, he effectively divided the top command of the Army of the Potomac against itself. The order went on to create a fifth corps, in the Shenandoah Valley, to be commanded by another radical Republican, Brigadier General Nathaniel P. Banks. Brigadier General James G. Wadsworth, another political appointee, was assigned to command the defenses of Washington. It was hoped that the creation of this new hierarchy of command would make it easier to control McClellan and his conservative subordinates, and would form a link between the corps commanders and their friends in the cabinet and the Committee on the Conduct of the War.[4]

These actions were taken without consultation with McClellan, and were squarely against his wishes. The commanding general was opposed to the formation of corps at the present time. It was his contention that such a move was premature, owing to the fact that none of his division commanders had proven themselves sufficiently on the field of battle to substantiate their promotion. McClellan favored keeping the division structure in place until such time as the sheep had been separated from the goats, and a realistic assessment could be made of their qualities of leadership. This was not a revolutionary idea. In fact, it was in accordance with events taking place within the enemy army. The Confederates maintained a command structure of the division being the largest organization within the army until September of 1862, by which time Generals James P. Longstreet and Thomas J. "Stonewall" Jackson had so distinguished themselves as to merit the added responsibility.

Lincoln was not yet done hedging his bet, however. In his President's General War Order No. 3, also issued on March 8, he laid out stipulations and conditions for the coming campaign. The president ordered McClellan to begin his campaign on or before March 18. He further directed that no movement could be made until provisions had been made to ensure the safety of Washington. McClellan and his new corps commanders would come up with the number of troops necessary to meet this condition. The order concluded by directing that no more than two corps of the Army of the Potomac, or about 50,000 men, would be allowed to depart for the new base of operations until such time as the enemy obstructions were cleared from the Potomac River in front of Washington.[5]

Lincoln's last order was remarkable in several respects. First, it once more set the date for the movement. As with his order setting February 22 as the date for an overland movement, he was unconsciously providing the enemy with warning of the coming offensive, and eliminating any possibility to surprise the Confederates. Second, his directive that the Rebel batteries on the lower Potomac be cleared before a movement to the Peninsula could be made in force made the projected date of March 18 completely unrealistic. The completion of this assignment would necessitate a campaign that would, in and of itself, require several weeks to accomplish. The assumption that it could be done in the ten days between the issuance of the order and the assigned date for the offensive to begin was optimistic in the extreme. If McClellan was to follow Lincoln's directive to the letter, he might find his army divided and defeated in detail. The two corps that the president agreed to allow to embark for the Peninsula might find themselves confronted by overwhelming odds before McClellan could be given permission to concentrate the remainder of his army there. The commanding general knew that Lincoln's fears were wholly unfounded. The Confederate positions along the Potomac would have to be evacuated as soon as his army was landed on the Virginia shore. Johnston would be forced to withdraw his army in order to mount a defense of his own capital. This could be accomplished without the need to mount a campaign that would require the useless expenditure of lives or time.

Lincoln was acting on advice from radical members of his own party, and particularly from his new secretary of war, Edwin Stanton. Stanton felt McClellan to be soft on the issue of slavery, and lacking in the necessary hatred of Southerners. Though he disliked both Lincoln and McClellan, he viewed the general as the greater threat to the administration's agenda, and sought to drive a wedge between them. He urged Lincoln to take a more prominent hand in military affairs, to oversee and overrule the decisions of his top commander. This was in stark contrast with the manner in which the administration dealt with General Ulysses S. Grant two years later. Grant was given a free hand to conduct his affairs in the way he saw fit, unfettered by executive interference. As Lincoln would state at that time, "Do you hire a man to do your work and then do it yourself?"[6] But such was not the case in March of 1862, and the Army of the Potomac would find that there were far too many cooks stirring the pot.

March 8, 1862, would also be a significant day because of news coming from the Virginia Peninsula. On that day, the Confederate ironclad *Virginia*, formerly the U.S.S. *Merrimac*, made its day-long rampage in Hampton Roads, resulting in the sinking of the U.S.S. *Cumberland* and the U.S.S. *Roanoke*. The U.S.S. *Minnesota* was severely damaged, and had run aground by the time the *Virginia* called off its assault and returned to port for the day. Aground and defenseless, the *Minnesota* was sure to be finished off when the *Virginia* returned on the following day. The administration had long been aware that the Confederates were constructing an

Jefferson Davis, president of the Confederacy. Davis and his top military advisors feared that the Federals would adopt an offensive campaign by way of the Peninsula, and felt that the Confederate forces were ill-equipped to deal with the Union's superior engineering and artillery (Military History Institute, United States Army War College).

ironclad vessel, and had taken steps to counter this by commissioning designer John Ericsson to build an armor-clad vessel for the Union. What the administration had not envisioned was the utterly defenseless nature of the wooden ships of the line when they came in contact with the *Virginia*. News of the *Virginia*'s foray arrived in Washington during a meeting between Lincoln and his cabinet. It immediately caused hysteria among those assembled. Secretary of the Navy Gideon Welles asserted that the most discomfited man present was Secretary Stanton, whom Welles described as being "almost frantic." Stanton wildly stated that the *Virginia* "could lay every city on the coast under contribution [tribute] could take Fortress Monroe; McClellan's mistaken purpose to advance by the lower Chesapeake must be abandoned, and Burnside (then at New Bern) would inevitably be captured. Likely the first movement of the Merrimac would be to come up the Potomac and disperse Congress, destroy the Capitol and public buildings." Welles wrote that Stanton flitted from room to room, waving his arms and raving almost incoherently. Lincoln was only slightly less disturbed than his secretary of war. He and Stanton repeatedly went to the window to look out, as if they expected to see the *Virginia* appear at any given moment. Welles tried to assure them that there was no need for such panic, as the U.S.S. *Monitor* was on the scene, and prepared to do battle with the *Virginia*. He also assured them that the *Virginia* could not possibly reach Washington, as her heavy draught would prevent the vessel from making it over Kettle Bottom Shoals, on the Potomac River. Despite his promises for their safety, Welles was not able to convince Lincoln and Stanton that the *Virginia* was not an immediate threat until word reached Washington that the *Monitor* had engaged the armored giant and compelled it to return to its anchorage. Stanton somehow held McClellan at least partly responsible for the happenings at Hampton Roads, and voiced "terms which clearly indicated his want of confidence in" the general.[7]

Panic caused by the *Virginia* had come close to signaling the death-knell of the Peninsula Campaign before it ever got started. But March 8 also signaled the elimination of a threat that had caused Northern leaders great consternation for some months. On that day, General Johnston started withdrawing his army from its positions at Manassas, Centreville, and along the Potomac to a new line at the Rappahannock River, many miles south. McClellan did not learn of Johnston's action until March 9, at which time he marched his army forward to Manassas and Centreville. The general explained that he wanted to give his men some practical experience of marching and campaigning in the field, and that the movement to Johnston's old lines would be a perfect opportunity to give the troops some practice before they embarked upon the operations on the Peninsula. The Army of the Potomac reached Manassas and Centreville on March 11, and took their first look at the fortifications the Confederates had prepared. McClellan seemed to have been completely vindicated in not wanting to throw his army against them. Brigadier General John Sedgwick wrote his brother that "McClellan did not underrate their strength or position. It would have been madness to have attacked them." Brigadier General George G. Meade told his wife, "It would have given us a great deal of trouble to have driven them out," and expressed relief when he said it was "a very good thing they evacuated them." McClellan, for his part, was more concerned with the condition of the roads than with the strength of the fortifications. He had anticipated that the Confederates had used their time wisely in constructing field works of an intimidating nature, but he had not anticipated the deplorable condition of the roads. An overland offensive, as Lincoln had proposed, would have found itself bogged down in the muddy quagmire of the spring thaw in Northern Virginia. Even though the Confederates had departed, McClellan advised Washington that it would be a good idea to transfer a portion of General Banks' corps from the Shenandoah Valley to the vicinity of Manassas, just in case Johnston had any ideas of returning to the area.[8]

While McClellan and his army inspected the Southern entrenchments in Virginia, President Lincoln called a cabinet meeting. Stanton took the floor to denounce McClellan's management of the army, and declared that he "reports nothing — and if he has any plans, keeps them to himself." The secretary's memory was indeed short and selective. He omitted the detailed communiqué of February 3, which had explained all of the general's reasons for opposing the overland route, and his alternate proposals. He also conveniently forgot about the meeting McClellan had had with Lincoln and himself just three days before, during which time the general had meticulously mapped out his plans for the coming offensive. Attorney General Edward Bates chose this moment to press his oft repeated belief that no officer should hold the position of general-in-chief. Bates felt that Lincoln, as commander-in-chief, was the final word in military affairs, and that all generals in the field should be subordinate to the president and the War Department, not to a single general. He was willing to concede that a general-in-chief could be retained, if Lincoln chose to do so, but he did not think that such a position should be granted to a general who was leading a particular army.[9]

Lincoln agreed with Bates, and informed the members of the cabinet that it was his intention to relieve McClellan from his responsibilities as general-in-chief. He accordingly issued orders to that effect: "Major General McClellan having personally taken the field at the head of the Army of the Potomac, until otherwise ordered, he is relieved from command of the other Military departments, he retaining command of the Department of the Potomac."[10] For the time being, Lincoln would leave the position of general-in-chief open, creating the possibility that McClellan might be reinstated at a later time. Effective immediately, all department commanders were instructed to report directly to the War Department for their orders. In addition, Lincoln created a new Mountain Department, and he assigned the darling of the radical Republicans, Major General John C. Fremont, to command it. All of the Union forces west of the Appalachian Mountains were combined into the Department of the Mississippi, and assigned to Major General Henry Halleck.

McClellan was unaware of any of the proceedings taking place in Washington. Once the cabinet meeting was adjourned, William Dennison, the governor of Ohio, was summoned and charged with the mission of informing the general of his demotion. Dennison was a friend of McClellan's, and was the person responsible for giving the general his first command when he assigned him to be major general of the Ohio state troops. The governor went to army headquarters in Washington where he met with Randolph Marcy, a member of McClellan's staff, and his father-in-law. Dennison explained the situation to Marcy, who then sent a message to McClellan: "Come to Washington tonight. Please telegraph me from Fairfax when you will be here, as Mr. Dennison desires to see you before you see anyone else." The general replied that he was too worn out to return to Washington that evening. As a result, McClellan first learned about his demotion when he read about it in the *National Intelligencer* the following day. The news did not come as a complete surprise, however, as he had written his wife Ellen, "The rascals are after me again." When Dennison arrived in Fairfax Courthouse, he related the conversation he had had with Lincoln concerning the demotion. McClellan seemed to be buoyed by these words, and determined not to take the demotion as a personal affront. He wrote to Lincoln, thanking him for the "official confidence and kind personal feelings you entertain for me." He went on to inform the president that "no feeling of self interest or ambition should ever prevent me from devoting myself to your service," and assured Lincoln that "under present circumstances I shall work just as cheerfully as ever before."[11]

General Henry Halleck had thrown his hat into the ring in what was to become a struggle for power within the Union military. McClellan advocated a move on Decatur, Tennessee, prepatory to a campaign against Chattanooga and East Tennessee. Both Halleck and Buel were to be cooperating to accomplish this goal, but Halleck had ideas of his own. Halleck believed that Corinth, Mississippi, was the key to the entire region, and felt that the capture of that place would secure all of western Tennessee for the Union. With western Tennessee firmly in Union hands, a drive against Chattanooga would result, he thought, in sure victory. Halleck disregarded McClellan's directives, and proceeded with his own plans, all the while offering the general-in-chief his sincerest expressions of support, while advocating that McClellan name him as the overall commander in the Western Theater. The fact of the matter was that Halleck was playing both sides against the middle. If McClellan would not consent to elevate him to a higher command, possibly Stanton would. On February 24, Halleck had written to McClellan to warn him of intrigue being planned by the Radical Republicans. Halleck said that a member of Congress had informed him that the "abolition party had decided to make either [Benjamin[Wade or [Nathaniel] Banks Lieut. Genl." Halleck went on to assure McClellan of his own personal devotion by stating he had informed the congressman "that the whole army had full confidence in you and that if you were superceded by *any one*, it would be utterly demoralized."[12] Halleck's letter caused a further rift between Stanton and McClellan, but it was just one of many such communications he was sending to both superiors. Halleck had been pressing McClellan to allow him to have 50,000 men from the Army of the Potomac, and grant him overall command in the West. With this force, he promised to end the war in that theater. When McClellan flatly refused, Halleck took his case to Stanton. The secretary of war considered the request, and even took it a step further by suggesting that McClellan go to the West himself, to assume command there in person. Such a move, Stanton speculated, would vacate command of the Army of the Potomac, and make it possible for Lincoln to assign a more energetic officer to that position, without opening a political Pandora's box by simply relieving McClellan.[13] McClellan refused to entertain either option, and the matter was dropped, but Halleck had promised action, and had ingratiated himself with the secretary of war, whose enmity he feared. Before many months had passed, this relationship would result in Halleck being called East to assume the position of chief-of-staff for the Union army.

Stanton was well aware that accusations of intrigue, on his part, were rampant throughout Washington. Though he personally conveyed expressions of his complete and unflappable support to McClellan, his back-room activities and ill-timed comments were being widely broadcast, and had brought him under open criticism by McClellan's supporters, most notably the Blairs. When Secretary William Seward suggested that the order to demote McClellan be issued in Stanton's name, so as to strengthen the position of the War Department and show that the secretary of war was running things in the military, Stanton balked at the idea. He stated that "a row had grown up" between himself and McClellan's supporters, and felt that the action would be ascribed to his personal animosity toward the general. Lincoln agreed, and the order was issued in his name.[14] If Stanton sought to eliminate any charges that he was making the removal of McClellan one of the prime objectives of his department, his actions at the conclusion of the meeting only added fuel to the fire. The secretary took the opportunity to launch a public tirade against the general in front of Lincoln, the rest of the cabinet, and several other prominent individuals. He went on record as damning "the imbecility which had characterized [McClellan's] operations."[15]

With only a week remaining to comply with Lincoln's order to begin the campaign by

March 18, the military situation within the Union army had been dramatically altered. McClellan was no longer general-in-chief of the Federal forces. As such, he would only be able to call upon the resources within the Department of the Potomac for his upcoming offensive. Even the men and material at Fortress Monroe, which would be within his immediate sphere of operations on the Peninsula, would be an independent command, and not subject to his orders. Secretary Stanton had assumed control of the various departments, and was dictating their actions and movements. The ensuing campaign would show that Stanton did little, if anything, to coordinate activities between the departments to facilitate the success of the campaign against Richmond. Even within McClellan's own army, steps had been taken to circumvent the general's authority by the creation of army corps, assigned to officers aligned to the radical Republicans, and not to the army commander. The way things were stacking up, an observer might come to the conclusion that everything that could be done was being done to ensure the failure of the campaign, not its success.

The withdrawal of the Confederate forces from their Potomac line necessitated a change in McClellan's plans for the campaign. Urbanna was now too close to Johnston's army, and McClellan felt that hazards were too great to subject his army to the possibility of an attack by the enemy before he had time to consolidate his position. Accordingly, he altered his destination to be the tip of the Virginia Peninsula. Fortress Monroe could be used as a base of operations, as well as a point of retreat, in case of disaster. An advance up the Peninsula from this point would allow the flanks of the Federal army to be protected by naval gunboats operating in the York and James Rivers. The navy would also still be able to supply the army by sea, which was highly preferable to overland transportation using rails or wagons.

Hoping to alleviate any further opposition to his plans from the administration, McClellan decided to submit his proposed alterations to a vote of his four new corps commanders, before submitting them to the War Department. On March 13, at Fairfax Courthouse, McClellan assembled his generals and described his proposal in detail. Heintzelman, Sumner, Keyes, and McDowell were all known to be anti–McClellan Radicals, and it was a matter of record that they had been appointed to their positions against the wishes of the army commander, but they nonetheless unanimously approved of McClellan's plan. In fact, they went further than McClellan could have hoped for in their support for the operation. In addressing Lincoln's concerns that a sufficient force be left behind to defend Washington from any Confederate incursions, they stated that it was their combined opinion that 40,000 men would be more than adequate for that purpose. They also made a recommendation concerning the force necessary to ensure success of the campaign. All four corps should be committed to the operation, they advised, augmented by the 10,000 men then stationed at Fortress Monroe. Lastly, they called for substantial assistance from the navy in turning the Confederate strongholds at Gloucester and Yorktown. Armed with the approval of the corps commanders, McClellan submitted his revised plans to the administration.[16]

Stanton answered McClellan's message by telling him, "All the forces and means of the government will be at your disposal." He even agreed that McClellan could have control over General John Wool's forces at Fortress Monroe.[17] Later that same day, Stanton sent a message to McClellan telling him that President Lincoln had agreed to the new proposals, with the following conditions:

1. Leave such force at Manassas Junction as shall make it entirely certain that the enemy shall not repossess himself of that position and line of communication.
2. Leave Washington entirely secure.

3. Move the remainder of the force down the Potomac, choosing a new base at Fortress Monroe, or anywhere between here and there, or, at all events, move such remainder of the army at once in pursuit of the enemy by some route.[18]

By all appearances, McClellan was going to get the support he desired from the administration, provided Lincoln's three conditions were met. But back-room events were still transpiring that told an entirely different story. Stanton had summoned to Washington Ethan Allen Hitchcock, the 64-year-old hero of the Seminole Wars and the Mexican American War. Upon his arrival in Washington, Stanton commissioned him a major general of volunteers, only the sixth appointment at that grade to be made at the time, and informed Hitchcock that he was to be a military advisor to both himself and President Lincoln. In addition, Hitchcock was appointed to be chairman of the Army Board, supervising the activities of the various bureau chiefs. But the best was yet to come. When Hitchcock reported to the War Department, Stanton made known his real intentions for summoning him to the capital. "On reporting to the Secretary, almost without a word of preface he asked me if I would take McClellan's place in command of the Army of the Potomac! I was amazed, and told him at once that I could not."[19] Hitchcock was, at that time, in very poor health, and the duties he was already assigned would take all of his physical strength and moral fortitude to complete. Stanton's personal animosity toward McClellan knew no limits. Though he was unwilling to openly cross swords with his top general in public due to the esteem with which McClellan was held by the army and the folks back home, Stanton's constant and continual attempts to sabotage his reputation and derail his career display an ugliness of character and purpose not often encountered in men of public service at a time of national crisis. Far from offering all of the succor and support within his power to command, the secretary was openly plotting the downfall of the commander of the Union's primary army on the eve of its greatest undertaking to date in the war.

On March 17, McClellan was ready to start moving his army towards the Peninsula from Alexandria. General Heintzelman's Third Corps would be the first organization to board the boats and get underway. From top to bottom, this transfer to men and equipment would be an amazing feat of organization and logistics, unlike anything the world had yet seen in the annals of military conflict. John Tucker, assistant secretary of war, had been charged with arranging transportation for the army, and he had met the challenge of amassing the fleet that would be needed in less than a month, even though his original estimate of the time needed to do so would not have allowed the expedition to set sail until the end of March. In all, Tucker would have the responsibility for transporting 121,500 men; 14,592 animals; 1,150 wagons; 44 artillery batteries; 74 ambulances; a pontoon train; and the enormous amount of equipment, arms, food, and clothing for such a gigantic force. To accomplish this, he gathered together a fleet of 113 steamers, 188 schooners, and 88 barges. It was with just pride that Tucker wrote: "For economy and celerity of movement, this expedition is without parallel on record."[20] A foreign observer who watched the proceedings admiringly referred to the expedition as "the stride of a giant."[21]

As the troops prepared to say goodbye to Washington, McClellan issued a proclamation to his army:

> To the Army of the Potomac
> Soldiers of the Army of the Potomac!
> For a long time I have kept you inactive, but not without purpose; you were being disciplined, armed and instructed; the formidable artillery you now have, had to be created; other armies were to move and accomplish certain results. I have held you back that you might give the death-blow

to the rebellion that has distracted our once happy country. The patience you have shown, and your confidence in your General, are worth a dozen victories. Those primary results are now accomplished. I feel that the patient labors of many months have produced their fruit; the Army of the Potomac is now a real Army — magnificent in material, admirable in discipline and instruction, excellently equipped and armed; — your commanders are all that I could wish. The moment for action has arrived, and I know that I can trust in you to save our country. As I ride through your ranks, I see in your faces the sure presage of victory; I feel that you will do whatever I ask of you. The period of inaction has passed. I will bring you now face to face with the rebels, and only pray that God may defend the right. In whatever direction you may move, however strange my actions may appear to you, ever bear in mind that my fate is linked with yours, and that all I do is to bring you, where I know you wish to be, — on the decisive battlefield. It is my business to place you there. I am to watch over you as a parent over his children; and you know your General loves you from the depths of his heart. It shall be my care, as it has ever been, to gain success with the least possible loss; but I know that, if it is necessary, you will willingly follow me to our graves, for our righteous cause. God smiles upon us, victory attends us, yet I would not have you think that our aim is to be attained without a manly struggle. I will not disguise it from you; you have brave foes to encounter, foemen well worthy of the steel that you will use so well. I shall demand of you great, heroic exertions, rapid and long marches, desperate combats, privations, perhaps. We will share all these together; and when this sad war is over we will all return to our homes, and feel that we can ask no higher honor than the proud consciousness that we belonged to the ARMY OF THE POTOMAC.

George B. McClellan
Major General Commanding[22]

The troops were indeed glad to be underway. One young Pennsylvania officer in McClellan's command wrote his brother about the voyage to the front:

Union troops drilling in their defenses in Washington. McClellan would stress the importance of proper military training as he converted an armed mob into an efficient and reliable army (Military History Institute, United States Army War College).

All our regiment is upon this one boat, which is considerably crowded, but I fortunately succeeded in getting a bunk and slept quite comfortably. We have two large schooners in tow, filled with cavalry horses and men, and our captain says we will not be able to reach our destination before tomorrow some time. There appears to be a total ignorance as to our destination, but I presume it must be Fort Monroe or Newport News—but no matter where—it is evident there is warm work before us sooner or later. As we passed Mount Vernon the men became silent and stood uncovered, while the band played the Star Spangled Banner, Hail Columbia and other stirring and patriotic airs.... We also passed the terrible batteries erected by the energetic secesh along the river, but which are now silent and deserted, much to the disgust of a number of the impatient ones who are ever anxious for a brush with the enemy.[23]

But this officer was among the minority of the troops crowded together like cattle on the transports. Most echoed the sentiments of Sergeant John Adams when he declared "In no place is the life of a soldier so hard as on a transport."[24] A soldier in the 69th Pennsylvania Infantry related a harrowing journey aboard the ferry boat *Champion*:

The captain of this boat objected to the entire regiment being placed aboard, its registered capacity being but for 500 persons, while the regiment numbered between 800 and 900 men. No attention, however, was paid to his protests, and the men, with their arms and camp equipage, were huddled aboard, and for nearly three days were foundering upon the waters of the Potomac river and Chesapeake bay. The men were obliged to work the pumps night and day to prevent the boat from sinking.[25]

Another Pennsylvania soldier, aboard the steamer *Wilson Small*, recorded that the vessel was so overloaded that ship's officers distributed the men to trim it properly, and "stationed

The 96th Pennsylvania Infantry drilling in their camp in Washington. Organized in the fall of 1861, it was one of the many new regiments that McClellan would mold into his Army of the Potomac which would swell to well over 100,000 men (Military History Institute, United States Army War College).

Confederate defenses near Centreville. Note the "Quaker guns" mounted along the works. These works proved to be extremely formidable, but the Confederates lacked enough artillery to fully arm the fortifications (Military History Institute, United States Army War College).

watchmen to see that the passengers kept still." Luckily, the *Wilson Small* made the voyage in 24 hours, not the three days taken by the *Champion*.[26]

McClellan did not accompany the vanguard of the army to Fortress Monroe. General Heintzelman was assigned to take command of the troops as they arrived at the Union stronghold until McClellan completed his supervision of the operation from Alexandria and could join them. The men disembarked at Hampton and marched inland, with Heintzelman making sure that no demonstrations were made that would give the enemy an indication of their ulterior motive, as he had been directed to do by McClellan.[27]

It would take several trips by the transports, and almost a month of time, to effectively relocate the entire Army of the Potomac from the environs of Washington to the Virginia Peninsula. Much would take place between the beginning of the operation and the time the army was once more consolidated and ready for offensive action. On March 20, General McDowell wired McClellan that he had just met with Lincoln and Stanton, and had been given distressing news. McDowell informed the commander that he had been informed that there was serious doubt that the navy would be able to do its part in the operations against Yorktown and Gloucester. The destruction of the enemy's batteries at these strongholds was of prime importance, and should be the first step to be taken before any movement up the Peninsula could be made. If the navy was not able to provide the warships necessary to silence the Southern guns, the invasion might fail before it ever got a chance to start. If the Army of the Potomac was forced to reduce the enemy positions by storm or by siege, a great amount of lives or time would be wasted. But the positions must be taken. Guns from

Yorktown and Gloucester could shell shipping vessels in the York River, and thus strangle the seaborne supply line McClellan desired to establish. McClellan shot off a quick message to Stanton: "Have you received my letter in regard to cooperation of the Navy? If so please see the President at once and telegraph the reply. On your reply much depends for as you will see from my letter I have now to choose between two methods of accomplishing an object." Stanton responded at once, telling the general, "In order to determine the precise cooperation you want with the Navy the President will go immediately to Alexandria, and desires you to meet him at the wharf."[28]

Louis Goldsborough commanded the North Atlantic Blockading Squadron that was assigned to assist the army during the campaign. Goldsborough did not feel his ships equal to the task of eliminating the Confederate shore batteries at Yorktown and Gloucester. He considered the safeguarding of his vessels to be his first priority, and declined to risk their destruction in a contest with the heavy, land-based enemy guns. In fact, Goldsborough was reluctant to release his ships of the line for any service on the York River until such time as the army had eliminated the threat of the Confederate batteries at Yorktown and Gloucester. As Goldsborough described the defenses at Yorktown, "This work is very formidable, both from its heavy cannon, its extensiveness, and its very elevated position, which enables it to throw a plunging fire upon the decks of these gunboats, as well as a horizontal fire from its rifled cannon." He went on to say that the Confederate emplacement "would destroy all the vessels, while it would receive little or no injury from our fire."[29] This was a long way from the combined effort McClellan had been promised when the plan was accepted, and it would necessitate an altering of his original plan of attack.

McClellan had previously mapped out the details of the entire operation, which heavily depended upon the hearty cooperation of the Navy. With naval warships to shell the Confederate position at Yorktown into submission, the general felt that the objective would not "require many hours" to capture. Without this cooperation from the navy, McClellan warned that the mission "may be prolonged for many weeks and we may be forced to carry in front several strong positions which by their aid [the navy] could be turned without serious loss of either time or men."[30] Without naval support, it was a certainty that considerably more time would be expended in removing the Confederate presence from the lower regions of the Peninsula. McClellan's goal was to reach West Point, the location he had chosen to establish a base of supply for his operations against Richmond. From there, he would be able to utilize the Richmond and York River Railroad for his subsequent push against the Confederate capital. Even at this early date, the general was looking to the James River as a better choice for his drive to Richmond. At present, the presence of the *Virginia* prohibited its use for his designs, but if that threat were to be eliminated, a James River line would be preferable to one established on the York. But the full cooperation of the navy was never to materialize. McClellan's prophecy concerning the resulting delays in reaching Richmond would prove itself to be all too correct. Though he had warned of the probable delays that would result from a lack of joint operations, when those delays came to pass, McClellan was charged with being dilatory in his movements, and afraid to fight.

On April 1, the transports loaded more elements of the Army of the Potomac, bound for the Peninsula. McClellan accompanied these troops, traveling aboard the U.S.S. *Commodore*. Little had been settled regarding the cooperation of the navy, and the general's detractors in the administration were still launching scathing attacks upon his generalship and fitness to command. George Gibbs, an old friend of McClellan's, felt that the general was making an extreme error in judgment by not addressing the activities of his enemies before departing the capital. Gibbs favored the establishment of relations with the moderate and conservative members of the Republican Party. McClellan should "tell them frankly your designs and so much of your plans as are proper to communicate." Gibbs felt that such a move would render moot the accusations that McClellan was under the control of the Democratic opposition. "You have secluded yourself from political associations and interests. I and others who know you, understand this, but the country don't." Gibbs went on to state that "this is a popular war and you ... must at least understand, if you do not bow to popular feeling." He declared, "A General in the field and away from the immediate political arena ... must have someone who is a man of the world and enters into the world.... If you leave [Washington] with your rear undefended your tenure of office is not worth a week's purchase."[31] But McClellan chose to ignore the warnings of Gibbs and other supporters. He would not embroil himself in any political struggles, feeling it beneath his office to participate in such base and vile trivialities. Instead, he determined that the path to vindication, both for himself and his army, lay in securing victories on the battlefield. Success on the Peninsula would silence his critics and restore his own good name in a way that could be achieved in no other manner.

The day before McClellan left for the Peninsula, he learned that his force was being reduced by the withholding of Brigadier General Louis Blenker's division. Blenker was to be assigned to Fremont's Mountain Department to reinforce his corps against the threat Stonewall Jackson was mounting in the Shenandoah Valley. On March 23, Jackson had attacked the division of General Nathaniel Banks at Kernstown, Virginia. Though the Confederates had been repulsed, the mere presence of a strong Confederate force in the valley, poised to march against Washington, caused the administration to hesitate in releasing McClellan's full force for operations against Richmond. When the commanding general arrived at Fortress Monroe on April 2, he was informed that General John E. Wool's garrison force had also been removed from his command, and he would have no authority over either Wool or his men. Thus, before the campaign ever got underway, McClellan learned that he would probably not receive the naval support he had been promised to reduce the enemy positions at Yorktown and Gloucester. What's more, he would have to accomplish the task with a force that had lessened by some 20,000 men.

Stonewall Jackson's activities in the Shenandoah Valley would cause the same sort of hysteria within the administration that the cruise of the *Virginia* had brought about, and would ultimately lead not only to a further reduction of forces for the Army of the Potomac, it would also shape the strategy and tactics McClellan employed on the Peninsula. Stanton had urged Lincoln to detach Brigadier General Joseph Hooker's division for service with Fremont's forces, along with Blenker's men, but this the president declined to do.

Before boarding the *Commodore*, McClellan had provided Adjutant General Lorenzo Thomas with a detailed breakdown of the forces assigned to the duty of protecting the capital. According to his calculations, the following troops had been designated for this purpose: 18,000 men in the defenses of Washington; 7,780 men at Warrenton; 10,859 at Manassas; 35,467 in the Shenandoah Valley; and 1,350 in the Lower Potomac. This totaled an aggregate force of 73,456 men.[32]

McClellan had miscalculated some of the numbers, however. He had mistakenly counted the troops at Warrenton twice, and had included in the totals at Manassas a few regiments that had not yet arrived from their positions in Pennsylvania and Maryland. Estimating the discrepancies to amount to some 7,000 men, the total McClellan left for the defense of Washington would still have been more than 67,000 men. In December of 1861, the chief engineer, General John G. Barnard, had submitted a report stating that the defensive works bristled with heavy guns, "about 480, requiring about 7,200 men to furnish three reliefs of gunners. The permanent garrison need consist only of these gunners, and even in case of attack it will seldom be necessary to keep full garrisons in all the works." Barnard's report intimated that a force of some 20,000 men would be sufficient to safeguard the capital.[33] When General Hitchcock was consulted regarding the adequacy of the troops left behind for the defense of Washington, he replied that McClellan knew better than anyone else what force would be sufficient for the job, as he had been in command of the building of the fortifications, and was in the best position to make such a decision. Hitchcock had been brought in by Stanton to replace McClellan. When that eventuality did not occur, he was still retained to advise the secretary and Lincoln on military matters. His appointment was intended to have the effect of being a check and balance to McClellan, but here he was, granting his consent to McClellan's plans and provisions—for the time being, at least.

When they had been canvassed concerning McClellan's Urbanna Campaign, his four corps commanders had rendered their opinion that a force of 40,000 troops would be more than adequate to safeguard Washington from any attack by the Confederates. Clearly, many more troops than that had been left behind for the protection of the capital. The problem was that McClellan had informed Adjutant General Thomas of his dispositions, and had not directly discussed them with either Lincoln or Stanton. Possibly, he was conducting his affairs as if he were still general-in-chief of the army, but those duties were now being performed by Stanton and Lincoln. As such, the general would have been well-advised to have discussed his dispositions with his civilian superiors in person, instead of relying on military channels.

General Wadsworth reported to Stanton that he had 20,477 men in the forts around Washington, with 19,022 present for duty. Though he would later admit that he never anticipated that the Confederates would make an assault against the city, Wadsworth informed Stanton that he felt a minimum of 25,000 men were needed to adequately defend the capital. Wadsworth did not consider the forces in the Shenandoah Valley or in northern Virginia to be part of Washington's defenses, and thus he felt that Lincoln's directive regarding the safety of the capital had not been complied with. Wadsworth stated that his command was "inadequate to and unfit for the important duty to which it is assigned." Stanton responded to Wadsworth's information with alarm. Hitchcock and Thomas were dispatched to Manassas to inspect the situation there, and to determine if McClellan had complied with Lincoln's directive concerning the safety of Washington. Though both officers agreed that the Confederates were not likely to advance on Washington by way of Manassas, owing to the fact that they had torn up the railroad lines south of there during their withdrawal to the Rappahannock, they still felt that the capital was not sufficiently guarded. Neither general considered General Banks' force in the Shenandoah to be part of the defenses of Washington. As such, they maintained that McClellan had not left enough troops behind to satisfy Lincoln's decree.[34]

When the president was informed of the findings of Generals Hitchcock and Thomas, he instructed Stanton to detain either McDowell's or Sumner's corps in front of Washington. As McDowell later recalled, "I think that one division of Sumner's corps had gone, (already departed for the Peninsula) and that my corps was the only one intact; and the Secretary decided the matter himself, and ordered me to remain."[35] The orders placed McDowell under the direct command of Stanton and Lincoln. He would no longer be considered a part of the Army of the Potomac, but would act as an independent force, under the supervision of the secretary of war and the president. McDowell protested against the order, and felt that it undermined the probability for success on the Peninsula. 1st Corps division commander, General William B. Franklin, said:

> McDowell told me that it was intended as a blow againt you [McClellan]. Stanton had said that you intended to work by strategy and not by fighting. That all of the opponents of the Administration centered around you. In other words that you had political aspirations. There were no friends of yours present to contradict those statements, of course, but McDowell told Stanton ... that he opposed the detachment of his corps from you.... He used all the arguments he knew of to convince Stanton that he was making a mistake.[36]

The question now arises as to whether Stanton indeed made a mistake, or whether he was intentionally trying to sabotage operations on the Peninsula. Hitchcock, Thomas and Wadsworth would all later testify before the Committee on the Conduct of the War that they were not fearful of the Confederates making a push toward the capital. If this is the case, then why was it so essential to have such a large contingent of troops available for the defense of Washington? Furthermore, Thomas and Hitchcock had both informed the administration that a Southern advance by way of Manassas was highly improbable, due to the destruction of the railways south of that point. Any Confederate advance, by that line, would necessarily be a slow and ponderous undertaking, as the Rebels would be forced to reconstruct the railways as they marched forward. This would give the administration ample time to collect an overwhelming force at Washington to contest the move. The only real avenue of advance open to the Confederates was the Shenandoah Valley, the "back door" to Washington. Banks and his corps were stationed in this important corridor, 35,000 strong, and guarded the only viable option open to the Confederates, should they decide to undertake offensive operations of their own. But neither Stanton, Lincoln, nor any of their advisors counted Banks' corps as being a legitimate part of the defenses of Washington, despite the fact that they guarded the only feasible route of approach open to the enemy. Blenker's division had been withheld. Wool's men had been removed from McClellan's authority. Now, McDowell's corps was being stripped from the striking power of the Army of the Potomac. In all, some 60,000 men had been detached from McClellan's original force, reducing his numbers by more than a third.

But Stanton was not only diminishing the striking power of the Army of the Potomac, he was still actively seeking to replace its commander. While all of these changes were taking place, Stanton was actively seeking a replacement to oust McClellan from top command. An obscure and unproven brigadier general, Napoleon B. Buford, was the secretary's choice. Buford had graduated from West Point in 1827, and had served as a lieutenant of artillery for eight years before resigning in 1835. He had recruited the 27th Illinois Regiment early in the war, and was appointed its colonel. In November of 1861, the regiment participated in its first engagement at the battle of Belmont, where Buford played a minor role. Nonetheless, he was promoted to the rank of brigadier general of volunteers on April 15, 1862. Belmont had been Buford's only experience under fire, and the first time he had ever commanded a detachment larger than an artillery battery, but somehow Stanton deemed him suitable for army command. In conversation, the secretary told Senator Browning of his intention to promote Buford to major general and give him McClellan's command. For whatever reason, this did not materialize, but Stanton was actively pursuing the option while the buildup on the Peninsula was taking place.[37] McClellan knew nothing about Stanton's efforts to replace him in command of the army. In fact, he knew nothing about the detachment of McDowell's corps from his army. That information, along with General Franklin's letter detailing McDowell's protest, would not be relayed to him until after he had reached the Peninsula and initiated his offensive movements.

By all appearances, Lincoln was not part or party to Stanton's behind-the-scenes intrigue against McClellan, but was being used as an unwilling accomplice. The secretary was playing both sides against the middle, in his quest to further the agenda of his friends in the Committee on the Conduct of the War, and Lincoln was being used as a tool toward that end. The radical members of the Republican Party viewed Lincoln to be soft on the question of slavery, and McClellan was seen as an absolute obstruction in the goal of establishing the abolition of slavery as the prime focus of the war. Both Lincoln and McClellan favored a conciliatory approach to the South, and a limited approach to the warfare being waged against that sector, hoping that a speedy end of the war would result in a reunification that brought about as little social upheaval as possible. In his first inaugural address, the president had assured the people of the South that he had no intention of interfering with their social or economic institutions in any way. This was in direct contradiction with the goals and objectives of the radicals, who sought to destroy everything Southern, and punish the errant states for their crimes against the Union. Indeed, many members of the radical faction feared that the war might be brought to a conclusion before the issue of the conflict had been shifted from defending the Union to freeing the slaves. Stanton had definitely aligned himself with Wade, Chandler, and the other influential members of the committee, and he viewed both Lincoln and McClellan with disdain, but was he actively doing all in his power to undermine the largest offensive operation the Union would mount during the war? His interactions with Lincoln, concerning McClellan, do not provide a positive indictment of this, but they do raise cause for suspicion. The following example illustrates a pattern that is repeated consistently in the recorded memoirs of individuals that came in close contact with both the secretary and the president. Senator Browning relates an incident where Lincoln was having doubts about McClellan's ability to perform his mission, feeling that he might be too cautious to achieve the desired results. Stanton entered the room and heartily declared that he did not believe any of the charges being made by politicians that McClellan was a traitor, and generally tendered his support to the general. Later, when Browning and Stanton were out of earshot of the president, the secretary made his true feelings known. The secretary

> expressed the opinion that McClelland [sic] ought to have been removed long ago, and a fear that he was not in earnest, and said that he did not think that he could emancipate himself from the influence of Jeff Davis, and feared that he was not willing to do anything calculated greatly to damage the cause of secession, and that if I would propose to the President to appoint Col. N.B. Buford of Illinois a Majr. Genl. And give him Command of the army here he would second my application.[38]

The all too numerous recorded incidents of Stanton saying one thing about McClellan in front of Lincoln, and the opposite when the president was out of earshot, form a definite picture of deceit and malice of purpose. Lincoln genuinely liked McClellan, and though he had certain reservations regarding the general's strategy and plans of operation, he respected his talent and appreciated the service he had already rendered the nation in the creation of the magnificent Army of the Potomac. What's more, Lincoln's conciliatory approach to the South more closely coincided with the sentiments of his top general than they did with the radical members of his own party. In fact, Lincoln had been accused of being soft on the South, just as McClellan had. Did Stanton feel that the war aims of both Lincoln and McClellan were too closely similar to make a frontal assault on the general directly to Lincoln? Was it feared that such a move might serve to push Lincoln more firmly into McClellan's camp, and further distance him from the agenda of the radicals? Or was this simply an effort, on Stanton's part, to exert his own influence over individuals he felt to be unsuited to the demands of the current situation? The answers to these questions must remain conjecture and speculation, as there is no definitive evidence that supports or denies any of the questions asked. What is clear, even to the casual observer, is that Stanton was conducting a campaign of his own, for reasons known only to him, that was setting the administration against McClellan, and negatively effecting the efficiency of the campaign. Even Lincoln's secretary, John Hay, who was a vehement critic of McClellan, was led to confide to John Nicolay that "Gen McC is in danger. Not in front, but in rear."[39]

Being the consummate politician he was, it is possible that Lincoln understood what McClellan did not: that the surest way to defeat the radicals and destroy their agenda, was to secure a great victory and an early end to the war. An early cessation of hostilities, with the subsequent reunification of the nation, would ensure that the nation would be restored with a minimum of upheaval to the social and economic systems of either section. The public was also pressing for an early end to the war. The voters were demanding positive action from the military, and their voices were being heard in Washington. The best way to accomplish this would be to place all the resources of the Union behind McClellan's effort to capture Richmond and end the war in the East. But Lincoln was tormented by doubt over the prudence of McClellan's proposed campaign, and these fears, stoked by Stanton, would cause him to withhold the men and means necessary to accomplish the very thing he sought. Part of the responsibility for this must rest with McClellan. His reluctance to discuss fully his strategy and plans with members of the administration left Lincoln relatively uninformed. Had he taken the president into his confidence, and explained all of the intricacies of the operation, it is possible the support he sought might have been forthcoming. As it was, political intrigue had caused the general to become suspicious of the administration, and reticent in his dealings with Lincoln and the members of his cabinet. Without reassurance from McClellan, Lincoln had only the cautionary advice of Stanton upon which to base his decisions.

Possibly the most amazing and inexplicable action taken by the war secretary came on April 3, when he issued General War Order No. 33. This edict closed all recruiting stations in the North, and suspended the further enlistment of volunteers for the army. Not only had the size of McClellan's army been severely reduced through the detachment of Blenker and McDowell and the refusal to place Wool under his command, the system for obtaining replacements for the casualties the army was sure to suffer in its drive for Richmond had been eliminated. This, just at the time when the Confederacy was adopting conscription to maximize its available manpower and ensure a steady flow of men into the ranks. It seemed to McClellan that the administration was doing its best to keep men away from his army, and it is little wonder that his distrust of the politicians in Washington intensified. He declared that "the results were wasteful and pernicious. There were enough, or nearly enough, organizations in the field, and these should have been constantly maintained at the full strength by a regular and constant influx of recruits, who, by association with their veteran comrades, would soon have become efficient."[40] But such was not to be the case. McClellan would have to make do with two-thirds of the force originally designated to accomplish the mission, without the possibility of replacements for the losses he was sure to incur. The deck seemed stacked against him as he prepared to meet his primary adversaries: the Confederate army, the tidewater terrain, and an unanticipated rainy season.

Three

Up the Peninsula

By the time McClellan landed at Fortress Monroe. The transports had been active for more than a week, and some 53,000 men, 42,000 of which were effectives, could be counted as present for duty. Heintzelman and Keyes would redeem the Union's reputation on April 5 by capturing Big Bethel, the scene of the first Federal defeat in the East a year earlier. McClellan feared the action might have been ill-timed. "I hope the movement on Big Bethel was well considered, in view of my wish not to prematurely develop our plans to the enemy," he had said, when hearing of the action.[1]

McClellan's desire to cloak his intended purpose was only natural. The ability to confuse or surprise an enemy often equates to victory on the battlefield, and McClellan hoped to benefit from both in the upcoming campaign. He need not have been concerned over the movement against Big Bethel, however, for the Confederates had already correctly ascertained his proposed strategy. Contrary to the sentiments expressed by McClellan's superiors in Washington, the Confederate high command held a most favorable opinion of the legitimacy of the operation. In fact, it was the move they had most feared McClellan would make when they planned against the possible thrusts the Federal forces might make in their spring campaign. While Lincoln and Stanton fretted over McClellan's removal of the Army of the Potomac from in front of Washington, most of the Confederate generals in Virginia were of the opinion that the water route to the Peninsula was the most promising plan the Federals could have adopted. General Johnston knew that such a move would place the Federals "at least two days' march nearer Richmond than the Army of Northern Virginia," and stated, "I did not doubt, therefore, that this route would be taken by General McClellan."[2] General John Magruder felt that an amphibious operation by McClellan would "probably embarrass us greatly," and feared that the Southern army would not be able to stop him.[3] In 1861, President Jefferson Davis had been advised that the best possible route of attack for a Federal army against Richmond would be up the Peninsula, possibly from the direction of Norfolk. General

General Joseph E. Johnston. One of the heroes of Manassas, Johnston would command the Confederate army concentrated for the defense of Richmond (Military History Institute, United States War College).

Joseph E. Johnston could see McClellan's proposed campaign as clearly as if he had attended a council of war with the Union commander and his generals. Johnston also thought the water route to the Peninsula to be the Federals' best course, and speculated on "the certainty that the Federal rifled cannon, mounted out of range of our obsolete 'smooth-bore' guns, could destroy the batteries of Yorktown and Gloucester Point; and the very strong probability that General McClellan's plan was to open the York River by demolishing those batteries with his powerful artillery. That being done, we could not prevent him from turning our position, by transporting his army up the river and landing in our rear, or by going on to Richmond and taking possession there."[4]

When Stephen Mallory, Confederate secretary of the navy, authorized the construction of the ironclad *Virginia*, it was with a view of eliminating this threat of invasion as much as it was to inflict damage on the Union fleet. The administration in Richmond had been heartened by the maiden voyage of the *Virginia*, and hoped that her rampage against the Federal warships at Newport News would be sufficient to convince the Federals that a water route to the Peninsula was impracticable. Judging from the reactions of Stanton and Lincoln, they were almost successful in accomplishing this goal. But the arrival of the *Monitor* on March 9, and the ensuing battle between the two armored giants, meant that the amphibious course would still be open to the enemy. The *Virginia* could not prevent the Federals from operating against the Peninsula if they chose to do so. The Confederates could only meet them, initially, with a force of about 25,000 men, stationed at Yorktown and Norfolk. When the initial reports came in of the landing of elements of the Army of the Potomac at Fortress

Large coastal gun in one of the Confederate fortifications at Yorktown (Military History Institute, United States War College).

Top: The Yorktown fortifications as they exist today. The original Revolutionary War earthworks were strengthened and expanded by the Confederates. *Bottom:* Photograph showing the remnants of the moated ditch in front of the Confederate works (photographs taken by author).

Monroe, McClellan's force was estimated to be some 35,000 strong. That number would continue to grow, as Davis made arrangements to shift his forces to meet the threat.[5]

The Confederate high command, both civil and military, realized readily what many in the Lincoln administration failed to grasp. McClellan's plan would fully utilize every facet of the Union war machine that was superior to that of the Confederates. The South could not compete with the Federals' naval power, as the Confederate Navy existed more in name than reality, and they anticipated the Union's North Atlantic Blockading Squadron would be playing a major role in the offensive. The South was also deficient in the fields of engineering and artillery, areas in which the North excelled. If Union forces were landed in sufficient strength to make a frontal assault upon them by Johnston's army unfeasible, then the Confederates would be forced to defend Richmond from behind a series of prepared works. McClellan was an engineering officer himself, and it was felt that he would not waste his army by obliging the Confederates and throwing it against these works. Instead, he would probably utilize his training and experience and conduct a campaign of siege warfare. The Confederates could not hope to withstand such a campaign, and would ultimately be pushed from position to position, under pressure of the Northern artillery, until the capture of Richmond became a foregone conclusion and only a matter of time. The only hope the Confederates had was that somehow, some way, the Federals might be tempted into battering their forces against one of Johnston's fortified works, or leave themselves vulnerable in a position where their superior navy, artillery, or engineering could not be brought to bear. The South must consolidate its forces and bide its time, waiting for a mistake to be made by the Union leadership that would enable the advantages McClellan was now holding to be lessened. The South must hold its breath and pray that the Federals made a misstep in their march toward Richmond. If not, then the capital and the cause might surely be lost, and the early prophecies of a short war might come to pass.

McClellan's first objective was to force General Magruder out of his defensive positions at Yorktown. Union intelligence reported that Magruder had between 15,000 and 20,000 men in his command. McClellan proposed to flank Magruder's force and cut it off from Richmond by moving around Yorktown's southern flank, to Halfway House, on the Yorktown-Williamstown Road. Such a movement would place Magruder in an untenable position. The Federals would be behind his prepared works, and between him and the rest of his army. Magruder would be forced to come out of his works to offer battle, in which case McClellan's superior numbers could be brought to bear on the open field. If he stayed where he was, his forces would be isolated and trapped, and the surrender of the garrison would be but a matter of time.

On April 4, McClellan sent orders to General McDowell regarding his intended role in the campaign, which was to begin the following day. As of this date, McClellan was not yet aware that McDowell's Corps had been detached from his army, and his attack force reduced by some 35,000 men. McClellan desired to have McDowell's men operate against the Southern defenses at Gloucester Point, hoping to capture both positions, and clear the lower portion of the Peninsula of Confederates in one fell swoop. As such, he instructed McDowell: "I think it will be advisable for you to land at least one division on the Severn in order to ensure the fall of Gloucester Point. I have therefore telegraphed to Franklin ... to get your First Division embarked as soon as possible (supposing you will be here by morning) to make the movement."[6] News that McDowell was no longer under McClellan's command came as a dreadful shock to the commander, and was the first indication that his plans for a speedy reduction of Confederate forces in the area were coming unraveled. Heavy

Open ground over which the Federal army would have to advance to attack the Confederate defenses (photograph taken by author).

rains and snow were turning the camps and roads into a quagmire of mud and impeding the movement of the troops — especially the cavalry and artillery. McClellan's proposed line of march, around the southern flank of Yorktown, was found to be impracticable when the soldiers trudged through the mud to reach their assigned goal. It was discovered that the Federal maps were wrong regarding the position of the Warwick River. The maps showed the Warwick to flow west to east, but the troops found that it actually flowed directly across their line of march, and that Magruder had fortified this natural obstacle, making it a formidable barrier to the Union advance. This revelation made a movement against Gloucester Point even more critical, but McClellan was convinced that a speedy capture of that place would make the defenses at Yorktown untenable, and force Magruder out of his works.

The Federal Navy might have expedited the evacuation of the works at Gloucester Point and Yorktown, but Commodore Goldsborough would not consent to sending his ships against the Rebel defenses. His concern over the vulnerability of his fleet against the heavy land-based guns mounted in the Southern works, caused him to withhold committing it to action. Furthermore, he would not consent to even allow his vessels to enter the York River until such time as McClellan had taken Yorktown and Gloucester Point, and silenced their guns. The arrival of McDowell's corps, and the capture of Gloucester Point now became paramount if the issue on the southern Peninsula was to be decided quickly. But McDowell, of course, was not coming. Amid the sound of heavy rain on his headquarters tent, and the more distant rattle of musketry from the defenses at Yorktown, a messenger arrived from Washington, bearing a communication from the War Department that would seriously alter all of McClellan's future strategy and tactics. "By direction of the President, McDowell's army corps has been detached from the force under your immediate command, and the general is ordered to report to the Secretary of War."[7]

This news devastated McClellan. He was contending with an entrenched and defiant enemy, miserable conditions of weather and terrain, faulty maps, an uncooperative navy, and now he was faced with a further reduction of manpower that amounted to almost 25 percent of his force. The general immediately sent a protest against the order to the War Department, taking care to voice his displeasure in measured and diplomatic terms:

> Headquarters, Army of the Potomac,
> Camp Near Yorktown, April 5, 1862.
>
> Brig._Genn. L. Thomas, Ajt.-Gen. U.S.A.:
> General: I have now a distinct knowledge of the general position of the enemy in my front. His left is at Yorktown; his line thence extends along and in rear of the Warwick river to its mouth. That stream is an obstacle of great magnitude. It is fordable at only one point (so far as I yet know) below its head, which is near Yorktown; is for several miles unaffordable, and has generally a very marshy valley. His batteries and entrenchments render this line an exceedingly formidable one, entirely too much so (so far as I now understand it) to be carried by a simple assault. I shall employ tomorrow in reconnaissances, repairing roads establishing a depot at Ship's Point, and in bringing up my supplies.
>
> Porter, the head of the right column, has moved as close upon the town as the enemy's guns will permit; he is encamped there, supported by Hamilton's division. Porter has been under fire all the afternoon. But five men killed. His rifled field-guns and sharpshooters have caused some loss to the enemy. Keyes, with two divisions, is in front of Lee's Mill, where the road from Newport News to Williamsburg crosses the Warwick river. He has been engaged in an artillery combat of several hours' duration, losing some five killed. At Lee's Mill we have a causeway covered by formidable batteries. The information obtained at Fort Monroe in regard to the topography of the country and the position and strength of the enemy has been unreliable. He is in strong force and very strong position. If the reconnaissances of to-morrow verify the observations of to-day, we shall be obliged to use much heavy artillery before we can force their lines and isolate the garrison of Yorktown. I ommitted to state that I hold the reserves in a central position until I can learn more of the condition of affairs. The present aspect of affairs renders it exceedingly unfortunate that the 1st corps has been detached from my command. It is no longer in my power to make a movement from the Severn river upon Gloucester and West Point. I am reduced to a front attack upon a very strong line. I still hope that the order detaching the 1st corps may be reconsidered. I do not feel that without it I have force sufficient to accomplish the objects I have proposed in this campaign with that certainty, rapidity, and completeness which I had hoped to obtain. The departments will, I trust, realize that more caution will be needed on my part after having been so unexpectedly deprived of so very large a portion of my force when actually having my troops under fire. I have frankly stated what I now consider to be the strength of the enemy's position; the reconnaissance of to-morrow may modify my opinion. Whatever the facts may be, I shall make the best use I can of the force at my disposal, determined to gain my point as completely and as rapidly as may be.
>
> Very respectfully, your obedient servant,
>
> Geo. B. McClellan
> Maj.-Gen. Commanding[8]

While the tenor of this message to his superiors was respectful and subdued, McClellan vented all of his anger over the decision in a letter to his wife, written that same evening. He ranted to Ellen, "It is the most infamous thing that history has recorded," and raged at "the idea of depriving a General of 35,000 troops when actually under fire!"[9] McClellan's ire over the order detaching McDowell was echoed by one of his corps commanders, Erasmus D. Keyes. In his diary, Keyes wrote: "What a time to do such a thing. It is a great outrage."[10] He wrote a lengthy letter of protest to Senator Ira Harris, of New York, outlining the reasons why he so strongly opposed the directive. Keyes told Harris that he had voted in favor of the Peninsula Campaign "with the distinct understanding that *four* army corps should be employed, and that the Navy should co-operate with us in the taking of Yorktown.... This army being reduced by 45,000 troops (Blenker's Division, as well as McDowell's Corps) ... and without the support of the Navy, the plan to which we are reduced bears scarcely any resemblance to the one I voted for." Keyes argued that "the great battle of the war is to come off here," and emphasized that "the plan of campaign I voted for, if carried out with the means proposed, will certainly succeed." He cautioned, "But with the reduction of force and means the plan is changed, and is now a bad plan, with means insufficient for certain success."[11] It is important to bear in mind that Keyes was one of the generals friendly to the Radical Republicans who had been appointed to corps command to check McClellan's authority and influence. As such, his complete endorsement of McClellan's original plan of operation, and his condemnation of the administration's subsequent interference, is of signal importance, as it comes from an officer not considered to be within the commanding general's circle of friends.

McClellan's intelligence regarding the strength of the enemy he opposed was faulty. In reality, General Magruder only commanded about 11,000 at Yorktown — two-thirds to one-half the number attributed to him. As such, he was hopelessly outnumbered by the 53,000 troops McClellan already had on hand. To the casual observer, it would seem that capturing Yorktown would be an easy assignment for an aggressive and emboldened commander, and McClellan has endured criticism and condemnation for failing to avail himself of his numerical advantage in a bold assault against Magruder's inferior forces. It has been alleged by his critics that no one but McClellan would have hesitated in making the attack. General John Barnard, McClellan's chief engineering officer, reported the enemy works to be "certainly one of the most extensive known to modern times." General Keyes wrote that "no part of (the enemy) line, so far as discovered can be taken by assault without an enormous waste of life." After the war, McClellan would write that "no one at that time thought an assault practicable; moreover, that when we saw the works abandoned by the enemy it remained the conviction of all that, with the raw troops we had, an assault would have resulted in simply a useless butchery with no hope of success."[12]

What McClellan found before him was this: The Confederate defensive position was some 12 miles long, running in a southwesterly direction from Yorktown to the James River. It had been constructed under the supervision of the Confederate Corps of Engineers, using some 1,000 impressed slaves as laborers.[13] Magruder's line stretched across the entire lower tip of the Peninsula. The Warwick River lay in front of the Southern line, and Magruder had made the most of this natural barrier by the construction of five dams that flooded the marshy ground along its banks, creating a formidable obstacle. Artillery emplacements were constructed to cover the breastworks of each of the dams, as they afforded the only viable avenues of approach to the Confederate line. An attacking force would be compelled to advance across these narrow causeways only a few men abreast, under a galling artillery fire, making it extremely difficult for the Federals to even get at the enemy. It would be impossible to advance on even a company front. While the Confederates were severely outnumbered in their Yorktown defenses, they would be able to achieve numerical superiority, at the point of attack, in front of any of these five causeways. Union troops would be funneled into a cross fire of artillery and musketry that was sure to reward any Union effort to cross with a bloody repulse. One need only remember the fiasco of General Burnside's corps at Antietam, where several hundred Confederates held his entire corps at bay for a number of hours because of the funnel created in crossing the bridge. These Rebels did not have the advantage of prepared works or heavy artillery support, both of which were available to the defenders of the Yorktown line. The British defensive earthworks from the Revolutionary War still existed along the Yorktown line. Magruder expanded and improved these positions, and loaded them with as many cannon as he could get his hands on. Parapets were 15 feet thick, and fronted by ditches 10 feet deep and 15 feet wide.[14] Gun emplacements were constructed on high ground at Yorktown and Gloucester Point to prevent passage of the York River from either shore. The surrounding area had experienced a stretch of snow and heavy rain for the previous ten days, causing the two primary roads to become almost impassable. Rations for the troops had to be carried to the advanced positions on the backs of the men.

From April 6 to April 16, the Union army busied itself in constructing works, bringing up artillery, and keeping a close eye on the activities of the Confederates in the Yorktown-Warwick line. Many Northern soldiers got their first taste of campaigning during this time, learning lessons that would stay with them for the rest of their time in the service. One New Yorker, a member of the 56th regiment from that state, described the march of his unit from Newport News to Yorktown, and the "severe lesson" learned, which the men "never forgot." Troops used to a camp existence soon learned that troops on the march should "carry in our knapsacks and otherwise just as little as we could possibly get along with and no more. Many of the men on that march threw away overcoats and blankets, beside many other articles, and the road was strewn with them for miles." By the time the 56th New York reached Yorktown and went into camp "war in earnest was soon experienced by the boys, who were continually under fire while on the picket line. Nearly every day a detail would be sent out skirmishing and scouting, also parties to dig the trenches and approaches. The roar of cannon and crack of the rifle continuously in the ear, along the whole line from river to river, day and night, kept us all in a fever of excitement."[15] McClellan was preparing his army for active operations against the enemy, and was ordering up his siege train, with its heavy guns, in preparation to blast the Confederates out of their strong positions. It was not the sort of rapid campaign that either the administration or McClellan desired, but the general was convinced that the reduction of his forces, and the refusal of the navy to take on the Rebel fortifications at Gloucester Point or Yorktown, had forced him to adopt the strategy he now employed.

The Confederate high command would benefit from the delay of the Army of the Potomac, and General John B. Magruder was, at least in part, playing a major role in bringing it about. Magruder had only two-thirds to one-half the number of men that Union intelligence credited him with having, and fielded only some 11,000 men with which to face McClellan. But "Prince John," as Magruder was called, owing to his passion for pomp and circumstance, would make the watching Federals think that their estimate of his strength had been understated, and that he had considerably more men in the Rebel defenses than had been reported. Magruder was a fan of the theater, and he used his theatrical expertise to advantage by putting on a grand show for the Yankees. In a game of bluff, he shifted and marched his regiments constantly, creating the illusion that his force was much larger than it actually was. Troops would be marched into view of the Federals, and would then disappear behind the Confederate works, only to march around the rear of the fortifications and out in view of the Federals again. Other troops would cheer, as if a new regiment had just arrived, making it appear to the Federals that Magruder's works were crammed with soldiers. This ruse was continued up and down the Confederate line, and, along with the daunting nature of the enemy's works, caused McClellan to believe that his only sensible course of

Top: A portion of McClellan's artillery being amassed at Yorktown for the army's siege operations against the Confederate works. *Bottom*: One of the Union's large siege mortars at Yorktown. McClellan planned to blast the Confederate defenders into submission through the use of his superior firepower (Military History Institute, United States Army War College).

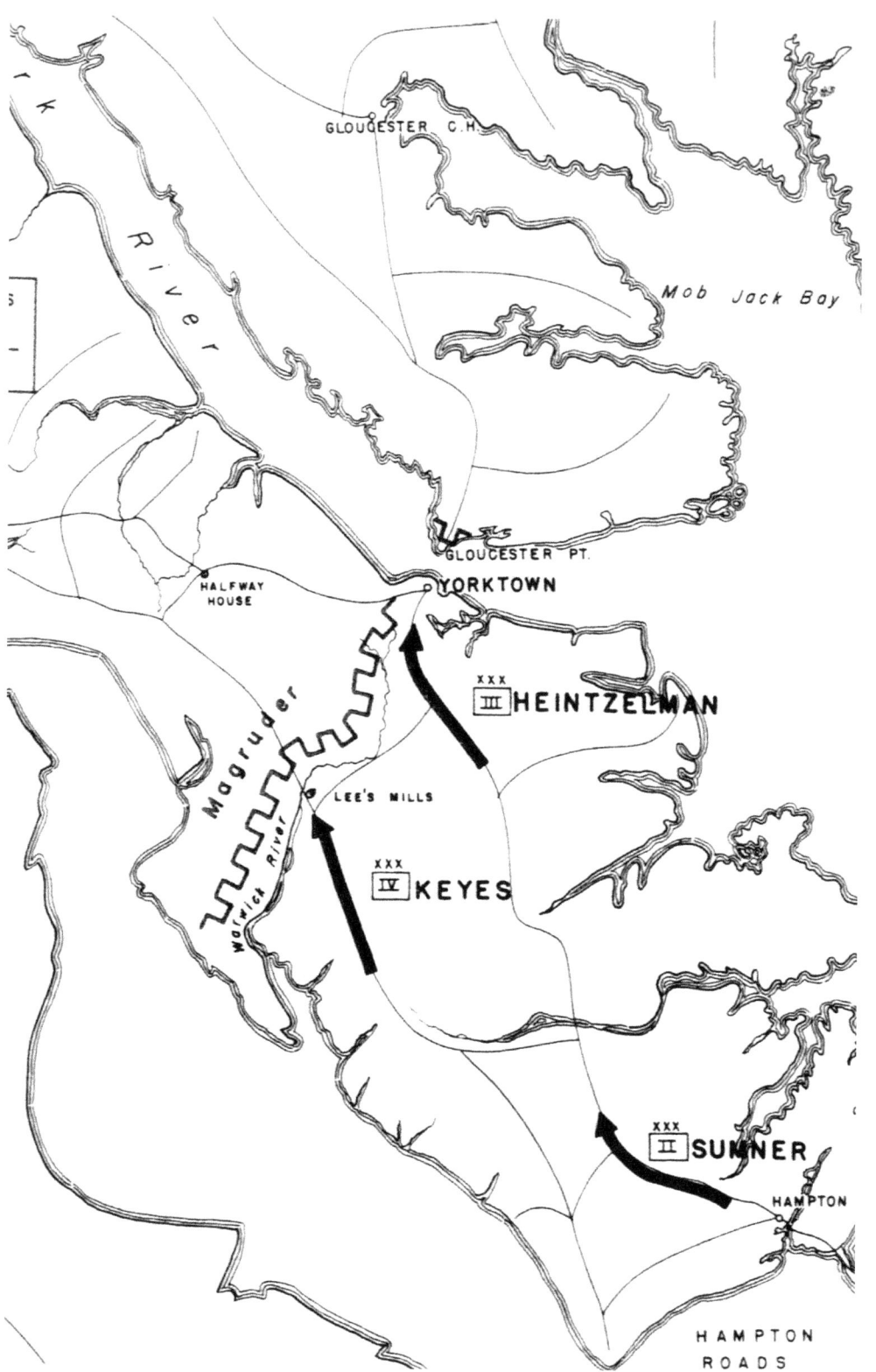

Map showing the relative positions of the contending forces at Yorktown (Military History Institute, United States Army War College).

action was a siege. The ruse worked, and if it was not Magruder's single greatest contribution during the war, it was definitely his most celebrated.

While Magruder's actions helped to stall the Union army in front of Yorktown, the Confederates were scrambling to assemble a sufficient force between McClellan and Richmond to safeguard the capital. President Jefferson Davis and his top field commander, General Joseph E. Johnston, found themselves opposed, in terms of strategy, in much the same manner as McClellan and Lincoln. Davis favored a concentration of Confederate forces at Yorktown, along Magruder's line. The Confederate president wished to keep the Federals as far from Richmond as possible. He also sought to keep as much of the Peninsula as possible in Southern hands. Johnston felt any attempt to hold the lower Peninsula to be foolhardy. He knew that the Federals could use their superior artillery to force the Confederate army out of their prepared positions, and feared that McClellan would use the Union navy to land troops behind the Rebel forces, cutting his army off from Richmond.

> Instead of delaying the Federal army in its approach, I proposed that it should be encountered in front of Richmond by one quite as numerous, formed by uniting there all the available forces of the Confederacy in North Carolina, South Carolina, and Georgia, with those at Norfolk, on the Peninsula, and then near Richmond, including Smith's and Longstreet's divisions, which had arrived. The great army thus formed, surprising that of the United States by an attack when it was expecting to besiege Richmond, would be almost certain to win; and the enemy, defeated a hundred miles from Fort Monroe, their place of refuge, could scarcely escape destruction. Such a victory would decide not only the campaign, but the war, while the present plan could produce no decisive result.[16]

Johnston was quite correct in fearing the entrapment of his army on the lower Peninsula. He was also sound in his judgment that fortifications could delay, but not stop McClellan's forward trek toward Richmond. As for the remainder of his strategy, he was taking a great deal for granted. Could the Confederacy marshal its resources in time to make an even fight of it at the threshold of Richmond? Would McClellan, with greater resources, superior artillery, and naval support, commit an error that would enable the Confederates to attack his army on even terms? Johnston must have known that his plan depended on several circumstances aligning in his favor, or else he would simply be allowing the Federals to advance unchecked to the very gates of Richmond, where the strength of the North's heavy guns could still pound the capital into submission. His plan was risky, but Johnston felt it to be far less so than that proposed by Davis, and he made every argument he could to sway the president. But Davis would not be swayed. Like Lincoln, he was being pressured to bring about action from his military, and a retrograde movement up the Peninsula, without a fight, would panic the government and the people back home, and could potentially demoralize the army. Davis was adamant. Magruder must be reinforced on the Peninsula, and an effort must be made to keep the Federals at arms length from Richmond. Lincoln, with great reservations, would allow McClellan to attempt his plan of campaign. Davis would not allow Johnston to attempt his.

Relations between President Davis and General Johnston were much strained before the campaign for the Peninsula ever began. The rift had begun in August of the previous year, when Davis and Johnston became embroiled in a public controversy over rank in the army. President Davis had nominated Samuel Cooper, Albert Sidney Johnston, Robert E. Lee, Joseph E. Johnston, and Pierre G.T. Beauregard for the rank of full general in the Confederate army. The Confederate Congress confirmed all five men, in the order submitted. According to military code, officers of the same rank resorted to date or order of commission when it came to deciding who was actually the ranking officer among them. This meant that Joseph

Johnston would be the fourth highest general in the army, behind Cooper, A.S. Johnston, and Lee. Johnston took offense to what he perceived to be a slight from Davis, as he had outranked the other three in the United States army at the time they all resigned their commissions. He pointed out that this was contrary to Confederate law, which dictated that generals of like rank would have relative rank according to the commissions they held in the old army. Cooper, A.S. Johnston, and Lee had been colonels when they resigned, while Joseph Johnston held the commission of a brigadier general. Davis maintained that Johnston's commission was for a staff officer, while all the others had been officers of the line. This was true. Johnston was serving as quartermaster general at the time he resigned. Davis felt that a staff commission was beneath that of a line officer, and based his nominations accordingly. Johnston submitted a lengthy written argument to support his claim to the top spot in the Confederate army, but Davis refused to budge. In a terse, two sentence reply, the president said, "I have just received and read your letter of the 12th instant. Its language is, as you say, unusual; its arguments and its statements utterly one-sided, and its insinuations as unfounded as they are unbecoming."[17] Johnston would remain the fourth-ranking general in the army. The personal animosity between the two men would, however, continue to grow and fester.

Confederate spies had reported the activity of the Union fleet gathered at Alexandria from the moment the first transports sailed down the Potomac. The government in Richmond speculated on the possible destinations of the Union military. Fortress Monroe, the Peninsula, and the coast of North Carolina were all viable options. President Davis reacted quickly, trying to counter all possible eventualities. Johnston was ordered to send the brigades of General John G. Walker and Cadmus M. Wilcox from his army in Northern Virginia to Richmond. The reinforcements were not allowed to tarry in the capital. Walker's brigade was sent immediately to North Carolina, and Wilcox's was forwarded to Yorktown. Major General Theophilus Holmes was also detached from service with Johnston's army. Holmes was assigned to take command of the Confederate troops in North Carolina. The transfer of Holmes created a command void in the army, which Johnston filled by assigning Major General Gustavus Woodson Smith to take Holmes' place, in command of the Rebel troops in the Fredericksburg area.[18]

By April 5, Davis had become convinced that the Federal army intended to operate on the Peninsula line, and he reacted accordingly. Johnston received orders to immediately detach the divisions of Generals Daniel Harvey Hill, David R. Jones, and Jubal A. Early and transfer them to the Peninsula. This left Johnston with but four divisions in his army: those of Generals Thomas J. "Stonewall" Jackson, in the Shenandoah Valley; Richard H. Ewell's, along the Rappahannock; James P. Longstreet's, at Orange Court House; and Gustavus W. Smith's, at Fredericksburg.[19] Johnston had correctly deduced McClellan's intentions in making his assault by way of the Peninsula. McClellan had also been correct in predicting what the Confederates would do to counter his movements. As Rebel units were rushed to defend Richmond, the enemy presence in Northern Virginia was significantly reduced. The force remaining would not be strong enough to pose any serious threat to Washington, given the aggregate total of defensive troops McClellan had left behind.

On April 10, General Johnston was summoned to Richmond personally, to meet with the president. Davis informed the general that his command was being expanded to include Norfolk and the Peninsula. He further instructed Johnston to leave only such troops in Northern Virginia as were absolutely necessary for defensive measures. The rest were to be forwarded to Richmond, as soon as possible. Johnston ordered General Ewell to guard the

Professor Thaddeus Lowe and his balloon *Intrepid*. McClellan made great use of this new technology to gain intelligence concerning the position and movements of the Confederates (Military History Institute, United States Army War College).

upper Rappahannock with his division, reinforced by a regiment of cavalry. Jackson was to remain in the Shenandoah Valley, where he was already severely outnumbered. Johnston told Jackson that Ewell's force would be at his disposal, should Stonewall find himself in need of reinforcement, and directed Ewell to comply with any such order from Jackson. General Smith was ordered to leave a mixed force, of brigade strength, in front of Fredericksburg. The remainder of his division, along with Longstreet's division, was to march at once for the capital.[20] These troops were also rushed to the front, where Magruder girded himself for the Union thrust that was sure to come.

From April 6 to April 16, McClellan probed and examined the Confederate line, looking for a weakness. He took full advantage of the newly created U.S. Balloon Corps, the aeronautical brainchild of Thaddeus Lowe, its creator and commander. Lowe had invented a portable gas generator, which enabled his balloons to travel with the army and operate in the field. Lowe took three balloons with him to the Peninsula, with crews and support staff numbering over 100 men. When fully inflated, Lowe's balloons would ascend to a height of 300 feet, from which point Lowe and his crew members could observe the surrounding area for a 15-mile radius. Lowe had even gone so far as to install telegraphs in his balloons, to more easily expedite the flow of information from the balloons to waiting officers on the ground. The balloon corps was a striking innovation in warfare for the Federal army. The Confederates were taken aback by the appearance of balloons rising into the Virginia sky, and feared that they would result in yet another advantage for the Union army. The Southerners were quick to respond by forming a balloon corps of their own. Using ingenuity in an effort to compensate for the superior resources of the Federals, the Confederates adapted a barge as a launching platform for one of their balloons, effectively creating the first aircraft carrier in military history. While the Balloon Corps sparked the imagination (and proved to be hazardous duty for those who went aloft), the information provided by these aeronauts did not materially affect the outcome of the campaign, and revealed little more intelligence than was being gained by land-based probes and reconnaissance. The balloons served as more of an inconvenience than anything else, a constant annoyance to those being observed. For this reason, movements and activities needed to be concealed from the spying enemy eyes, and one Confederate general felt that this alone made the balloons worthwhile. "Even if the observer never saw anything, his balloons would have been worth all they cost, trying to keep our movements out of sight," he wrote.[21]

By April 16, McClellan was certain that he had located the soft-spot in the Rebel defenses—at Lee's Mill, in the center of the Confederate line. He ordered Brigadier General William F. Smith's 2nd Division of the IV Corps to make a reconnaissance in force at a place called Burnt Chimneys, a dam site one mile north of the mill. An artillery barrage preceded Smith's attack, and was successful in silencing two of the three Rebel guns guarding the breastwork of the dam. Smith chose Brigadier General William T. Brooks' Vermont Brigade to spearhead his assault. Brooks' men found a ford across the Warwick, and two companies of the 3rd Vermont splashed across the stream and drove off the Confederate defenders on the opposite shore. Brooks sent three companies of the 4th Vermont across the breastwork, and four companies of the 6th Vermont crossed at the ford, in support of the 3rd Vermont. The 15th North Carolina Infantry had been in front of the Vermonters, but most of the men in the regiment were busy constructing entrenchments for their camp when Brooks launched his assault, and were some 100 yards to the rear of the rifle pits. These men quickly grabbed their muskets and rushed forward, led by regimental commander Colonel Robert M. McKinney. McKinney was shot down in the vanguard of his men, leading to momentary confusion in the ranks. This was compounded when a subordinate officer issued an unauthorized order to fall back. Colonel William T. Wilson's 7th Georgia Infantry was on the scene, however, and with fixed bayonets they charged through the retreating North Carolinians, and fell upon the two companies of the 3rd Vermont. Colonel Lucius M. Lamar's 8th Georgia Infantry supported Wilson, as did three companies of the 2nd Louisiana Infantry. Casualties were mounting, and the 3rd Vermont was being pushed back, out of their recently captured position. Brooks' supporting companies blunted the Confederate counter-stroke, and helped to stabilize the front for the time being. It appeared as if the Army of the Potomac would be able to hold this breach in the Confederate line, and if more troops had been committed to the effort, it is possible that the Warwick line might have been broken, and Magruder forced to abandon his formidable works. In reality, the possibility was indeed a small one. Fearing that the Federals might try an attack in force at this point, the Confederates were already massing to meet it. Brigadier General Howell Cobb, in command at this point of the line, had already committed the 7th and 8th Georgia and a portion of the 2nd Louisiana to the action. He formed the 16th and 24th Georgia Regiments and the Cobb Legion to receive the Federal attack, and steeled himself to hold until reinforcements arrived. Those reinforcements were not long in coming. Brigadier General Lafayette McLaws was on his way with the 10th Louisiana, 15th Virginia, 11th Alabama, and elements of the 17th Mississippi Infantry Regiments. These troops were marched, under fire, to take up a line of battle in reserve of Cobb's men. In addition, McLaws placed the remainder of his division under arms, ready to move as circumstances required. Brigadier General Robert Toombs advanced his brigade forward, throwing two of his regiments into the fray, and holding the remainder in reserve.[22] In the end, the Vermonters were pushed back across the stream, and the reconnaissance came to naught.

One Vermonter described the action from the Union point of view. He credited Colonel Edwin Stoughton, said to be the youngest colonel in the Federal army at the time of his appointment, with firing the first shot of the engagement.

> He had deployed Companies B., Captain Platt, and G., Captain Foster, as skirmishers, and accompanied them in person through the woods to the edge of Warwick Creek, above the dam. As they arrived in sight of the earthwork on the other side, Colonel Stoughton took a musket from a man and discharged it at the works, within which the morning ceremony of guard-mounting was in progress. His men followed the example, and drew from the enemy a brisk response, both of small arms and artillery, till the latter was silenced by the fire of the Vermonters, and by Union batteries.

Once the first attack by the Vermonters had been repulsed, "the remaining four companies, A., F., I., and C., advanced to the end of the dam to take part in the second attempt to carry the Confederate works, but were withdrawn by General Smith's order, before crossing the creek."[23]

McClellan has been accused of missing a golden opportunity to split the Confederate line at Lee's Mill and capture the Yorktown defenses in one bold rush. This has been ascribed to an over-cautious streak in the general that caused him to be unable to assume daring offensive actions. The allegations of Stanton and the members of the Joint Committee on the Conduct of the War that McClellan intended to conduct his campaign by strategy, instead of by fighting battles, was revived, and the general's failure to push forward a general assault at Lee's Mill was used as proof positive that these claims were true. An examination of the facts show that McClellan acted responsibly in not enlarging the size and scope of the reconnaissance. The Vermonters had effected a lodgment in the Rebel works, but only because the Confederate defenders facing them had been pulled from the line at the time of the attack. The enemy responded by bringing several brigades forward, turning the supposed weak spot into one of the strongest points on the line. Cobb had committed six regiments to the front, and Tombs had added another two. Two of Tombs' other regiments were in reserve, as well as four regiments from McLaws' command. In addition, the remainder of McLaws' division were under arms, and ready to march at a moment's notice to the sound of the guns. This meant that the Confederates had 16 regiments at the point of attack or in reserve immediately behind the front line. They also had substantial reinforcements standing by, ready to join the fray at any time their participation should become necessary. The Federals would be forced to attack across the breast of the dam, or at the ford of the Warwick that had been discovered, resulting in their attacking columns being funneled into the action over narrow avenues of approach. To order such an attack in the face of the enemy force described, would have resulted in a bloodbath for the attacking units, and a costly repulse for the Army of the Potomac. Prudence and good judgment guided McClellan's actions, not a lack of personal courage or resolve. This prevented the general from ordering the four Vermont companies poised to attack across the dam, forward to their destruction.

Failing to find a weak point in the Rebel lines that would afford justification in making an attack against the fortifications, McClellan busied himself in pushing forward his own works, and in making preparations for his siege train to arrive. Once the big guns were on hand and positioned, he was sure that the Confederates could easily be blasted from their stronghold. Most of the Federal troops were employed in fatigue duty when not manning the skirmish line or mounting guard details. The manual labor was frequently interrupted by skirmishing, but the Federal approaches continued to inch toward the Rebel works with menacing regularity. The progress was slow and steady. It was assured to produce positive results, but it lacked the dash and glory of a pitched battle.

A large number of the Federal soldiers had never seen blacks before joining the army, and for most, the first slaves they ever encountered were when they entered Virginia. Now, these Northerners were seeing something they never thought possible: armed blacks fighting for the Confederacy. To be sure, they had seen black laborers working within the Rebel works, but these were mostly impressed slaves. Armed black combatants were quite another story. Several reported incidents show that black Confederates actually took an active part in the combat along the Yorktown line. One black sniper took refuge in a chimney in Yorktown, shooting at any exposed target he could find in Camp Scott. He picked off several Union soldiers from his position, despite the pleas of the Northern men for him to desert and join them. In the end, a regiment was marched forward to fire a volley at the sniper's hiding place, resulting in the black soldier being shot through the head. Two more black snipers were reported by Alfred Bellard, of the 5th New Jersey. The two had been firing at Bellard and his comrades from the cover of a hollow tree. One of the snipers was killed when he left his cover, presumably to relieve himself, and the other was wounded. Bellard reported that two white Confederates later tried to retrieve the body, but were driven off by Union fire. Still more black Confederates were seen serving a cannon at Yorktown, loading and firing the gun at the Federal lines. Both men were eventually felled by a Yankee sharpshooter.[24] These incidents were but the first reported glimpses of armed black soldiers serving within the Confederate army during the Peninsula Campaign. Northerners would come face to face with greater numbers of Black Confederates when they drew nearer to Richmond.

Black Confederates were not the only surprise Federal troops found within the enemy lines. General Johnston's advance elements began arriving during the first week in April. When Brigadier General Winfield S. Hancock's brigade captured a few prisoners, one Alabama private from Johnston's army defiantly stated that the general was on the scene with 500 guns and about 100,000 men.[25] The number of guns was a gross exaggeration, and the number of men was almost twice that in Johnston's army, but the information sent shock waves through Union headquarters. Pinkerton operatives had wildly overestimated the number of troops in Johnston's command ever since McClellan had taken charge of the army, and the general had come to believe these reports. When the Alabama private stated the number at 100,000, McClellan was all too quick to accept it as fact. His intelligence reported Johnston having that many men and more, so it became apparent to him that Johnston was present along the Yorktown line with his entire army. It also fortified his belief that a siege was his only viable option.

Johnston was indeed on the scene, but he did not have nearly the force attributed to him. Upon inspecting the defenses, he came to the conclusion that the position was untenable. Federal ships could easily outgun the heavy artillery at Yorktown and Gloucester Point, enabling McClellan to turn his left flank and transport the Federal army all the way to West Point, cutting the Confederates off from their base at Richmond. Johnston did not know that Admiral Goldsborough feared the guns in the Confederate forts as much as Johnston feared the guns of the Union Navy, and had already reneged on undertaking his part in the operation. Johnston did not change his mind when he discovered that the Union army intended to lay siege to the Confederate line, instead of turning the position with their naval guns. Once McClellan got his heavy siege guns in place, it would be only a matter of time before the Confederates would be blasted out of their fortifications. On April 30, Johnston sent a message to General Robert E. Lee, President Davis' military advisor, stating. "We are engaged in a species of warfare at which we can never win. It is plain that General McClellan will adhere to the system adopted by him last summer, and depend for success upon artillery and engineering. We can compete with him in neither."[26]

The Confederate concentration was not yet complete, and Johnston was unwilling to risk the destruction of his army against such overwhelming odds. He decided that his best choice was to abandon the Yorktown line and withdraw toward Richmond. Such a move would surrender the lower Peninsula to the Federals, to be sure. But it would allow Johnston time to reinforce his army, and to choose the time and place he would offer battle to the enemy. However, there was a danger that McClellan might divine his intentions, and attack his army while it was retreating from Yorktown. Johnston needed to steal a march on McClellan. He needed to extricate his forces before the Federals realized what was happening and had time to react. With the Union army in such close proximity, and watching his every move, it would be a tricky task to perform. Secrecy and stealth could only accomplish so much. He would need a great deal of luck to pull off the evacuation.

During the first week in May, McClellan's preparations were nearing completion, and he was almost prepared to open on the Rebel works with his heavy guns. Magruder's defenses had held the Army of the Potomac in front of Yorktown for almost a month, causing consternation back in Washington, and a rift between President Lincoln and his chief general. On May 1, Lincoln responded to a request from McClellan for heavy Parrott guns to be sent to his army from the capital. The president, falling victim to intrigues of Stanton, was starting to believe that Little Mac did not intend to fight. He tersely responded: "Your call for Parrott guns from Washington alarms me, chiefly because it argues indefinite procrastination. Is anything to be done?" McClellan's answer destroyed Lincoln's premise and showed that he was doing all he could to facilitate the speedy reduction of the enemy works. "I asked for the Parrott guns from Washington for the reason that some expected had been two weeks, nearly, on the way and could not be heard from. They arrived last night. My arrangements had been made for them, and I thought time might be saved by getting others from Washington. My object was to hasten, not procrastinate. All is being done that human labor can accomplish."[27]

Forrest Little, a soldier in the 5th Vermont Infantry, agreed with McClellan, and believed his strategy to be correct. "General McClellan is working it so we shant [sic] have to loose [sic] many lifes [sic] in the battle of Yorktown. He is doing the thing slow but sure. I think he knows what he is about. If these Rascality [sic] Congress men will only let him alone we shant [sic] have no Bull run nor Pittsford (Pittsburgh) Landing affair."[28]

Johnston was aware that time was running out for his army in Yorktown. The night of May 3 was selected for the evacuation. Despite all their efforts at concealment, however, spying enemy eyes observed activity that should have forewarned the Federal army that Johnston was preparing to flee the trap. As early as May 2, two Federal signal officers, Charles Herzog and W.H.R. Neel, reported that the Confederate works at Lee's Mill had been abandoned. On the morning of May 2, Lieutenant A.B. Jerome reported Rebel barracks in Yorktown being destroyed. Confederate wagons had also been observed moving to the rear, presumably to get them out of the way of a rapid retreat. The report of the destroyed barracks was dismissed as not necessarily meaning that the enemy intended to withdraw. The information regarding the evacuation of the defenses at Lee's Mill never made its way to army headquarters. It was stopped at division or corps headquarters, and McClellan was never made aware of the occurrence.[29] Even if the intelligence had reached the general, it is questionable if it would have made a difference. The most recent observations of Professor Lowe's balloon corps revealed nothing to indicate that the Confederates were planning to abandon their lines. McClellan was certain that Johnston planned to offer battle at Yorktown, and felt sure that the Confederate army had the numbers to make it a fearful contest. At nightfall on May 3, Johnston began pulling his troops out of the line and marching them north, toward Richmond. The movement was covered by a heavy, random artillery bombardment, which lasted until approximately 2:00 A.M. By 4:30 A.M., a signal station in the center of the Federal line reported that the enemy works in their front seemed to be evacuated. A personal inspection of the fortifications confirmed the initial report, and the news was sent to army headquarters. Soon after daylight, a message was received from Moore's House, in the city: "Our flag flies over Yorktown."[30]

A member of the 56th New York Infantry Regiment described the events leading up to his regiment entering the Yorktown lines. On the morning of May 4, a staff officer rode into the camp of the 56th and issued orders for the men to be ready to move in two hours, with three days' rations.

> Promptly on time the regiment marched out of camp, through the woods into an open field in front of and within easy artillery range of the enemy's works; a line of battle was quickly formed, each man, in response to orders, threw off his roll of blankets, haversack and canteen, which were placed together, each company's things in a pile, and a guard left with them, preparatory to making a charge on the works along the entire line. Between our regiment and the earthworks was a wide slashing made by felling trees outward from the line of works, which made a tangle of trees and tree tops, which it was very difficult to make our way through, especially as the limbs of the trees had been cut off near the outer ends with sharp axes, making a sharp point to each limb. At the order, the line immediately moved forward on a charge, crawling through, under and over the almost impenetrable tangle, which was at last accomplished, much to our astonishment but satisfaction, without a gun being fired on either side. Climbing the embankment and forming a line inside was the work of but a few minutes, when it was found that the enemy had evacuated the works, taking everything with them, probably the night before.[31]

The Confederates had indeed taken everything they could, but a great quantity of material had to be left behind, including 77 pieces of heavy cannon. The South was in dire need of heavy ordnance, but Johnston did not possess the means to remove them.[32]

The 22nd Massachusetts Infantry claimed the honor of raising the first flag over the captured city of Yorktown. The regiment had been performing picket duty when the men discovered that the Rebels had abandoned their works. As regiments performing such duty were not permitted to carry their flags, Colonel Jesse Gove sent a man back to their camp to bring their flag forward. Gove planted the flag on the enemy works with his own hands, officially claiming Yorktown for the Union. Before departing, one Confederate soldier had posted a public message for the Yankees that would occupy the town on a private dwelling:

> To the Future Yankee Occupants of this Place:
> We have retired to the country for a short time to recruit our health. We find that with your two hundred thousand men you are too modest to visit this place, and we give you an opportunity to satisfy your curiosity with regard to our defenses, assuring you that we will call upon you soon. We hope a few days residence in a house once occupied by men will induce enough courage in your gallant hearts to enable you to come within at least two miles of white men hereafter. Be sure to have on hand a supply of pork 'n beans when we return; also some codfish and "apple sass." When we learn to relish such diet we may become like you — Puritanical, selfish, thieving, God-forgotten, devil-worshipping, devil-belonging, African-loving, blue-bellied Yankees. Advise father Abraham to keep his Scotch cloak on hand, to keep soberer, and your wise Congress to hunt up two thou-

sand five hundred millions of specie to pay the debt you have incurred in winning the contempt of every live man. We have on hand a few tools which we devote to the special duty of loosening the links of your steel shirts. Couldn't you get a few iron-clad men to do your fighting? Are you not horribly afraid that we will shoot you below the shirts? When are you coming to Richmond? Couldn't you go up the river with us? There is one score which we will yet settle with you to the death. Your fiend-like treatment of old men and helpless women reads you out of the pale of civilized warfare, and if rifles are true and knives keen, we will rid some of you of your beastly inclinations.... We despise you as heartily as we can whip you easily on any equal field.

Most heartily at your service, whenever you offer a fight.

J. Traviso Scott
Company A, Sixth Georgia Volunteers.[33]

Though the city had fallen, and the enemy had fled, Union troops in Yorktown still needed to exercise caution. "Before evacuating Yorktown, the enemy had placed torpedoes in the ground close to every object of interest or attraction about the town, so that danger was in our way at every step."[34] The booby traps were everywhere, and a number of curious Federals were killed or wounded by their detonation. The employment of these indiscriminate killing devices was a new development in the war, and was roundly criticized by Union officers. Captain Francis Donaldson thought that this "conduct on their part will only reflect upon their cause, which must indeed be a bad one when such measures of revenge are resorted to."[35]

One Union officer related an incident regarding the booby traps where "a soldier, taking his seat with his companions on a green knoll, near to a well, saw lying at his feet a pocket-knife. As he picked this up he found around it a small cord; without thinking of the concealed danger, he gave the knife a sudden jerk to break the cord. This was followed by an explosion which blew the soldier into a hundred fragments." This same officer also related the steps the Union army took to find and remove the hidden bombs. Confederate prisoners were immediately put to work "unearthing the concealed shells."[36]

Brigadier General Gabriel Rains was in command of the Confederate rearguard. Rains was fond of explosives, and given to conducting experiments in that field. It was under his direction and supervision that the booby-traps had been placed in and around Yorktown. Rains continued to place his deadly surprises along the line of retreat until Colonel Moxely Sorrell learned of his actions. "Hearing this I reported the matter to Longstreet, who instantly stopped it. He caused me to write Rains a rather severe note, reminding him that such practices were not considered in the limits of legitimate warfare, and that if he would put them aside and pay some attention to his brigade his march would be better and his stragglers not so numerous. This officer did not remain long on duty in the field."[37] McClellan protested the use of the booby-traps, but the Confederates had stopped the practice before his indignant message ever reached Johnston.

Mines and booby traps were not the only innovations unveiled at Yorktown. The Federals had introduced a new weapon of their own during the siege. A machine gun, invented by Wilson Ager and promoted by salesman J.D. Mills, first made its appearance on the siege lines at Yorktown. The weapon, commonly known as the "Coffee Mill Gun," had a single barrel mounted on artillery wheels. Cartridges were loaded into a hopper mounted on top of the weapon. A hand crank fed the cartridges from the hopper into the barrel, where they were detonated. The gun fired at a rate of 120 rounds per minute, by design, as the inventor understood that a higher rate of fire would over heat the barrel and make the gun inoperable, unsafe, or both. It was President Lincoln who tagged the invention with the name of "Coffee Mill Gun," during a test of the weapon in Washington, because of the similarity in design to a coffee mill. McClellan had approved an order to have 50 of the Ager Guns manufactured. Colonel Charles H. Van Wyck's 56th New York Infantry, of General Naglee's Brigade, had one of the machine guns, and used it during the operations against the Confederate defenses. A New York reporter who observed the gun in action said, "The balls flew thick and fast, and the Yankee invention must have astonished the other side." A number of Ager Guns were with the Army of the Potomac on the Peninsula, and would see service during the campaign. Several Pennsylvania regiments were armed with them, including the 49th Pennsylvania, which bears the distinction of having the first machine gunner wounded in battle. Private George Wills was wounded in the thigh while operating the Ager Gun assigned to that regiment.[38] The Confederates had been working on a rapid-fire weapon of their own, which would make its battlefield debut later in the campaign.

Back in Washington, the administration was still laboring under the impression that McClellan's actions were far too ponderous and timid. Senator Charles Sumner, of Massachusetts, stated that Lincoln and his cabinet were in accord that the general should be relieved of his command. News of the capture of Yorktown prompted a stay of execution, however, and bought more time for McClellan, as the administration decided to "let the matter stand for the present."[39] McClellan's actions, upon receiving news of the Confederate evacuation, were anything but ponderous and timid. He ordered an immediate pursuit of the enemy, whose rear guard was commanded by General J.E.B. Stuart. Brigadier General George Stoneman was instructed to give chase with all the available cavalry and horse artillery. Stoneman's troopers were to be supported by infantry, marching on both the Lee's Mill and Yorktown Roads. Stoneman had with him four batteries of artillery, the 1st and 6th United States Cavalry, the 8th Illinois Cavalry, and Captain Charles Barker's Squadron of Illinois Cavalry. Brigadier General Joseph Hooker's division was to follow the cavalry, and provide Stoneman with infantry support. Seeing the opportunity to trap the Confederates out in the open, McClellan made plans to advance General William B. Franklin's division up the York River, to land behind the fleeing Rebels. General Sumner, commanding on the Federal left, was ordered to repair the bridges over the Warwick River, advance by the Lee's Mill Road, and place the divisions of Generals William F. Smith, Darius Couch, and Silas Casey in front of the Confederates, holding them in place to afford Stoneman an opportunity to gain the enemy's rear. About eight miles from Yorktown, Stoneman caught up with the rear guard of Johnston's army. After driving them out of their position, the general pushed his troopers forward, in an attempt to seize the intersection of the Yorktown and Lee's Mill Roads, about two miles south of Williamsburg. When Stoneman's advance arrived at the intersection, they found it guarded by a strong earthwork, Fort Magruder, containing a regiment of cavalry, two regiments of infantry, and an artillery battery. Stoneman sent word back to Hooker, requesting immediate support. The defenders at Fort Magruder did likewise, and a build up of forces was soon taking shape outside of Williamsburg.[40]

In the meantime, McClellan was focusing his energies on pushing Franklin's division up the York, and getting behind the Confederates. In a best-case scenario, he would be able to cut Johnston's army off from its base at Richmond, and force the Confederates to fight out in the open. At the very least, he should be able to separate Johnston from his wagon train, depriving the enemy of desperately needed munitions and supplies when he finally brought them to battle. Poor weather conditions, and inadequate wharf facilities at Yorktown, made the business of embarking Franklin's men a tedious process, and it would take two full days before the division could be landed at their desired position. McClellan kept a watchful eye on developments from Stoneman's and Sumner's fronts, and retained the divisions of Generals Fitz-John Porter, John Sedgwick, Israel B. Richardson, and George Sykes for deployment in support of the movements of Stoneman, Sumner, or Franklin, wherever the need was the greatest.[41] McClellan was not trying to merely harass the retreating enemy, he was attempting to bring them to bay and force a battle. His actions were swift and decisive, and his decisions were predicated upon the intent of trapping Johnston's army in the open, and not giving the Confederates the opportunity to once more oppose him from behind daunting works, as had been the case at Yorktown. The activity and energy exhibited by the general during this pursuit was in stark contrast to the allegations being made by his detractors in the administration, that he had no desire to fight, and was far too slow and tedious in his movements. If the Confederates could be brought to ground, he would yet have the opportunity to prove his critics wrong, and show that his strategy had been right all along. Everything depended on Stoneman and Hooker being able to keep the Confederate army in place, forcing them to go on line to defend their rear from assault, enabling Franklin's movement up the York to arrive at a point behind the enemy between Johnston's army and the Southern capital. Timing was everything. If all of his movements went according to plan, McClellan could catch Johnston in an untenable position, and make him pay for his decision to abandon his strong works at Yorktown. Speed was of the essence, however — a fact not lost upon his counterpart in the Confederate army. The race to Richmond was on, and the possible outcome of the war hung in the balance. Goldsborough's flotilla even sprang into action. Upon learning that the heavy gun positions at Yorktown had been evacuated, the Federal ships steamed into the channel between there and Gloucester Point, ready at last to lend material aid to McClellan's forward thrust.

Four

To the Edge of Victory

When General Stoneman arrived at Fort Magruder, he determined the place to be too strongly held by the enemy to risk a general assault with the men he had on hand. Nonetheless, he ordered Major L. A. Williams to make a demonstration with his 6th U.S. Cavalry, to check the enemy until Hooker's infantry could arrive. Williams' troopers sallied forth, only to be met by a galling fire from the fort's defenders, and were saved from destruction only by the gallant charge of the regiment's rear squadron, which enabled Williams' men to extricate themselves from the field. In the meantime, Stoneman learned that Hooker's vanguard was still some two hours distant. The general determined to pull his troopers back and await the arrival of Hooker's infantry.[1] Though Stoneman had been unable to make a dent in the defenses at Fort Magruder, he had been successful in forcing Johnston to halt at least a portion of his army to meet the menace to his rear.

Thus far, both the retreat and pursuit were being hampered by frightful conditions. A torrential downpour on the night of May 3 may have helped to conceal the Confederate withdrawal from their lines, but it created miserable conditions for the soldiers on both sides. A Confederate colonel later recalled the difficulties endured by the men in their march to Williamsburg. "The horrible roads are well remembered even now by all those who passed them on that dark and rainy night. The mud and water were ankle and sometimes knee deep, and infantry were often called to help the weary horses drag wagons from holes and ruts in which the wheels had sunk to the very axels."[2] Worn-out Confederates often dropped by the roadside to catch a few moments' sleep before plodding onward. The Federal pursuit took place over the same roads the Southerners had used, which by this time had been churned into an absolute sea of mud through the plodding of thousands of feet and hooves, and the heavy wheels of artillery and supply wagons. Speed was of the essence for both commanders, but nature was contriving to slow the efforts of both sides. The Confederate retreat was toilsome and difficult. The Union pursuit was even more so, due to the fact that the enemy had all but destroyed the road through their passage.

General John B. Gordon, then colonel of the 6th Alabama Infantry, left an account of the retreat that is both touching and humorous. Along the line of march Gordon found one of his

> youngest soldiers—he was a mere lad—lying on the roadside, weeping bitterly. I asked him what was the matter. He explained that his feet were so sore that he could not walk any farther and that he knew he would be captured. His feet were in a dreadful condition. I said to him, "You shall not be captured," and ordered him to mount my horse and ride forward until he could get into an ambulance or wagon, and to tell the quartermaster to send my horse back to me as soon as possible. He wiped his eyes, got into my saddle, and rode a few rods to where the company of which he

Top: Looking southeast along current day Route 60, in Williamsburg, Virginia. The Confederates retreated, and the Federals advanced, along this road from Yorktown in May of 1862. *Bottom:* The spot where Fort Magruder was located. The city of Williamsburg has overrun the battlefield, and the location of the fort is now the site of the Fort Magruder Hotel & Conference Center (photographs taken by author).

was a member had halted to rest. He stopped his horse in front of his comrades, who were sitting for the moment on the roadside, and straightening himself up, he lifted his old slouch-hat with all the dignity of a commander-in-chief and called out: "Attention, men! I'm about to bid you farewell, and I want to tell you before I go that I am very sorry for you. I was poor once myself!" Having thus delivered himself, he galloped away, bowing and waving his hat to his comrades in acknowledgement of the cheers with which they greeted him.[3]

News of the rear guard action at Williamsburg was received with suspicion by General Johnston. "I became convinced that it was a mere demonstration, intended to delay our march — that the Federal army might pass us by water." Johnston sensed a trap, and was not about to allow himself to be drawn into a general engagement at Williamsburg. As he stated it, his only purpose was to "hold the ground long enough to enable our baggage-trains to get out of the way of the troops."[4] Johnston had no intention of obliging McClellan and offering battle to the Union forces nipping at the heels of his retreating army. All the same, the threat had to be dealt with, as the Union pursuit had been speedy enough to catch up with the rear guard, and endangered the Confederate wagon train. The train had to be protected, and given time to clear the area. As such, Johnston needed to administer a check to the Union advance, and buy time for his precious wagons of supplies and munitions. Fort Magruder, with its connected works, provided him with an opportunity to deliver that check with a minimum of risk to his own army.

Johnston had pushed the divisions of Generals John Magruder and Gustavus Smith forward, toward Richmond. Those of James Longstreet and Daniel H. Hill were left behind to support Stuart's cavalry, with Longstreet in overall command. Neither commander antic-

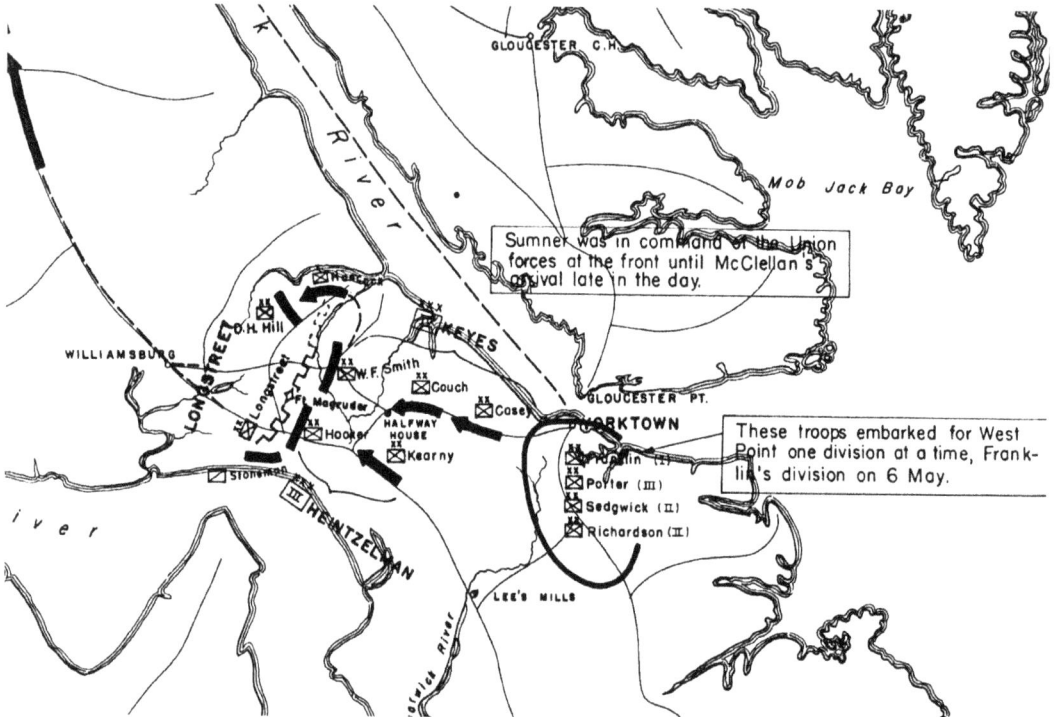

Map showing the relative positions of the opposing forces at Williamsburg (Military History Institute, United States Army War College).

ipated a serious engagement at Williamsburg. McClellan remained in Yorktown, arranging the details to transport Franklin's division up the York. He assigned command of the Union pursuit to General Sumner, his senior corps commander. Johnston remained with the main body of his army, confident that Longstreet could manage affairs with the rear guard.

Union infantry arrived in front of Williamsburg just before dark on May 4. The rain that had made the march so deplorable continued to fall, drenching the troops on both sides, and causing weapons to become useless due to drenched powder. Sumner deployed Hooker's division on the left, opposite Fort Magruder. William F. Smith's division took position on the right. The front was extremely narrow at this point. Marshes on either flank shortened the line the Confederates needed to defend to only four miles. At the center of the line stood Fort Magruder, some 600 yards wide, and protected by a deep ditch. The line also contained 13 redoubts, and supporting rifle pits, but Fort Magruder served as the linchpin of the defenses. General Sumner decided to attack the works at daylight on the morning of May 5. Regrettably, he neglected to issue any specific orders concerning the assault to either Hooker or Smith.[5]

Edwin Vose Sumner was 65 years old during the Peninsula Campaign. He had been in the service of his country since 1819, and was by far the senior of any of McClellan's commanders when it came to age or experience. While he was a good soldier, astute at following orders, Sumner was not inclined to issuing orders. The result of his lack of communication was that the assault was delayed until 7:30 A.M. on the 5th, and then it was only brought about by the impetuous nature of one of his division commanders. Joe Hooker had been chafing at the bit ever since daybreak. Ambitious and confident, Hooker sought to make a name for himself at Williamsburg by winning laurels on the battlefield. An artillery officer who observed him that morning related that the general had his back up for a fight. "His great idea was to go ahead quick until you ran against the enemy, and then fight him."[6] Hooker advanced his skirmishers to engage the enemy occupying the rifle pits in front of Fort Magruder, and the fight was joined. He next ordered up the six guns of Battery H, 1st United States Light Artillery, and ordered the cannoneers to shell the Confederate line, preparatory to a general advance. Confederate gunners responded, however, and their fire killed two officers in the battery, causing hysterical fear among the men. The Union artillerymen deserted their guns and ran for the rear. Officers tried to reform the battery, but the men refused to rally. The 6th New York Battery was ordered up and went into position beside the guns of the 1st U.S. The New Yorkers not only manned their own guns, but took charge of the abandoned ones as well, and soon Hooker had 12 cannon belching death and destruction at the enemy works. Hooker ordered his battle line forward, and for the next two hours the Federals made headway toward the enemy fortifications. During this time, Sumner did nothing to support Hooker's move. He had some 28,000 men in the immediate vicinity of Williamsburg, all save Hooker's remaining idle. General Longstreet took notice of the inactivity of the rest of Sumner's units and decided it would be safe to concentrate his entire force against Hooker. He counterattacked, mounting three different charges, and drove the Federals back for a distance of nearly one and one-half miles. As the Confederates surged into the Union ranks, small arms fire gave way to hand-to-hand fighting. Seven Union battle flags were captured, and the 9th Alabama Infantry and the 19th Mississippi Infantry overran and captured all 12 guns of the 1st U.S. and 6th New York Batteries.[7]

Private Alfred Bellard, of the 5th New Jersey Infantry, was engaged on this part of the field. He related how the famed Louisiana Tigers had advanced upon his brigade in the first charge, bearing the stars and stripes, in an effort to prevent the Federals from firing on them. "The ruse did not succeed and buck and ball was poured into them so thick from the 6th, 7th, and 8th (New Jersey) who were immediately in their front, that they were well satisfied to get back as quick as their legs could carry them." But when the third Rebel charge broke the Union line, Bellard reported the men

> fell back under a galling fire.... As the fight was going against us and the men being about used up, the regimental bands were ordered to consolidate and play.... And as soon as the bands struck up three cheers for the red, white and blue, two guns were run out on the road. A shower of grape and canister was sent into the advancing rebels who were seen coming down the road. And as cheer upon cheer rent the air, the infantry, who had a few moments before been on the skedaddle, now rushed in with renewed vigor, as did also the stragglers who had previously been got together as a sort of forlorn hope.[8]

It was now approximately 4:00 P.M. The battle had been raging all day, though it had been an unequal contest, Hooker's division being forced to go it alone against the Confederates. Finally, Sumner sprang to action by ordering Major General Phil Kearny's division forward in support of Hooker. The choice of Kearny was indeed a curious one. Not that Kearny wasn't itching for a fight — he was. Having been promoted to division command only three days before, he was eager to prove himself worthy of his new responsibilities. But his division had only just arrived on the field. They had been the last division in the line of march, and had spent all day in reaching the field. For whatever reason, Sumner chose these weary, foot-sore troops to support Hooker, instead of one of the rested divisions that had been in the vicinity all day. Kearny voiced no protest over the selection — quite the contrary. When he received the order to attack, the general drew his sword in his right hand, clenched the reins of his horse in his teeth, and rode toward the sound of the heaviest fighting to determine the strength and position of the enemy. He had lost his left arm in the Mexican American War, but the disability seemed to make him only more determined to prove his mettle. Two staff officers were killed during his reconnaissance, but Kearny returned to his men unscathed. He ordered his regiments forward, and when some of the men hesitated to plunge into the blazing inferno he turned to them and shouted, "Don't flinch boys! They're shooting at me, not at you." The comment brought forth a round of laughter from the men, and Kearny yelled, "That's it boys! That's it! Go in gaily!" The Union line swept forward, striking the Confederates and driving them back. They even recaptured seven of the 12 cannon that had previously been lost to the enemy. The Confederates had already taken five of the guns off the field — all that they had spare horses for. Kearny's men eventually regained most of the ground that had been lost, pushing the Rebels all the way back to the clearing in front of Fort Magruder.[9]

Thus far, the battle had been a series of charges and counter charges, with neither side being able gain a decisive advantage. Longstreet had been able to hold off the Union pursuit for the entire day and had fulfilled his mission of buying time for the Confederate wagon train to be evacuated from the area. If he could now safely disengage and extricate his forces from the Union front, the engagement at Williamsburg would be a tactical victory for the South. Events were transpiring on the Confederate left flank, however, which could trap Longstreet and his men and turn the battle into a strategic victory for the North.

Brigadier General Winfield Scott Hancock's brigade found itself in a position to possibly determine the outcome of the day. That morning, a reconnaissance of the Confederate position had revealed that two of the redoubts on the far left of the enemy line were unoccupied. Sumner directed a flanking movement be made in that direction, and Hancock was selected for the purpose. A 38-year-old West Point graduate with a fine service record, and a born leader (despite his reputation for voluminous repertoire of profanity on the battlefield), Hancock had strained at the bit as Hooker's and Kearny's forces engaged the enemy approximately two miles south of his position. He had reached his assigned point on the Confederate line, with the 2,500 men of his brigade, at 12:00 P.M., and had sent skirmishers forward. Noting the exposed nature of his own right flank, he had twice requested reinforcements, but was refused both times by Sumner. Worse yet, at about 2:00 P.M., as Hooker's men were being driven from the field, he received orders from Sumner to withdraw. Hancock delayed following the order, hoping Sumner would change his mind, but by 5:00 P.M., he was preparing to comply and fall back. It was while making preparations for the withdrawal that Hancock's force was first discovered by General Longstreet. General Magruder, the architect of the defenses, lay ill that day, and it is probable that Longstreet, unfamiliar with the works as he was, did not even know that the two redoubts on his left were unoccupied. Longstreet had a strong reserve, the division of Major General Daniel H. Hill, the hard-fighting North Carolinian, and brother-in-law of Stonewall Jackson. Hill's brigade commanders were certain that they could drive the Yankees back (not knowing that they planned to leave anyway), and requested permission to launch an attack. Longstreet was hesitant to grant his permission. In his mind, he had already completed his mission of covering the withdrawal of the Confederate supply train. The attack on Hancock's men might be costly, and was an unnecessary action. At length, however, permission was granted. General Johnston had recently arrived on the field, and statements differ as to whether it was he or Longstreet who finally approved the attack.[10]

Brigadier General Jubal A. Early's brigade, some 2,300 strong, was chosen to make the assault. Brigadier General Gabriel J. Rains' brigade was ordered to support Early. The Confederates advanced in a battle line of four regiments. The 24th Virginia was on the left, and the 5th North Carolina was on the right. The center was held by the 23rd Virginia and the 38th Virginia. Early was to command the regiments on the left, and took position with the 24th Virginia, his old regiment. Hill, who was accompanying the attack, was to command the regiments on the right, and placed himself with the 5th North Carolina. The two flanking regiments went forward rapidly, and soon outdistanced the two regiments in the center, which seemed content to engage the enemy at long distance. Seeing the separation between the regiments, the commander of the 5th North Carolina executed an unusual movement by marching his men completely across his own brigade front to form them on the right flank of the 23rd Virginia. The two regiments then surged forward to the attack.[11]

As the Confederate wave surged forward, Hancock was heard to say, "You must hold this ground or I am ruined."[12] He had tarried in following Sumner's order to give up the ground because of his conviction that the position he held was too important to give up. If that disobedience now ended in disaster, Hancock knew that his military career would probably be over. The Confederates pressed forward gallantly, as Hancock cautioned his men to aim low and gave the order to fire at will. General Early was hit in the shoulder and had to be removed from the field. The gray tide swept forward, amid the crash of Hancock's artillery, and the constant rattle of the Federal musketry. Hancock would later praise the enemy for the extreme bravery of their charge, but bravery alone could not overcome the disadvantages the Confederates were contending against. Owing to the fact that only half of Early's brigade was actually taking part in the charge, the Confederates were outnumbered about two to one. The Union troops were also afforded the protection of the captured Confederate works. As a result, the assault was unable to close with the Federals, and was stopped 20 paces from the Union line. Hancock sensed that the time was right for a counterattack. Lieutenant George Armstrong Custer, an officer whose star was in ascendancy, and who would later distinguish himself as the boy-general of the Civil War, happened to be near Hancock during this time. Custer described the scene in his journal: "With that excessive politeness of manner which characterizes him when everything is being conducted according to his liking, Hancock, as if conducting guests to a banquet rather than fellow-beings to a life-and-death struggle, cried out in tones well befitting a Stentor: 'Gentlemen, charge with the bayonet.'"[13]

Hancock's troops responded immediately, and the unexpected rush of the Federals caught the Rebels completely by surprise. The Confederates recoiled, then began a precipitate retreat from the field. But the Federals were upon them before many Confederates could make good their escape. Approximately 500 prisoners were captured from Early's brigade by the time the pursuit was called off. This was in addition to the numerous losses that had been inflicted in the form of those killed and wounded. For his part, Hancock's brigade had sustained but 31 total casualties in the engagement, making his victory one of the most glorious achievements of the war to date.

General McClellan had arrived on the field at Williamsburg at approximately 5:00 P.M. News of the developments there had caused him to lay aside the work he was doing to facilitate the transfer of Franklin's division up the York River, and ride the 13 miles to Williamsburg to assume control of the fighting himself. By the time he got his bearings, the action in Hancock's front was already underway. McClellan described the situation when he arrived: "I found everything in a state of chaos and depression. Even the private soldiers saw clearly that, with force enough in hand to gain victory, we, as the pursuers, were on the defensive and content with repulsing attacks, and that there was no plan of action, no directing hand."[14] He ordered Hooker and Hancock to be reinforced, and took steps to reestablish communications between the two wings. As these steps were being taken, word arrived at headquarters that Hancock had not only repulsed the Confederates, he had attacked and driven them from the field. McClellan rode at once for Hancock's position. Along the way, he passed the line of Confederate prisoners being marched to the rear. Upon joining Hancock, McClellan saw exactly what his subordinate had seen when he tarried in obeying Sumner's order to withdraw. The commanding general congratulated Hancock and his men on the victory they had achieved. Though the coming of darkness and the most recent cloudburst had curtailed operations for the day, McClellan made preparations to resume the contest on the following morning. That night, he sent a report of the action to Washington, praising Hancock's actions. "Hancock was superb today," he wrote in a telegram to his wife.[15] The epithet stuck. For the remainder of his life, he would be known as "Hancock the Superb." The youthful George A. Custer would also realize his first distinction of the war at Williamsburg, when he captured a battle flag from the attacking Confederates.

McClellan's arrangements to resume the battle on May 6 proved to be in vain. Longstreet's mission to protect the supply train had been accomplished, and Johnston saw no need to remain in Williamsburg any longer. On the night of May 5, he began pulling Longstreet's men out of the line and marching them northward. Both sides would claim victory at Williamsburg. The Confederates maintained that they had successfully prevented the Union army from preventing their retreat, and had given the Federal pursuers a serious check in the process. The Federals would claim victory on the basis of Hancock's thrilling charge that inflicted serious casualties on the enemy and rendered the Confederate defenses untenable. Losses were high on both sides, especially when one considers that this was a holding action in which only a relatively small portion of the armies participated. Union losses were listed as 456 killed, 1,410 wounded, and 373 missing, for a total of 2,239. The Confederates reported casualties in killed and wounded of 1,570, with another 133 listed as missing, for a total of 1,703.[16] Given the fact that Hancock's brigade captured some 500 prisoners by itself, it is obvious that the Southern losses were under reported. It was also obvious that the Confederates had scored a tactical victory in the engagement. Longstreet had indeed accomplished all that he had been ordered to do in protecting the retreating Rebel army. In fact, the fighting at Williamsburg resulted in even more substantial benefits to the Southern cause. It had given Johnston the opportunity of pushing the divisions of Generals Smith and Magruder rapidly forward, in a northwesterly direction, toward Barhamsville. It had also necessitated McClellan directing two of his divisions, those of Generals Sedgwick and Richardson, away from their intended embarkation at Yorktown. The time bought at Williamsburg had allowed Johnston to get a significant portion of his army well up the Peninsula, and out of harm's way from the waterborne blocking movement he anticipated McClellan to be making. It also meant that McClellan's blocking force, for the time being, had been reduced by two full divisions. As such,

General Winfield S. Hancock. His hard-fighting and skillful leadership at Williamsburg forever earned him the sobriquet of "Hancock the Superb." (Military History Institute, United States Army War College.

the rear guard action at Williamsburg produced more fruitful results than even Johnston anticipated. Another result of the battle was that it reinforced McClellan's beliefs regarding the corps commanders that the administration had forced upon him. The general had argued all along that the army should not be formed up into corps until such time as division officers had been able to prove their leadership qualities on the field of battle, ensuring that only the best and brightest received promotions. Sumner's lack of activity at Williamsburg only served to convince McClellan that he had been right in his assumptions, and caused him to worry over the command structure that had been forced upon him. Steps would need to be taken in an effort to circumvent the hold of the four Republican appointed corps commanders over the army.

On May 6, the Army of the Potomac marched out of its positions in front of the Confederate defenses and took possession of the town. As the Union troops walked over the ground that had been the scene of conflict the previous day, one soldier noted "the sight that greeted our eyes was a most ghastly one, hundreds of dead of both armies were strewn in every direction, trampled on, and half buried in the mud. Numbers of wounded were moaning piteously for help, while dead and dying horses, broken wagons, and abandoned guns lay scattered in all directions. As soon as our men took possession of the field, details were set to work to bury the dead and care for the wounded; long trenches were dug and

General Edwin V. Sumner. Sumner's inaction at Williamsburg possibly cost the Union an opportunity to cut off and destroy a portion of Johnston's army. He would redeem himself magnificently at Fair Oaks, however (Military History Institute, United States Army War College).

the dead laid therein, side by side."[17] When the dead and wounded on the field had been tended to, the soldiers marched the two miles that separated the battlefield from Williamsburg. The reception they received was far from friendly: "The citizens acted at first as if they expected the most inhuman treatment from our men; at every house a white flag was displayed in token of surrender, but not a single case of inhumanity was heard of from our boys. On the contrary, guards were placed at every house to prevent our soldiers from intruding on the inmates."[18]

On that same day, President Lincoln arrived at Fortress Monroe, accompanied by Secretary of War Stanton and Secretary of the Treasury Salmon P. Chase. The president had come to personally observe McClellan's progress, and to judge for himself if anything could be done to hasten the advance of the army. He also wished to see if something could be done to eliminate the threat still posed by the Confederate ironclad *Virginia*. The Rebel monster had been in dry dock for several weeks, getting the necessary repairs for the damage incurred during its engagement with the *Monitor*, but it was now ready for offensive action again, and the president feared the influence it might now exert over the campaign. Stanton had proposed that an expedition be launched to capture Norfolk, thereby depriving the *Virginia* of its port, and rendering it useless to the Confederacy. He felt that 10,000 men would be sufficient for the job, properly supported by the navy. McClellan had no men available for the enterprise, so Major General John E. Wool, the 78-year-old commander at Fortress Monroe, was selected for the mission, along with his garrison force. The operation began on May 8, with President Lincoln in direct command. From the deck of the flagship *Minnesota*, Lincoln oversaw a combined operation against Sewell's Point. A flotilla, led by the *Monitor*, was charged with the assignment of shelling the Confederate works, prepatory to an amphibious landing by Wool's men. One officer aboard the *Minnesota* described Lincoln as being "dressed in a black suit with a very seedy crepe on his hat, and hanging over the railing, he looked like some hoosier just starting home from California with store clothes and a boiled shirt on." When the *Virginia* steamed out of Norfolk and took up position at the intended landing site Lincoln was forced to grudgingly call off the operation and seek another spot for his landing. Chesapeake Bay was chosen because it was situated at a point where the channel was narrow, protected by the guns of Fortress Monroe on one side, and Fort Wool on the other. The threat from the land-based guns was thought to be enough to prevent the *Virginia* from attempting to enter the channel. On the night of May 9, General Wool went ashore with 5,000 men to begin his march on Norfolk. Lincoln stayed at Fortress Monroe, directing the operation and overseeing the departure of reinforcements for Wool. But Wool would need no reinforcements. The Confederates had divined his purpose and declined to allow themselves to be caught in a trap at Norfolk. The garrison commander, Major General Benjamin Huger, had already evacuated the city, taking his 9,000 men to join Johnston, and had left behind only a small detachment charged with the job of destroying the Gosport Navy Yard. That work was not yet completed when Wool's men reached the outskirts of the city, causing Mayor William W. Lamb to spring into action. Lamb met the vanguard of Wool's army to offer the formal surrender of the city. By means of a lengthy ceremony, he bought the demolition crew the necessary time to complete their work. Left without a port, the fate of the *Virginia* was sealed. Her draught was too great to sail up the James to Richmond, and Federal fortifications barred her passage into the Chesapeake River. It was unthinkable that she be allowed to fall into Union hands, so the only option left open was to destroy the pride of the Confederate Navy. She was sailed to Craney Island, where a fuse into her powder magazine was lit. At precisely 4:58 A.M. on the morning of May 11, the magazine exploded and the *Virginia* was blown to pieces. Norfolk was in Union hands, but more importantly, the ironclad menace that had so worried Union operations in the region was eliminated.[19]

While all this activity was taking place, McClellan was pushing forth his plans for capturing an even bigger Confederate prize, and it seemed as if Richmond was well within his reach. On May 7, Franklin's Division effected a landing at Eltham's Landing, a plantation near West Point, in an attempt to cut off the Confederate line of retreat. West Point was situated on a peninsula created by the confluence of the York, Pamunkey, and Mattapony Rivers, and was the terminus of the Richmond & York River Railroad. McClellan planned to use this line to supply his troops in their march to Richmond. Franklin's assignment was to interpose his forces between Johnston's army and the Confederate capital, thus blocking the enemy's retreat. But upon landing, Franklin chose to dig in around West Point, and no blocking movement was undertaken. Satisfied at creating a beachhead, the general waited for the divisions of Sedgwick, Porter, and Richardson to arrive before contemplating any aggressive operations. General Johnston was concentrating his army Barhamsville, a few miles south of the river, and immediately recognized the danger Franklin posed to his command. "The security of our march required that he should be dislodged, and General Smith was intrusted with this service."[20]

Johnston's intentions were for Smith to check Franklin's movements, and prevent him from hindering the Confederate retreat. Major General William H.C. Whiting did not understand his commander's purpose, however. Instead of taking up a position to block Franklin, he ordered his division to attack the Federals with the brigades of Wade Hampton and John Bell Hood. On the morning of May 7, Whiting's division moved forward toward Eltham's Landing. Hood's Texas brigade formed the left of the line of battle, with Hampton's brigade on the right. General Hood had instructed his men to march with unloaded weapons since they had not seen much action, and the general feared an accidental discharge that might reveal their approach and alert the enemy. Hood led his brigade on horseback, about 15 paces in front. When he came to a cabin on the brow of a hill overlooking the slope that led down to the landing, his orders concerning the unloaded muskets almost cost him his life. As Hood crested the ridge, he found himself face-to-face with Federal pickets posted on the opposite side of the slope. Hood sprang from his horse and ran back to his men, shouting "Load your guns" and "forward into line" as he came. The Yankees fired a volley at Hood's men before scampering back to their main line. One Union corporal, however, could not resist the opportunity to take a shot at the Rebel commander. He lowered his musket and took deliberate aim at Hood, but a shot rang out from Hood's line and the Yankee fell dead. Private John Deal, of the 4th Texas, had disobeyed orders, and had loaded his musket during the march. His disobedience had saved his general's life.[21]

The unexpected encounter soon developed into a lively firefight, as Hood's line came under a heavy fire from the Federals. Hood detached the 18th Georgia Infantry and a battery of artillery to remain at the cabin. With the 1st Texas formed on the left and the 4th Texas on the right, Hood advanced the remainder of his brigade to close with the enemy. Hampton's brigade, joined by Hood's 5th Texas, was formed to the right of the 4th Texas. The 1st Texas bore the brunt of the fighting, as the Federals made a flanking movement against Hood's left. Observing that his left was about to give way, Hood gave an order that was to become synonymous with his style of leadership: Charge! The 1st Texas responded beautifully, and the flank was saved. The entire Confederate line then surged forward, driving the enemy from their forward positions, and forcing them back toward the protection of their gunboats in the York River.[22]

A Union observer witnessed the battery Hood had left at the cabin open on the retreating Union soldiers and felt that "it was a moment of serious danger, and the most rapid action was necessary to avert the impending catastrophe."[23] The fighting continued unabated for several hours, and by 12:00 noon, the Federals had been driven back one and one-half miles. But the retreat had brought the Federals under the protection of their navy gunboats. The shipboard guns opened on the Rebels, and brought the gray tide to a standstill. General Whiting ordered the batteries of Major Stephen D. Lee and Captain James Reilly to the river bluff to shell the vessels, but the range was found to be too great for the Southern field pieces. Unable to silence the Union's big guns, Whiting realized that it was fruitless to continue the attack. By early afternoon, the fighting at Eltham's Landing had ended, and Whiting's men were on their way back to Barhamsville.[24] When Whiting's men rejoined the army, General Johnston had Hood summoned to his headquarters. "General Hood," he asked, "have you given an illustration of the Texas idea of feeling an enemy gently and then falling back? What would your Texans have done, sir, if I had ordered them to charge and drive back the enemy?" Hood responded in a serious tone: "General, I suppose they would have driven them into the river, and tried to swim out and capture the gunboats."[25] Johnston's orders may have been exceeded, but the check delivered by Hood and Hampton served to put Franklin on the defensive and allowed Johnston all the time he needed to safely continue the withdrawal of his army. McClellan's object in making the amphibious landing had been thwarted due to the hesitancy of his subordinate and the over-aggressiveness of the Confederate commander on the scene. The Union commander would have to content himself with establishing a portion of his army on the line of the Richmond & York River Railroad, and the knowledge that he had secured a defendable base of supplies for his future movements. The chance to block Johnston's line of retreat was now lost, and the decisive battle of the campaign would now most probably be fought with the enemy's backs to Richmond.

Confederate leaders realized they had escaped a fatal blow to their cause by evading McClellan's blocking movement at West Point. However, they still doubted the ability of the military to deliver a significant check to the Army of the Potomac that would safeguard Richmond and prevent the capital from falling into enemy hands. McClellan's vast army seemed to be on the verge of total victory. The loss of the *Virginia* meant that the Confederates could no longer contest control of the James River by the Federal fleet, and the possibility loomed large that Union gunboats would be able to steam right up to Richmond and bombard the city. Panic gripped both the administration and the populace. The Virginia Legislature voted to burn the city, rather than allow it to be captured by McClellan. Plans were set forth to relocate the Confederate archives to South Carolina, and the treasury gold was crated and prepared for shipment aboard a train that was kept under constant steam. Many residents evacuated the capital, including President Davis' wife, Varina, and their children. Congress went into adjournment, with many of its members taking the opportunity to leave the city and return home. Those who could not leave prepared for the worst by hiding their valuables and setting aside quantities of tobacco to trade with the conquering Yankees. Jefferson Davis asked General Robert E. Lee, his military advisor, where the best place for the Confederate army to make a stand would be if Richmond fell, and Lee responded that the Staunton River, 100 miles to the southwest, would provide the best natural barrier to the Union forces. In an uncharacteristic departure from his usual calm demeanor, Lee then blurted emotionally, "But Richmond must not be given up. It shall not be given up!"[26]

Lee's admonition served as a precursor of the events that were to follow. The panic in Richmond seemed to disappear almost as suddenly as it had come, being replaced by a dogged determination that evidenced itself through the grit and determination of the Southern people. As Edward Pollard, the Southern journalist, recounted, "Inert and speculative patriotism was aroused to exertion; mutual inspiration of courage and devotion passed from heart to heart through the community, and with the restoration of public confidence, came at last vigorous preparations."[27] The Virginia Legislature demanded that the city be defended at all costs, and allocated $200,000 to purchase obstructions for the James River and another $200,000 to help cover the expenses of the evacuation of women and children from Richmond. Governor John Letcher called for the organization of companies for home defense, and provisions were made to collect and destroy the valuable tobacco stored throughout the town. Local women were also quick to rally to the cause, making large quantities of bedding to be used in the city's hospitals.[28]

The Virginia Legislature showed ample foresight in passing the bill allotting money for river obstructions, as the next test of military preparedness would come by way of the water, and not McClellan's ground forces. Brigadier General Oliver O. Howard stated that "McClellan did not like to have his principal supplies dependent on the York River," and that he "already meditated working over to the James River to thus secure by the help of the navy a safer base and, as he thought, a better approach to Richmond."[29] On May 10, McClellan had told Stanton that "should Norfolk be taken and the Merrimac destroyed I can change my line to the James River and dispense with the West Point Railroad."[30] Several days later, in a discussion with Admiral Goldsborough, he discussed the possibility of a transfer of the army to the James, laying the plans for such a move as the Army of the Potomac drew nearer to Richmond.[31] By all these accounts, it can be readily seen that McClellan contemplated a change of base to the James River line approximately six weeks before the Seven Days Battles were commenced. During those battles, the general would shift his army to a position on the James, and would be accused by his critics, and by numerous historians that followed, of making a retreat, not a change of base. In his *The Peninsula Campaign 1862*, Joseph P. Cullen voices the opinion of many historians when he states, "It was not until he wrote his official report, when the campaign was over, that McClellan suggested the James River approach and claimed Washington's interference prevented it."[32] By the aforementioned accounts, it is evident that this plan was conceived long before it was actually carried out, and that it was not the result of hindsight, but rather a part of McClellan's overall strategic planning. The historical record refutes the claim that McClellan offered the change of base argument only to cover for his own failures on the Peninsula. The facts show that he had determined the James River line to be a better avenue of approach to Richmond than the route from the York River, and had been pursuing the possibilities of making that change long before it was actually accomplished. Circumstances beyond McClellan's control prevented him from making the movement until July, when he did so in the face of an all-out Confederate offensive.

The Confederate high command anticipated that McClellan would make a move to the James at some point in the campaign, and feared the potential disaster to follow. General Johnston wrote, "I suspect that McClellan is waiting for iron-clad war vessels for James River. They would enable him to reach Richmond three days before these troops ... should such a move be made, the fall of Richmond would be inevitable."[33] Robert E. Lee deduced that utilizing the James River line would be McClellan's "best policy.... (I)t is fair for us to conclude that his operations in front of Yorktown will be re-enacted in front of the obstructions on the James River."[34] Apprehension over McClellan's anticipated move caused Johnston not to stop his withdrawal until he was across the Chickahominy River and could secure his right flank behind Drewry's Bluff. President Davis and General Lee, both fearing the same possibility, felt that the more prudent course of action would be to engage the Union army before it had the opportunity to get within striking range of Richmond.

On May 11, McClellan had urged Stanton "that our gunboats and iron clad boats be sent as far as possible up the James River without delay."[35] Stanton concurred, and met with Secretary of the Navy Gideon Welles. Accordingly, Welles sent a message to Admiral Goldsborough, directing him to "push all the boats you can spare up James River, even to Richmond."[36] Captain John Rogers was selected to command the flotilla, consisting of the ironclads *Galena* and *Monitor*, and the wooden gunboats *Aroostook, Naugatauck, and Port Royal*. On May 15, Rogers and his fleet had reached a point on the James River only seven miles below Richmond. There was a sharp bend in the river here, dominated on the west side by high ground known locally as Drewry's Bluff, which towered 90 feet above the James and provided a commanding view of the river for several miles. On top of this bluff the Confederates had constructed Fort Darling, under the supervision of Colonel George Washington Custis Lee, Robert E. Lee's son. Six heavy pieces of coastal artillery had been mounted within the fort's walls. The defenses of Fort Darling were complemented by a water battery, containing two more heavy guns, and the wooden gunboat *Patrick Henry*. About 300 yards downriver from the bluff Lee's men had scuttled old ships and sunk stone-filled cribs to create obstructions for the Federal ships, which left only a narrow channel for passage. Rifle pits had been dug along the banks of the river, filled with sharpshooters to harass any Union seaman who dared expose himself on the decks. At 7:35 A.M., the Confederates spotted Rogers' flagship, the *Galena*, at the head of the Union flotilla. The *Galena* was allowed to steam to a point approximately 400 yards below the obstructions before the guns of Fort Darling were ordered to fire. The *Galena* quickly suffered two hits, but Rogers continued forward until he was 600 yards from the fort. He then maneuvered so as to bring a broadside volley to bear and opened fire. The other Federal ships joined in the fray, and the concussion from the big guns on both sides was enough to shake the windows in Richmond.[37]

Rogers instantly saw that his ships were at a severe disadvantage, as they could not elevate their guns sufficiently to do any serious damage to the fort, while the Confederates enjoyed the benefit of a plunging fire down upon the Union vessels. Nevertheless, Captain Rogers determined to make a fight of it with his own ship and the *Monitor*, ordering the vulnerable wooden ships to withdraw out of range of the Rebel guns. By 9:00 A.M., however, it was discovered that the guns of the *Monitor* could not be elevated to threaten Fort Darling, and she was ordered to return down the river and join the wooden ships. The *Galena* would carry the fight to the enemy alone. Rogers was wounded in the early stages of the engagement, but he refused to leave his post or relinquish command.

> The *Galena* opened with her port battery of six 9-inch guns and two 100-pounder Parrotts, doing considerable execution and actually silencing the enemy's fire for a time. From the first, however, the Confederate gunners had her range, and poured down shot and shell without stint upon the gallant craft. About ten o'clock the fort reopened fire with great energy. Reinforcements of trained gunners said to be the crew from the destroyed *Merrimac* had arrived, and with a cheer that echoed across the James, resumed the battle, which now waxed hot and furious. Nearly every shot struck the *Galena* with terrible effect, and her decks were soon slippery with human blood and covered with the dead and dying and splintered fragments from her sides. A solid ten-inch shot struck the after 100-pounder, killing and wounding a score of men. At the same instant an eight-inch shot struck her amidships, followed immediately by another which killed a gunner and several men. This same shot struck and exploded a nine-inch shell that was standing on the deck, the fragments of which killed a powder boy who was passing a ten-pound cartridge, which in turn was exploded, killing and maiming another score of men, and filling the ship with smoke so that it created the idea that the *Galena* was on fire.[38]

The narrowness of the channel prevented Rogers from maneuvering, and forced him to wage this unequal contest from a stationary vessel. The after 100-pounder gun was still intact, but its entire crew of 23 men had been killed or wounded. Marine Corporal John Mackie called out to the other Marines aboard the ship to spring to action. He and his comrades removed the dead and wounded from around the gun and then took charge of the piece themselves, keeping it in the fight for the remainder of the engagement. For his gallant service, Mackie would later be awarded the Congressional Medal of Honor. Quartermaster Jeremiah Regan would also receive the nation's highest award for his actions on this day. A white flag that had been used to signal the wooden ships downriver had become caught in the rigging of the *Galena*, giving the appearance that the ship was surrendering. Regan, "heedless of the shells from the fort and the rain of bullets from the sharpshooters who lined the river bank, sprang into the forerigging," climbed up, "and cleared the flag, throwing it, rolled up in a ball, toward the enemy's works. When he regained the deck after this perilous deed, Captain Rogers asked him why he threw the flag away in that manner, and Regan replied: 'I wanted to show the Johnnies that we have no use for white flags now or at any other time.'"[39]

By 11:00 A.M., the *Galena* had suffered about 50 direct hits from the Confederate guns. The railings had been shot away, and her smokestack had been riddled to resemble Swiss cheese. Her deck was lined with the killed and wounded, but still Rogers stood firm. Then a shot from the *Patrick Henry* ripped through the bow gun port, setting the *Galena* on fire. This was the final blow. At 11:05 A.M., Captain Rogers gave the order to break off the engagement and withdraw back down the river. The Confederates had achieved a great victory, with a reported loss of only 15 killed and wounded. Rogers' flotilla had been turned back, and the city of Richmond had been spared from the menace of the Union Navy.

McClellan had not been idle during the navy's attack on Fort Darling. The campaign was not progressing as rapidly as he might have hoped, but his strategy was proving to be correct, and even the Radical Republicans were forced to admit that the campaign was thus far a success. Congress voted him their thanks for his victory at Yorktown "with but little sacrifice." His old friend Samuel Barlow wrote that even "the most noisy abolitionists now fear to say anything openly and the politicians among them are trying to get on your side without delay."[40] McClellan was beginning to feel that his strategy and actions were receiving vindication among the masses. In a letter to his wife, he asked, "Are you satisfied now with my bloodless victories? Even the abolitionists seem to be coming around." He also informed her that he anticipated "a very severe battle on the Chickahominy.... Secesh is gathering all he can in front of me — so much the better — I will finish the matter.... I have implicit confidence in my men and they in me!"[41]

The matter of the Confederate concentration caused McClellan anxiety, however. He had always been far too willing to accept as fact the inept estimates of enemy strength given to him by the Pinkerton operatives that were supposed to be providing the army with intelligence. Now, these agents set the number of soldiers the South was gathering before Richmond to be approximately 240,000 men.[42] John Tucker, one of Secretary Stanton's own assistants, telegraphed the War Office from Fortress Monroe "that 200,000 troops are in the immediate vicinity of Richmond and that Johnston has a strong force."[43] The Army of the Potomac, at this time, numbered just over 100,000 men. In McClellan's mind, he had already achieved brilliant success in the face of overwhelming odds. Certain that he was nearing the decisive battle of the campaign, the general would once more press the administration to release to him the troops that had been withheld from his army at the outset of the operation. McClellan was sure that his recent performance would convince the government to do so. He was also sure that he would need these reinforcements in the coming struggle. For their part, the Confederates would be doing all in their power to convince the Lincoln administration otherwise, and to ensure that reinforcements never reached the Army of the Potomac.

On May 10, McClellan had his headquarters at Roper's Church, 15 miles west of Williamsburg. His army was concentrated in the nearby vicinity, and was preparing for a forward movement to New Kent Court House the following day. As more of the Peninsula was falling under control of the Army of the Potomac, the general felt the need to set down his expectations for the conduct of his troops as it applied to the civilian inhabitants of the region. He told his officers to "give the most stringent instructions to prevent depredations upon the persons and property of the inhabitants." He stated that "the good conduct of the troops thus far has had the happiest effect, and the general commanding indulges the hope that no effort will be spared ... to maintain the good name which we have thus gained." The soldiers were to conduct themselves in such a manner as to at all times protect "the private property of the inhabitants, and treat them with courtesy and kindness." To McClellan, this was a war of reunification. The enemy they were fighting against were errant friends and brethren, not fiends or savages. His orders regarding the treatment of Confederate civilians were predicated upon the belief that they would soon be returned to their rightful place in the Union and to citizenship in a reunited nation. The army must conduct itself as liberators, not as conquerors, and depredations against the Southern populace would be sternly dealt with. McClellan warned his soldiers that any man caught stealing from Confederate civilians would be "immediately placed in irons, tried by a military commission, and punished to the extent of the law."[44]

McClellan's objective for the army was White House on the Pamunkey River, a tributary of the York, which was reached on May 15. White House was a large plantation where George Washington had courted Martha Custis. The historic link that the property had to the founding father made it sacred soil to Americans both Northern and Southern, but it also had substantial ties to the Lees of Virginia. Robert E. Lee's wife, Mary, was the granddaughter of Martha Custis Washington, and the property was currently owned by General Fitzhugh Lee, the nephew of both Robert E. Lee and Confederate Adjutant General Samuel Cooper.

Disregarding the affiliation the property had with the current Confederate leaders, McClellan viewed White House as a shrine to Washington and the revered rebels of an earlier age. Guards were placed around the house to prevent curious soldiers from entering, and McClellan opted to establish his headquarters in a tent erected upon the grounds, rather than desecrate the home by occupying it. He would write Ellen of the emotion aroused by his surroundings, and by the memory of Washington: "I rode over a horrid road to [White House] this morning; spent some time at Washington's house, or at least his wife's, and afterwards rode to the front, visiting in the course of my ride the old church where he was married.... As I happened to be there alone for a few moments, I could not help kneeling at the chancel and praying that I might serve my country as truly as he did."[45]

White House provided access to a landing where the Richmond & York River Railroad crosses the Pamunkey River, and here is where McClellan determined to establish his supply base for the army. Ships steaming up the York, and then the Pamunkey, would bring 500 tons of supplies a day to White House. These same ships would also bring five locomotives and 80 rail cars from Baltimore (which the general had secured to transport the supplies from his base) to the front, as his army moved upon Richmond. The trains would be a welcome sight to the soldiers, and especially to the teamsters of the army. The rain that had been their constant companion ever since the army landed on the Peninsula was continuing with no letup in sight. Transporting supplies and ammunition over roads that had become rivers of mud had become increasingly difficult. Indeed, it was reported that the roads were so bad that it took one wagon 36 hours to travel a distance of five miles between the landing and White House.[46] The engines and cars would significantly improve the transportation situation and get the army out of the ruts and onto the rails. With the base established, supplies began pouring into the Army of the Potomac. It also seemed that McClellan's constant requests were about to be granted, and that men would soon be pouring into the army as well.

On May 17, General McDowell received the following orders from Secretary Stanton: "Upon being joined by Gen. Sheilds' division you will move upon Richmond by the general route of the Richmond and Fredericksburg Railroad, cooperating with the forces under Gen. McClellan, now threatening Richmond from the line of the Pamunkey and York Rivers. While seeking to establish as soon as possible a communication between your left wing and the right wing of Gen. McClellan, you will hold yourself always in such a position as to cover the capital of the nation against a sudden dash of any large body of the rebels."[47] Lincoln immediately sent McDowell further instructions: "You will retain the separate command of the forces taken with you; but while co-operating with General McClellan you will obey his orders, except that you are to judge, and are not to allow your force to be disposed otherwise than so as to give the greatest protection to this capital which may be possible at that distance."[48] McClellan received word of the intended movement through the War Department, when Stanton advised him:

> General McDowell has been ordered to march upon [Richmond] by the shortest route. He is ordered — keeping himself always in position to save the capital from all possible attack — so to operate as to place his left wing in communication with your right wing, and you are instructed to cooperate, so as to establish this communication as soon as possible, by extending your right wing to the north of Richmond.... You will give no order ... which can put him out of position to cover the city (Washington).... The President desires that General McDowell retain the command of the Department of the Rappahannock and of the forces with which he moves forward.[49]

At first glance, McClellan was delighted by the news. He would have preferred that McDowell's men be transported by water, rather than marching overland, but so long as they were coming, he was willing to concede that point. The addition of the 1st Corps would increase the size of the Army of the Potomac by about 40,000 men, and would seriously reduce the odds which the commanding general thought to be facing him. Upon further reflection, however, McClellan noted several flaws in the administration's decision. First, McDowell was given the authority to act independently of the Army of the Potomac. True, he was to cooperate with McClellan when their forces were joined, but only to the extent that he did not stray from Lincoln's assignment that he at all times post his army between the enemy and Washington. McDowell would have the discretion to countermand any order McClellan gave to his corps if he deemed it to be contrary to Lincoln's directive. The coordination of any tactical or strategic plans, under such circumstances, would be extremely difficult. The second fault McClellan found with the orders he had received caused him grave concern. By order of the president, he would be compelled to extend his right flank northeast of the Chickahominy River, in order to form the desired junction with the advancing 1st Corps. At the same time, he would be obliged to operate against Richmond with his left flank, on the southwest side of that same river. His army would be divided by the Chickahominy, and in danger of being defeated in detail by the Confederates. The general voiced these concerns in a letter to Secretary of State William Seward: "Indications that the enemy intend fighting at Richmond. Policy seems to concentrate everything there. They hold central position, and will seek to meet us while divided. I think we are committing a great military error in having so many independent columns. The great battle should be fought by our troops in mass; then divide if necessary."[50]

McClellan was undertaking a little division of his own, in preparation for McDowell's arrival. The operations of the preceding weeks had confirmed his apprehensions over the formation of corps, and the subsequent promotion of corps commanders. Frustrated by the performance he had thus far witnessed, particularly at Williamsburg, the commanding general sought to reorganize the Army of the Potomac in such a way that would both give him greater control over its movements, and reduce its dependence on officers whom McClellan did not yet deem suitable to their responsibilities. He had tried to address this situation in a message to Stanton, in which he requested authority to scuttle the corps structure and return to an organization by divisions. At the very least, he sought permission to relieve any corps commander he felt to be incompetent. Stanton replied that he was free to suspend the corps organization and to reorganize in any way "you see fit." But a letter from Lincoln accompanied Stanton's message, and it beckoned McClellan to consider the matter more thoroughly. The president urged his commander to weigh carefully his options before making such a change. He reminded McClellan that the four corps commanders had been put in place for political reasons by the Radical Republicans, and cautioned that their removal would be poorly "received in quarters which we cannot entirely disregard." He asked if McClellan felt himself "strong enough, even with my help — to set your foot upon the necks of Sumner, Heintzelman, and Keyes all at once?"[51] Lincoln's words served to convince McClellan that this was an inopportune time to initiate a public confrontation between himself and the Radical Republicans who controlled the Joint Committee on the Conduct of the War. He would retract his request to be able to remove any of the existing corps commanders, or to eliminate the corps structure that had been established. Instead, he would use Stanton's permission to reorganize the army in any way he saw fit to establish a little more balance in the command structure, and give him more control over his subordinate generals. He would embrace the corps concept by expanding it. Two additional corps would be created. The corps of Sumner, Heintzelman, and Keyes would be reduced to two divisions each. William B. Franklin would retain his own division, and would be given one more to form the 6th Corps. Fitz-John Porter, McClellan's most trusted subordinate, would command the newly created 5th Corps, three divisions strong. Under the reorganization, the three appointees of the Radical Republicans would have control over six of the army's divisions, while McClellan's personal choices would command five divisions. It was as close as the commanding general could come to reshaping the army to conform to his personal preference without causing a political feud with the current corps commander's supporters. At the same time, it ensured that he would not be entirely overpowered by adversarial subordinates when McDowell's corps joined the army.

With his new command structure in place, McClellan now took steps to execute his part of the orders issued by Lincoln. Sumner's 2nd Corps, Franklin's 6th Corps, and Porter's 5th Corps were instructed to fan out in a northwesterly direction from the railroad, on the north bank of the Chickahominy. The resulting line stretched for ten miles from the railroad to the extreme right, occupied by Porter's corps, near Mechanicsville, just six miles northeast of Richmond. This disposition of his right wing was made to facilitate the junction with McDowell's corps when it marched south from Fredericksburg. McClellan deployed his left wing south of the Chickahominy, sending Keyes' 4th Corps and Heintzelman's 3rd Corps westward along the Williamsburg Road. The major problem in this disbursement of forces was the Chickahominy River itself. At most times of the year, it was little more than a sluggish and meandering stream. But the river was known for its unpredictability. Any sudden rainstorms could cause it to turn into a raging giant, flooding the swampy marshland that normally bordered its banks for one-half to one mile from either shore, and making it impossible to ford. The rains of the last few weeks had caused the river to swell to heights not seen by the local residents in more than 20 years.[52] To make matters worse, the retreating Confederates had destroyed the bridges across the river. On May 20, General Silas Casey's division reached Bottom's Bridge, or what was left of it, 12 miles east of Richmond, on the Williamsburg Road. Casey was able to get some troops across the river, and immediately set the engineers to work making repairs on the span. When McClellan arrived on the scene the following day, he was surprised to find that there was no sizeable force of Confederates on the opposite bank to contest his crossing, as was the case at the railroad bridge and the bridge at Mechanicsville. The "enemy was there in only small force, and, as it was of the utmost importance to secure a lodgement on the right bank of the stream, I ordered Casey's division of the 4th corps to ford the river at once and occupy the heights on the further bank." Work on the bridge was stepped up, the "troops were directed to throw up defenses to secure our left flank, and the 3rd corps was moved up in support."[53]

McClellan realized the river posed a threat to his communications and supplies, and served to eliminate the ability for the two wings of his army to act in concert, or to support one another. For that reason, no fewer than 11 bridges were begun along the Chickahominy in the 12-mile stretch from Bottoms Bridge to Mechanicsville. The river itself was no great challenge — it could be bridged by short spans almost anywhere along its course. The problem arose from the swampy bottom land on either side of the river. This necessitated the construction of lengthy approaches of logs laid in corduroy fashion. Up river from Bottoms Bridge, two regiments of Sumner's 2nd Corps built a pair of spans. One of the regiments used grapevines to lash together the logs. Both bridges were completed by May 30. The Grapevine Bridge, as the improvised span came to be known, would play a critical role in the upcoming battle.

By May 24, Keyes' 4th Corps had advanced west on the Williamsburg Road, and dug in near a crossroads called Seven Pines. Porter's 5th Corps had driven the Confederates out of Mechanicsville and taken possession of the town. This meant that the extreme left and right flanks of the Union line were only five to six miles away from Richmond. Soldiers in Keyes' and Porter's Corps could see church spires in the city, and could hear the bells chime in their bell towers. Neither side could know it, but this would be as close as the Army of the Potomac would come to the Confederate capital. May 24 would be the date that saw a series of events set in motion that would lead to the Confederate Army of Northern Virginia taking the initiative in the campaign and becoming the hunter instead of the hunted.

It was on that day that the administration in Washington learned of the defeat of Major General Nathaniel P. Banks' troops at Front Royal, in the Shenandoah Valley, by forces under the command of General Thomas J. "Stonewall" Jackson. The fighting had taken place the previous day, when General Richard Ewell's men captured the garrison at Front Royal and compelled Banks' men to retreat northward. Banks correctly advised Washington that his estimate of Jackson's strength was approximately 15,000 men. The news of the defeat and subsequent retreat of Banks' column caused great panic in the capital. The spectre of a gray-clad army marching down Pennsylvania Avenue gripped the politicians, and it became their paramount mission to eliminate Stonewall and the threat he posed. This is exactly what the Confederates desired. Robert E. Lee had assigned Jackson to the Valley for just such a purpose. Lee had hoped that Jackson could cause sufficient commotion to prevent the Federals from concentrating all of their available forces in front of Richmond, and gathering together a multitude capable of crushing the Army of Northern Virginia. The strategy worked. On May 24, Lincoln sent a message to General McDowell informing him, "You are instructed, laying aside for the present the movement on Richmond, to put 20,000 men in motion at once for the Shenandoah.... Your object will be to capture the forces of Jackson and Ewell."[54] Later that same day, Lincoln wired McClellan, "In consequence of Banks' position, I have been compelled to suspend McDowell's movements to join you."[55]

McClellan's response to the president was measured and soldierly. "Telegram of 4 P.M. received. I will make my calculations accordingly."[56] His personal feelings were quite another matter. The general felt that McDowell's withdrawal toward Front Royal was "a serious and fatal error; he could do no good in that direction, while had he been permitted to carry out the orders of May 17, the united forces would have driven the enemy within the immediate entrenchments of Richmond before Jackson could have returned to its succor, and probably would have gained possession promptly of that place."[57]

McClellan was not the only high-ranking officer to see the folly of the administration's action. General James Shields sent a formal protest to Secretary Stanton from Fredericksburg, stating that reinforcements from there could not possibly reach Banks in time, and warning that a "panic there ought not to paralyze this movement just now prepared on the eve of execution." When McDowell received his orders, he telegraphed Stanton that he was preparing to comply with the directive, but added, "This is a crushing blow to us." In a message to General Wadsworth, McDowell wrote, "It is idle to think of taking any force from this point to go after any force ... in Banks' rear.... If they are really in his rear, nothing from here can get there in time to afford him any help.... Try and get over the flutter into which this body seems to have thrown everyone. If the enemy can succeed so readily in disconcerting all our plans by alarming us first at one point, then at another, he will paralyze a large force with a very small one."[58] These Union generals correctly assessed the purpose of Jackson's movements, and warned the administration of the consequences of falling prey to them.

Jackson was kicking up a fuss in the Valley, nothing more. The force he had with him was not nearly large enough to contemplate a rush on Washington. Wadsworth had more than enough garrison troops, entrenched behind strong defensive works, to have made such a move a fool's errand. What's more, Jackson did not have sufficient strength to stand against the Union forces already in the Valley. Fremont and Banks outnumbered him by almost three-to-one already. The only viable option open to Stonewall was to adopt a strategy of hit and run — to accomplish by speed and maneuver what he could not hope to achieve by strength of numbers. If he hoped to keep his small army in the field, he would need to meet and defeat the various detachments of the Union army before they could concentrate in front of him. Stonewall proved to be the master of hard marching and hard fighting, however. His rapid marches in the Valley gained for his men the sobriquet "foot cavalry," and the vicious attacks he launched caused his very name to strike fear in the ranks of the Union army. On May 25, Jackson once more defeated General Banks' men at the First Battle of Winchester, causing Banks' men to retreat across the Potomac River into Maryland. The affair at Winchester was enough to cause Lincoln to lose all grasp of reality. On the day of the battle, he sent a frantic message to McClellan that shows the extent to which the government had fallen under the spell of Jackson.

> The enemy is moving north in sufficient force to drive Gen. Banks before him; precisely in what force we cannot tell. He is also threatening Leesburg, and Geary on the Manassas Gap Railroad, from both north and south; in precisely what force we cannot tell. I think the movement is a general and concerted one, such as would not be if he was acting upon the purpose of a very desperate defense of Richmond. I think the time is near when you must either attack Richmond or give up the job and come to the defense of Washington. Let me hear from you instantly.[59]

If McClellan is to be ridiculed, as he has been, for accepting the grossly inaccurate estimates of Confederate strength reported by his intelligence service, then Lincoln must stand the same sort of censure for this frantic message. Counting McDowell's corps, the forces under Banks, Fremont, and Wadsworth, the Federal government already had some 80,000 men at its disposal for the defense of Washington. Did Lincoln really think that Jackson had enough men with him, or indeed that there were enough men under arms in the Confederacy, that the addition of the Army of the Potomac, and a force of nearly 200,000 men, would be necessary to defend the capital from Stonewall's threat? McClellan responded to Lincoln's message by advising him that "the object of the (enemy) movement is probably to prevent reinforcements being sent me." He went on to assure the president that "the mass of the rebel troops are still in the immediate vicinity of Richmond, ready to defend it."[60]

Jackson's forces next concentrated on the columns under Fremont and Shields that were pursuing him. On June 8, Jackson's men fell upon Fremont at the battle of Cross Keys, driving the Federals from the field. He then executed a forced march to Port Republic, where Shields' column was checked and compelled to retreat. His band of 15,000 men had met and defeated superior forces four times in little more than two weeks from May 24 to June 8. During that time, he had inflicted some 3,400 casualties on the Union army.[61] More importantly, he had frozen some 60,000 Union troops in the Valley, and another 20,000 at Fredericksburg, and kept them from swelling the ranks of the Army of the Potomac, in front of Richmond. Against the advice of prominent officers, Lincoln and Stanton had allowed Jackson's little Army of the Valley to neutralize a Federal force more than five times its size. If one adds Wadsworth's Washington garrison into the equation, more than six times Jackson's numbers were employed in safeguarding the capital from a threat that could never have been brought to fruition. If the administration had ordered the concentration of the forces they already had in the Valley, Jackson would not have dared to assail them, as he would have been facing an army that outnumbered him by almost three-to-one, with another force larger than his own still in Washington. Had the government proceeded with its plans for McDowell to reinforce McClellan, Stonewall would most surely have been summoned from the Valley for an all-out defense of Richmond. Either way, the tables would have been turned, and Jackson's force would have been the one to be neutralized. The Confederates had only one hope of success in the Valley — that fear would magnify the illusion of Jackson's offensive capabilities to the extent that panic dictated the decisions made by the Federal government. In the end, this plan worked to perfection. Following the battle of Port Republic, Jackson eluded the efforts of the Union forces to catch or contain him, and headed for Richmond in a series of forced marches.

Back on the Peninsula, McClellan made plans for his final thrust against Richmond based on the assumption that McDowell's reinforcements were only being delayed, and not cancelled. As the general said, the orders to McDowell stated that the movement to the Peninsula "was simply suspended, not revoked."[62] Accordingly, the right flank of the Army of the Potomac remained extended toward Fredericksburg, in anticipation of the eventual arrival of the 1st Corps. General Lee had ordered the brigade of Brigadier General Lawrence O. Branch to advance from Gordonsville and take up a new position at Hanover Courthouse, 15 miles north of Richmond. He also ordered Brigadier General Joseph R. Anderson's brigade to Hanover Courthouse from its position just south of Fredericksburg. This meant that the Confederates had placed a blocking force of some 12,000 men between McClellan and McDowell. The Confederates at Hanover Courthouse also posed a threat to McClellan's lines of communication and supply, being positioned on the right rear of his army, from whence they could make a thrust against White House. Porter was assigned the task of driving the Confederates out of Hanover Courthouse, and was further charged with the destruction of the Virginia Central Railroad, the last remaining major line of communication between Northern Virginia and Richmond. Porter selected the division of Brigadier General George W. Morell to spearhead the movement, supported by the infantry commands of Bridagier General George Sykes and Colonel Gouverneur K. Warren, and the cavalry of Brigadier General George Stoneman. Morell's and Warren's men moved forward at 4:00 A.M. on the morning of May 27, from their position at New Bridge, preceded by an advance guard of two regiments of cavalry and a battery of artillery, under the command of Brigadier General William H. Emory. Sykes' and Stoneman's men were instructed to follow an hour later. Morell's force, accompanied by Porter, was to advance directly at Hanover Courthouse to make a frontal attack upon the Confederates. Warren was to march his command by a road that followed the Pamunkey River, from which place he could assail the Rebel position in flank and rear. The march was conducted for 14 miles in a "pelting storm of rain" that forced the Yankees to wade through deep mud on the way to their objective.[63]

Morell's advance made contact with the enemy approximately two miles from Hanover Courthouse, and the 25th New York Infantry, Berdan's sharpshooters, and a section of artillery were pushed forward to hold the Confederates in place until Morell could come up with his main body. Morell's brigades quickly routed the Confederates when they reached the field, and Porter pushed the men forward toward the courthouse, in an effort to strike the enemy camp. At this time, Porter received word that his left flank was being attacked by a large force of Rebels, being the command of General Branch. The Federal line was about to confront this threat, and the Confederates were taken in front and flank, and speedily routed from the field. Porter had relieved the immediate threat to McClellan's right

Top: Artist's depiction of the fighting at Hanover Courthouse (Military History Institute, United States Army War College). *Bottom:* Hanover Courthouse as it appears today (photograph taken by author).

flank. Union casualties were 355 in killed, wounded and missing, while Porter reported burying some 200 Confederate dead, and capturing 730 more. May 27 and 28 were spent carrying out McClellan's order to destroy Confederate communications to Northern Virginia, and in the process of this task, actually made contact with several scouts from McDowell's command, who expected to receive orders from Washington to march on Richmond at any moment.[64]

But McDowell's imminent approach was not forthcoming. McClellan realized that Porter was too far advanced to hold his position for an extended time, and he ordered the 5th Corps to be pulled back to Gaines's Mill on May 28. On that same day, the commanding general sent Secretary Stanton a message that showed the frustration he was experiencing with his civilian superiors. "It is the policy and duty of the Govt. to send me by water all the well-drilled troops available.... I am confident that Washington is in no danger. Engines and cars in large numbers have been sent to bring down Jackson's command.... The real issue is the battle about to be fought in front of Richmond."[65] McDowell echoed McClellan's sentiments by stating to Stanton, "I do not consider Washington City in any danger."[66] But the administration would not relent. McDowell's forces were to hold fast where they were. McClellan was sure that the decisive battle of the campaign would take place any day, and he was becoming increasingly infuriated with the politicians in Washington whom he saw as hampering his efforts to end the war and save the nation. Then, on May 29, the general was stricken with a bout of neuralgia and malaria, which he had originally contracted during the Mexican American War, forcing him to retire to a sickbed for the next two days.[67]

May 30 saw little activity along the Union line, only some minor shifting of units along the front. On the right wing, on the north bank of the Chickahominy, Sumner's 2nd Corps was positioned at the Grapevine Bridge. Franklin's 6th Corps held the center, near New Cold Harbor and Gaines's Mill, and Porter's 5th Corps extended the line westward, with his right flank in the vicinity of Mechanicsville. The left wing of the Army of the Potomac, on the south bank of the river, saw Heintzelman's 3rd Corps in the vicinity of Bottom's Bridge. Keyes' 4th Corps was several miles west of the bridge, in the vicinity of Seven Pines, along the Williamsburg Road. General Silas Casey's division formed the extreme left of the Union line, about three-quarters of a mile west of Seven Pines. This would be the positioning of the Union Army on May 31, when Joe Johnston unleashed his army in the battle of Fair Oaks.

Five

Counteroffensive at Fair Oaks

Stonewall Jackson's operations in the Shenandoah Valley were not the only offensive movements being undertaken by the Confederates besieged in Richmond. Davis, Lee, and Johnston were all well aware that some sort of assault needed to be mounted before the Federal government regained its composure and released McDowell's reserves to McClellan. In the event that this took place, the Confederate defenders would find themselves not only deficient in artillery and engineering, they would be facing an enemy army that outnumbered them by approximately two-to-one in infantry. If a junction of McClellan and McDowell was allowed to be made, there was little the Army of Northern Virginia would be able to do but fight a delaying action. Barring an egregious mistake by McClellan, it would simply be a matter of time before Richmond fell and the Confederate army would have to flee or perish. A bold stroke was needed to snatch the initiative away from the Federals and avert almost certain disaster. The Army of Northern Virginia could retreat no further. Johnston must now stand and fight. The Union army, by placing the Chickahominy River between its two wings, had presented the Confederate commander with an opportunity to isolate and destroy a portion of the Army of the Potomac, before McClellan's entire horde could be brought to bear.

Johnston was spurred to action on May 27, when Confederate cavalry near Fredericksburg reported McDowell's forces to be on the march south. The news caused a flurry of activity at Johnston's headquarters, and he prepared to meet the threat. The Army of the Potomac must be attacked before McDowell's men reached it, and Johnston determined to strike his main blow on the north side of the Chickahominy, against the three Federal corps under Sumner, Franklin, and Porter. Major General Ambrose P. Hill was given command of Branch's and Anderson's brigades. He was assigned to attack the extreme right of the Union line. Major General Gustavus W. Smith would be in overall command on the Confederate left, and his division would assist Hill in making the attack on Porter's 5th Corps. Major General John Magruder's division along with Major General Benjamin Huger's division were to attack Franklin's 6th Corps, in the vicinity of New Bridge. The divisions of Major Generals James P. Longstreet and Daniel H. Hill would stay on the south bank of the Chickahominy River. They were to assault the right flank of the Union army on that side of the river, Heintzelman's 3rd Corps, near Bottom Bridge. It was hoped that these combined assaults would drive the Yankees back from their advanced positions and make the junction with McDowell a difficult proposition. The attack was set for May 29, but on the night of May 28, while Johnston was holding a war council with his generals, a courier arrived from Major General James E.B. Stuart with information that McDowell was not marching on Richmond. He was, in fact, returning to Fredericksburg.[1]

With the threat of McDowell's forces being temporarily eliminated, Johnston turned his attention to Heintzelman and Keyes, south of the Chickahominy. Keyes' position, at Seven Pines, was several miles distant from Heintzelman, at Bottom Bridge. Both corps were separated from the rest of the army by the river. If Johnston could gather superior forces to throw against the Federal left, he could possibly crush the 3rd and 4th Corps before the rest of the Army of the Potomac could be funneled over bridges to assist them. If he could rout and cripple these two corps, he would reduce McClellan's fighting strength by approximately 40,000 men. Such a crushing defeat might even induce McClellan to withdraw his entire army from in front of Richmond to refit and reorganize. Johnston accordingly made plans to concentrate his forces on the south side of the Chickahominy. Twenty-three of Johnston's 27 brigades were ordered massed to deliver the knockout blow against the Federal left. General Gustavus Smith was assigned the task of checking any Federals from the right wing who tried to come to the assistance of the left. If none came, he was to add the weight of his brigades to the assault on the Federal left by attacking the left flank of Heintzelman's corps. As the second highest-ranking officer in the Army of Northern Virginia, Smith should have been in command of the main assault. His division was on the far left of the Confederate army, however, and Johnston felt that it would cause too much confusion, and cost too much time, to shift it to the right. For that reason, the honor of leading the main assault against the Federals fell to General Longstreet, he being the senior of the three division commanders on the right flank of the army.[2] The Confederates received a stroke of good fortune when it began to rain violently on the afternoon of May 30. The downpour was causing the Chickahominy to rise by the hour, and as Johnston planned his attack for the following morning, there was a distinct possibility that the river would be in full flood stage when the Confederates struck. If that became the case, the Yankees on the south side of the river might find themselves completely cut off from their comrades to the north.

General Erasmus D. Keyes. His corps occupied the left flank of McClellan's army, and was close enough to Richmond that his men could see the spires of churches in the city (Military History Institute, United States Army War College).

General Samuel P. Heintzelman. His corps, and that of Erasmus Keyes, formed the isolated left wing of the Union army that Johnston sought to crush in his offensive (Military History Institute, United States Army War College).

Smith B. Mott, quartermaster of the 52nd Pennsylvania Infantry, recorded that "on the night of May 30th a fearful storm prevailed. Rain fell in torrents. The country was flooded; the Chickahominy overflowed its banks, the swampy

Above: General Daniel Harvey Hill. His division shouldered the load in the attack on the first day, and fought virtually alone for a large part of the engagement (Military History Institute, United States Army War College). *Left:* General John B. Gordon. His regiment sustained severe casualties during the engagement, as did the rest of Rodes's brigade, of which it was a part (Military History Institute, United States Army War College).

ground through which that stream flowed became impassable, and the bridges were so much damaged as to, for a time, practically isolate the two corps—Keyes's and Heintzelman's—from the other three corps with McClellan on the left bank."[3] Gilbert Hays, of the 63rd Pennsylvania Infantry, gave an even more graphic account of the storm:

> About 3 o'clock in the afternoon the sky assumed a coppery color, which was frightful to behold. Flashes of lightning of the most vivid character followed each other so rapidly that the whole sky seemed to be aflame, while the thunder crashed and roared in a manner that caused a thrill of fright to strike the hearts of the bravest. The rain fell in perfect sheets and the wind blew a hurricane. The storm partially ceased about 6 o'clock and the boys prepared their scanty supper. In a short time the thunder, which was muttering in the eastern part of the heavens, began to grow louder, and it was soon apparent to all that the storm was returning. All the old soldiers of that portion of the Army of the Potomac will remember as long as they live, that terrible night of thunder and lightening and tempest.
> All night long the fearful war of the elements continued, and during the night a number of men in our division were killed by lightning. The storm ceased about daybreak, and on the morning of the 31st the sun rose bright and clear. The camp was soon astir and the boys were drying their clothing and laughing and joking as usual. The sluggish Chickahominy in our rear was now a raging torrent and that portion of the army that had crossed it was completely separated from the rear portion on the other side.[4]

The Confederates were experiencing the same fearful storm, and they were getting even less sleep than the Federals. One member of the 17th Virginia Infantry remembered the deluge, and said that when it started to slacken, after midnight, "the men were endeavoring to quiet themselves down for at least a short nap, when a courier rode hastily to the Colonel's quarters, the long roll beat and the cry of 'Turn out! Turn out!' resounded on all sides. The order to prepare two days rations was issued, and the men instructed to be ready to march at a moment's notice."[5] This scene was being repeated throughout Johnston's army. Many Rebs would get no sleep that night. It is doubtful if many men would have been able to sleep even if they had the opportunity, however. All knew that the great battle they had so long anticipated would commence as soon as the sun rose, and the combination of fear and excitement that caused their hearts and minds to race would have made it extremely difficult to close their eyes in quiet repose.

A common misconception about the battle of Fair Oaks is that the Confederate attack on that field was a surprise to the Federals. Nothing could be further from the truth. Keyes' Corps was close enough to the Southern line that the Federals could hear orders from the Rebel officers, and could listen to the tramping of feet as regiments were shifted to and fro along their front. General Casey's division was engaged in sharp skirmishing on May 29 and 30. The fighting was so hotly contested on May 30 as to cause Casey to call for support from Brigadier General John J. Peck's brigade. Casey and Keyes recognized the increased activity for exactly what it was, a probing of their line in preparation for a general assault. Indeed, it was because they expected an attack that Casey selected a position one and one-half miles west of Seven Pines to construct a redoubt with connecting rifle pits, and felled trees in his front to impede the movement of any assaulting force. For these reasons and more, Alexander Webb, the general who would later so distinguish himself at Gettysburg

Union artillery at Fair Oaks. McClellan planned to move by posts in his Richmond offensive, using engineering and artillery to overpower the Confederates (Military History Institute, United States Army War College).

Union soldiers in unfinished redoubt on the battlefield (Military History Institute, United States Army War College).

to be awarded the Congressional Medal of Honor, stated adamantly, "It will readily be seen that there was nothing in the nature of a surprise about the rebel attack on the 31st."[6]

The historian of the 11th Maine Infantry wrote that by May 30, everyone was certain an attack was imminent:

> The movements of the enemy, as reported by the officers of the picket line, for a day or two had shown that the rebels were making ready to attack, the picket fighting increasing steadily in intensity, until this day, it sounded almost as if a general engagement was in progress. And early in the morning of the 31st, men of D Company had captured Lieutenant Washington, of General Johnston's staff, at a point indicating that the anticipated movement was now on foot. So threatening were all the signs that General Keyes gave orders to have all his troops under arms and in position by eleven o'clock, directing Colonel Bailey, his Chief of Artillery, to have his batteries fully manned.[7]

Without question, the Federals anticipated an attack any day. They just did not know exactly when, where, and in what force. The activity of Branch's and Anderson's brigades, near Hanover Courthouse, had caused McClellan to initially believe that the Confederates intended to launch a counteroffensive in that area. Indeed, this had been Johnston's plan until he received word that McDowell's corps was returning to Fredericksburg, and not marching south to join with the Army of the Potomac. McClellan's efforts to build 11 bridges across the Chickahominy evidences a strong desire to be able to shift forces back and forth across the river, in response to any eventuality that might arise. His army was in a precarious position. It was important that lines of communication be established and maintained between the two wings in order to counter any movement the enemy might make. The commanding general tried to anticipate any eventuality by constructing what was essentially a bridge a mile along the 12 miles of riverfront occupied by the army's line. What was not anticipated was the prospect that these bridges might be rendered useless, leaving the army separated, and the corps unable to support one another. But that is precisely the situation that arose because of the terrific rainstorm that took place on the night of May 30.

Under normal circumstances, the Chickahominy was an unpredictable and treacherous river. Union engineer John C. Palfrey, when describing the river, said, "It was hard to say at the best of times where its banks were, and of which no man could say to-day where its banks would be to-morrow."[8] The violent rains had caused the river to swell to a raging torrent. The swampy ground that usually bordered its banks became filled with rushing, muddy water. The corduroy approaches to the bridges became submerged or washed away, and many of the bridges themselves became precarious, if not downright impassable. Events could not be playing out in a more opportune manner for Johnston and the Confederate army. His plan had been to assail a portion of the Army of the Potomac while it was separated from the main body, and nature was now assisting to ensure that the Federal left wing was not only separated, but virtually cut off.

There had been only one flaw in Johnston's plan, and that should have proved of little consequence. When the Confederate commander shifted his attention from the Federal right wing to the left, he was under the assumption that only Keyes' 4th Corps had actually crossed the river. The fact that Heintzelman's 3rd Corps was also in the vicinity, and on the south side of the Chickahominy, was intelligence that was unknown to Johnston.[9] Johnston planned to annihilate the 4th Corps, pitting 23 of his brigades against the six that Keyes could array against him, and giving his a superiority of nearly four-to-one. Even with the addition of Heintzelman's corps, the Union would have but 12 brigades in the area, and the Confederates would enjoy an advantage of approximately two-to-one.

Johnston's orders were for D.H. Hill's four brigades to advance east, along the Williamsburg Road, and attack Keyes' line from the front. Hill was to be supported by the division of General Longstreet. Major General Benjamin Huger was to simultaneously attack the Union left flank via the Charles City Road, while Brigadier General William H.C. Whiting, leading Gustavus Smith's division, was to assault the Union right flank. Silas Casey's division was the only Union force opposed to the Confederates in this line of battle.

Silas Casey had been one of the most senior officers in the army before the war. An 1826 graduate of West Point, he had already served for 35 years when hostilities erupted. He had seen combat in the Mexican War, where his service was so distinguished as to win him brevet promotions to major and lieutenant colonel. At the outbreak of the war, Casey was in command of the 9th United States Infantry Regiment. Despite his vast experience, Casey was passed over for promotion by numerous junior officers, and did not receive a general's star until August of 1861. The fact that he had written a manual of infantry tactics that would be adopted by the United States Military in 1862 seemed to make him a logical choice as a drillmaster when McClellan assumed command of the army.[10] Accordingly, he was assigned to command of Camp Lloyd in Washington, and was charged with the task of turning the raw recruits in the Army of the Potomac into trained soldiers. Casey was employed in training the most recent crop of enlistees when McClellan issued orders on March 13 for the men at Camp Lloyd to be organized into a division, with Casey as their commander, prepatory to the move to the Peninsula. As such, Casey's division contained the greenest and least trained soldiers in the army, posted to the most advanced and exposed position occupied by the left wing. They were also among the most poorly armed troops in the army. Owing to the fact that they had been latecomers to the service, and the best long-arms were already taken, they were issued whatever weapons were available, largely inferior Austrian muskets.

Casey's position was roughly three-quarters of a mile west of Seven Pines. His line was extended at right angles from the Williamsburg Road. South of the road, the line extended to the edge of White Oak Swamp, where the left flank was fairly protected. North of the road, the line extended for approximately one mile to Fair Oaks, a station on the Richmond & York River Railroad. Just northeast of Fair Oaks was a massive expanse of marshes and dense woods that stretched three miles to the Chickahominy. This portion of the line was thinly manned, and was the weak spot of the Union defenses.[11] Casey attempted to bolster his defensive ability by constructing a series of rifle pits and a pentagonal shaped earthen redoubt — Fort Casey. Work on the fortifications was well underway, but was not completed on the morning of May 31. In addition, the rainstorm of the previous night had served to fill the works with water. A line of abatis was constructed in front of and behind the works. Casey maintained a picket line far in advance of his main line. The ground he had chosen to defend had previously been under cultivation, and open fields stretched for almost 800 yards in front of his line. The picket line had been pushed forward to a point where these fields bordered woods to their front. Fort Casey was manned by six cannon, with a regiment from Brigadier General Innis N. Palmer's brigade immediately in front of it. The rifle pits, north and south of the Williamsburg Road, were held by the brigade of Brigadier General Henry W. Wessels. In advance of the rifle pits, the first battle line was held by three regiments of Brigadier General Henry M. Naglee's brigade north of the road, and by three regiments of Palmer's brigade to the south.[12]

The Richmond & York River Railroad as it appears today. The Federals used this line to transport supplies to the front from their base at West Point (photograph taken by author).

Site where Casey's Redoubt stood as it appears today, near the present day Sandston Branch of the Henrico County Library (photograph taken by author).

Early on the morning of May 31, Casey roused his men, and though they were hungry and wanted to prepare breakfast, the general put them right to work on the unfinished fortifications. The heavy skirmishing of the previous two days had convinced him that the defenses would soon be needed. His suspicions seemed to be confirmed at approximately 9:00 A.M., when pickets from the 100th New York Infantry captured Lieutenant Washington, one of General Johnston's staff officers, immediately in their front. Though Washington refused to divulge any information during interrogation, Casey was sure that something big was brewing, and he alerted Keyes accordingly. His suspicions were bolstered by the fact that a report from his officer of the day revealed that trains had been heard running back and forth from Richmond to the Confederate line all night, a sure sign that an enemy build-up was in progress. Between 11:00 A.M. and noon, a mounted vedette reported from the picket line with news that a large body of the enemy had been sighted advancing along the Williamsburg Road. Casey ordered the 103rd Pennsylvania Infantry forward to support the picket line. This order was barely given before another rider reported the Confederates advancing in force. His warning was punctuated by the explosion of two enemy artillery shells directly over the camp. Casey knew that an attack was imminent. He ordered the work details to cease, and put the entire division under arms.[13]

Casey could not have known it, but the Confederates were experiencing great difficulty coordinating their attack. Johnston had ordered the assault to be made at daylight, and it was now several hours behind schedule. Generals D.H. Hill, Huger, and Smith all had been issued written orders from Johnston. General Longstreet, being present at headquarters when the orders were drafted, was given his orders verbally.

Five • Counteroffensive at Fair Oaks

General Hill, supported by the division of General Longstreet (who had the direction of operations on the right), was to advance by the Williamsburg road to attack the enemy in front. General Huger, with his division, was to move down the Charles City road in order to attack in flank the troops who might be engaged with Hill and Longstreet, unless he found in his front force enough to occupy his division. General Smith was to march to the junction of the New Bridge road and Nine-mile road, to be in readiness either to fall on Keyes' right flank or to cover Longstreet's left. They were to move at daybreak.

Johnston goes on to state that the heavy rains of the previous night prevented the "prompt and punctual movement of the troops," which led to the delay. According to Johnston, Huger's division was tardy getting into position, and "Major General Longstreet, unwilling to make a partial attack, instead of the combined movement which had been planned, waited from hour to hour for General Huger's division. At length, at 2 P.M., he determined to attack without these troops. He accordingly commenced his advance at that hour, opening the engagement with artillery and skirmishers. By 3 o'clock it became close and heavy."[14]

Johnston's official report of the events of May 31 seems to be inconsistent with other recorded statements, as well as with the historical record. In Johnston's recounting, Longstreet was merely awaiting the arrival of Huger at his assigned position, and the delay would appear to have entirely rested upon the tardiness of that officer. No mention is made of the errors committed that morning by Longstreet himself. Indeed, Johnston's report goes so far as to cloak the mistake made by his right wing commander by inferring that he was to follow Hill on the Williamsburg Road. That was not the case. General Gustavus Woodson Smith provides a different version of the story, supported by several officer's statements, as well as the original copy of Smith's report of the action. Smith asserts that Longstreet himself was a major reason for the delay of the attack. According to that officer, Longstreet was to have advanced his division by way of the Nine Mile Road, which would have placed them in support of Hill, but would have brought his division out immediately at Fair Oaks. When Smith's division, under the command of General Whiting, attempted to reach the Nine Mile Road, early in the morning on May 31, their path was obstructed by Longstreet's command, who were breaking camp and loading baggage wagons. Whiting became impatient over the delay, and sought to contact Longstreet to remedy the situation. When he requested information regarding the exact location of Longstreet, Johnston informed him that he was probably with his division, moving down Nine Mile Road. An aide was sent with a message for Longstreet, but word was soon received that the general was not where Johnston imagined him to be. In fact, there was no sign of his division anywhere along the road. The aide sent word that he would try to ride across country, to the Williamsburg Road, to see if he could locate Longstreet's troops. When Johnston learned that Longstreet was not where he should have been, he directed Lieutenant Washington to locate him, and to give him instructions to march at least three of his brigades back to Nine Mile Road, so long as the change would not involve a serious loss of time. This all took place at approximately 9:00 A.M., and it was this same Lieutenant Washington who was captured by the pickets of the 103rd Pennsylvania.[15]

Smith contends that Johnston contacted him, following the submission of his official report of the battle, to ask that he amend his statements, and delete some of the information contained. Johnston wrote a letter to Smith asking him to make a "modification — or ommission make note to author rather" to his report. "I refer to the mention of the misunderstanding between Longstreet and myself in regard to the direction of his division." He asserted that since this concerned "Longstreet and myself alone, I have no hesitation in asking you to strike them out of your report — as they in no manner concern your operations."[16] Smith consented to grant Johnston's request, but he kept a copy of his original report, which included several paragraphs regarding the absence of Longstreet's division from the Nine Mile Road. Johnston assumed part of the blame in his letter to Smith by referring to a "misunderstanding" between him and Longstreet. But there was definitely no misunderstanding on the morning of May 31. Longstreet was not where Johnston meant for him to be, and Lieutenant Washington was captured in the act of trying to locate that officer and return at least a part of his division back to its intended jump-off point. Why did Johnston cover this mistake in his own report, and why did he ask Smith to delete any mention of it from the report he submitted? Why is Huger specifically named as the cause of the delay, while Longstreet is held blameless? The answers to these questions may never be known, but the record shows that Huger was not the only officer who was not where he was supposed to be at the appointed time. The whole truth is that Huger was offered as a scapegoat in the affair, and he seems to be the officer that was blameless. When Longstreet departed from his assigned line of march, he countermarched off the Nine Mile Road, thus delaying Whiting from being able to use the road until his men had left the scene. He then took his troops south, toward the Williamsburg Road, where he encountered Huger's division at a makeshift bridge across the Gilles Creek. The creek was swollen by the recent rains, and the only way across it was by way of the bridge, in single file. Longstreet insisted that Huger's division wait until his own had crossed, and Huger was thus frozen in place by the bottleneck created by Longstreet. It was through no fault of his own that his division was not at its appointed place in time to launch an early morning assault. The delay was the sole responsibility of Longstreet, the officer assigned to command the assault by that wing of the army, and therefore Huger's superior officer.[17] This delay would have severe consequences in the outcome of the fighting on May 31, and it is for that reason that so much attention has been given to its cause, and to the officer responsible for bringing it about.

    D.H. Hill had been up all of the previous night preparing for the assault. By 6:00 A.M., he had three of his four brigades on the Williamsburg Road, and was ready to march to the attack. The three brigades Hill had with him were those of Brigadier Generals Winfield S. Featherston, Samuel Garland Jr., and Gabriel J. Rains. Featherston was unable to perform his duties due to illness, so Colonel George B. Anderson assumed command of the brigade. Brigadier General Robert E. Rodes' brigade was on the Charles City Road, with orders to hold his position until relieved by General Huger's troops. The fiasco at Gilles Creek caused Rodes to be greatly delayed in rejoining Hill, and as Hill's orders were not to attack before all his brigades were present, Johnston's entire timetable was coming unhinged. Hill was becoming more and more frustrated with each passing hour. By noon, he sent a message to Longstreet requesting permission to launch the attack, with or without Rodes. This request was refused. Then, at approximately 1:00 P.M., Hill sent another message, that Rodes was finally on his way, and would be able to join in the assault. Longstreet gave the order to go in, and the signal guns were fired.[18]

    On the left, or northern side, of the Williamburg Road, Garland's brigade advanced behind a skirmish line. Anderson's brigade was in support of Garland. On the right, or southern side of the road, the skirmish line was to be followed by Rodes' brigade, supported by Rains. The only problem was that only two of Rodes' regiments had thus far arrived on the field. The remainder were still enroute from the Charles City Road, and were to be funneled into the line as they came up. What resulted was a difference of 15 minutes between the time the left wing, under Garland, advanced, and the time Rodes' right wing stepped off.[19]

Garland's brigade advanced with five regiments: the 5th North Carolina, 23rd North Carolina, 24th Virginia, 38th Virginia, and 2nd Florida. The 2nd Mississippi Battalion, also a part of the brigade, had been deployed as skirmishers. On first glance, it would be assumed that Garland had a mighty strike force at his disposal, but such was not the case. Previous battle losses, sickness, and the like had greatly reduced the number of soldiers in these regiments. The sum total of the men in his command amounted to only 2,065 effectives, including the skirmishers from the 2nd Mississippi Battalion. The 5th North Carolina, the smallest of Garland's regiments, mustered but 180 officers and men when it marched forward to meet the enemy. Garland stated that the ground over which the men marched was

> almost insurmountable. The recent rains had formed ponds of water throughout the woods with mud at the bottom, through which the men waded forward knee-deep, and occasionally sinking to the hips in boggy places, almost beyond the point of extrication.... Still all pushed onward with alacrity — so fast, indeed, that when the skirmishers became heavily engaged the regiments pressed upon their heels and the fire became hot along our whole front before emerging from the woods. The regiments were brought into line of battle to support the skirmishers, who, without retiring behind them to reform, became in many places intermingled in their ranks, and so continued throughout the day. We drove the enemy before us out of the woods back into the abatis, where they had several regiments drawn up behind a fence to support them.... We had now reached the edge of the wood, where the abatis impeded our farther advance, and the troops were under heavy fire.[20]

Garland's men were not only facing fire from the front, they were also being subjected to enfilading fire into their right flank, owing to the fact that the advance of Rodes' brigade had been delayed. At this crucial time, Garland was attacking Casey's entire division with his solitary brigade.

General Howard remembered Garland's assault as being so "abrupt and overwhelming that but little resistance was made by those in advance of the main line. The pickets and regiment just sent forward, leaving the dead and badly wounded, were quickly swept away by their advancing enemy."[21] General Webb recalled how the retreat of the picket line, joined by "a large number of sick, camp followers and skulkers, flowed in a steady stream to the rear, thus giving the impression that Casey's division had broken in panic, and left the field without making any firm or resolved resistance." Webb stated that the first intelligence sent to McClellan had given this notion, causing the commanding general to telegraph Secretary Stanton, "Casey's division, which was the first line, gave way unaccountably and discreditably."[22] McClellan would later retract this statement in his official report, and would attempt to set right his previous slander of Casey and the men in his division. The greenest and most poorly armed division in the Army of the Potomac met its baptism of fire with gallant tenacity, and retreated only after being overwhelmed and outflanked.

High winds had prevented Professor Lowe from ascending in his observation balloon on the 31st. The only intelligence being received at army headquarters were the reports coming in from Keyes and Heintzelman. McClellan was aware that the Rebels were building up their forces against his left wing, and both of the corps commanders on the south side of the Chickahominy warned that an attack was imminent. When McClellan heard the first sounds of battle, he attempted to rise from his sickbed to try to take charge of the situation. Malaria had sapped his strength, however, and he was not yet fully up to the crisis. He had taken the precaution of issuing orders to General Sumner that would prove to be a turning point in the battle. Sumner was instructed to have his corps ready to march to the relief of the left wing at a moment's notice. Still smarting from his mediocre performance at Williamsburg, Sumner made sure that this assignment would be carried out to the fullest. Taking McClellan's orders a step further, Sumner marched his divisions out of camp at a little after 1:00 P.M., and led them down to Sunderland Bridge and Grapevine Bridge, where he held them in readiness for the anticipated order to advance.[23]

The 103rd Pennsylvania was the first unit Garland's brigade encountered when it approached the edge of the woods. The regiment numbered some 450 officers and men. For several minutes, the Keystoners held their ground against more than four-to-one odds, buying precious time for Casey to recall his fatigue parties and get his regiments into line. When the 103rd's commander, Major Audley Gazzam, was informed that the regiment was being flanked on the right, he ordered the men to withdraw as quickly as possible. The thick undergrowth of the woods made an orderly withdrawal difficult. When Casey's artillery opened on the woods, before the Pennsylvanians had successfully extricated themselves, the retreat turned into a frantic rout. Under fire from the enemy to their rear, and their own artillery to their front, the men of the 103rd broke and ran as fast as their legs could carry them.[24]

Garland said that when his brigade reached the edge of the woods, its further progress was impeded by the abatis to their front. General Naglee's regiments were making things hot for the Confederates, pouring a heavy fire into their ranks. Garland first ordered his regiments in the center and left of his line to move by the left flank to get around the abatis and was in the process of ordering the right portion of his line to skirt the obstruction by the right flank. An examination of his line, however, revealed that the regiments were becoming bunched up as they came out of the woods, which was causing the men to suffer terribly from the enemy fire. Garland determined to meet the problem head-on, and ordered his men forward, straight through the obstacle. The 2nd Florida, on the left, was the first

One of the Union Bridges over the Chickahominy River (**Military History Institute, United States Army War College**).

Chickahominy River as it appears today at the site where the Grapevine bridge once stood (photograph taken by author).

regiment to get through, with the 38th Virginia on its right. Garland's command was taking heavy casualties and was in need of support, but all of the general's aides and couriers were either employed, or had fallen as casualties. There was no one to send back to Anderson to request help. Garland trusted that Anderson would hear the heavy musketry, and given his military experience, would understand that he was needed and march to the sound of the guns. Anderson responded exactly as Garland anticipated. Three of his regiments marched forward to join Garland's men, while a fourth regiment was sent out to the left, to envelop the Union right flank. In the meantime, the 2nd Florida and 38th Virginia pressed the assault once they were past the obstruction, and pushed forward to a fence that had previously marked the line of Naglee's men. In the process, they captured a two-gun section of Union artillery. But the attackers were paying a fearful price. Casualties were extreme, especially among the officer corps. In the 2nd Florida, ten of the 11 company commanders had been lost, as well as two of the field officers. Similar casualties were experienced in all of Garland's regiments. The engagement on this part of the field was rapidly becoming a soldier's fight, with non-coms and privates taking the initiative and pressing the assault.[25]

The 52nd Pennsylvania was one of Naglee's regiments that was facing Garland's desperate attack. A member of the regiment recalled how Garland's men "flung themselves upon our lines in front and both flanks with a desperate courage born of a belief that circumstances had at last placed a wing of McClellan's army helpless at their mercy. As daring as was the advance not less obstinate was the resistance."[26] The Pennsylvanian was right, the fight being waged by Naglee's men was indeed taking its toll on the Confederate attackers. When the skirmish line, supported by the 103rd Pennsylvania, had been forced to retire,

General Casey had given the order for a counterattack. Naglee sent forward the 100th New York, 104th Pennsylvania, and 11th Maine.

> The regiments sprang forward toward the enemy with a tremendous yell. In our way was a high worm fence, which cut our former line of battle, but the boys sprang over it into the same inclosure [sic] with the enemy, where we formed and renewed the fight. The battle now raged with great fury and the firing was much better than before.... At about 3 P.M. the enemy being largely re-enforced, pressed us in front and flank, and seeing that we could not hold our position much longer unless re-enforced, I dispatched an officer to General Casey for that purpose. The colonel of the One hundredth New York being killed; the colonel of the One hundred and fourth being severely wounded; the major mortally wounded; the lieutenant-colonel being absent; half our men having fallen killed or wounded.[27]

Sergeant Hiram Purcell would win the Congressional Medal of Honor for his actions during this part of the engagement. Purcell was carrying a regimental color during the retreat of the 104th Pennsylvania when he noticed that the regiment's other color had been left behind. He immediately rushed back into the very faces of the advancing enemy, and despite the hail of bullets all around him, rescued the second flag and brought it off the field.[28]

Garland's command was still pressing forward, but the wheels were beginning to come off the cart. The stubborn resistance of Naglee's men was taking its toll. Though the Confederates still held the upper hand, Naglee's men were bleeding them almost dry. The loss of so many officers was starting to cause confusion in the ranks, and the assault was in danger of stalling. Garland must have support on his right if the attack was to be successful, but, as yet, he was still fighting alone. Where was Rodes?

Rodes was advancing toward his assigned place in the line as fast as he could. General Hill was with him, doing all in his power to hurry the much-needed brigade along. Hill ordered Rodes to make straight for the abatis. General Rains was ordered to make a march around the right flank, and to place his brigade in the rear of the Federal works. As Rodes was deploying, he could see a heavy column of Federal reinforcements double-quicking on the Williamsburg Road to meet him. General Hill ordered Captain J.W. Bondurant's six-gun battery to shell and disperse the enemy, but Bondurant was unable to hold his ground. The guns from Fort Casey soon found the range and drove Bondurant back before he could effect any material damage on the Federal infantry. Captain Thomas H. Carter then rode up and asked Hill permission to lead his five guns of the King William Artillery forward to take a crack at the Yankees. Hill felt that little could be accomplished, given the manner in which Bondurant had been driven off, but he agreed to allow Carter to try. This was the first action the King William Artillery had been in, and the gunners were eager to prove themselves. Carter wheeled his cannon into position, and immediately opened on the advancing infantry. The guns in Fort Casey responded, but this time their aim was high, and the shells flew harmlessly overhead. While the fighting was at its highest, and the decision was still in doubt, Lieutenant William Carter approached his brother and commander to inform him that he had been badly wounded. William opened his shirt to reveal a bullet wound in the center of his chest. "I am afraid it is mortal," Thomas said. "Mount your horse, find an ambulance and surgeon and go to Richmond. May God bless you." Thinking that he would never see his brother again on this earth, Captain Carter returned to the business at hand and continued shelling the Yankees. After the battle, he would be pleasantly surprised to discover that William was not only still alive, but was expected to make a full recovery.[29]

The reduced efficiency of the gunners inside Fort Casey was to be expected. The Confederates had positioned sharpshooters in the woods in Rodes' sector to snipe at the artillerymen, and their efforts were paying off. Colonel Guilford D. Bailey, Casey's chief of artillery, was shot through the forehead and killed. Major Van Valkenburgh, who had assumed command of Battery A, 1st New York Light Artillery when Bailey was promoted, was shot dead shortly after Bailey fell. Lieutenant Rumsey, the adjutant of the battery, was also killed. All of the staff and field officers of the artillery had fallen, the gunners had suffered fearful casualties, and most of the artillery horses had been killed. Casey's big guns were almost out of the fight. At this point, General Naglee entered the fort and took personal charge of the cannon, directing their fire in an attempt to stay the Rebel onslaught.[30] But Naglee was to achieve no reversal of fortunes. Once Carter's Confederate guns had driven back the Federal column, he turned his attention to the guns in Fort Casey. General Rains had reached his assigned destination, behind the Union line, and opened a deadly fire into the rear of the fort. Rodes had assumed his place to the right of Garland's brigade, and the combined force was pushing forward.

Major Bryan Grimes, commander of the 4th North Carolina, had exhorted his men forward, crying, "Charge 'em! Damn 'em, charge 'em!" He was leading his regiment on horseback when an artillery shell severed the animal's head, and the beast went down, trapping Grimes' leg beneath it. The men of the 4th North Carolina thought their commander to be dead, and the regiment began to falter, but Grimes, still trapped beneath the horse, waved his sword and yelled "Forward! Forward!" The 4th kept their place in the line, and once Grimes had been gotten out from under his horse, he picked up the regimental flag and continued to lead his men on foot.[31]

All three of Casey's brigades were now reeling from the ceaseless pounding they were receiving in front, flank, and rear. The blue line waivered, then simply melted away, as soldiers broke for the rear as fast as they could. Rodes' men dashed into the abandoned fort and turned its guns on the fleeing defenders who had so recently occupied it. After two hours of hard fighting, Casey's division had been whipped, and the battlefield was in the possession of Hill's men, along with Casey's camp, his works, and his guns. Hill had achieved this victory himself. Longstreet's division had taken no part in the fighting, and had definitely not followed Johnston's orders to support Hill's attack. On the contrary, Longstreet seemed to be doing all that he could to keep his men out of the fight. Brigadier General George E. Pickett's brigade was ordered to march north, away from the fighting, to guard the York River Railroad, even though General Johnston was already there with Whiting's division. Longstreet sent three more brigades, under the overall command of General Cadmus Wilcox, to the Charles City Road, where Huger already had two brigades. These five brigades were kept marching and countermarching for the next few hours, with no apparent intent or reason. Longstreet kept the final two brigades in his division in reserve. That left him with a reserve force, but evidently no attacking force.

One can only imagine what might have been the outcome of the battle if the Confederate assault had been delivered by ten brigades instead of only four. Hill had broken Casey's division. He had forced it from prepared, if unfinished, defenses, and had driven it pell-mell from the field. In the process, he had sustained grievous casualties to his own command. Had he been supported as Johnston intended it is probable that the victory would have been more complete, and the cost would have been substantially lower. As it was, Casey's men were beaten, but not broken. Couch and Casey were able to rally a substantial number of them three-quarters of a mile in the rear, and establish another defensive line along the Nine Mile Road.[32]

Given the aforementioned chain of events, it is obvious why Moxley Sorrell, Longstreet's chief-of-staff, brushed off the first day's battle at Fair Oaks with a single paragraph when he wrote his memoirs. It is also obvious that he intended to cover the actions of his old commander when he wrote that paragraph.

> There shall be no attempt to describe or discuss this battle. G.W. Smith with a large command was on our left. General Johnston with him and Major General Huger with a strong division was expected to support our right, but for some reason we did not get it. D.H. Hill with his four brigades and our six, attacked with great fury. Smith's attack on the left was retarded and unsuccessful. We made quick progress, but with heavy losses in our ten fine brigades. The enemy could not stand before them and Casey's division, posted at Seven Pines, gave way after heavy losses and was crushed. Cannon and colors fell into our hands. Darkness was then coming on and no supports, much to Longstreet's chagrin.[33]

It is unmistakable that Longstreet did not follow Johnston's plan of attack, and it is just as evident that Longstreet was personally responsible for a large measure of the delay in making the attack. Johnston, for whatever reason, determined not to assess blame for the shortcomings, and even went so far as to ask Smith to strike any mention of it from his report. Sorrell makes no such magnanimous gesture. He clearly assigns the blame for the delays to Johnston, Huger, and Smith, and he leaves the reader with the distinct impression that Longstreet and Hill carried the fighting, when it was Hill, unsupported by Longstreet, who had routed Casey from his works and sent his division reeling.

Casey had called for support, and was desperately trying to rally his men and form a new line. Hatless, his long white hair flowing, he was raging among the retreating men, trying to stop their flight with pleas, threats, and exhortations. One observer witnessed his efforts and turned to a comrade to say, "Did you ever see an old woman when her suds were boiling over?" The comrade replied that he had not. "Well, look at old Casey, he puts me in mind of one."[34] General Keyes was responding to Casey's calls for help as the refugees from the battle came streaming down the Williamsburg Road. The commander of the 4th Corps was ordering General Darius Couch's men into battle to try to stem the tide, but he was doing so in a piecemeal fashion. Regiments from Brigadier General John J. Peck's brigade were thrown together with regiments from Brigadier General Charles Devens' brigade to form a patchwork line. The 55th New York and the 10th Massachusetts were ordered forward to check the Confederate advance. The 10th Massachusetts advanced about 450 yards to a line of rifle pits. Finding the pits filled with water, the men laid down behind them, taking advantage of the cover afforded by the ground thrown up in their front. The 55th New York was about 150 yards in front of the Bay Staters, and had taken up a position in the midst of a row of felled trees. Some distance to the rear, the 7th Massachusetts, along with Captain Jeremiah McCarthy's Battery C, 1st Pennsylvania Light Artillery, had formed a line of battle on a slight elevation. The 36th New York extended the line to their left. The 93rd and 102nd Pennsylvania regiments had been on the left of the 10th Massachusetts, but they were ordered away right, placing the flanks of the 10th in a precarious position.[35] The 55th New York was engaged almost immediately upon taking up their position. The Confederates made this "a very hot place" for the New Yorkers, and in a few short minutes, their line "began to melt away, and those that were left fell back before the murderous fire of the enemy." The 10th Massachusetts was then ordered forward to a point just short of the line recently held by the 55th New York. In some respects, the men of the regiment were glad to be moving up. While in their position behind the rifle pits, they had been subjected to a murderous cross fire from front and rear. The threat from the front came in the form of small arms fire from the Confederates; that from the rear in the form of defective artillery shells being fired by

McCarthy's battery, that were exploding above the prone men and doing as much damage as the enemy bullets, if not more.[36]

The companies in the center of the line were suffering fearfully from enemy musket fire, but because of "high bushes and brush in their front" could not see their assailants, "and could only fire by guesswork at the enemy's position." The view was much clearer for the men in the companies on the left and right flanks of the regimental line. These troops could plainly see that the Confederate line overlapped the Federals on either side. When an enfilading fire was opened on the left flank, the regiment fell back, very much in danger of being surrounded. They continued to give ground until they had retired to the vicinity of their camp, when Colonel Briggs rallied the men and led them in a counter-attack that drove the Confederates back beyond the line of the rifle pits. General Keyes now joined the regiment in person, and led it far to the right, where it once more engaged the enemy, firing volley after volley into the faces of the tiring attackers. It was here that Colonel Henry Briggs received his third and final wound of the day. Briggs had previously been struck in the chest by a mini ball, but had been spared injury because of the steel breastplate he was wearing underneath his tunic. These early versions of a bulletproof vest had become popular in the army in this second year of the war. Soldiers would later discard them as being too heavy and cumbersome, while providing too little protection, but in Briggs' case, the armor had done its job. He was next struck in the foot by a spent ball. Upon falling back to the secondary line, the colonel's luck ran out, and he was shot by a bullet through both hips. The lieutenant colonel of the 10th Massachusetts was unfit for duty due to illness, and the major had been detailed as brigade officer of the day, so the command passed to Captain Orzo Miller.[37] Miller was able to rally the command, despite the fact that it was now facing the fiercest fighting it had experienced. Casualties were severe.

> The scene at this time was awfully magnificent. The faint smoke of the musketry arose lightly all along the line just so that the heads of the men could be seen through it, sudden gusts of intense white smoke burst up from the mouth of the cannon all around; bullets shredded the air, and whistled swiftly by, or struck into fences, boxes, or with their particular chuck into men; and far up into the air shells burst into sudden flame like shattered stars, and passed away in little clouds of white vapor, while others filled the air with a shrill scream, and hurried on to burst far in the rear. Every second of time had its especial tone, and every inch of space was packed with death.[38]

But the 10th Massachusetts held. Their fierce struggle held the enemy in check until darkness fell.

In the meantime, Keyes had dispatched Peck to hold the left of his line. The 93rd and 102nd Pennsylvania had been ordered away from their position to the left of the 10th Massachusetts to rejoin Peck's 62nd New York in a line along the principal road connecting the Williamsburg Road with the Charles City Road. Keyes sent orders for the 62nd New York to march to the extreme right of the Union line, to the support of General Couch. This left Peck with only two regiments of his brigade on the left. General Heintzelman inquired if Peck could advance from his position, in order to take some of the pressure off of the Federal right. He immediately retracted the suggestion, however, upon learning that Peck had only two regiments, and was holding an important line where several country roads connected the Charles City Road to the Williamsburg Road. Heintzelman directed Peck to hold his position "at all hazzards." About an hour later, at 4:30 P.M., the situation on the right had become critical, and Peck received orders to double-quick his regiments to that part of the line. The 93rd Pennsylvania and 102nd Pennsylvania went into line immediately upon reaching the field, and pressed forward to relieve their hard-pressed comrades. For half an hour, the lines went back and forth, as Peck's men were pushed back, reformed, counter charged, and were pushed back again. Finally, unable to withstand the pressure from the reinforced Confederate line, Peck's men were compelled to withdraw from the field. His men fell back to Couch's camp, where they took up position in rifle pits, along with troops from Brigadier General Hiram G. Berry's brigade.[39] Penrose Mark, of the 93rd Pennsylvania, remembered that the bullets had "fairly rained upon us like hail.... It was truly a shower of death." The regiment had almost expended all of its ammunition. A barricade was thrown up across the road, and Colonel J.M. McCarter, a former Methodist preacher, announced that the position must be held, "or our dead bodies left upon the field.... By this time the cannonading and musketry had become terrific, and a desperate effort was made by the Rebels to outflank us, and to prevent this we received orders to move to the right. Many a poor fellow bit the dust and men were dropping like flies. A charge was made, but the deadly fire of the Rebels was hard to withstand, closed in mass, by Brigades, four regiments deep."[40]

The action on the flanks became a prime focus for both armies. Rodes was advancing against the left wing of the Federal line, and his troops were skirting the edge of White Oak Swamp. In many cases, they were trudging through flooded marshland, where the water was hip-deep. The wounded had to be propped up against trees to keep them from drowning. Rodes had expected to be supported by Rains' brigade on his right, but Rains found the terrain in his front to be even more difficult than that which Rodes was dealing with, and his advance literally got stuck in the mud. At this time, a vicious counterattack slammed into Rodes' line, as Phil Kearny arrived on the field with two brigades. Kearny had been three miles back on the Williamsburg Road when he got the order to come to the relief of the embattled defenders along Couch's line. He met General Casey when his troops neared the fighting, and that officer urged him, "If you will regain our late camp the day will still be ours." His impression of Casey might be revealed in a letter he would later write to his wife: "Another haphazard battle where I was sent for to redeem the blundering and shortcomings of others."

The general put his brigades on the march to the south of the Williamsburg Road, and made straight for the right flank of Hill's division. As the battle was joined, he galloped up and down his line, exhorting his men, completely oblivious to the leaden storm all around him. When one of his colonels asked where Kearny wanted his regiment to be, the general responded, "Oh, anywhere! T'is all the same, Colonel, you'll find lovely fighting along the whole line." Kearny had with him the men of Brigadier General Hiram G. Berry's brigade. The 2nd Michigan was on the left of his first line of battle, with the 5th Michigan extending that line to the right. The supporting line consisted of the 37th New York on the left and the 3rd Michigan on the right. Brigadier General David Birney's brigade had been detached and sent north of General John Ambercrombie's brigade to form the right flank of the defensive line. When Brigadier General Charles D. Jameson's brigade arrived on the scene, General Heintzelman directed that one regiment be sent to the support of Peck's brigade. The 87th New York was detached for that duty. Jameson's other two regiments, the 63rd Pennsylvania and the 105th Pennsylvania, took up a line on the north and south sides of the Williamsburg Road, with their left flank formed on the right of Kearny's line. The battle raged for nearly one and one-half hours, as Kearny's troops pushed the Confederates back, almost to Casey's camp. The Rebels reformed and counterattacked, turning Kearny's right flank, and threatening to envelop his command and pin it against the White Oak Swamp. Kearny recognized the seriousness of the situation. He ordered the 37th New York to face about, and had them charge into what had been their rear to prevent the Confederates who had gotten behind them from cutting off their line of retreat. His regiments then withdrew to the protection of their fortified camp, the place they had started from a few hours earlier.[41]

Rodes' brigade had received the full impact of Kearny's assault, and some of the most desperate fighting it did that day was against Kearny's men. Rodes had suffered a painful wound in the arm earlier in the engagement, but had refused to leave the field for two hours, until weakness from loss of blood forced him to turn command over to Colonel John B. Gordon of the 6th Alabama. Gordon was much embarrassed and surprised by this turn of events. He was not only junior in commission to the other regimental commanders in the brigade, he was also the youngest member of the group. As Gordon was riding up and down his line, trying to encourage the men, he passed his brother, Augustus Gordon, "only nineteen years old, but captain of one of the companies. He was lying with a number of dead companions near him. He had been shot through the lungs and was bleeding profusely. I did not stop; I could not stop, nor would he permit me to stop. There was no time for that — no time for anything except to move on and fire on." Augustus would miraculously survive this wound, only to be killed two years later, at the battle of the Wilderness, by a wound to almost exactly the same place. "My field officers and adjutant were all dead," Gordon wrote. "Every horse ridden into the fight, my own among them, was dead. Fully one half of my line officers and half of my men were dead or wounded. A furious fire still poured from the front, and re-enforcements were nowhere in sight." Gordon recalled that "the losses were appalling.... Of forty-four officers of the line, but thirteen were left for duty. Nearly two-thirds of the entire command were killed or wounded." Gordon may have stretched the losses in Rodes' command somewhat, but he was undoubtedly thinking of the carnage in his own regiment when he did so. The 6th Alabama had 59 percent casualties in the battle, the most suffered by any Confederate regiment in a single engagement during the war.[42]

Longstreet's brigades had taken no part in the fighting prior to the arrival of Kearny's brigades on the field. Hill had been desperately calling for assistance, but succor from the right wing commander was not forthcoming. Finally, Longstreet ordered the two brigades he had designated as his reserve into the fight. Colonel James L. Kemper's brigade was sent to assist Gordon's roughly handled men. On their march to the front, Kemper's men had to pass through the human debris of the battle. The slain lay on every side, and a "Long stream of wounded made their appearance on their way back to the rear, in every species of mutilation. Some were borne on stretchers, others swung in blankets from whose folds blood and gore dropped in horrible exudations, staining the ground and crimsoning the budding grass." The men hurried on past a wrecked Confederate battery where Private Alexander Hunter, of the 17th Virginia Infantry, took note that all of the gunners and horses lay dead or wounded, save for a little boy, the powder monkey. "He cowered behind a wheel of one of the guns, with eyes protruding, hands clasped, teeth clenched and a face wearing a look of horrified fright — face so white, so startling in its terror, that it haunted me for days after."[43] These sights might have been demoralizing if Kemper's men had had time to dwell upon them. Kemper had to cover more than a mile to reach the battlefield, and he wanted to get there in time to make a difference in the outcome. George Wise, another member of the 17th Virginia, reported that they "double quicked, marching at a rate of seven miles an hour." When the men reached a point behind Casey's old camp, they were given a few minutes to catch their breath. Kemper's four regiments were put into line amid "one of the heaviest assaults of lead and canister that we had ever passed through. The order to charge was given, and the men moved briskly to their work."[44]

A member of the 17th Virginia recalled the "incompetence and ignorance of our commanding officers" at this moment in time. The officers had been in such a rush to get at the Yankees that the order to form line of battle was never given. Instead, the regiment surged forward in column of fours, "like a lance, instead of spreading out in a line." The Virginians were forced to endure fire from all sides, while many of the troops in the massed column could not shoot back.

> From the half circle on the other side of the camp the enemy rained a constant fire upon the struggling mass. Order disappeared, discipline fled before that tempest. Within five minutes all was over. Men fell in groups. The noise of the Federal bullets ripping through the canvas of the tents added to the horrors of the moment. Men screamed as the balls struck them, the officers shouted out unmeaning cries, the flag went down; (Sgt. W.T.) Morrill, the color-bearer and the tallest man in the regiment, sank to the earth; Corporal (C.W.) Diggs caught the colors and he fell, too. A private grasped them. He raised the staff and in a second he sank face downward with a bullet through his heart. Another gallant private, named Harper, seized the staff from the dead man's hand and bore the colors the rest of the day. In five minutes seventy-four officers and men out of our regiment fell. Then there was a blind rush for shelter.

The Confederates made for Casey's redoubt and abandoned rifle pits, which "proved now our salvation. But for them none save a few would have escaped alive."[45]

Kemper's men were hugging the earth behind the Federal works.

> I have listened to some heavy firing and to the music of many missles [sic] singing through the air, but I never heard the like of the noise made by shot and shell, as I lay there securely behind that redoubt. They came so fast that at least twenty men were struck down by the overtaking balls as they were climbing over the works. There was a ceaseless pour of shot and shell, the bullets were hissing like snakes, without a moment's cessation. Every second they would strike the work and bury themselves in the damp earth, or, hitting higher, scrape the top and send the mud spattering over us. As I glanced around I could see the soldiers of different regiments and brigades cowering beneath the parapet, but few daring or having curiosity enough to lift his head over the works to take aim at the running line of fire that showed where the foe lay concealed. Indeed, it was a dangerous experiment. I saw two men not a dozen feet from me ... raise their heads and both fell back dead, with their heads shattered by bullets. The very sky seemed to be alive with little fiery devils who sang their song, each to its own tune, as they flew over the work. The canister sounded worse than all, and as the bits would strike against the earthwork it would make the bravest cower closer to the ground.... For fully an hour did this infernal fire keep up; for fully an hour did we lie there and listen to the sound of projectiles striking the earthwork.... Behind the works where we were the ooze and mire was so deep that it reached to our waist belts. Many of the Federals were killed here by Rodes' men and had found a grave without burial, for their corpses had sunk beneath the surface. We could feel that we were standing on their bodies, but the danger all were in prevented any remarks. [All around the] breastworks the water lay in pools and several of our wounded, falling in these puddles, had absolutely drowned. One of my regiment that I examined was not mortally wounded, but dropping face downward in the water he had been suffocated; his mouth and throat were filled with liquid mud.

Kemper's men remained behind the works until late in the evening, when the fire from the Union line slackened and died off. They then formed a line of battle and moved forward, to the line of trees from which the Federals had poured such a murderous fire on them. The Federals were gone. They had stopped Kemper's men cold, and then had fallen back to form a new line.[46]

While Kearny had had attacked Kemper, on the left of the Union line, with Berry's brigade, there seems to have been some measure of confusion with the deployment of Birney's brigade, to the right of Ambercrombie. Heintzelman had ordered that the brigade advance forward, in support of the Union right, as Birney had done. His brigade took up a position to the right, and slightly behind that of General Ambercrombie. Heintzelman, however, felt that Birney had stopped short of his assigned goal, and he placed the general under arrest the following day, and preferred charges against him for failing to perform his duty. Heintzelman would say, "Early in the afternoon ... an order was sent, on the application of General Keyes, to General Kearny, to send a brigade up the railroad to his assistance. The order sent to General Kearny was to send a brigade up the railroad to the front, and General Birney's was ordered up. I learned, after I arrived on the field of battle, that the brigade was halted on the railroad a very short distance from the camp." General Kearny rose to Birney's defense, categorically stating that his subordinate "never disobeyed orders" and referring to him as a "superior officer." He went on to point out that the wooded terrain was the cause of the confusion, stating that in such surroundings orders can sometimes "conflict." He also asserted that Birney's advance had been instrumental in saving Couch's division and pointed to this as proof "of his affecting what was intended." In the end, Birney would be acquitted of the charges, and would render illustrious service to the Union for the remainder of the war.[47]

Kemper's brigade had relieved some of the pressure from Rodes, but it had suffered heavy casualties and a severe repulse in doing so. Longstreet's other brigade had far greater success against the right of the Union line. General Naglee had been able to keep his brigade fairly well in hand when the rest of Casey's division fled the field. He had reformed his line behind a second row of abatis to the south of Fair Oaks Station, where he was joined by elements of Couch's division, and by General Couch himself. The Federals were able to stop the advance of the two Confederate brigades under Garland and Anderson, and the fighting was some of the fiercest seen on the field that day. One Union soldier described the scene: "Thousands of muskets in streaming volleys, with the sonorous roar of cannon and the hoarse screams of the combatants, created an uproar as if fiends had been unleashed to prey on each other. Storms of bullets and canister tore wide passages through the trees and mangled the bodies of men."[48]

Just when it looked as if Garland and G.B. Anderson were destined for a bloody repulse, the brigade of Brigadier General Richard H. Anderson, commanded by Colonel Micah Jenkins, came onto the field. Jenkins marched his men into the woods to the north of the clearing where Garland and Anderson were struggling against the stiff Union defense. He was able to drive back Ambercrombie's men, and veered to the right, cutting across the Nine Mile Road, to the north of Seven Pines. A member of Company B, 23rd Pennsylvania Infantry, one of Ambercrombie's regiments, remembered how the men gathered "up arms from the wounded and stragglers." When Jenkins' men attacked, this company opened a particularly heavy fire upon the Confederates, "each man having at least six guns loaded."[49] But the fire from the 23rd could not stem the tide. The men of Deven's brigade were taken in flank, in their Seven Pines entrenchments, and the rest of Couch's men scampered from the scene. The Union line was broken, and it seemed as if victory was within the grasp of the Confederates. Colonel Jenkins stated:

> I advanced my regiment (Palmetto Sharpshooters) through the abatis under a very heavy fire, which was repaid with interest after crossing. Finding after crossing that the Sixth Regiment South Carolina Volunteers and mine were isolated, I instructed Colonel (John) Bratton to keep his left touching to my right; and the enemy's line, after a stubborn resistance, having given way to our attack, I perceived that we had pierced his line, and having dressed the line, I executed, under fire from the right front, a change of front obliquely forward on our right company. Directing the two regiments forward in line, we drove the enemy to the front and right, passing over their second camp and through a swamp. At this point the enemy, heavily re-enforced, made a desperate stand,

and our fighting was within 75 yards. Not pausing even to load, and pouring my volleys at close range as I advanced, I never allowed a broken line to get through their new lines before I pushed on the new line and drove them back, losing heavily myself, but killing numbers of the enemy. Our advance continued in this steady manner, the enemy steadily giving back. The ranks of the enemy having broken to our right and front and the fire having lessened, I halted the lines, dressed them, and then changed front obliquely forward. Following the retreating enemy either fresh troops or heavy re-enforcements, met us, and in front of their third camp offered us battle with greatly superior numbers. Without pausing our lines moved on him, and our steady advance was not to be resisted. After a most obstinate resistance and terrible slaughter the enemy gave back to our left and right across the Williamsburg road.[50]

It was this movement by Jenkins that emboldened Kemper to launch his attack on the opposite end of the Confederate line. Kearny's timely arrival on the field had prevented the enveloping pincer movement that Kemper and Jenkins were attempting.

The 23rd and 61st Pennsylvania regiments were among the reinforcements reported by Jenkins in his report. General Couch was accompanying these regiments to direct them to their proper place in the line. As the 61st was marching through the woods, an enemy column was spotted 50 yards away, moving by the flank. Couch ordered Colonel Oliver Rippey to right file and move the length of the regiment, then face to the front and attack the Confederates. As Rippey gave the order, a Rebel officer could be plainly heard issuing orders for a mirror movement to his own men. The result was that the opposing lines were formed some 20 yards apart, and a brisk fire fight immediately ensued. Colonel Rippey was killed early in the action. Lieutenant Colonel George Spear was wounded and captured along with Major George Smith. This left Captain Robert Orr in command of the regiment. General Couch formed the 23rd Pennsylvania on the left of the 61st, but that regiment had moved slightly to the rear to avoid being flanked. Jenkins' Confederates now overlapped the 61st on both flanks, and had gotten behind Orr's men. The men of the 61st refused several demands for their surrender, and fought gamely until their supply of ammunition was exhausted. Only then did Orr give the order to fall back. By this time, however, their line of retreat was blocked by Jenkins' men, and the men of the 61st had to cut their way out. "Instantly a fierce hand-to-hand fight ensued, officers using their swords and revolvers and the men their empty muskets as clubs. The contest was necessarily short, as the rebel line in front came rushing over the abandoned position, yelling like fiends and ordering men of the 61st to throw down their arms and surrender. But this demand was unheeded, the rebels in the rear were brushed out of the way, except thirty-five of them, who were swept into the Union line as prisoners." The regiment had escaped envelopment, but found itself cut off from the main body. It withdrew to the north of Fair Oaks, along with General Couch, who also found himself separated from the remainder of his command. Of the 574 men that the 61st Pennsylvania took into the fight, 55.4 percent would fall as casualties. In fact, the 92 men killed in the regiment would account for over 11 percent of the total battle deaths suffered by the Union in the entire battle. The 61st would suffer more losses than any other Union regiment at Fair Oaks, and only ten other regiments in the entire war suffered greater losses in a single battle.[51]

While a portion of Couch's men withdrew eastward on the Williamsburg Road toward Savage Station, the remainder were cut off from the main body and withdrew north, across the Richmond & York River Railroad, to a point above Fair Oaks Station, a few miles from the Grapevine Bridge. The regiments that were forced to withdraw north of the railroad included the 23rd and 61st Pennsylvania, the 67th New York, and the 7th Massachusetts. The 31st Pennsylvania, 65th New York, and Captain James Brady's Battery H, 1st Pennsylvania

Five • Counteroffensive at Fair Oaks 107

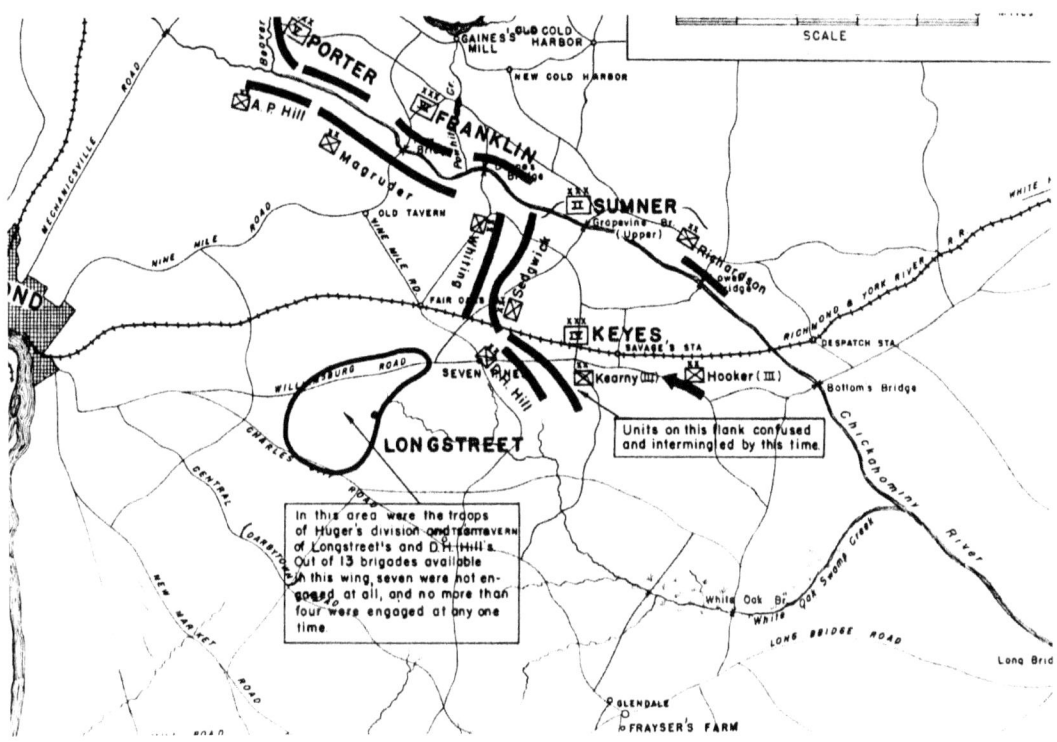

Top: Map showing the relative positions of the opposing forces at Fair Oaks (Military History Institute, United States Army War College). *Bottom:* Virtually nothing remains of the Seven Pines Battlefield. It has been completely developed and is now part of Metro Richmond (photograph taken by author).

Light Artillery, were already posted at Fair Oaks Station. General Keyes' main line had been pushed back nearly two miles, and its right flank had been severed from the main body. The Confederates had captured the camps of both Casey and Couch, and had forced the enemy to retire to their third and final line of defense. All of this had been accomplished by only six of the 23 brigades Johnston had intended to participate in the attack. Thus far, D.H. Hill had substantially shouldered the burden of the fight himself, with late assistance from two of Longstreet's brigades.

Where was the rest of the Confederate army, and why was Johnston allowing Hill to fight the engagement unsupported? The answer to that was to be found in a rare natural phenomenon known as an acoustic shadow. An acoustic shadow takes place when factors such as wind currents, weather, geographic terrain, temperature, or elevation affect sound waves and cause them to deflect in an abnormal manner. The result is that the sounds can be heard at a substantial distance from their source, but are muffled or muted to those nearby. Acoustic shadows played a part in several Civil War battles, most notably Iuka, Perryville, Chancellorsville, Gettysburg, Fort Donelson, and Five Forks, and one played a defining role in the battle of Fair Oaks. While General Sumner could clearly hear the sound of the engagement several miles away, Johnston, only half as far removed from the scene of the fighting, could not hear the musketry at all. The only sound that could be distinguished at his headquarters was muffled cannon fire, leading the commanding general to the assumption that an artillery duel was being fought and the main attack had not yet begun. General Robert E. Lee had ridden to Johnston's headquarters and had expressed the notion that he heard muffled rifle fire, but Johnston dismissed it out of hand. By this time, he was so distraught over the miscarried plan of attack that he was heard to say, "I wish all the troops were back in camp."[52] There is no question that an acoustic shadow was present at Fair Oaks, or that Johnston and his staff could not hear the sounds of the battle as they were taking place. There is, however, a great unanswered question as to why he allowed so much time to elapse before making inquiry as to the condition of affairs with the right flank of his army. Hill had already been fighting for more than two hours before Johnston dispatched a staff officer to see what was causing the delay. He had ordered the attack to be made early on the morning of the 31st, and by the time he sent an officer to the right to ascertain the situation there it was already past 3:00 P.M. Longstreet may have been directly responsible for creating the delay due to his failure to follow his commander's plan of attack, but Johnston bears accountability for not taking charge of the situation and making sure that his orders were being followed. Johnston definitely showed a lack of decisiveness and leadership in allowing so much time to elapse before taking an active role in the proceedings.

It was approximately 4:00 P.M. when Johnston's staff officer returned to headquarters with news that Hill was not only engaged, but had driven the divisions of Casey and Couch from the field. Longstreet was requesting support from the left to sustain the offensive. Johnston immediately ordered Gustavus Smith to send forward his division under General Whiting to attack the right flank of the Federal forces opposing Hill and Longstreet. Whiting had been posted along the Nine Mile Road, northwest of Fair Oaks. Johnston decided to lead the division into the attack himself, and guided the 10,000 fresh troops toward the Union right flank. Hill had already achieved great success against Keyes' corps, and if Johnston could now crush the Federal right, a complete victory might yet be salvaged from this day of bungled orders. Whiting's brigade, under the temporary command of Colonel Evander Law, was first in the line of march. It was followed by the brigades of Brigadier Generals James J. Pettigrew, Robert Hatton, and Wade Hampton. General John Bell Hood was issued orders to lead his brigade south of the Nine Mile Road and effect a junction with the left of the Confederate line, then under Jenkins. This disposition effectively kept Hood out of the fight. Pursuant to orders, he advanced toward where Longstreet's left was assumed to be, but he did not reach his assigned position until sunset.[53]

Johnston was pushing the other four brigades forward, toward Seven Pines. He did not know that Jenkins was already across that road, effectively splitting the Union army. When the head of his column reached a point only a mile from Seven Pines, General Whiting expressed concern that a large force of the enemy might be on his left flank, concealed in the woods to the northeast of Nine Mile Road. Johnston felt that there were Union troops there as well, but he surmised that they were merely the refugees from Casey's captured camp, and estimated their strength to be minimal. The commander was in a hurry to reach Seven Pines, and he dismissed Whiting's warning with the admonition, "Oh, General Whiting, you are too cautious!"[54] But Whiting's caution was not unfounded. General Couch had formed a line of battle parallel to the Nine Mile Road, on either side of the Adams House, with the 61st Pennsylvania, 23rd Pennsylvania, and 65th New York, from left to right. The 67th New York and 7th Massachusetts were in support of the main line, along with the six ten-pounder Parrott guns of Captain James Brady's Battery H, 1st Pennsylvania Light Artillery. Johnston had just concluded his rebuke of General Whiting when Brady's guns opened fire on the Confederate column. It was now almost 5:00 P.M. Colonel Dorsey Pender's 6th North Carolina was at the head of the column, in the vicinity of Fair Oaks Station, when Brady's guns were unleashed. Pender called out orders for the regiment to change front and move forward toward the battery at the double-quick. The three companies on the left of the line moved against the supporting infantry, while the seven on the right took on the guns. The distance between the combatants was approximately 150 yards, and Brady's gunners used it to advantage, pouring a sheet of canister into Pender's ranks and throwing the companies on the right back in disorder. Pender rallied his men and led them forward again, this time supported by other regiments in Law's brigade. This time the Confederates got to within 75 yards of the guns before they were once more thrown back by the hail of canister and small arms fire. The Confederates formed for a third attempt, and the Union gunners braced themselves against the worst. The battery had run out of canister, and the prospect of stopping a massed infantry charge without them seemed slim. Brady was determined to hold his position, however. Loading his guns with exploding shells, the fuses cut to point-blank range, he awaited the next assault. The Confederates came on boldly, and reached a point only 20 yards from Brady's guns, but the advance stopped there. The exploding shells tore the attackers to pieces, and the Confederates were swept back in confusion. Pender took charge of the situation and rallied the broken regiments. President Jefferson Davis was on the field and witnessed the colonel's "courage and coolness." He rode over to compliment Pender, and called him "General" in his salutation. It was no slip of the tongue—Pender had caught the eye of a very important benefactor, and in two days he would indeed be a general.[55]

General Smith had been in the rear of the column when the lead brigade was assailed at Fair Oaks. He immediately took charge of the trailing brigades, ordering Wade Hampton to continue his march parallel to, and on the right side of the Nine Mile Road, which would put him in position to link up with Pettigrew, and extend his line to the left. Smith then hurried General Hatton's brigade directly down the road, ordering him to hold himself in reserve, prepared to support Whiting, Pettigrew, or Hampton, as the situation demanded. Once these movements were in progress, Smith proceeded to Fair Oaks and the sound of the guns. He was sure that a combined attack by his entire division would be sufficient to overwhelm the Yankee defenders in the vicinity.[56]

Smith was quite correct that the battered remnants under Couch were no match for his entire division, but he was not the only commander hastening toward the sound of the guns. General Edwin V. Sumner was about to redeem the lackluster performance he had turned in at Williamsburg, and restore his reputation as a hard-fighting, competent officer. The order to move his corps to the support of Heintzelman and Keyes came at 2:30 P.M. Sumner had Brigadier General Israel Richardson's division waiting at Sunderland Bridge, while Brigadier General John Sedgwick's division was at Grapevine Bridge. Sunderland Bridge had water cresting two feet above its flooring, and Richardson was able to get only one brigade across before the bridge collapsed. The situation was not much better at Grapevine Bridge. The rushing water had loosened the ropes that held the log flooring together, creating gaps in the span, and the middle of the bridge seemed about to be swept away by the current. When Sumner approached the bridge, an engineering officer told him that it would be impossible for him to cross. "Impossible?" Sumner roared, "Sir, I tell you I can cross. I am ordered." A staff officer recalled "A group of officers with serious, thoughtful countenances and bespattered with mud from head to foot stand discussing as to whether it is safe to trust the troops on so frail and apparently unsafe a structure." Sumner's iron will fortified the men, and they determined to follow where he led. Sedgwick's men started across, with Brigadier General Willis A. Gorman's brigade in the lead. Grapevine Bridge swayed, but the weight of the column of men held the floor in place. It took nearly two hours for Sedgwick's Division to effect the crossing, but by 4:30 P.M., Gorman's Brigade was approaching the Hanover Road, just north of Fair Oaks.[57] Richardson shifted the remainder of his division over to Grapevine Bridge as well, and crossed behind Sedgwick. These two divisions would be all the troops that Sumner would be able to get to the south side of the Chickahominy. The bridge collapsed following Richardson's crossing.

When Couch learned that Sumner was on his way, he immediately sent word to Heintzelman and Keyes that he would hold his position until reinforcements arrived. Sumner reached the field with the vanguard of Gorman's brigade, and assumed command of Couch's regiments. Couch informed him that his right was in danger of being turned, and Sumner dispatched Colonel Alfred Sully's 1st Minnesota to the right to extend Couch's flank to the right. Sully's regiment was formed on either side of the Courtney house. Gorman's other three regiments were directed to the left. There they formed a line perpendicular to Couch's, facing northwest and directly on the right flank of Whiting's brigade. From right to left, Gorman's line consisted of the 82nd New York, the 34th New York, and the 15th Massachusetts. When Brigadier General William W. Burns' brigade arrived, his 69th Pennsylvania filed in to the left of the 61st Pennsylvania. The 72nd Pennsylvania went into line to the left of the 69th, and connected to the right of Gorman's 82nd New York, where an angle of almost 90 degrees was formed. Brigadier General Napoleon Dana only had two of his regiments with him when he arrived on the field. The 19th Massachusetts and 42nd New York had been detached to guard the river crossing and assist the artillery. Dana was ordered to place his regiments on the left flank, and he formed the 20th Massachusetts to the left of Gorman's line and extended his flank to the left with the 7th Michigan to a point adjacent to Fair Oaks Station.[58] The Union line thus resembled a backward "L," with the shaft running parallel to the Nine Mile Road and the base being parallel to the road to Grapevine Bridge, known locally as the Nine-Mile Road. With approximately 9,000 men on hand, Sumner was more than ready to meet Whiting's division.

General Sedgwick reported that Sully formed his line under a "very sharp fire," and the remainder of Gorman's brigade, along with Couch's regiments, "became almost instantly and hotly engaged." The Union line threw back "repeated and furious charges of the enemy, finally charged him in turn with the bayonet with such impetuosity as to rout and drive him from his position."[59] The action Sedgwick described was the assault by Pender's 6th North Carolina, and the subsequent attacks of the rest of Law's brigade. It was about this time that General Sumner ordered Sedgwick to take charge of the right wing of the line, Sumner assuming personal direction of the fighting on the left. Sedgwick found little to do in his new assignment. Sully's 1st Minnesota was well posted and soundly supported, and there seemed no imminent danger of that flank being forced from its position.

On the left, Lieutenant Edmund Kirby's Battery I, 1st United States Light Artillery, had come on the field to support Brady's guns. Together, they now had 11 cannon with which to pound away at the Confederates. The gunners kept up a constant fire of canister, case, shot and shell, subjecting the Southerners to an irritable storm of fire. In little more than two hours, the artillerymen would fire more than 500 rounds of ammunition at Whiting's men. The Confederates could do little to combat the fearsome barrage. Whiting had no artillery of his own to provide counter-battery fire, and the infantry was forced to slug it out alone against fearful odds.[60]

General Johnston, who was then near Fair Oaks, said that when Law's brigade attacked, "so much strength was developed by the enemy, that General Smith formed his other brigades and brought them into battle on the left of Law's. An obstinate contest began, and was maintained on equal terms; although the Confederates engaged superior numbers in a position of their own choosing."[61] In actuality, the numbers were pretty much even. The Union artillery, however, was proving to be a deciding factor.

Smith put his brigades into the fight. Pettigrew's brigade went forward against the men of Burns' and Ambercrombie's brigades, on the left of the shaft of the Union line. Hampton assailed the Federal right, against the remainder of Ambercrombie's men, and the 1st Minnesota. The attacks were repulsed, and Johnston sent word to Smith to call up all available reinforcements as soon as possible. The only body of soldiers who were not already on the field, and, at the same time, were easily accessible, was a reinforced brigade of General Magruder's division, stationed along New Bridge Road. Smith forwarded Johnston's orders, and then issued one of his own. Directing General Whiting to concern himself only with the troops on the Confederate right, Smith took personal command of all units on the left, leaving Whiting to oversee only his own brigade, under the command of Law. Fearing that Union reinforcements from across the Chickahominy might advance against Longstreet's left and rear, Smith determined to bolster his left to counter such a movement. Hatton's brigade, along with a reserve regiment from Pettigrew's command, was about 200 yards north of the Nine Mile Road. Smith gave Hatton orders to advance in support of Pettigrew and Hampton, and the Tennessee Brigade went into the woods with Pettigrew on its right and Hampton on the left.[62] The previous day, General Hatton had addressed his men, telling them, "Boys, before the dawn of another day, we will be engaged in deadly conflict with the enemy."[63] Regrettably, his admonition would prove all too correct for him and his Tennesseans. Hatton was killed at the side of General Smith as soon as his brigade arrived at the front in line of battle.[64]

The scene was horrific. The rattle of musketry and the crash of the artillery reverberated through the woods, while roads and fields were flooded into a seemingly bottomless morass. Many of the Confederates were forced to stand in water three feet deep as they battled against the foe. A combatant, D.B. Easley, stated that many of the wounded were buried in mud "half way [up] their bodies." In such conditions, it is almost certain that some of the wounded drowned.[65] Henry Childs, a member of Hatton's brigade, described the fight: "Above us and all around us grape and bombs were falling thick and fast, tearing up the earth in front and rear ... and deadly missiles and treetops were falling around us."[66] James J. Marks was among the men in the line opposing Hatton's brigade, and he felt that the tempest of lead being fired from the Union line was so intense "that not even a small bird could fly unscathed where fell this storm of bullets."[67]

The situation was no better for the brigades on either side of Hatton. General Pettigrew was reported as being mortally wounded and was captured, along with several of his men, by members of the 69th Pennsylvania Infantry.[68] Though Pettigrew would survive his wound, and would later take a conspicuous part in Pickett's Charge at Gettysburg, his men were getting as good as they gave, and better, and were being repulsed all along the line. On the left, Wade Hampton was wounded. He had ridden to the front of his line, where he instructed the men, "Do not fire a shot until you can feel the enemy on your bayonets. Forward!"[69] A mini ball struck him in the foot while he was leading the charge. Surgeon E.S. Galliard immediately administered aid to the general and removed the bullet. Hampton refused to dismount from his horse, and the doctor performed the surgery with the general still in the saddle.[70] Once the bullet was removed, Hampton also refused to leave the battlefield, despite the intense pain he was suffering. Maybe he was attempting to live up to the letter he had written his sister, Mary, a few short days before, when he contemplated his immediate future. "Whatever the result to our army may be, it may please God to take me. Rest assured then should this be the case, that I have always loved you very much & thanked you for your devotion to me & mine. Keep up your care to all the dear ones I leave.... I have done my duty as a soldier & none of my name need be ashamed of me. God bless & keep you all."[71] Hampton's brigade made three separate charges against the Union line. They got to within 15 to 20 yards before being thrown back each time.[72]

The battle on Smith's part of the line lasted for approximately two hours, until darkness brought a close to the hostilities. Despite their heroic efforts, the Confederates had not been able to dislodge Sumner from his position, and Smith ordered a withdrawal to reform his lines. In the meantime, an event was taking place that would have serious consequences upon the battle and the command structure of the Confederate army in the East for the remainder of the war. At approximately 7:00 P.M., General Johnston "received a slight wound in the right shoulder from a musket-shot, and, a few moments after, was unhorsed by a heavy fragment of shell which struck my breast." President Davis and General Lee were in the immediate vicinity, and hastened to Johnston's side. Johnston was about to be loaded into an ambulance when the president arrived. Though the two men had experienced a prolonged feud between them, Davis was noticeably moved by seeing his top general writhing on a stretcher. Johnston opened his eyes and extended his hand in greeting. When asked the extent of his wounds, Johnston replied that he was not sure, but he felt his spine had been injured. Davis offered to have the general taken to the executive mansion, in Richmond, but the general's staff declined the gesture. Johnston was loaded into the ambulance and taken toward the capital. He was still lucid enough to recount that he had not traveled a mile from the battlefield before the firing stopped for the night.[73]

Davis next went in search of General Smith. Being second in rank to Johnston, the command of the army would naturally fall to him. Davis was troubled by his interview with Smith. The general was worn out by the demands of the day, and he appeared nervous and unsure of himself when the president inquired about his plans for the following morning. Smith declared that he did not know what he planned on doing. He needed to receive word of how the battle had gone with Longstreet and Hill before he made any decision. The general expressed the opinion that he might have to withdraw the army closer to Richmond. Davis tried to encourage him by saying that the Federals might pull back themselves, during the night, leaving the Confederates with "the moral effect of victory." The interview concluded, and Davis, accompanied by General Lee, returned to Richmond by the shortest route.[74]

The day's fighting had been inconclusive. The Confederates had driven Keyes' corps from its works and camps, but the Union left wing was neither broken nor destroyed. Keyes and Heintzelman had assumed new positions, and were ready to continue the contest whenever the enemy chose to do so. One facet of the battle had been a complete success for the Confederates, however. A secret weapon the South had been working on since the winter of 1861 had seen its battlefield debut, and had come through the test with flying colors. Captain R.S. Williams, of Covington, Kentucky, had invented a rapid fire weapon that was more of a small cannon than a machine gun. The weapon was a one-pounder, with a 1.57 inch bore. The barrel was four feet in length, and was mounted on a howitzer carriage. The firing mechanism was controlled by a hand crank, on the right side of the barrel. The weapon, named the Williams Machine Gun, had a rate of fire of 65 rounds a minute, and an effective range of 2,000 yards. Captain Williams had been attached to General Pickett's brigade, and during the battle he opened fire on the enemy, at long range, with his unusual weapon. The test proved to be a complete success, and the Confederate government authorized several batteries of the guns to be built. The Williams Gun also made an impression on the Union troops it was used against. Several Northern officers who were captured later in the engagement inquired to find out what the strange weapon was that had fired upon them.[75]

Six

Another Grim Day of Battle

The first day of fighting had been a confused and incomplete affair. The battle had been fought with little or no supervision from either Joseph E. Johnston or George B. McClellan. Indeed, with the severe casualties sustained by the officer corps of both sides, it had largely degenerated into a "soldier's fight" on many portions of the field. In Hill's division, 33 percent of the regimental and brigade commanders were killed or wounded. In Keyes' 4th Corps, eight of nine generals were either wounded, or had their horses shot out from under them.[1] Casualties among regimental and brigade commanders were about 25 percent. The loss of officers at the company level was much higher for both armies. That it was fought with fierce courage and determined heroism — by both sides— was evident by the large number of casualties sustained. The Confederates had been successful in driving Keyes' and Heintzelman's men from the field, and they had captured the camps and works of both Casey and Couch, but they had not achieved their objective of destroying or crippling a significant portion of the Army of the Potomac. The men of Keyes' and Heintzelman's corps were holding new positions, and were prepared to defend them against any further assaults. Two divisions of Sumner's corps were now across the river, substantially bolstering the Union position. Though the Federals had taken the worst of the fighting thus far, the dogged resistance they mounted enabled them to stave off disaster and prevent the Rebels from achieving their objective. The coming of darkness had ended the combat for the time being, but all were sure that the following morning would bring a resumption of hostilities and the decisive action that would favor their side with the crown of victory.

For many men on both sides, this had been their first fight, their first glimpse of the elephant they had heard so much about. A soldier in the 11th Maine Infantry related how many of the men in his regiment took the day's events with a matter-of-fact sort of attitude. This was the 11th Maine's first engagement, and the first time the men had ever been under fire. The fact was that "the men had no experience to compare it with, so [they] just took it as a fairly sample engagement, about the sort of thing they must go through, all in the day's work, and nothing to make any particular fuss about."[2] If the fighting on May 31 was considered a "day's work," then it was surely a very hard day's work. Private Alexander Hunter, of the 17th Virginia Infantry, described how the men of his regiment interacted after the fighting had subsided: "A soldier after a battle is in a peculiar and self-complacent humor; he has escaped death and mutilation, so he loves to sit and recall the incidents of the battle, narrate his narrow escapes, and listen to his comrade's tales."[3]

When the men from Hill's and Longstreet's brigades withdrew from their advanced positions, many in the ranks had the opportunity to search for spoils from the camps of Couch and Casey. A member of the 17th Virginia remembered how the ground was "surrounded on all sides by the dead and dying. It was a soul-harrowing position. On our return to the rear we passed through the camps, where many secured blankets and 'grub'—two invaluable acquisitions to cold and hungry men."[4]

It had indeed been a "soul-harrowing" position. Colonel John B. Gordon reported casualties of approximately 60 percent in his 6th Alabama Regiment. The 2nd Florida had captured the flag of the 8th New York, along with 45 to 50 prisoners, but they had paid heavily for the honor. All of their field officers were killed or wounded, and ten out of 11 of their company commanders had fallen. Overall, the regiment had sustained casualties of around 45 percent. The 38th Virginia had also captured a flag belonging to the 104th Pennsylvania Infantry, and had suffered losses only slightly lower than the 2nd Florida in doing so. It was the same story with all the regiments in Hill's division, as well as in Kemper's brigade and Jenkins' brigade of Longstreet's command. The Confederates had dictated the tone of the battle, but they had paid a severe price. General Oliver O. Howard felt that Sumner's unexpected appearance, combined with the wounding of General Johnston, had served to throw the enemy into a panicked state. "At 4 P.M. they were confident, jubilant; at dark they had lost their head and confusion reigned."[5]

Howard commanded a brigade in Brigadier General Israel Richardson's division. Richardson had followed Sedgwick across the Grapevine Bridge, but his division did not reach Fair Oaks in time to participate in the fighting, arriving on the field two hours after Sumner had led his reinforcements to the aid of Couch. Howard was at the head of his brigade as they neared the front. He had sent a staff officer, Lieutenant Nelson A. Miles, ahead to scout the situation and find out where his troops were needed most. Howard remembered: "As we approached the front a thick mist was settling in and a dark, cloudy sky was over our heads, so that it was not easy at twenty yards to distinguish a man from a horse." Miles met Howard at the edge of a swamp where the Confederates had charged and been pushed back. In the inky darkness, Howard had no idea that fallen men were all around him. "General, you had better dismount and lead your horse, for the dead and wounded are here," said Miles.[6]

> A peculiar feeling crept over me as I put my feet on the soft ground and followed the young officer. Some stretchers were in motion. A few friends were searching for faces they hoped not to find. There were cries of delirium, calls of the helpless, the silence of the slain, and the hum of distant voices in the advancing brigade, with an intermittent rattle of musketry, the neighing of horses, and the shriller prolonged calls of the team mules, and soon the moving of lanterns guiding the bearers of the wounded to the busy surgeons; all these things made a weird impression and a desire to be freed from following in the wake of the ravages of war.[7]

As Howard walked carefully forward, he was hailed by a weak voice coming from the ground. He walked over and inquired of the man what regiment he belonged to. The reply was "The Fifth Mississippi." When Howard asked what the fallen foe wanted, the Confederate responded, "I am so cold!" The wounded soldier was already covered, and Howard knew that it was the chill of approaching death, and not the night air that was causing his discomfiture. "You have a good warm blanket over you," the general observed. "Yes," said the man, "some kind gentleman from Massachusetts spread his blanket over me, but, sir, I'm still cold." The incident gave Howard reason to think about just the sort of war these young men were fighting—one in which a soldier would fight to the death to hold his position on the firing line, but would give up his only blanket to ease the sufferings of a fallen enemy he had so recently been fighting against.[8]

An officer in the 10th Massachusetts Infantry recalled that he had been so involved in performing his duty during the battle, that he "had no heart to feel for the sufferings of my men, until the battle was over." Once the firing subsided, he had time to take stock of his surroundings. "Then, and not before, did I realize the horrors around me."[9] Many of the survivors on both sides echoed the sentiments of the Massachusetts officer. The battle had monopolized their attention during the day, and their only thoughts had been of doing their duty and surviving. When night fell and the firing stopped, many of the exhausted combatants simply fell to the ground and tried to get some much needed sleep. A member of the 15th Massachusetts remembered that "it was a night of drizzling rain and inky darkness. All were wet to the hips, many had lost their shoes in the mud and the bodies of the dead and wounded were on every side. You could not move without falling over them — the air was filled with shrieks and groans."[10] For the most part, the dead of the Army of the Potomac would have to wait to receive attention from their comrades. Most of the Union fallen lay within the lines now held by the Confederates. Southern burial details did their best to commit the bodies of their comrades to hasty, shallow graves, but they simply did not have the resources or time to see to the interment of their enemies. Most of the Union dead would have to lie where they had fallen until the outcome of the battle had been determined.

After the battle, Union soldiers would claim that a large number of black troops had fought on the Confederate side. It was alleged that as many as two full regiments of Colored Troops were in the Southern ranks. What's more, the accusation was made that these same black troops refused to show quarter to the fallen Yankees, killing the wounded, mutilating the dead, and robbing all of their possessions.[11] Whether these accusations are true or not is impossible to say. The trail of historic evidence is too thin to either prove or disprove the claim conclusively, and it remains to this day a source of controversy and speculation. It is certain, however, that there are too many reports of the presence of black men fighting for the Confederacy, to discount or ignore the fact that more than a few men of African-American descent were actively supporting the Southern cause. This, at a time when the North was still over a year away from adopting the policy of allowing blacks to even enlist in the army.

For the civilians in Richmond, the war was brought forth with stark reality, as the flood of wounded pouring into the city soon over taxed the army medical facilities. The people of the city opened their hearts and their doors to the wave of suffering humanity. Civilian doctors pitched in to assist the military surgeons. Local women collected medical supplies, made bandages, and served as volunteer nurses. Many women even ventured out to the battlefield to rescue wounded soldiers and bring them back to their own homes for care.[12] Richmond was quickly becoming one vast hospital, and most people believed that this was merely the beginning, that the decisive, and possibly the bloodiest, portion of the campaign was yet to be fought.

The people of Richmond were right. There would be more fighting, and there would be more casualties. Both sides were preparing to renew the contest on the following morning. Jefferson Davis was much concerned over the lack of confidence he observed in his meeting with General Smith. It seemed to him that his top generals in the East were all opposed to fighting, and especially opposed to attacking. He had watched General Johnston withdraw his army up the Peninsula to the very gates of Richmond, without stopping to offer the enemy a serious check. Davis had become so incensed by Johnston's retrograde movements that he had issued an ultimatum to the general: "If you will not give battle, I will appoint someone to command who will."[13] Now, Smith seemed indecisive, and vacillated over his course of action, suggesting that a retreat from the recently won field might be necessary. Smith's lack of aggressiveness caused Davis to send word to Robert E. Lee that orders were being cut placing him in command of the army, which Davis now officially named the Army of Northern Virginia. Other factors contributing to the president's decision were that a full general was needed to command the army. He had no intention of promoting Smith to that lofty grade, and therefore, his command of the army could be but a temporary assignment until a successor was found. On a more personal note, Smith was close friends with both General Johnston and P.G.T. Beauregard, with both of whom Davis had been involved in a personal and public feud since shortly after Manassas.[14] As of that time, Smith was not aware of the impending transfer of command. He made his preparations for the following morning completely ignorant of the fact that before another sunset had taken place his time in top command would be over.

Smith received his first reliable intelligence concerning the proceedings of the day when J.E.B. Stuart reported to Smith's headquarters a short time after dark. Stuart had been picketing the Charles City Road and White Oak Swamp with his cavalry, on the extreme right of the Confederate line. The cavalryman reported the right wing had carried the Federal positions at Seven Pines, and had pushed eastward from there. He was not sure how far east of Seven Pines the attack force had penetrated, however, as darkness had brought a close to the fighting. Stuart also reported that there were no Yankees south of the Williamsburg Road. The gap between Longstreet's wing and Whiting's was estimated to be a mile in length. Smith had received no contact from General Longstreet, and Stuart offered to send one of his guides to find him and bring him to army headquarters. Thus far, Longstreet had made no effort to communicate his position or condition to his superiors. By midnight, Smith had still heard nothing from Longstreet. A message from Stuart had arrived shortly before stating that he had failed to locate the general by 10:30 P.M. At 12:40 A.M., Smith sent a courier in search of Longstreet with a message requesting information regarding the position of his men, their condition, and his views regarding operations to be taken in the morning.[15]

Longstreet finally made his appearance at headquarters at 1:00 A.M. He conferred with Smith for the next two hours. Smith was astonished to learn that the lion's share of the fighting had been done by Hill's division. He had assumed that the entire right wing had been thrown into the fight, and the news that only a portion of Longstreet's division, and none of Huger's had participated in the battle came as a revelation. Longstreet was very complimentary of Hill, calling him an officer of "ability, courage, and skill."[16] Smith was still formulating his plans for the following morning, and seemed torn by doubt over the exact disposition and intent of the Union army. It was clear that Sumner's corps, or a large portion of it, had crossed the Chickahominy. How many more Yankees had crossed, the new commander had no way of knowing. Smith had no intelligence regarding the condition of the bridges across the river, and did not know if he would find the entire Army of the Potomac in his front at daybreak. At approximately 9:00 P.M., he had received a message from Brigadier General Lafayette McLaws.

> I am at the position opposite the New Bridge. The colonel in command informs me that there is a heavy force opposite this point, and that this evening the pickets reported that the enemy had been throwing heavy objects in the river. As pontoon boats have been seen there, it is supposed they are making a pontoon bridge. The force to guard this point is two regiments.... We have no force to fill up the gap between this and your left except two regiments of Kershaw's, and Semmes's brigade.... If this position is forced your command will be in great danger, as you are aware.

Brigadier General Ambrose P. Hill, in temporary command of the left wing of the army, reported that all was quiet in the vicinity of Meadow Bridge, but there was heavy firing coming from Mechanicsville.[17]

Smith decided to hedge his bet by adopting a strategy that, in his mind, covered all eventualities. Longstreet was ordered to move Huger's division from the Charles City Road to the Williamsburg Road. One brigade was to be detached to support General McLaws at New Bridge. A.P. Hill was ordered to assume a defensive posture at Meadow Bridge. Brigadier General David R. Jones was directed to defend the river bluffs between the two bridges. The remainder of the left wing would hold its positions, and guard against any thrust across the river by the Yankees. Longstreet, with his own division and those of D.H. Hill and Huger, was to resume the offensive on the right and see if they could not complete the objective of destroying Keyes' and Heintzelman's corps. The meeting ended and Longstreet went to the right to prepare for the morning's attack. Smith sent a message to General Lee, informing him of his actions. Lee answered Smith's message in a letter written at 5:00 A.M. on the morning of June 1. "It will be a glorious thing if you can give a complete victory. Our success on the whole yesterday was good, but not complete."[18]

D.H. Hill had established his headquarters in General Casey's captured tent, and Longstreet rode there to give him his instructions in the early morning hours of June 1. As the two officers talked, skirmishing began between the opposing lines, and three bullets ripped through the walls of the tent. The skirmishing was still going on when the meeting ended, and Longstreet took his leave of Hill. In parting, Longstreet told Hill, "You have taken the bull by the horns and must fight him out."[19] He had given Hill precious little more instructions than to fight it out with the bull. Longstreet gave no orders on how the battle was to be fought. He had opposed Smith's plan, and seemed to be giving only token obedience to it. Seven Pines and Fair Oaks offered the only significant cleared patches of ground in the area, and the ground over which his troops must attack was roadless and heavily wooded. He had voiced a concern to Smith that in attacking the Federals to the north, his right flank would be exposed and vulnerable to an enemy counterattack. Smith had told him that he was free to call upon the forces under A.P. Hill and Magruder for support if such an eventuality took place. But Longstreet was still not convinced, and so stubbornly opposed the attack that Smith had to order him to make it. This did little to ensure compliance from Longstreet. He had little faith in Smith's leadership or qualities of command. As he would later write, "it was evident that our new commander would do nothing and we must look to accident for such aid as might be drawn to us during the battle."[20]

When Longstreet met with D.H. Hill, he told him only to "develop" the enemy's front with a few brigades.[21] He had no intention of throwing his entire force into an attack he opposed. The action would be limited in nature. Sufficient force to accomplish any significant results would be withheld, just as they had been withheld on the previous day. Also like the previous day, the forces under D.H. Hill's command would bear the brunt of the fighting. Hill's own command had been almost used up in the fighting of the previous day. When the fighting resumed, Hill would be commanding a mixed force of brigades coming from Longstreet's and Huger's divisions. Hill directed that the brigades of Brigadier Generals Cadmus M. Wilcox and Roger E. Pryor march out the Williamsburg Road to relieve Jenkins's brigade on the far right. This force was intended to block against any westward movement the Federals might make. From right to left, the brigades of George E. Pickett, Lewis Armistead, and William Mahone, supported by Raleigh E. Colston's brigade, would serve as Hill's main attack force, facing north from Seven Pines. Jenkins's brigade was placed on the left of Mahone, with Hood to his left. All of these forces were south of the railroad, and with the exception of Wilcox and Pryor, all were facing in a northward direction. The left wing of the Confederate army was formed on the north side of the railroad, facing in a somewhat easterly direction, along the Nine Mile Road. Forming on Hood's left, and going from right to left, there were the divisions of Pender, Pettigrew, Hatton, and Hampton. The Federal forces were all north of the Railroad. Richardson's division was formed along the track. On his left was the brigade of David B. Birney. To Birney's right were the brigades of Francis Meagher, William French, and Oliver O. Howard. From Howard's right, the line formed almost a right angle, in a northeasterly direction, with the Federals facing northwest. Napoleon Dana's brigade was to the right of Howard, with the rest of Sedgwick's division extending to the right. The remnants of Couch's command continued the line and formed the extreme right of the Federal position. On the Federal left, the remnants of Heintzelman's and Keyes' corps were formed south of the railroad, on either side of the Williamsburg Road, facing west. Brigadier General Joseph Hooker was to the front. As such, the Confederate line resembled a sort of open "S," while the Federal line looked somewhat like a fish hook. Hill was not exactly sure what force opposed him, but he surmised that Sumner's corps was on his left, with Heintzelman and Keyes to his center and right. Once the dispositions had been made on the right, the soldiers waited for the order to attack.

On the Union side, preparations for the renewal of the battle were also taking place. The Union troops were entrenching their positions. If the Confederates resumed their attack on the morning of June 1, they would have to do so against field works. General McClellan had roused himself from his sick bed and was making his way for the front. He arrived there early in the morning, greeted by the jubilant cheers of his men. After receiving a briefing on the current situation, McClellan approved the dispositions Heintzelman and Sumner had made, and ordered no tactical changes to the alignment of the troops. The commanding general's contribution to the previous day's battle had been extremely limited, being namely the ordering of Sumner's corps to the sound of the guns. This had proven to be a crucial factor in the outcome of the fighting, however. For the most part, the corps commanders on the scene had been responsible for the conduct of the battle. That situation was going to remain the same on the second day of fighting, even though the commanding general was now present on the field.[23]

At first light, General Hill sent the brigades of Pickett, Mahone, and Armistead forward to assault the Federal line. He seemed to be opposed to the attack, and one is left to speculate if it was the idea of attacking at all that he objected to, or rather the fact that he was being left to shoulder the burden of assault alone once more. His orders to his brigade commanders were vague and indecisive. To Mahone, he merely stated, "Take your brigade in there." The most critical flaw, however, was that he neglected to inform any of the brigade commanders of the overall strategy of the attack. Consequently, each commander assumed that his brigade was the only one making the attack, and

General Oliver O. Howard. His brigade would be instrumental in blunting the Confederate assault on the second day of fighting. He would win the Congressional Medal of Honor for his efforts, but it would cost him an arm (Military History Institute, United States Army War College).

General William "Billy" Mahone. The performance of Mahone's men on the second day led to an altercation that almost ended in a duel between him and General D.H. Hill (Military History Institute, United States Army War College).

General Cadmus Wilcox. His brigade was stopped and pushed back by Joe Hooker's division (Military History Institute, United States Army War College).

none of the three attempted to maintain flank contact with each other. This would produce a dangerous situation where each brigade advanced with both of its flanks exposed and vulnerable.[23]

At approximately 6:00 A.M., the brigades of Pickett and Armistead made contact with the Union line, and the battle commenced. Pickett's attack struck the left flank of the Union position, held by the troops of David Birney's brigade. Armistead hit the center of the defenses, at Orchard Station, against French's brigade. The Federals quickly repulsed the assaults, and mounted a counterattack against Armistead that sent his brigade reeling back in confusion. This left Pickett's Brigade alone, and his left flank vulnerable and exposed. Hill tried to eliminate the danger by ordering Mahone to take his brigade in on Pickett's left. But Mahone's men were fresh from Norfolk, where they had performed garrison duty for their entire enlistment, thus far. This would be their first time in battle, and they broke and ran to the rear at the initial Federal volley delivered in their direction. Hill rode forward in an attempt to stem the tide. He cried out to the troops to make a stand, and not disgrace the Old North State, but most of the men in Mahone's brigade were Virginians, and cared little for the reputation of North Carolina.[24]

On the Union side, the night of May 31 was spent in preparing for the resumption of hostilities. This would be the first engagement any of the men in Richardson's division would be involved in, their first time to "see the elephant." One would have thought that the regiments had seen a great deal of fighting based on their morning reports and musters. The 52nd New York Infantry was pretty much representative of the other units in the division in terms of its size at the time of the battle. When the regiment marched onto the field at Fair Oaks, it was at less than half strength, numbering but 387 men.[25] At full strength, the regiment should have mustered more than 1,000 officers and men. Sickness accounted for a great number of the absentees, as the malarial swamps of the Peninsula had served to seriously thin the ranks of the Federal army, placing many men in the hospital. The 52nd would face its first battle with diminished numbers that later in the war would have signified a veteran regiment that had made resolute stands on many hard-fought fields.

In the pre-dawn hours, Richardson's line was formed as follows: Colonel Edward Cross' 5th New Hampshire Infantry, from Howard's brigade, was covering the entire line, serving as picket guard. General French's brigade of four regiments served as the front line. Howard's remaining three regiments were formed a few hundred yards behind French, and formed the second line of defense. Meagher's brigade of three regiments formed a third line, behind Howard.[26] General French stated:

> At 2 o'clock on the morning of the 1st of June, Colonel Cross, commanding the Fifth New Hampshire (Howard's), who had been thrown out as the division advance guard, awakened me to point out that three regiments of the enemy had, unconscious of our presence, gone into bivouac in the woods about 100 yards on the right of my line. Communicating at once with the general of division, and receiving authority, I changed front to the right, placing my regiments *en echelon* until the break of day. I found that the enemy, under pressure of Dana, whose brigade was on my right, had deserted their position, when the line established the night before was resumed.[27]

The error committed by the Confederate regiments had become fairly common that night. Opposing camps were in close proximity. The terrain was unfamiliar, and the woods and swamps served to disorient a large number of soldiers, making it difficult to know exactly where friend and foe were positioned. Many combatants from both sides became confused in the darkness and "unwittingly walked into the wrong camp."[28]

At 5:00 A.M., General Richardson authorized French to move his line the length of a three regiment front so as to connect with Birney's brigade on the far left. Before making this movement there had been a gap of three-quarters of a mile between French's left and Birney's right. The space was quickly filled

General Dan Sickles. In his first battle, Sickles not only handled his troops in a credible manner, he also brought some levity to the grim struggle when his men captured an omnibus from a Richmond hotel and forwarded it to headquarters with a note suggesting that the officers visit the hotel when they captured Richmond (Military History Institute, United States Army War College).

by French's regiments, with the addition of the 81st Pennsylvania, from Howard's brigade. Moments after the movement was made, the Confederates attacked along French's entire front. Swampy ground and dense foliage had allowed the Rebels to advance to within 50 yards of French's position without being detected. The Confederates opened fire on the New Yorkers and Pennsylvanians who made up French's command, announcing their presence in a most disconcerting fashion. But the Union line stood firm and resolute, delivering a devastating return fire into the Southern ranks, and the attack was almost immediately repulsed.[29]

General Hill's official report of the fighting on June 1 does not mention an attack being made by the Confederates. Instead, he begins his narrative on the proceedings of the day with the Federal counterattack that followed this action. An examination of the reports of Union and Confederate officers substantiates that the Southerners made the first aggressive actions of the day, however. In Pickett's report, the general clearly states that he was ordered to make an attack, and even makes reference to the vague orders he was given by Hill to make the assault. When Pickett asked Hill the whereabouts of the enemy, "He said they were some distance in advance — in fact, I had no definite idea where, as I saw no one and had not had time to examine the nature of [the] ground or the position."[30]

Pickett went forward with Armistead's brigade on his left and Pryor's on his right. Wilcox's brigade was to the right of Pryor's. On the Union side, French's line connected with Birney, on the far left. From left to right were the 81st Pennsylvania, 52nd New York, 53rd Pennsylvania, 57th New York, and 66th New York. General French states that after the first attack was repelled, "the heads of several columns of the enemy threw themselves upon the intervals of the regiments on the right and left of the Fifty-second New York."[31] An officer in the 57th New York remembered, "The firing rolled in long continuous volume, now slacking, now increasing, until it seemed as if pandemonium had broken loose and all the guns in the world were going off at once."[32]

Colonel James Miller, commander of the 81st Pennsylvania, saw the outline of a line of troops in his front, and he immediately deployed his men for battle. He was in the act of giving the command to fire when one of his officers cried out that the men in front of them were Union troops. Miller called out for the men to identify themselves, and a chorus of voices announced that they were Virginians. They were part of Armistead's brigade, and the announcement was followed instantaneously by a volley that killed Miller and many of his men. The shock of the volley, and the death of their commanding officer, sent the survivors of the regiment into a panic, and it started to crumble. Captain Robert M. Lee Jr. was able to rally six of the companies and keep them in line, but four more retreated from the field. General Howard dispatched Lieutenant Nelson A. Miles of his staff, to find and take charge of these four companies. Miles soon found the whereabouts of the wayward companies and brought them back on line at the railroad.[33]

The attack against the 57th New York had been furiously delivered at a distance of 40 yards. The regiment stood the first Confederate volley, and returned it in kind. Colonel Samuel K. Zook then ordered his men forward, driving the attackers back. Having no orders for pursuit, Zook halted his command and dressed his line. A second Confederate assault materialized from the thick underbrush, and Zook's men came under another galling fire. General French arrived on the scene at this moment, and directed Zook to move his command obliquely to the right. The two companies on his right were to extend the line to the south, facing east. Zook's line thus resembled the letter "L." The movement was no sooner completed than the 57th received a third attack from the Confederates. The Southerners attempted to turn the right of Zook's line. The placement of the two companies on the right completely surprised the attackers, however, and caused the Confederates to face a fierce fire from both front and flank. After a desperate effort, the Rebels were thrown back in great confusion.[34]

On the Confederate right, Pickett was advancing against the troops under Birney's command. In a sharp contest, the Virginians drove the Federals through an abatis, and past a crossroad leading to the railroad. Pickett was doggedly pushing his men forward, and was preparing to renew his attack against a second line of defense the Yankees had established at a second line of abatis, when he discovered that Armistead's brigade had disappeared on his left. Pickett immediately rode to his left to learn the status of Armistead's brigade, and "found nothing between me and [the] railroad except the gallant Armistead himself, with a regimental color and some 30 persons, mostly officers, with him." Pickett at once realized the danger to his left flank, and sent a courier to General Hill asking for reinforcements to be sent forward to fill in the gap that had been created. No response was forthcoming from Hill, and Pickett dispatched a second messenger to the general, while he called off his forward movement and assumed a defensive posture amid the line of abatis. Pickett continued to send messengers to Hill, until all of his staff officers had been used up. The last message stated that if Hill "would send more troops and some ammunition to me we would drive the enemy across the Chickahominy." Pickett believed that his brigade was massed at the pivotal position on the battlefield, and would later state that a great opportunity to destroy the left wing of the Union army was lost through a failure to support his attack. In reality, Pickett was greatly outnumbered, and it is doubtful if he could have achieved any greater success than he was having by holding his own against the attacks being mounted in his front. Pickett, at length, went in search of Hill himself. Hill asked if the brigade might not be withdrawn from its position, but Pickett protested against such a move, citing the terrible losses that would be suffered by attempting to disengage and retreat in the face of an enemy assault. Hill then agreed to send two regiments from Colston's brigade to Pickett's support, extending his line to the left, where Armistead's brigade had been.[35]

As previously stated, it was at this point that Hill ordered Mahone's Brigade in to bolster the line and provide renewed impetus for the attack. When these troops were quickly put to flight, Hill went into a rage. The general invoked a tirade against Mahone's Virginians, but he could not get them to move from the positions of safety they were crouching behind. Finally, Hill stood up in his stirrups and called out to Colonel Alfred Scales, 13th North Carolina, of Colston's brigade: "Colonel Scales, come and occupy the position that these cowardly Virginians have fled from!" Scales immediately responded to the order, as well as to the further command to "run over the cowards." He literally marched his men across the backs of the prostrate Virginians, who retaliated by yelling insults to the North Carolinians, reminding them of the poor performance they had turned in at Hatteras and Roanoke.[36]

Mahone approached Hill and told him he should stop abusing his men, as they had been ordered to withdraw from the fight. At this point, Hill turned all of his rage upon Mahone. He demanded to know why the general would have issued such an order. "Do you not see that you have left a gap open for the enemy to pass through and break our line in two? But if you ordered them out, I beg the soldier's pardon for what I have said to them and transport it all to you." William Mahone had been nicknamed "Little Billy" by the troops because of his stature. He was only about 5 feet six inches in height, and weighed in at around 100 pounds. But he was 100 pounds of pure nerve and determination. Hill's words stung him deeply, and the rage that he flew into fully matched that of his commander. He was so incensed by Hill's insult that he approached General Pryor the following day to ask if he would deliver a challenge for a duel to Hill. Pryor talked him out of the idea by convincing him that such a move would only serve to damage his reputation. Hill's personal courage was well known within the army, as was his aversion to dueling. Pryor told Mahone that people would think he was trying a cheap trick, knowing in advance that Hill would never accept his challenge. Mahone agreed and dropped the idea, but he would be an avowed enemy of Hill's from that time on.[37]

Hill was not the only one funneling additional men into the fight. General Richardson was stacking up reinforcements behind French's position, preparing to lend support wherever it might be needed. General Oliver O. Howard had been ordered to march the 61st and 64th New York Regiments to the rear of the left of French's line. Howard was already in this supporting position when he learned of the death of Colonel Miller of the 81st Pennsylvania, which had previously been detached to lengthen French's line, which facilitated his sending Lieutenant Miles to restore order among the four companies that had retreated from the field. The 5th New Hampshire, Howard's fourth regiment, was held back in reserve when Richardson ordered Howard forward. When Colonel John Brooke reported that his 53rd Pennsylvania was running low on ammunition, General French ordered Howard's two regiments to the front. Brooke was instructed to have his men lie flat on the ground to allow Howard's men to pass through their lines.[38]

Up to this point, Howard's men had been crouching behind the railroad embankment, seeking shelter from the Confederate fire. This was due to no lack of courage on the part of the New Yorkers. While they were exposed to the Confederate small arms fire, they were unable to respond because Brooke's men were between them and the enemy. When Howard received his orders, he took his place in front of the 64th New York, detailing his aid, and brother, Lieutenant Charles Howard, to position himself in front of the 61st New York. When Howard yelled out the command to move forward, both regiments responded with a "glad shout." Howard was hit in the right forearm by a small caliber musket ball before reaching French's line. His brother left his post with the 61st long enough to bind up the wound with a handkerchief. Howard then crossed through Brooke's prone line and pushed forward against the Confederates, breaking their first line and sending it rearward.[39]

Major William Spencer, of the 61st New York, recalled that he

> started for the battle willingly, almost gaily. I wouldn't have changed places with any man north of Mason & Dixon's line. At last, after nine months of drilling and marching, after picketing and camp drudgery and road-building, I was to see battle and take all its glorious risks, and — of course — live, to tell of the rare and thrilling experience. If I had known that within two hours every tenth man and every fifth officer in that regiment would be shot to death, and many others wounded, I could not have gone forward with so light a heart.

Spencer's first experience at being under fire would forever change his misconceptions about the "glory" of war. As the regiment pushed forward toward French's line, Spencer reported that it lost all semblence of alignment, due to woods, underbrush, and swampland. "It was not a march; it was a rush. There were no ranks, but only a crowd of men pushing ahead." Once the regiment had passed through Brooke's line, Colonel Francis Barlow halted the men to reform them into line. He instructed the troops that there was to be no firing until he gave the command, and then led them forward against the enemy. "From this point there was danger enough for anyone who was seeking adventure.... About two hundred yards in front of the 53rd Pennsylvania's position, or a quarter of a mile beyond the railroad, our regiment came upon the enemy, although but few of us saw them by reason of the underbrush and battle smoke. As we halted, it was necessary to restore our alignment in some measure, and while we were doing this we received a volley from a regiment all ready for us, and only a few rods in front. This made havoc in our ranks, but as soon as possible we poured a volley into the enemy and reduced their fire."[40]

Howard's men had advanced and driven the Confederates back almost to the starting point of the previous day's fighting.

> We had come out of the woods on a gentle rise of ground, near the Nine-Mile Road, within sight of Casey's camp of the day before and had encountered a portion of Pickett's Brigade, at point blank range. The 61st with the 64th New York, a smaller regiment on our left, were considerably in advance of any other part of our line, for the reason that Colonel Barlow was bound to advance until he found an enemy before he ordered his men to shoot. And now for a little while the firing was hot and heavy, and the results in our ranks were awful.... I observed that the air all around me was pierced by unseen messengers of death.... I saw comrades here and there suddenly drop their muskets and collapse, or crawl away to the rear with a wound. After a while the smell of fresh blood, mingled with that of burnt powder, added a new element of horror. At one moment a ghastly sight confronted me, when one whom I had known as a tall, awkward country youth, who could hardly learn to keep step, came staggering toward me, leaning on his musket, with one of his eyes hanging out on his cheek and his face covered with blood. Here was a sergeant in my company, sitting before me, and asking me to look where a bullet had plowed through his scalp, and there was a lieutenant and friend in the next company with bullet wounds through both thighs, begging me to have him taken from the field.... I am free to confess that while nothing could have induced me to skulk or to seek shelter, the effect of the battle on me was neither exhilarating nor infuriating, but depressing and almost sickening. I wondered why I was not hit, and was dreading the expected bullet nearly all the time, while trying to look as if I didn't care."[41]

General Howard was with the 64th New York, alongside the 61st, during the fighting Spencer described. The brigade commander was not quite so fortunate when it came to eluding enemy fire, however. Howard recalled how the command

> pressed our way over uneven ground to the neighborhood of the crossroads at Seven Pines, where our men the day before had left their tents standing. Behind those tents was found a stronger force of Confederates, kneeling and firing. We approached within thirty or forty yards and, halting on as favorable ground as possible, promptly and efficiently returned their fire. When at last we halted near the standing tents and I had passed to the rear of the line which was rapidly firing, my gray had his foreleg broken and, though I was not then aware of it, I had been wounded again, my right elbow having been shattered by a rifle shot.

Lieutenant William McIntyre saw the condition of Howard and his horse, and rushed to assist his commander. McIntyre helped Howard from his horse and took him to a sheltered place. "General, you shall not be killed," he told Howard. While McIntyre was performing his humanitarian act, he was struck and killed by an enemy bullet. Howard felt himself becoming faint from loss of blood, and he called out to Colonel Barlow to assume command. Barlow inquired if he was to take command of the entire brigade, and Howard responded that he was only to take charge of the two regiments currently engaged. Colonel Edward Cross was senior to Barlow, and Howard would not deny him his rightful claim to exercise the command of the brigade.[42] Howard could not know it, but Cross would not get to exercise command of the brigade, as he would soon fall wounded himself.

Barlow noticed that the two regiments were far out in front of the rest of the Union line, and feared that the Confederates might be able to assail him on his unprotected flanks and rear. He sent word back to Colonel Brooke, asking him to bring his 53rd Pennsylvania forward to help rectify the situation. In the meantime, Barlow resumed fire on the enemy in the woods and camp to his front, until, at length, there were no more Confederates before him. By the time the 53rd Pennsylvania got into position, the fighting on that portion of the line had concluded for the day.[43] Colonel Barlow summoned Major William Spencer and instructed him to make his way back to the railroad to see if any Rebels had gotten between Barlow's force and the main line. If he found no enemy, he was to continue onward until he made contact with a colonel or general of their own army, and inform them of Balow's extreme need for reinforcements and ammunition. Spencer had hardly gotten started before several shots rang out, coming from the direction of the railroad. This was soon followed by a tremendous volley from a force Spencer estimated to be of regimental strength. The major ducked for cover, and once the firing had ceased, he continued forward to discover that the 69th New York, of Meagher's brigade, was immediately in his front. No enemy had gotten between Barlow and the rest of the Union force. It was the members of the Irish brigade who were now firing on their fellow New Yorkers; luckily, their volley produced few, if any, casualties. Spencer went in search of General Meagher. The general proved a hard man to convince. He told Spencer that his regiment had been fired upon by the enemy, and he had ordered them to return fire. He also found it hard to believe that Barlow was in front of him with his command. Spencer was finally able convince him the danger his fire was placing the 61st New York in, and Meagher ordered it stopped. When the major repeated Barlow's request for reinforcements and ammunition, Meagher dismissed the application by stating that his orders prevented him from advancing beyond the railroad. Spencer returned to the 61st to inform Barlow that there was no enemy behind him, and that he had failed in procuring help or ammunition. Neither would be needed, however. Barlow was soon after ordered to withdraw from his advanced position, back to the main line. His part in the battle was ended.

Barlow's men had blunted the Confederate attack on their portion of the line, but it had been accomplished at heavy cost. In the 61st New York, more than 25 percent of the men had fallen as casualties. One hundred and ten of the 432 men it had taken into the fight had been killed or wounded, including eight officers. The casualties were such that Barlow was forced to reorganize the regiment into eight companies, instead of the ten that usually make up a regiment.[44] General Howard's wound would necessitate the amputation of his right arm above the elbow. The next day, as Howard was awaiting evacuation to White House Landing, General Kearny came to visit him. Kearny had lost his left arm in the Mexican American War. He tried to give Howard comfort by telling him: "General, I am so sorry for you; but you must not mind it; the ladies will not think less of you!" Howard laughed as he looked at Kearny's right hand, and noticed that it was the same size as his own left hand. "There is one thing we can do, general, we can buy our gloves together!" The generals never got to split a pair of gloves though, as this was the last time they would see one another before Kearny was killed at the battle of Chantilly a few months later.[45]

The main fighting now shifted to the east of where Howard's regiments had been posted, beyond his left flank. The attack was concentrated on the portion of the line being held by the left of the 81st Pennsylvania, and the right of Birney's brigade. Birney would not command his brigade during the battle. Shortly after he had positioned his regiments in line he received word that he had been placed under arrest by order of General Heintzelman, and would face a court martial because of his supposed failing to carry out his orders on the previous day. Command of the brigade then fell upon Colonel John Henry Hobart Ward, of the 38th New York Infantry. Birney's brigade had been greatly reduced by illness and detachments to the extent that it numbered little more than a full-sized regiment. The 4th Maine Infantry counted only about 450 officers and enlisted men in the ranks, while the 40th New York mustered only 231 men, or about two full-sized companies.[46] Ward was facing Pickett's Virginia Brigade in his front, but as previously noted, Pickett was all alone in front of the Union line. Armistead's brigade had already withdrawn from his left, and no replacements were forthcoming. Pickett petitioned Hill to send reinforcements, and Hill requested Longstreet to release more men for the attack. Longstreet did not respond to the request. He could already sense that the attack was shaping up to be an abortive failure, and did not want to intensify the size and scope of it by committing any more units to the attempt. For his part, Longstreet had been bombarding General Smith with requests to unleash Whiting's division, on the Confederate left, in support of the attack on the right. This Smith refused to do. Unlike General Johnston on the previous day, Smith could clearly hear the sounds of battle coming from the right flank of his army, and he correctly deduced that that assault was being made by a force far below the three divisions he had ordered to undertake the action. His battle plan called for the left to attack once the right was fully engaged, and Smith knew that only a fraction of Longstreet's men had thus far been sent into the fight. Accordingly, he declined to send Whiting forward into a piecemeal affair, knowing that the effect of such a move would only be to subject Whiting to a repulse from a concentrated and entrenched enemy in his front.[47] Pickett was out on a limb that was being sawed off behind him. There was little Hill could do to help him. All of the brigades Longstreet had assigned to him had been committed, and he had no reserve to draw upon for Pickett's support. Hill was being left to fight it out alone as he had been on the previous day. But unlike the previous day, there were now the better part of three Federal Corps in his front, and they were ready and waiting for him.

Ward had established his line with the 7th Massachusetts, of General Charles Devens' brigade, on the right, its skirmishers making contact with the left of French's line, held by the 81st Pennsylvania. The 4th Maine was to the left of the 7th Massachusetts, and its line bent southward, across the railroad. To the left of the 4th Maine, extending in an oblique

Looking north from the intersection of Nine Mile Road and the Richmond & York River Railroad as it appears today. This is the location where Fair Oaks Junction stood (photograph taken by author).

Contemporary artist's depiction of Union troops gathering the dead for burial following the end of the battle (Military History Institute, United States Army War College).

line to the south and facing southwest, were the 38th New York, the 40th New York, and the 3rd Maine. At approximately 8:00 A.M., General Hooker appeared on Ward's left flank, pushing his division westward on both sides of the Williamsburg Road against the brigades of Roger A. Pryor and Cadmus Wilcox. Ward was forced to withhold fire from a large portion of his command as Hooker's troops marched past, to avoid hitting them. In the meantime, Colonel Elijah Walker, of the 4th Maine, detailed one man from each of his ten companies to advance some distance in front of his line to act as scouts, and report of any enemy activity. The regiment was near the Susan Allen House, at the edge of a tract of woods, and Walker desired to know exactly what was in front of him. Fred Rogers, a member of the scouting detail, reported that the detachment went forward until they came to the edge of a swamp which could not be crossed. The detail was in the act of skirting the swamp to the left when Rogers came across a Confederate soldier with a musket in one hand and a white flag in the other. Rogers noticed a wounded Confederate officer in close proximity to the surrendering enlisted man, lying under a tree. As he was attempting to ascertain the identity of the officer, five more Confederates approached — all of them weaponless and offering to surrender. They had with them Captain John D. McFarland, of the 13th Pennsylvania Infantry, who had been captured earlier in the battle. Rogers soon discovered that the wounded officer was Colonel John Bratton, of the 6th South Carolina Infantry. The prisoners were taken to the Allen House, which was being used as a hospital by the surgeons of the regiment. Bratton remained there to receive medical attention, and the rest of the captured Confederates were sent to General Kearny's headquarters.[48] As Hooker went into action against Pryor and Wilcox things heated up in Ward's front.

Ward ordered a change of front of the 3rd Maine, 38th New York, and 40th New York, to counter fire from Pickett's men. These three regiments were ordered to fire a volley and charge. The Federals charged upon Pickett's tired and isolated men and drove them back. The Confederates attempted to rally, but they were met by a destructive flank fire from the 7th Massachusetts and 4th Maine. The three attacking regiments kept the pressure up, and, as Colonel Ward stated, "the rout was complete." Ward's attack had been successful, but it had also been costly. Colonel Thomas Egan, of the 40th New York, reported that 96 of his 231 men had fallen as casualties during the action.[49]

In the meantime, Hooker was slowly advancing against the line held by Pryor and Wilcox. The Confederates were holding their own and giving ground slowly and grudgingly. Hooker had the 5th and 6th New Jersey, in the advance, followed by the five regiments of Brigadier General Daniel Sickles' Excelsior Brigade. Though he acknowledged that the advance was slow and tedious, Hooker felt that the pressure they were placing on the Confederate line was sure to be successful. Unknown to Hooker, Hill had issued orders for Pryor and Wilcox to withdraw. Having no more troops to commit to the battle, and receiving no reinforcements from Longstreet, Hill had determined to cut his losses and call off the attack. Pryor and Wilcox were dumbfounded when they received the directive from Hill. Both officers felt that they were holding firm, and felt victory to be within their grasp. Wilcox would later write that "the men were eager for the fight, and everything seemed to indicate a success as full and complete as the previous day."[50] The general felt that "the engagement was going on as well as could be desired," but when he got Hill's order to withdraw, it "was instantly done."[51]

The Confederates were just beginning to withdraw when Hooker became alarmed about the exposed position of his New Jersey regiments. He sent all of his staff officers back to hurry along Sickles' Excelsior Brigade. When the New Yorkers arrived at the front, Hooker ordered a bayonet charge by all of his regiments. The Federal line surged forward just as the Confederates were obeying Hill's order to quit the field. The result was that Pryor's and Wilcox's men were routed in "wild confusion, throwing away their arms, hats, and coats, and broke through the forest in the direction of Richmond."[52]

During the assault, men of the Excelsior Brigade captured a horse-drawn omnibus that the Confederates had been using as an ambulance. On the side was painted the legend, "Columbus Hotel, Richmond, Va." Sickles sent the omnibus back to General Heintzelman with the suggestion that he visit the hotel when he got to Richmond. Heintzelman laughed heartily at the joke, and commented, "It seems that those damned fellows of Sickles have got into Richmond and are keeping hotel."[53]

The time was now approximately 2:00 P.M. The battle, for all intents and purposes, had ended, though no one on either side yet knew it. Sporadic picket firing, and an occasional artillery shell, kept all of the combatants alert and prepared for a renewal of the fighting, but neither side seemed willing to take an aggressive posture. Hill spent the remainder of the afternoon supervising the gathering of some 6,700 muskets and rifles from the battlefield.[54]

The main drama for the day may have concluded on the battlefield, but another one was playing out at that time along the Nine Mile Road. At 1:00 P.M., General Robert E. Lee had ridden out of Richmond with his staff, enroute for Gustavus Smith's headquarters. He surely felt the weight of responsibility bearing down heavily upon his shoulders. In a letter to his daughter-in-law, Lee would say that the wounding of Johnston had "rendered it necessary in the opinion of the Pres. that I should take his place." But the general certainly did not covet the position. "I wish his mantle had fallen on an abler man, or that I was able to drive our enemies back to their homes," he would go on to state.[55] When Lee met with Smith, President Davis was already there. The three discussed the events of the day, and were interrupted by a courier bearing a message from General Longstreet. Longstreet's note, dated 1:30 P.M., stated, "The attack this morning was made at an unfortunate time. We had but little ammunition.... I sincerely hope that we may succeed against them in their next effort. Oh, that I had ten thousand more men." This message from Longstreet is indeed perplexing. In the first place, none of the brigades that took part in the attack on June 1 had been engaged the previous day. Therefore, they should all have had a full complement of ammunition, and the shortage referred to is questionable. Second, what would Longstreet have done with the addition of 10,000 more men? He already had a sizeable force at his disposal, consisting of three full divisions, and had only committed five brigades to the battle. General Smith passed the note to President Davis and General Lee, both of whom read it without making comment. Davis left the headquarters at 3:00 P.M., and Lee took his leave several minutes later.[56] The change in command was complete. Gustavus Smith had been commander of the Army of the Potomac for only about 18 hours. A new era was now at hand.

That afternoon, Lee issued a broadside to the troops advising them of the change in command.

> The unfortunate casualty that has deprived the army in front of Richmond of the valuable services of its able general is not more deeply deplored by any member of his command than by its present commander. He hopes his absence will be but temporary, and while he will endeavor to the best of his ability to perform his duties, he feels he will be totally inadequate to the task unless he shall receive the cordial support of every officer and man.
>
> ... he feels that every man has resolved to maintain the ancient fame of the Army of Northern Virginia and the reputation of its general and to conquer or die in the approaching contest.[57]

A significant number of men had already fallen in the previous two days. More than 6,000 Confederates had been killed or wounded. The Federals had sustained losses of more than 5,000. Many of the dead and wounded from the fighting on May 31 still lay where they had fallen, their comrades unable to reach them. To these were added the casualties of the June 1 fighting. One Union soldier described the terrible scene presented by the battlefield. He stated that "the ground was covered in every direction with the corpses of the enemy. Their faces were turned black under the hot sun and swelled almost to bursting. It was horrible to look upon, and the stench was almost unbearable. They lay in every conceivable condition just as they had fallen. Whole companies had seemingly been shot down in their tracks, so closely did they lie."[58] A member of the 2nd New Hampshire remembered how a "terrible stench which arose from the decaying bodies, aided by hard labor and the swamp water we were obliged to drink, began to tell on the health of the men, and our sick list increased to a frightful degree." He saw "hundreds of shallow graves, from which the heavy rains had washed the dirt until the arms and legs of the dead protruded above the ground, and hundreds of the dead, as yet unburied, were scattered through the abatis which lined the Williamsburg road."[59]

President Davis and General Lee rode back to Richmond together late that afternoon by way of the Williamsburg Road, which took them past the positions held by General Longstreet's command. When they located the general, Davis and Lee found quite an assemblage gathered around him, including Generals J.E.B. Stuart, Theophilus Holmes, and Howell Cobb; and Cabinet Secretaries George Randolph, Stephen Mallory, and John Reagan. During the fighting, Postmaster Reagan had made a special delivery of his own when he

Seven Pines National Military Cemetery as it appears today (photograph taken by author).

picked up a dropped musket and fired it at the Yankee line.[60] Davis was unimpressed by the events of the day, and he surely wondered if he had made the right decision in appointing Lee to command of the army. Many of Johnston's top officers voiced resentment at having a staff officer placed in command over them. Few men in the Confederacy, at this date, were aware of Lee's organizational talents, or leadership potential. Davis only hoped that his own intuition and ability to judge character were not misplaced. The fortunes of Richmond, and indeed the entire Confederacy, were now in the hands of this yet unproven Virginian.[61]

For his part, General McClellan claimed a great victory had been achieved by Union arms, and he telegraphed Lincoln and Stanton with word that his army had prevailed in the first great battle of the campaign. To be sure, although the Confederates had pushed back Casey's and Couch's divisions on the first day and had captured the works and camps belonging to these divisions, it was the Southerners who were forced to give ground on June 1, and Union forces recovered much of the ground they had lost the previous day. When General Lee ordered the army to retire to the positions they had held prior to the assault on May 31, the Confederates effectively surrendered all that they had won, and left the Federals in command of the battlefield. This, combined with the fact that their offensive completely failed to attain its objective—the destruction of the left wing of the Union army—must cause the objective observer to rate the battle of Fair Oaks as a Union victory, and McClellan was correct in calling it such. But both armies had been fought out and fatigued by the battle and the hardships caused by the almost constant rains. A foreign observer noted that "after such a struggle the two armies, composed of soldiers but little inured as yet to the hardships of war, were equally in need of rest."[62]

Seven

Lee Takes the Offensive

General McClellan telegraphed Washington that his army had won a great victory over the enemy at Fair Oaks. His critics among the radical faction of the Republican Party—especially those who were members of the Joint Committee—continued to denounce him for the manner in which he was conducting the campaign, and allegations questioning his loyalty were still circulated around the capital, but the mainstream of popular opinion in the North supported both the general and his actions. Combined with the victories at forts Donelson and Henry, and with the bloody repulse of Albert Sidney Johnston's army at Shiloh, McClellan's victories at Yorktown, Williamsburg, and now Fair Oaks seemed to the masses to be proof that the Southern Confederacy was teetering on the edge of collapse, and that the war could not last much longer. Everything was going as planned, even if it was progressing at a slower pace than some might have desired, and as a result, McClellan enjoyed the confidence of the majority of the people in the North. Even the staunch Republican newspapers conceded that the commander seemed to have matters well in hand, and grudgingly stated, "McClellan appears to have been right in all his calculations."[1] Horace Greeley, publisher of the *New York Tribune*, went so far as to editorialize that the activities of McClellan's army were such that "we consider this war substantially over."[2] The Confederates had gambled in an effort to check the Union advance, but after early successes, had been thrown back with a bloody repulse. The nation now prepared for the final stages of the campaign, the advance against and eventual capture of Richmond.

There were those critics, even in the army, who contended that McClellan had missed a golden opportunity to end the campaign and capture the city when he failed to follow up his victory at Fair Oaks with an immediate advance. The fact of the matter was that such a move was logistically impossible at the close of the battle. The almost constant rains and floods had washed away all of the bridges across the Chickahominy River except Bottom's Bridge. For McClellan to have concentrated all of his army on his left wing would have necessitated marching the right wing 23 miles down the left bank of the river to Bottom's Bridge, and thence up the right bank of the river to Fair Oaks—the entire route through the sea of mud that was now the Chickahominy Valley. McClellan correctly decided to focus on rebuilding the spans across the river that had been washed away, so as to open a strong line of communications between the two wings. This undertaking, however, would take approximately three weeks to complete. The engineers were faced with constructing spans that crossed not only the river, but also the extended swamps on either side that had been caused by the flooding.[3]

The general's critics in the army were vastly in the minority. The overwhelming majority of the officers and men not only supported McClellan, they almost worshipped him.

Indeed, he remains today one of the most popular leaders in American military history. The adoration with which he was held by his men rivaled that which Robert E. Lee would come to enjoy later in the war. As anyone who has ever been in the military can tell you, soldiers in the ranks will not long suffer a fool for a leader, and it speaks well for the general that these men would follow wherever McClellan led. So great was McClellan's influence with the men that Union officers used it to help win a battle that he was not even involved in. On the first day of fighting at Gettysburg, it was known that Joe Hooker had been relieved as commander of the army, but it was not yet generally known that George G. Meade had been chosen to replace him. Union officers spread the rumor that McClellan had been reinstated, and the troops on McPherson's Ridge took heart that their "Little Mac" was back, and fought like poet warriors. McClellan returned the fond sentiments of his men, and had a father's pride in their accomplishments. In a proclamation issued on June 2, he told them: "I have fulfilled at least part of my promise to you. You are now face to face with the rebels, who are at bay in front of their Capital. The final and decisive battle is at hand.... The result cannot be for a moment doubtful.... Wherever you have met the enemy you have beaten him. Wherever you have used the bayonet he has given way in panic and disorder. I ask of you now one last crowning effort." He not only praised their recent accomplishments, he also promised them, "Soldiers! I will be with you in this battle and share its dangers with you. Our confidence in each other is now founded upon the past. Let us strike the blow which is to restore peace and union to this distracted land. Upon your valor, discipline and mutual confidence that result depends."[4]

Public opinion in the South mirrored that in the North. The string of reverses that had thus far typified Confederate fortunes in 1862 had started with Brigadier General George H. Thomas' victory at Mill Springs, Kentucky, and had degenerated from there. Hatteras, North Carolina, Port Royal, South Carolina, and the crucial city of New Orleans had all fallen to the Federals. Albert Sidney Johnston's defensive line in the west had crumbled, and large portions of Tennessee were now under Union control. The effort to relieve Richmond had proved a failure, and had cost the South the services of Joseph E. Johnston, the savior at Manassas, and one of the Confederacy's first heroes and best-known commanders. His replacement, Robert E. Lee, was still an unknown quantity to most people in the South, and most of the facts that were known about him at the time were less than an endorsement of his ability. His first field command in the war, in 1861, had been in the mountainous region of western Virginia that would eventually secede from the state and become West Virginia. Lee's mission was to coordinate activities between the two principal commanders in the region: Brigadier Generals John B. Floyd and William W. Loring. Lee's plan of campaign was complicated, and the difficult terrain served to exacerbate

General Robert E. Lee. The wounding of Joseph E. Johnston resulted in Lee being elevated to command of the Confederate army at Richmond (Military History Institute, United States Army War College).

its execution. Lee's forces were defeated in minor battles at Cheat Mountain and at Rich Mountain, and the Confederates were forced to retire. The campaign had placed a stain on Lee's otherwise spotless record. The failure of this campaign was the only measuring stick most people in the South had to judge their new commander, and though their hopes and prayers were with the general, he enjoyed little of their confidence. Strangely enough, it was this same campaign that had catapulted McClellan to national prominence and paved the way for him to become commander of the Army of the Potomac when his forces emerged victorious over Lee's at the battle of Rich Mountain. Lee and McClellan had met before, and Lee had gotten the worst of it. Everything, including history, seemed to be on the side of the Federals. The *Richmond Examiner* voiced the opinion of many when it stated, "Evacuating Lee, who has never yet risked a single battle with the invader, is commanding general."[5]

Lee's counterpart held a similar disparaging view of the general's capabilities to command. When McClellan learned of the change in command he was overjoyed. "I prefer Lee to Johnston," he stated. "The former is too cautious and weak under grave responsibility — personally brave and energetic to a fault, he yet is wanting in moral firmness when pressed by heavy responsibility and is likely to be timid and irresolute in action." Joseph E. Johnston's opinion of Lee could not have been more opposite to McClellan's. When a friend suggested to Johnston that his wounds might prove a calamity to the Confederacy, Johnston stated emphatically, "No, Sir! The shot that struck me down is the very best that has been fired for the Southern cause yet. For I possess in no degree the confidence of our government, and now they have in my place one who does possess it, and who can accomplish what I never could have done — the concentration of our armies for the defense of the capital of the Confederacy."[6] By "our government," Johnston was surely talking about one man: Jefferson Davis.

Jefferson Davis was one of the few people in the Southern government who had complete confidence in Lee's abilities, but even he held a dismal opinion of Southern chances to thwart Federal designs to capture the capital. Lee's correspondence with the president did little to dispel these feelings of impending doom. The general warned, "McClellan will make this a battle of Posts. He will take position from position, under cover of his heavy guns, and we cannot get at him without storming his works, which with our new troops is extremely hazardous." In conclusion, he referred to the failed offensive at Fair Oaks: "You witnessed the experiment Saturday." Lee told Davis that it would take an army of 100,000 men to defend the city against a siege. He also divulged his plans for the upcoming campaign. His intention was to construct a strong ring of earthworks around the city that could be held by a relatively small command, which would enable him to marshal a strike force with which he could attack the enemy if an opportunity presented itself. He also planned to mount a piece of heavy artillery on a railroad flat car to provide firepower to impede McClellan from bringing up his siege guns. But the commander confessed that he was meeting resistance to these plans. Many of the officers and men in the Army of Northern Virginia felt that the construction of works signified a defeatist attitude, and that they were wasting time in a fool's errand that could result in nothing but the fall of Richmond. In many circles, the new commander had already been dubbed "The King of Spades." Lee complained to Davis, "Our people are opposed to work. Our troops, officers, community and press. All ridicule and resist it. It is the very means by which McClellan has and is advancing. Why should we leave to him the whole advantage of labor?"[7]

Lee next made a proposal that would have branded him as being mad with a majority of the Southern people, had they been privy to his plans. He suggested to Davis that

Stonewall Jackson's command in the valley be reinforced, and that those reinforcements should come from the Army of Northern Virginia. Lee's army was already considerably less than the 100,000 he advised the president would be necessary to defend the capital against the Federals, and now he was proposing to further reduce their number by sending a portion of that army away from the city. Edward P. Alexander, the young officer who would rise to be Lee's chief of artillery, was initially one of his greatest detractors, and believed that Lee lacked the aggressiveness to be a good combat leader. Shortly after Lee had assumed command of the army, Alexander met Colonel Joe Ives, who was assigned to President Davis' staff. Alexander expressed his misgivings concerning Lee, and received a response that he remembered for the rest of his life. Ives informed him, "If there is one man in either army ... head and shoulders above every other in audacity, it is General Lee! His name might be Audacity. He will take more desperate chances and take them quicker than any other general in this country, North or South; and you will live to see it, too."[8] The coming weeks would prove Ives correct, and make a believer out of Alexander.

Lee correctly judged that the flooded countryside would serve as an ally to the Confederates, and would stymie McClellan's efforts as effectively as any counteroffensive he could mount at that time. While the Federals struggled against the elements, Lee pieced together his plans to seize the initiative in the campaign before McClellan could bring up his heavy guns and pin the Confederates down behind their earthworks. The new commander knew that the Federals must prevail in such a contest. If he could not find a way to change the campaign from a war of posts to one of maneuvering, all would be lost. The first phase of Lee's strategy would take place far from the capital, in Richmond, and Stonewall Jackson would be the principal actor. The Shenandoah Valley would serve as Lee's fulcrum as he tried to pry McClellan out of his entrenchments, and old Stonewall would be the lever.

Bridging the Chickahominy was not McClellan's only concern. The recent engagement had confirmed his previous notion that a transfer of the army to the James River would be preferable to his current position. In the days immediately after the battle, he conferred with Admiral Goldsborough about the possibility of a future movement of the army to that locale, and on June 3, he ordered that a reconnaissance be made to open communications with the Union gunboats there.[9] The rains continued to fall, and by June 7, McClellan was forced to report that the Chickahominy had risen three to four feet, and that both banks of the river were submerged. "The whole face of the country is a perfect bog. The men are working night and day, up to their waists in water, to complete" the bridges.[10]

The Chickahominy region was simply no place to maintain an army at this time, but McClellan was not exactly free to choose his area of operations just yet. The orders to extend his right wing north and east of Richmond for a proposed juncture with General McDowell's Corps were still in force. So long as his actions were guided by these directions, the army would have to remain where it was. If McDowell's 40,000 reinforcements were indeed sent to McClellan's assistance, many of the problems being caused by the inhospitable terrain might be overcome through increased numbers. If not, the Army of the Potomac was still astride the Chickahominy, in a dangerous position that could invite attack by a bold and aggressive opponent.

A well-known historian voices the sentiments of many in the field when he states, "He [McClellan] seemed unalarmed by the division of his army even after Johnston attacked the portion south of the Chickahominy, and nothing indicated dissatisfaction with his own selected base at White House Landing. Indeed, for moving siege guns to the front, the York River Railroad gave him facilities that could be found nowhere else. From the evidence, the idea of abandoning the enormous base built at the White House would seem to be a later development, as in early June he received more positive assurances that McDowell would join him."[11] It is amazing to this writer how these sentiments prevail, or how they even found their way into the history books in the first place. The evidence to the contrary is both credible and overwhelming. As previously stated, McClellan had met with Goldsborough as early as May 10 to discuss the possibilities of changing base to the James. The naval operation against Drewry's Bluff was undertaken a few days later in an effort to facilitate such a move. Testimony before the Joint Committee supports the fact that the general desired to shift his forces to this new base of operations, and McClellan has left numerous recorded statements in the historical record to show his dissatisfaction with the vulnerability of the base at West Point. The fact is, McClellan knew what Grant would discover some two years later, and what the Confederate high command feared: that the James River line was the most practical avenue of approach for the capture of Richmond. Had the government consented to send McDowell's corps to the Army of the Potomac via a water route, this change might have been made prior to the battle of Fair Oaks. The orders for McClellan to keep his right wing extended toward Fredericksburg, in anticipation of McDowell's arrival, had prevented that. It was still preventing such a move in early June, and would result in the vulnerability of McClellan's position being fully exposed by the enemy.

McClellan was first and foremost an engineer. He brought his engineering talents to all he did in the army, and conducted his campaigns with the calculating, scientific eye of an engineer. To his critics, he seemed slow and meticulous, but his movements were deliberate and well thought out. A historian has stated,

> The aura of his presence, the attitude by which men knew him, epitomized the ideal of the era, McClellan was in fact the most modern of generals then active: he was an executive. His talents were in organization and administration. This accounted for his quick rise in industry, his postwar success as a state government executive, and the organizational structure he built in the Army of the Potomac. This structure permitted the army to continue functioning through successive failures in command, changes of command, inner political divisions and crushing defeats by a physically inferior enemy.

But the same historian finishes the statement by saying that "as a combat general, McClellan hated to go near a battlefield."[12] This evaluation differs greatly from one given by an officer in a better position to judge the merits and liabilities of the general, a foe he faced on several hard-fought fields of battle: Robert E. Lee. Historians praise Lee's perception in evaluating the character and ability of his counterparts as one of the prime reasons he was able to attain such success on the battlefield, yet they regularly discount his judgment when it comes to McClellan. After the war, when Lee was asked which of the Union generals he considered to be the greatest, "he answered most emphatically 'McClellan by all odds!'"[13] Strange that we credit Lee with almost supernatural powers of evaluation when it came to divining the intentions and capabilities of officers like Pope, Burnside, and Hooker, but discount completely his opinion regarding McClellan. The Seven Days Battles are commonly used by historians to prove that McClellan was not a combat general, and narrowly escaped the destruction of his army by Lee's inferior forces. The truth of the matter, as will be seen in the following pages, is that McClellan's operations were conducted in a masterly fashion, against an enemy army that for the only time in this theater of operations was numerically equal to the Federals, and in most instances he delivered a severe repulse to his adversary.

Lee was doing all he could to ensure that McDowell's corps never reached McClellan. His bold plan called for the detachment of Whiting's division, plus another brigade, from the Army of Northern Virginia to be sent to Stonewall Jackson in the Valley. The move was intended to play upon the fears of the government in Washington, that a Confederate rush against the Union capital was in the offing. Instead of making the move in secret, it was almost advertised, as Lee wanted the Lincoln administration to know exactly what he was doing. The Confederates had no intention of mounting an offensive against Washington. Union forces in the area, as well as the strong fortifications built under McClellan's supervision, made any such endeavor pure folly. Lee was playing a game of bluff and audacity, and it worked to perfection.

On June 7, McClellan received word from Secretary Stanton that Brigadier General George A. McCall's Pennsylvania Division, some 9,000 strong, would soon be joining him. McCall's men had been detached from McDowell's corps, and were being sent to the Peninsula via the water route. The following day, McDowell received orders to move "as speedily as possible in the direction of Richmond, to cooperate with Major-General McClellan," as soon as his corps returned to Fredericksburg from their venture into the Valley.[14] McCall's men began arriving at White House on June 11, and McClellan assigned them to Porter's corps, as his third division. As McCall's men were arriving, McClellan received a message from Stanton that stated: "Be assured, General, that there never was a moment when my desire has been otherwise than to aid you with my whole heart, mind and strength since the hour we first met and ... you have never had and never can have any one more truly your friend or more anxious to support you."[15] General Montgomery Meigs, the quartermaster general of the United States Army, shows that Stanton's words of friendship and support were far from sincere. The administration had ordered General Ambrose Burnside to report to Washington from the North Carolina capes for the purpose of promoting him to command of the Army of the Potomac to replace McClellan. Burnside protested against the move, but was compelled to obey orders, and made the trip to the Peninsula. Lincoln, however, bowed to his "earnest request," and "left him with discretion, after acquainting McClellan with the contents of the order in his pocket, not to deliver it, if any assurance of progress could, under this pressure, be obtained from him. Burnside obtained such assurances as he thought justified him in not taking command of the army on the Peninsula, and returned to the President and reported leaving McClellan in command."[16] In fact, Burnside was in McClellan's corner. He had told the general that he believed, from his observations, that there was a great deal of Union sympathy in North Carolina, and expressed the opinion that if the Army of the Potomac could take Richmond it would "at once bring North Carolina back into the Union."[17] Hitchcock, Buford, and now Burnside had all been offered command of the Army of the Potomac, and all the while, McClellan was receiving effusive promises of support from the administration. Many historians claim that McClellan exhibited paranoia toward the Lincoln administration. Paranoia is an unfounded fear. The commander was well aware of all of the "back room" deals that the administration had been contriving to replace him, and his fears were founded upon the sure and certain knowledge that his superiors did not have his best interests, or that of his army, foremost in their minds.

McCall's division was to be the last support McClellan would receive from the government. Jackson's antics in the Valley, combined with news of the reinforcements he had acquired, had exactly the effect that Lee had envisioned when he made the daring move. Instead of marching to join McClellan, McDowell's corps was to become part of a new army the administration was forming: the Army of Virginia. Major General John Pope was assigned to command the new organization, comprised of the corps of Generals McDowell,

Fremont, and Banks. From June 12 onward, no more mention of reinforcements from McDowell's corps came from Washington.

General Lee was receiving reinforcements from all over the South. Some 16,000 troops arrived in Richmond from North Carolina. Another 5,000 came from South Carolina, with approximately 6,000 coming from Georgia. Stonewall Jackson's army was also to be part of Lee's, bringing the grand total for the Army of Northern Virginia to some 90,000 men. McClellan would show approximately 105,000 men on his rolls, but when one subtracts the non-combatants and those not present for duty, his total effective strength was 91,169.[18] As such, McClellan would be the only Union general during the war to face the Army of Northern Virginia under Lee, when it was not at a significant disadvantage in numbers. George G. Meade would come next closest at the battle of Gettysburg.

As was often the case, McClellan believed reports from his intelligence that the Confederates had many more men than they actually did. The general estimated the strength of Lee's army to be in the neighborhood of 200,000, a little more than twice its actual strength. Believing himself to be severely outnumbered made it all the more important to the general that his method of advancing post to post under cover of his artillery and protected by works for his infantry, be strictly adhered to. McClellan spent the first two weeks of June completing his bridges across the Chickahominy and strengthening his defensive works. This work was interrupted slightly by the daring ride General Jeb Stuart made with his cavalry completely around the Union army, beginning on June 12. Stuart's mission was to scout the position of the Federal army, and see if the right flank was susceptible to attack. In a dashing raid that propelled him to become one of the most famous cavalry commanders of the nation, Stuart discovered that McClellan's right flank was indeed vulnerable and then completed his circuit of the Army of the Potomac — defeating all of the small Federal units that stood in his path, and outrunning the pursuit that was organized to catch him. The raid took three days. By June 15, he was once more safely within Confederate lines.[19]

General James E.B. Stuart. His ride around the Federal army gained him national fame, and provided General Lee with valuable information concerning the strength and disposition of McClellan's forces (Military History Institute, United States Army War College).

On the very day Stuart began his circular ride, McClellan warned Washington that his right wing was exposed. After finding out that McCall was being sent to him, and while he still was under the impression that McDowell was to follow, he tried to impress the seriousness of the situation upon Stanton. The commander lobbied Stanton to send McDowell's forces by the water route, instead of marching them overland. McClellan cited the poor condition of the roads, caused by the flooding, as

The Hanover Tavern. Jeb Stuart suffered his only casualty during his ride around the Federal army near here (photograph taken by author).

well as the destruction of the railroad bridges south of Fredericksburg, as factors that would necessarily slow McDowell's march and extend the time it would take for him to reach the vicinity of Richmond. He then issued the following almost prophetic warning: "An extension of my right wing to meet him may involve serious hazard to my flank and line of communications and may not suffice to rescue from any peril in which a strong movement of the enemy may involve him.... The junction of his force with the extension of my present position will not admit of delay.... The enemy are massing their troops near our front."[20]

As early as June 12, McClellan was already aware that Lee was up to something, and he considered his right flank and his supply base at West Point to be endangered, but he continued to plan for his final approach to Richmond. On June 15, the day Stuart's ride was completed, he ordered General Casey to make a small reconnaissance to New Market, near the James River, while Brigadier General William W. Averell's cavalry was dispatched to reconnoiter all of the known roads leading to the James. That same day, he ordered a transfer of ammunition and supplies, by transport, from White House to Harrison's Landing, on the James.[21] If, as many historians allege, McClellan's first thoughts of a change of base came after the beginning of the Seven Days Battles, and were an attempt to save his army from annihilation, why then did he begin the transfer of supplies fully two weeks before those battles were joined? He was preparing for the eventuality he knew was to come, rather than reacting to events after they had transpired. The historic record shows that he anticipated the moves the Confederates were going to make and took steps to counter them.

By the middle of June, the weather had become clear and hot, the ground was drying, and the bridges across the Chickahominy were nearing completion. All of the Army of the

Potomac, except the three divisions of Porter's 5th Corps, were now on the south side of the river. Porter's corps was posted so as to defend the supply base at West Point, and maintained a line that was approximately three miles long, stretching from Dr. Gaines' house, by Powhite Creek, to just northeast of Mechanicsville. At Mechanicsville, the Union pickets were but four and one half miles from Richmond. On June 19, McClellan moved McCall's division from the Gaines property to Beaver Dam Creek, about two miles nearer to Mechanicsville. McClellan was preparing to open his offensive against the Confederate position at Old Tavern, a spot where the Nine Mile Road joined to the New Bridge Road. It was situated on a plateau on which the Confederates had placed artillery that commanded the immediate area. Old Tavern must be taken as the first objective in the general's post to post campaign.

McClellan decided that his offensive would begin on June 26. In preparation for the move against Old Tavern, he ordered General Heintzelman to advance his line westward from Seven Pines, along the Williamsburg Road, to the vicinity of Oak Grove. Kearny's and Hooker's divisions were assigned the task of pushing forward the Union line, and at 8:00 A.M., they made contact with forces under the command of General Benjamin Huger, and the battle variously known as Oak Grove, French's Hill, and King's Schoolhouse began. The fighting became relatively hot right from the beginning, and a fierce fire was maintained by both sides. General Lee was concerned over the safety of his line, as it was severely undermanned and inexperienced. General Huger's division consisted of three brigades, but the aggregate total present for duty had been reduced by casualties, sickness, and absentees to only about 6,000 men. Lee had ordered Brigadier General Robert Ransom, who had just recently arrived with his North Carolina brigade from Petersburg, to bolster Huger's line. Ransom's men were completely green, however, having been in the army for only two months. This would be their first time under enemy fire. Lee's misgivings proved to be unfounded. Ransom's men performed admirably, and Huger was able to hold against the Federals. In fact, he was mounting such a good defense that General Heintzelman, for reasons unknown, decided to call off the attack and withdraw his troops. When McClellan found out about Heintzelman's order, he immediately reversed it and sent Hooker and Kearny forward again. Lieutenant Theodore Dodge, of the 101st New York, described the fighting and the possible cause of the withdrawal order. Some of the fighting had taken place in woods, and Dodge explained that units became confused by the obstructed vision. He related how his regiment had been caused to deliver a volley into friendly troops by the diminished field of sight. He also recounted

General Joe Hooker. Following the end of the engagement at Fair Oaks, Hooker criticized McClellan's caution and advocated an immediate assault by the entire army against the Confederate forces at Richmond (Military History Institute, United States Army War College).

how the Confederates had been reinforced, and had "poured a fearful volley into our pickets, who retired upon us in confusion, passed through our ranks and left us between them & the Rebels. At the moment we could not see exactly what had happened, and the order to fall back at double quick was given." By the end of the day, the Federals had pushed Huger back about a half mile, and had achieved their objective. Though the fighting had been determined on both sides, the casualties were relatively light, as Civil War battles go. The Union forces had sustained 626 losses, as compared to the 441 suffered by the Southerners. More importantly, Heintzelman's line was now less than five miles away from Richmond. The next day would see the Army of the Potomac take another important step in the road to Richmond and the fateful battle that all felt would end the war and bring peace to the nation.[22]

General Lee had more reasons to be concerned over McClellan's forward movement than simply the number and experience of Huger's defending force. Lee had planned his own offensive operations, which were, by coincidence, also to take place on June 26. Lee feared that McClellan had possibly divined his intentions, and was beating him to the punch. McClellan was indeed aware that Lee was up to something, but his actions were not in response to any definite intelligence along those lines. A captured dispatch from the Union commander helped to calm Lee's nerves. The dispatch stated that the intention of the offensive along the Williamsburg Road was being made solely for the purpose of securing a more advanced position on his drive toward Richmond.[23]

Lee's plan was for a concentrated attack of his army against the right wing of McClellan's forces, commanded by General Porter. General Magruder was instructed to hold the

Left: General Richard Ewell. Lee sent Ewell and his division to Jackson in an effort to deceive the Federals about his true intentions in front of Richmond. The ruse worked to perfection (Military History Institute, United States Army War College). *Right:* General Thomas J. "Stonewall" Jackson. His brilliant Valley Campaign tied down large numbers of Union troops who might otherwise have been sent to reinforce McClellan (Military History Institute, United States Army War College).

main Confederate line, with a force of only 25,000 men, while Lee massed the rest of the army, joined by Stonewall Jackson's force, against Porter. Magruder would be outnumbered three-to-one in his defensive lines, and if McClellan decided to mount an attack with his left wing before Lee's offensive took shape, the result could be disastrous to the Confederacy. Magruder had been ordered to stage the same sort of theatrics that had won him such fame at Yorktown. He was to put on a show of force that would convince the Yankees that the line was being held by a much greater number of men than were actually present. This was Magruder's forte, and he at once set about the marching and countermarching of his regiments that had so deceived the Federals some six weeks before.

McClellan was indeed aware that Jackson's command was in the vicinity, however. On June 24, a captured deserter from Jackson's command provided a detailed report of Jackson's movements, as well as the strength and disposition of his forces. All signs pointed to the fact that the information from the deserter was credible, and McClellan correctly deduced that Jackson was intending to fall upon his line of communication with West Point. Accordingly, on the night of June 25, he ordered General Porter to send out a small force of cavalry and infantry to find Jackson and impede his progress. He also called off his own offensive operations for the following day. Stonewall's force would have to be dealt with before any further steps were taken on the road to Richmond.[24] The only problem was that the Union commander incorrectly guessed that Jackson's intention was to interrupt his movements by threatening his line of supply and communication. Stonewall's force was seen as an annoyance, just like the rain that had been falling for the past two weeks, and not as the vanguard of a powerful offensive thrust.

On June 16, Jackson had received instructions from Lee ordering him to bring his army to Richmond as soon as possible for the intended offensive against the Federals. The transfer of Whiting's division to Jackson had been widely publicized by the Confederates, and was universally known by the Federals. This movement was to be conducted under the utmost secrecy, however. Jackson was to slip out of the Valley as quietly as he possibly could, and no one was to know where he was headed. On June 17, his troops began their march for Richmond. Jackson did not even take his own staff officers into his confidence, though many correctly guessed their destination. The men in the ranks, on the other hand, seemed to be completely mystified. John Worsham, a soldier in the 21st Virginia Infantry, thought that "on reaching Gordonsville we would file to the left, and fall upon the enemy under McDowell at Fredericksburg, or our destination was Washington.... None of us had a single thought of Richmond." At Charlottesville, Jackson was asked by a citizen, "General, where are you going?" Stonewall responded, "Can you keep a secret? Yes? Ah, so can I," and rode off without further discussion. By June 25, his columns had reached Ashland, in close proximity to Porter's forces. Here, he acquired the services of Major Jasper Whiting, an officer very familiar with the countryside in which he was to be operating, and who had been assigned to his staff as a guide.[25]

General Lee's plan called for Jackson's force to get on Porter's flank and into his rear, screened by Jeb Stuart's cavalry. As soon as Jackson was engaged, A.P. Hill would attack Porter's fortified position at Mechanicsville. D.H. Hill was ordered to support Jackson, while Longstreet was held in reserve to be thrown upon the Union troops when they were forced to retire. Lee had massed 60,000 men for this assault on Porter's corps. He was gambling that he could break the V Corps line and capture McClellan's supply base before Porter could receive substantial assistance from the rest of the Union Army, or before Little Mac realized what was taking place and made an attack of his own against Magruder's outnumbered defenders. Lee was careful to issue written orders to his commanders, in an attempt to avoid the sort of confusion that had doomed Johnston's offensive at Fair Oaks.[26]

Lee's first offensive seemed destined to the same lack of execution that had typified Johnston's attempt to save Richmond. A.P. Hill waited for hours to hear the sound of Jackson's engagement, but silence ruled the day. As time wore on, the impatient and hot-blooded Hill began to strain at the leash. Jackson was not coming, however, and Hill was waiting in vain for the sounds that would indicate he was engaging the Federals. Because of his lack of knowledge of the terrain he was operating in, and the tired condition of his troops, Stonewall did not advance against Mechanicsville. Instead, he went into bivouac at Hundley's Corner and remained there for the rest of the day.[27] By 3:00 P.M., Hill had reached the end of his patience, and he began to cross the Chickahominy at Meadow Bridge, in preparation to making the assault with or without Jackson. Three companies of Pennsylvania "Bucktails" were guarding the bridge, but were quickly brushed aside. Lee observed Hill's movement and wondered as to its meaning. There was no indication that Jackson had made his attack, so why was Hill moving up? The commanding general rode forward to meet with Hill and discover the true state of affairs. In the meantime, Longstreet's and D.H. Hill's Divisions were put in motion toward Meadow Bridge.[28]

As A.P. Hill moved forward, his men came under heavy fire from Porter's fortified position at Beaver Dam Creek, about a mile east of Mechanicsville. General George McCall's Pennsylvanians were holding this key point in the line. This was to be the first time under fire for the men in McCall's division, but all of the advantages seemed to be leaning their way. They would be fighting from behind prepared works, with the formidable Beaver Dam Creek to their front. To get at them, the Confederates would have to cross open fields, where they would be exposed to merciless fire from the Union infantry and artillery. Hill sent Brigadier, Generals James Archer and Charles W. Field forward to attack McCall's line. Brigadier General Joseph R. Anderson's brigade was sent on a wide flanking march to get on the flank of and behind the Pennsylvanians. Brigadier General Maxy Gregg's brigade was to be held in reserve at Mechanicsville to await developments. As Archer and Field moved forward, Federal artillery tore gaping holes in their lines. When Captain William R. Pegram's Virginia Battery tried to respond, they were cut to pieces, losing 47 men in a matter of a few minutes. Archer and Field were stopped cold, but Anderson kept his brigade moving forward, searching for the Federal flank. His 34th Georgia, and 3rd and 14th Louisiana made steady progress until they found the object of their mission, where they ran into Colonel Hiram Berdan's 1st U.S. Sharpshooters and two companies of Pennsylvania Bucktails.[29] In May, the Sharpshooters had been issued breech-loading model 1859 Sharps rifles, with the capacity of firing eight to ten shots per minute, three times the firepower of men armed with standard-issue muzzle-loading weapons. Berdan's men brought this advantage to bear against Anderson's Confederates, raking the enemy line with rapid and constant fire.[30]

General Porter stated that the rapid volleys of musketry and artillery from his line had "strewed the road and hill-side with hundreds of dead and wounded, and drove the main body of the survivors back in rapid flight to and beyond Mechanicsville. So rapid was the fire upon the enemy's huddled masses clambering back up the hill, that some of [Brigadier General John] Reynold's ammunition was exhausted, and two regiments were relieved by the 4th Michigan and 14th New York of [Brigadier General Charles] Griffin's brigade."[31]

At Hundley's Corner, three miles away, Jackson could hear the sounds of battle coming from Hill's engagement. All that was necessary for him to do was to march his men a mile or two forward, and he would be in position to turn Porter's flank. Instead, he inexplicably bedded his men down for the night, without so much as sending a message to Lee telling him where he was, or what he was doing. Jackson's actions on June 26 were so contrary to his normal performance that it prompted one Confederate officer to state that he must have been under some sort of "spell."[32]

By 5:00 P.M., General Lee was convinced that no positive results could be obtained from further assaults, and he tried to issue orders for Hill to call off his attack. The message to Hill did not reach him, however. The Confederates reformed and went forward again, only to be met with the same disastrous results. D.H. Hill's division was now reaching the field, and Lee sent his lead brigade, under the command of Brigadier General Roswell S. Ripley, to support the Rebel assault. Ripley's four regiments met with the same fate that had befallen A.P. Hill's hard-pressed men, and were badly cut up. The 44th Georgia was repulsed with a loss of 335 men out of the 514 it had taken into the fight. By 9:00 P.M., darkness mercifully brought an end to the engagement. The Confederates had lost 1,484 men killed and wounded, while McCall's men had sustained casualties of only around 250.[33]

Lee's initial offensive stroke had failed miserably. Only about one-fourth of the men he had assigned to make the attack had actually become engaged, and these had been easily dispatched by Porter's well-entrenched troops. As at Fair Oaks, Hill's men had borne the brunt of the fighting, only this time it was A.P. Hill's men that had shouldered the load, assisted by a brigade of D.H. Hill's division late in the day. The Confederates had tipped their hand, without any gains to show for it. McClellan would now be fully apprised that Lee had concentrated his forces against Porter, and could act accordingly. Would he concentrate his own forces north of the Chickahominy, or would he launch an immediate attack by his left wing against Magruder and the city of Richmond? As night fell on the battlefield of Mechanicsville, Lee could only watch and wait.

McClellan had anticipated an attack against his line of communications, and had been aware of Jackson's presence in the immediate area. He had instructed Porter to take steps to counter any such move, and had called off his own offensive for the 26th, awaiting developments from Porter's sector. On June 25, he had sent a message to Secretary Stanton predicting the action the Confederates would take, and attacking what he saw to be the government's lack of support for his army and himself. He wrote:

> I incline to think that Jackson will attack my right and rear. The rebel force is stated at (200,000) two hundred thousand, including Jackson and Beauregard. I shall have to contend against vastly superior odds if these reports be true. But this army will do all in the power of men, to hold their position and repulse any attack.
>
> I regret my great inferiority in numbers, but feel that I am in no way responsible for it, as I have not failed to represent, repeatedly, the necessity of reinforcements, that this was the decisive point, and that all the available means of the government, should be concentrated here. I will do all that a General can do, with the splendid army I have the honor to command, and if it is destroyed by overwhelming numbers, can at least die with it, and share its fate.
>
> But if the result of this action, which will probably occur tomorrow, or within a short time, is a disaster, the responsibility can not be thrown on my shoulders, it must rest where it belongs. Since I commenced this, I have received additional intelligence confirming the supposition in regard to Jackson's movements, and Beauregard's arrival. I shall probably be attacked tomorrow, and now go to the other side of the Chickahominy, to arrange for the defense of that side. I feel that there is no use in my again asking for reinforcements.[34]

Was this message a cry of despair or an Elizabethan show of bravado? Though Alan Pinkerton's agents were reporting the Confederate army in front of Richmond to number 200,000 men, surely McClellan realized those estimates were inflated. He had correctly guessed the size of Magruder's force at Yorktown, and Jackson's in the valley, almost to a man. Did McClellan actually believe that the Confederacy was capable of amassing such a tremendous force here in Virginia, given the thousands of miles it had to defend and the limited population it had to draw from, or was he grandstanding in a final all-out effort to have McDowell's men released to him, once and for all? We can never be completely sure one way or the other, but this writer believes that the general's purpose in writing this message was to chastise the administration for what he felt to be its lackluster support of his army, and to embarrass it into finally fulfilling its promise to reinforce him.

When the battle ended at Mechanicsville, McClellan began taking steps to safeguard his right flank. Jackson had not taken part in the day's fighting, but the Federals knew he was poised to strike on their flank and rear, and the position at Beaver Dam Creek was no longer tenable. McClellan ordered Porter to fall back to a previously prepared line at Gaines's Mill, along Boatswain's Creek, approximately four miles east of Beaver Dam Creek. Only a small rearguard was left at Beaver Dam Creek to slow the Confederate's progress. Porter formed his line of battle with General George Morrell's division on the left, and General George Sykes's division of U.S. Regulars on the right. McCall, whose division had borne the brunt of the fighting the day before, was held in reserve. The position was extremely strong, and was formed along a crescent-shaped plateau. The fieldworks were supported by some 80 pieces of artillery. All in all, it was a more formidable position than Beaver Dam Creek, which had proved too hard a nut for the Rebels to crack.[35] What's more, the position was in close proximity to Grapevine Bridge, which would allow McClellan to feed reinforcements to the north side if they were needed, and would give Porter an avenue of escape if fortunes turned against him.

General Porter had established his headquarters at the center of his line, near New Cold Harbor. The site selected was the Watts House, a 30-year-old structure standing on farmland that had been in the Watts family for approximately 100 years. Three of the Watts grandsons would shortly be experiencing a homecoming of sorts. They were all soldiers in the 15th Virginia Infantry, in Brigadier General Lafayette McLaws' division. In addition to his own divisions, he would soon have the services of Brigadier General Henry W. Slocum's division, as McClellan had already issued orders for it to come to the 5th Corps' assistance. With the addition of Slocum's men, Porter would have a force of some 35,000 at his disposal with which to face the 60,000 under Lee's command.[36]

Lee's forces approached the Union position with Longstreet on the right, near the north bank of the Chickahominy, A.P. Hill in the center, and Jackson and D.H. Hill on the left. At about 12:00 noon on the 27th, A.P. Hill's men made contact with the Union rearguard at a gristmill known as Gaines' Mill, and the battle that would bear the same name was joined. Hill pushed his regiments forward, and by 2:30 P.M., he was sending his men against the center of the Federal line, under the cover of his artillery. Brigadier General Maxy Gregg's South Carolina brigade was Hill's leading unit in the assault, and they charged into "one living sheet of flame." Despite the withering fire, three regiments of Gregg's brigade managed to cross Boatswain's Creek and attacked Sykes's line. The 5th New York Zouaves mounted a counterattack that one Confederate remembered as "the most desperate charge I ever witnessed," and drove back the 1st South Carolina Rifles, inflicting casualties of 60 percent.[37] The Zouaves would suffer heavily as well. One of McCall's soldiers who observed the fighting thought it was one of the fiercest conflicts he had seen. The Zouaves charged into the face of Gregg's attack "with frantic yells.... The Zouaves poured into their ranks a deadly fire, and then, with a wild shout charged bayonets.... Then ensued a conflict as terrible as human beings can make it.... Neither side appeared to think of loading their muskets, but depended entirely on the bayonet ... by the time we reached the ground the gallant fellows had beaten the rebels back into the woods and out of sight. They had, however, paid dearly for their victory, as about 300 ... lay dead or terribly wounded on the field." Gregg's brigade suffered 815 total casualties, the most that any brigade on either side would lose on the field that day.[38] Confederate General Josiah Gorgas would view the field after the fighting had ended, and would record in his diary that the ground was "covered with their dead — in one field there are forty or fifty of the Zouaves lying."[39]

On the south side of the Chickahominy, men of General William F. Smith's Division, of Franklin's 6th Corps, could clearly hear the fighting taking place across the river. On the opposite shore, they could see Confederate soldiers advancing, and were ordered to form a picket line facing them. This had no sooner been accomplished than Southern artillery opened fire on the Federals, pinning them to the ground. Federal artillery was quickly brought up, and a duel of the big guns lasted for nearly an hour before the Confederate batteries were silenced. "In the intervals of our own deafening fire we could hear the cannonading going on with unintermitted fury on our right, and still the heavy gray columns were pouring in upon Porter. We all felt that we ought to attack to make a diversion, though we did not know that the 5th corps alone were still gallantly standing off the assault of sixty thousand men." The writer was also not aware that orders had been received for Smith to follow Slocum with his division, but when he formed his brigades, another barrage from three Confederate artillery batteries prevented him from moving to Porter's assistance.[40] The Rebels who had opened on Smith and prevented him from following Slocum were part of Longstreet's command, who were on the Confederate right.

Along Porter's front, the Union line was holding firm. A.P. Hill's order to attack had been carried out in piecemeal fashion, with Gregg's brigade attacking the Federals alone, followed by the brigades of Branch and Anderson. All of the brigade commanders found stiff resistance in their front, and Hill sent Pender's brigade to support Branch and Field's brigade to support Anderson. Archer, whose brigade was on the extreme right of Hill's line, was left unsupported, and went forward with his flanks exposed. Hill had only been able to get four of his artillery batteries up and into line to support the attack, and they were cut to pieces by the massed Federal guns. Hill's attack was cut down, and repulsed with heavy casualties. Longstreet had been ordered to make a feint, in support of Hill's assault, but with Hill's men now out of the fight he knew that the circumstances had changed. Instead of conducting a diversion, Longstreet ordered his division forward for an all-out frontal assault on the Federal line, striking the brigades of Brigadier Generals Daniel Butterfield and John H. Martindale, of Morrell's division. Longstreet's assault met with the same results as had Hill's. Longstreet would later write with admiration for the strength of the Federal position, "I was, in fact, in the position from which the enemy wished us to attack him."[41]

It seemed as if the Confederates were about to repeat the failed operations of the previous day. Only a portion of Lee's army had engaged the Federals, and Jackson was yet to be heard from. The fighting had been raging for almost two hours when Stonewall finally sent D.H. Hill's division against the right flank of Sykes' position. Hill got his men across Boatswain's Creek, through the tangled and swampy underbrush on the other side, and they emerged in a space of open ground some 400 yards from Sykes' position. Three batteries of artillery opened on them as they formed the line of battle to press the attack. A Union observer watched with awe. "We witnessed as complete a move by the enemy as could be made on drill or parade. They came out of the woods at double-quick, with guns at right-shoulder

Top: Beaver Dam Creek as it appears today. The area has been virtually untouched since the time of the battle. *Bottom:* Slope down which the Confederates advanced to attack the Union line at Gaines's Mill (photographs taken by author).

shift, and by a move known as 'on the right by file into line' formed the line of battle complete. We had not long to admire them. Forward they came, intending to strike our line on the right. Not a gun did they fire until within less than 50 yards, when after a volley they gave a yell, and charged, five lines deep."[42]

The impetus of Hill's attack forced Sykes's men to give ground, but the line was still holding firm. On the Confederate right, Longstreet launched another attack against Morrell's line, and though Cadmus Wilcox's brigade was able to make some initial headway, they were eventually thrown back. A soldier in Jackson's command who would serve on many of the bloodiest fields in the conflict thought that this "was the heaviest musketry I heard during the war."[43] James E. Hall, a member of the 31st Virginia Infantry, thought the "firing of the artillery was brisk, but the rolling of musketry surpassed anything I ever heard — one continuous roar."[44] Porter was being tested all along his line, but was thus far getting the better of the fighting, and was inflicting severe casualties on the attacking gray lines. It looked as if he might be able to hold his position until nightfall, when he could retire to another prepared position and invite the Confederates to dash their strength against his line. It was at this moment that General Whiting sent forward the two brigades of his division, in line of battle to the left of Longstreet. John Bell Hood and Colonel Evander M. Law marched their brigades forward with orders not to fire until they had closed with the enemy. Their troops scrambled down the bank of Boatswain's Creek, and pushed on across. Here, they met the men of Morrell's division, arrayed for battle in three lines. The first line was at the foot of the slope on the opposite bank. The second was halfway up the slope, and the third was formed along the crest. Hood's and Laws' men fired a volley into the faces of Morrell's first line that shattered it and sent the survivors fleeing pell-mell up the slope toward

Position of Sykes's division at Gaines' Mill (photograph taken by author).

safety. The second Union line was swept away by the flight of the first, as well as by the charge of the Confederates, who were following on the heels of the retreating Federals. The Union line began to crumble, and Whiting's troops kept the pressure on, not allowing the officers an opportunity to rally their confused and frightened men. The 4th Texas Infantry led the charge, breaking through the third Union line and gaining the crest of the slope near the Watts House. Losses in the regiment were indicative of those suffered by all the units in Hood's brigade that day. Of the 530 men the 4th Texas had taken into the fight, 256 had fallen killed or wounded.[45] When Jackson later surveyed the ground over which Hood's men had charged he paid the Texas Brigade a great compliment by saying, "The men who carried this position were soldiers indeed!"[46]

Porter's position was pierced. He had already committed McCall's and Slocum's men to the fighting, so he had no reserves with which to plug the hole that Whiting's division had caused. Sykes' regulars were giving ground on the right, but Hill could not break his line. All along the Union front the attackers were gaining the crest, and the tide of battle was shifting against the Federals. A general retreat was now taking place along Porter's center, and the Confederates were keeping up the pressure, capturing artillery pieces and pockets of men that were not fleet enough of foot. Brigadier General Philip St. George Cooke tried to stem the tide by ordering a cavalry charge to try to buy time for the infantry to rally and reorganize. The Prince de Joinville, a French observer, witnessed the mounted attack. "Then came the order for cavalry to charge ... I saw the troopers draw their swords with the sudden and electric impulse of determination and devotion." The Union troopers charged into the face of massed Confederate infantry, where the superior firepower of rifled muskets showed that grand mounted cavalry charges were destined to become a part of military history, not military tactics. "The charge failed against the dense battalions of the enemy, and the broken regiments galloping through the artillery and flying infantry only increased the general disorder." One-fourth of the troopers had been shot down in a matter of only a few minutes.[47]

Porter had massed 14 pieces of artillery behind the crest of the river bank with which to shell the pursuing Confederate units back to the river bed, but Cooke's mounted charge made this concentration all for naught. By the time the combined charge of the 5th U.S. Cavalry and a portion of the 2nd U.S. Cavalry had degenerated into a rout, wild-eyed horses were galloping through the artillery, carrying away artillery horses in their wake, and making it impossible for the gunners to work their cannon. The end result was that all 14 guns were captured by Whiting's men.[48] Porter would later claim that Cooke's unordered charge had been the key factor in precipitating the retreat of his infantry, but the historical record does not support that. Porter's center was already collapsing, and many men were running for the rear before Cooke ordered his troopers forward. The cavalry may have impeded the work of the artillerymen, and aided in the capture of the guns, but it did not cause the retreat of Porter's center.

General Law, whose brigade Cooke's charge fell upon, was more gracious in his estimation of the cavalry charge. Law stated, "Whatever may be said to the contrary, it is certain that the batteries, having no infantry supports, did not check our advance for a moment. The diversion by the cavalry, on the other hand, did delay their capture for the short period it took to repulse it, and gave time for the artillerists to save some of their guns."[49]

To General Israel Richardson once more fell the task of marching his men to the relief of a roughly handled portion of the army. The brigades of Generals French and Meagher had been ordered across the Chickahominy in support of Porter, but by the time they arrived on the field, the line at Gaines' Mill had already given way. In the gathering darkness of dusk, Richardson's brigades formed their lines and provided Porter's retreating men with a rallying point on which to concentrate. The sudden appearance of fresh Union troops also prevented any sorties by Confederate units that had been pursuing the 5th Corps men. The fast approaching darkness made it impossible for Lee or his subordinate commanders to reform for an organized pursuit, and so the battle was ended on the plateau overlooking Boatswain's Creek.

The cost of the Southern victory at Gaines' Mill had been high. Indeed, the Confederate forces had suffered almost 50 percent more casualties in killed and wounded than had been sustained during the two days fighting at Fair Oaks. A total of 8,751 Southern soldiers had fallen. The Federals, being on the defensive, had lost less than half the number of killed and wounded suffered by their attackers. Eight hundred ninety-four had been killed, and 3,107 were wounded, for a total of 4,001. But the Union losses were compounded by a large number of troops taken prisoner in the waning moments of the battle. Two thousand eight hundred and thirty-six were listed on the rolls as missing, with the vast majority of those being captured by the Confederates during the retreat.[50] Brigadier General John F. Reynolds had been commanding one of McCall's brigades during the fighting at Gaines' Mill. In the confusion of the retreat, he became cut off and separated from the main body, and was captured the following day.[51] Reynolds was not yet well known beyond the limits of the officer corps of the old army, but in a little more than a year, he would play an instrumental role in enabling the Union army to hold Cemetery Ridge and win the battle of Gettysburg; the effort would cost him his life.

In his first two engagements, Robert E. Lee was already showing signs of the oneness of purpose that would come to define many of his wartime campaigns. A master of Napoleonic principles, Lee understood that a battle was not necessarily decided by which army had the superior number of forces on the field. Battles were more often decided by which commander was able to marshal superior force at the point of attack. Lee had attempted to concentrate an overwhelming superiority at Mechanicsville, and again at Gaines' Mill. He was let down in these two early endeavors because of the failure of his subordinate commanders to coordinate their attacks, resulting in piecemeal assaults that were easily blunted by the Federals. Mechanicsville had resulted in a bloody repulse. Gaines' Mill had seen victory snatched from the jaws of defeat because of the fortuitous and timely charge of Whiting's division, not because Lee's plan had been executed fully. In the future, Lee's subordinates would become infinitely more adept at executing his plans, and Lee would continue to rely on massing superior numbers at the point of attack throughout the war. This tactic would bring him fame in some of his greatest victories, like 2nd Manassas and Chancellorsville. It would also provide some of his most tragic and heartbreaking defeats, such as those at Malvern Hill and Gettysburg.

Colonel Edward P. Alexander, the artillerist who served as chief of ordnance for the Army of Northern Virginia, attributed the failures to the complexity of the Confederate command structure. Alexander noted that the corps structure had not yet been adopted by the army, leaving the division as the largest unit of organization in the army. Lee had ten divisions in his army, and Alexander noted that all of them "received orders direct from Gen. Lee.... This gave too many independent commands to be effectively handled by the commanding officer."[52] General Lafayette McLaws thought that there was very positive outcome from the engagements that had thus far taken place. In a letter to his wife, dated June 28, McLaws stated, "General Lee is rapidly regaining, if he has not already regained entirely, the confidence of the army and the people as a skillful and even dashing officer."[53]

Eight

Race for the James

On the night of June 27 McClellan, at his headquarters at Savage's Station, issued orders for the army to proceed as quickly as possible with the change of base to the James. His army would have to screen the movement of some 5,000 wagons loaded with essential supplies, 25,000 horses and mules, and 2,500 cattle. Porter was ordered to concentrate his forces on the main body, south of the Chickahominy. All in all, it was a logistic nightmare. McClellan's supply train, his immense herd of horses and cattle, and his 85,000 troops were crowded into a narrow corridor between the Chickahominy and White Oak Swamp. The only way across the swamp was over the White Oak Bridge, creating a bottleneck of epic proportions. If the Confederates chose to attack, McClellan would be compelled to stand and fight to protect his supply train until it reached the comparative safety of the James River.

McClellan knew that the move he proposed would be a tricky thing to pull off, and he must have believed that he was being forced to make the effort under less than desirable conditions owing to what he felt to be a lack of support from the government. In this state of mind, the general took the opportunity to compose one of the most astonishing messages a commander in the field had ever sent to a superior. At 12:20 A.M., on the morning of June 28, McClellan sent the following to Secretary Stanton:

General Fitz-John Porter. His corps would shoulder the bulk of the fighting during Lee's initial thrusts in the Seven Days Battle (Military History Institute, United States Army War College).

> I now know the full history of the day. On this side of the river (the right bank) we repulsed several strong attacks. On the left bank our men did all that men could do, all that soldiers could accomplish, but they were overwhelmed by vastly superior numbers, even after I brought my last reserves into action. The loss on both sides is terrible...
>
> If we have lost the day we have yet preserved our honor, and no one need blush for the Army of the Potomac. I have lost this battle because my force was too small.
>
> I again repeat that I am not responsible for this, and I say it with the earnestness of a general who feels in his heart the loss of every brave man who has been needlessly sacrificed to-day.... Please understand that in this battle we have lost nothing but men, and those the best we have.

In addition to what I have already said, I only wish to say to the President that I think he is wrong in regarding me as ungenerous when I said that my force was too weak. I merely intimated a truth which to-day has been too plainly proved....

I feel too earnestly tonight. I have seen too many dead and wounded comrades to feel otherwise than that the government has not sustained this army. If you do not do so now the game is lost.

If I save this army now, I tell you plainly I owe no thanks to you or to any other person in Washington.

You have done your best to sacrifice this army.[1]

This message became known as the "Savage's Station Dispatch." When the telegram arrived at the War Office, a couple of men in the telegraph office deleted the last paragraphs before presenting it to Stanton. The secretary soon learned of the deleted text, however, and was able to get a copy of the message in its entirety. Strangely, Stanton never brought the matter up other than commenting on it privately to contemporaries. He had been trying to oust McClellan from command of the army for quite some time now, despite his constant professions of loyalty, and here he had in his hands a document so insubordinate in its tenor that it could have served as grounds for the accomplishment of the objective he sought. Stanton could easily have used McClellan's ill-chosen words to seek his removal from command, and to stain his reputation among his supporters in and out of the military. Why did Stanton hold his tongue? Not a man to shrink from a challenge, or suffer an indignity, he was still a man of cold calculations and well-laid plans. Is it possible that Stanton felt that McClellan was on the verge of suffering reverses in the field that would do far more irreparable damage to his reputation than a few poorly chosen words might accomplish? We may never know what was in the secretary's mind at this time, but his complete lack of a public response to such an inflammatory and disrespectful message from a subordinate certainly gives rise to speculation.

McClellan did not know it, but his apprehension over the situation he currently found himself in was somewhat overstated. On the other side of the river, the Confederates were momentarily at a loss as to the strategic situation. General Lee had assumed that the Federals would fall back to make a fight for their base of supplies at White House, or else begin a retrograde movement back down the Peninsula, in the direction of Williamsburg. He had made plans to intercept the Federal retreat at Bottom's Bridge and the railroad bridge, but no enemy was to be found at either location. When Confederate forces arrived at White House, they found smoldering and smoking piles of surplus supplies that had been destroyed prior to the evacuation of that place. McClellan had not acted in the manner Lee expected him to, and had left the enemy somewhat bewildered. It would take all of June 28 for Lee to finally divine his counterpart's intentions and react to them. That gave McClellan a long day's headstart to push along his wagons toward the James, and prepare to meet the attack he was sure was coming.

Lee had intended to use the threat against the base of supplies, at White House, to pry McClellan out of his defenses and make him fight in the open. In the process, he had also hoped to crush the right wing of the Army of the Potomac and gain an advantage in numbers. Porter had completely thwarted his designs at Mechanicsville. At Gaines' Mill, he had been forced to give up the field, but not until the Confederates had been severely bled and weakened. Lee was confronted by the fact that McClellan had escaped his trap, and now had his army concentrated on the south side of the Chickahominy, behind field works. He was not planning to fight for White House, and he was not retreating back down the Peninsula. That left only two options. Either McClellan was going to strike straight for Richmond, or he was going to shift his army to a new base of supply on the James River. As Magruder was reporting no aggressive action along his front that would indicate that Richmond was the target of McClellan's movements, Lee concluded that he must be retiring toward the James. An opportunity to achieve his objective of destroying McClellan's army might still be possible if Lee could catch the Federals in a vulnerable position during their withdrawal. He immediately began drawing up plans to exploit the situation and try to force the Federals into a decisive battle in the open, before they could reach the comparative safety of the James River and their screen of gunboats.

According to Lee's strategy, another pincer movement was put into motion. Generals Longstreet and A.P. Hill were to cross the Chickahominy River at New Bridge, and link up with General Huger's division. These three divisions were then to strike south, in an effort to intercept the Federals below White Oak Swamp. The intention was for these divisions to act as a blocking force to hold the enemy in place until the second part of the pincer could be brought to bear. General Magruder was to move his division eastward, along the Richmond & York River Railroad, toward the Federal rear. He would be joined by the four divisions under Jackson, who were to cross the river over the Grapevine Bridge. With Huger, Longstreet and Hill in front, and Jackson's force to the rear, the Federals would be caught in a trap and would be forced to flee or fight. Lee expected the blocking divisions to be in place by June 30. On the morning of June 29, Magruder advanced his 11,000 men eastward along the Williamsburg Road to a point three miles east of Fair Oaks, in preparation for the upcoming junction with Jackson. His position would place him exactly south of the Grapevine Bridge, and in a perfect spot to meet old Stonewall. But when Magruder arrived at the designated location, he found that half of the Union army was facing him, drawn up in line of battle, and supported by some 40 pieces of artillery at a place known as Savage's Station. Magruder pulled his forces back and waited for Jackson, but for the third time in four days, the famed "Foot Cavalry" was late in arriving.[2]

As Magruder waited, his men were treated to an awesome display of pyrotechnics, as the Yankees destroyed the supplies and ammunition they could not carry with them on their march. Bursting shells and exploding barrels of whiskey shook the ground and colored the sky. At approximately 5:00 P.M., Magruder ordered up a heavy siege gun that had been mounted on a railroad flatcar. The car had been adapted with armored plating, and had been constructed on General Lee's orders as a way to deal with the siege guns McClellan was expected to employ against Richmond. The rifled 32-pounder fired through a porthole in the armored plating, and was pushed along the railroad track by a locomotive. This was the first use of railroad artillery in military history. Magruder ordered the gun to open fire on the Federals' massed artillery, which was done with minimal results. The Federals responded with a murderous barrage, which mortally wounded Brigadier General Richard Griffith. Having received word that Jackson was detained in rebuilding the Grapevine Bridge, and would not be arriving on the field any time soon, Magruder elected to attack the Federals with the forces he had on hand. But Magruder sent less than half of his division forward, supported by only one battery of artillery. The battle of Savage's Station was on.[3]

General McClellan had already left the station by the time Magruder launched his attack. The commanding general had gone to White Oak Swamp to supervise the progress of the army over the sole bridge at that point. He had failed to appoint an overall commander for the forces around Savage's Station, leaving Heintzelman, Sumner, and Franklin to act independently of one another. In fact, Heintzelman, feeling that his corps was not needed at Savage's Station, had already taken the responsibility upon himself to begin the march to White Oak Swamp. Heintzelman had not bothered to inform either General Sumner or

Franklin of his intended evacuation of the area, and it was not until the Confederates launched their attack that either officer realized that he was gone.[4]

The Federals were drawn up with Franklin's men on the south side of the Williamsburg Road, and Sumner's extending north of the road to the railroad. Burns' brigade occupied the front line of Sumner's position, with Sedgwick's other two brigades behind him. Richardson's division was to the right and rear of Burns. When the Confederate railroad gun began its assault against the Union line, General Franklin went in search of Sumner, the senior officer on the field, to receive his orders. Sumner directed Burns to make an attack in his front against the Confederate forces that had been observed there, and Burns went forward with three regiments. Burns extended his line of battle so that it stretched from the Williamsburg Road to the railroad, causing him to be weak in the center. When the Confederates counterattacked, they pierced Burns' center, and the general went down wounded. General Sumner personally led two regiments forward to plug the hole, and the Confederates were driven back. South of the Williamsburg Road, Franklin had pushed forward Brigadier General William T. Brooks' brigade. Brooks' men were sustaining heavy casualties, but they were driving the enemy back. Brooks himself was felled with a painful wound to his leg, but refused to be taken from the field. Darkness brought a close to the fighting, with Magruder's men retiring and the Federals in full possession of the field.[5]

Soldiers in Brigadier General Joseph B. Kershaw's brigade recalled the fighting along Burns's front as a desperate and determined struggle. One remembered how the "bullets whistled past my ears without interruption and not singly, but in two's and three's at a time.... Men were falling all around." Another stated that it was "the hottest fire I was ever in," and said he "never saw balls fly thicker; it seems a miracle almost that so few were hurt, but still our loss was great." A member of the 1st Minnesota agreed with the statements of his enemies, and said that men in his regiment were "falling in alarming numbers."[6] The battle had been of short duration, and had been fought by only a portion of both armies, but it had been waged savagely on both sides. The 5th Vermont, of Brooks' brigade, lost 209 of the 428 men it had taken into the fight, and Brooks' brigade, as a whole, suffered 439 casualties.[7]

Total casualties were about even, with approximately 1,500 on each side falling in the battle. Union losses balloon, however, when one considers the 2,500 wounded men who were abandoned when Sumner and Franklin departed Savage's Station that night to follow the rest of the retiring army. Those wounded not able to move under their own power were left behind to the mercies of the enemy. On June 30, Magruder's men buried their dead and tended to their wounded. They also did what they could to assist the Union doctors who had stayed behind to care for the abandoned wounded. Gregory De Fontaine, a member of the Confederate army, left behind a shocking account of the miseries he saw:

> I beheld another sight, which few men, thank God, have ever witnessed. In the middle of the [hospital] yard something was lying upon the ground. At the first glance I supposed it to be a roll of dirty blankets, but observing that it had motion, I walked up to it. "Don't look there," said one of the Yankee nurses, "or you will see what will follow you to your dying day." Just at that moment the blanket was turned down by the object underneath — you could hardly call it a human being — and a faint voice ejaculated "Water!" I could hardly believe my senses. There lay a man with the right side of his face, including the eye, nose, right ear, and the entire right lobe of the brain shot away, and a deep cavity in their place, in which might have been inserted two large fists. Maggots, mosquitoes, ticks, flies and vermin of every description filling the gaping hole by the millions. They were crawling through his hair, in his mouth, over his face, and some had entered and were eating out the half closed eye on the opposite side. The man had been wounded ... and for nearly

Top: Union field hospital at Savage's Station. Note the primitive conditions, with men lying outside on the ground (Military History Institute, United States Army War College). *Bottom:* Location of fighting at Savage's Station (photograph taken by author).

three weeks had lingered in the condition I have described — a mass of corruption, suffering the torments of the damned and yet unable to die.[8]

By all accounts, Savage's Station was a drawn battle, as the combatants occupied almost the same ground at its conclusion as they had before it was fought. General Law thought that it was a victory for Union arms, however, as the Confederates had failed to keep the Union forces in place until reinforcements could come up, and the Yankees "accomplished the main purpose of the battle, which was to gain time for the passage of trains, artillery, and troops across White Oak Swamp."[9]

June 30 dawned a hot and sunny day, all the more sweltering because of thunderstorms that had fallen the previous night. The Army of the Potomac had evaded Lee's trap at Savage's Station, and by 10:00 A.M., all of the Federals were safely across the White Oak Swamp. Franklin burned the bridge across the swamp after his men had crossed, placing another obstacle in the path of enemy pursuit. To some, it might have seemed that the Federal army was now in the clear. Quite the opposite was true. The Army of the Potomac was strung out for six miles from the White Oak Swamp to the James River, and McClellan realized that he would need one more day to safely get his wagons and artillery to the protection of the navy's big guns. McClellan personally examined the entire route of march, from the swamp to the James River, and realized, "Our force was too small to occupy and hold the entire line ... exposed as it was to be taken in reverse by a movement across the lower part of the swamp, or across the Chickahominy below the swamp." McClellan and Lee were both suffering from a want of reliable information concerning the various roads and terrain features of the country in which they were operating. The maps being used by both commanders were incomplete, and, in many instances, incorrect. McClellan's limited information revealed only one road that his army could use in its march to the James, but this was intersected at many points along the line by roads the Confederates might use to try to cut him off. "It was therefore necessary to post troops in advance of this road ... so as to cover the movement of the trains in rear." McClellan issued orders for the posting of the troops, directing each corps commander to hold their positions until the trains had passed, at which time they would be free to take up the march toward the concentration point at Malvern Hill.[10]

Keyes' and most of Porter's corps had already reached Malvern Hill, leaving McClellan seven divisions with which to guard his line of march. Two divisions were left at White Oak Swamp under the command of General Franklin, to contest any crossing by the enemy at that point. The other five divisions were three miles south of the swamp, halfway to Malvern Hill, at a crossroads known as Glendale. This was a critical point because of the fact that the two routes of retreat from the White Oak Swamp both emptied into a single road, the Willis Church Road, causing a bottleneck for the advancing trains and infantry. The place was also susceptible to attack by means of roads leading to Richmond. Lee was well aware that McClellan's situation offered him an excellent opportunity to bring the Union army to bay, and he issued the necessary orders to launch a combined offensive by his entire army. Colonel E.P. Alexander echoed his commander's sentiments. "In spite of all the odds against us, it is my individual belief that on two occasions in the four years we were within reach of military successes so great that we might have hoped to end the war with our independence, had we gathered the rich victories which seemed easily possible.... This chance of June 30th '62 impresses me as the best of all."[11]

Jackson was to press the Union rear, under Franklin, at White Oak Swamp. Longstreet and A.P. Hill were to advance on Glendale via the Darbytown Road. Huger was on the Charles City Road, from which he could assail Franklin's left flank and rear. Holmes was

Contemporary picture of White Oak Swamp, as it was during the campaign (Military History Institute, United States Army War College).

Spot where the Federal army retreated across White Oak Swamp (photograph taken by author).

on the New Market Road with orders to throw his forces against McClellan's retreating supply train before it reached Malvern Hill. Magruder was initially ordered to support Longstreet and Hill, but was diverted from that assignment to assist Holmes. As General D.H. Hill put it: "It was the critical day for both commanders, but especially for McClellan. With consummate skill he had crossed his vast train of five thousand wagons and his immense parks of artillery safely over White Oak Swamp, but he was more exposed now than at any time in his flank march. Three columns of attack were converging upon him, and a strong corps was pressing upon his rear. Escape seemed impossible for him...."[12]

One of Jackson's men described Stonewall's pursuit matter-of-factly "We marched to the vicinity of White Oak Swamp, where skirmishers were thrown forward; some of our artillery was brought into position, and firing commenced. Gen. Jackson ascertained that the enemy had made a stand here. We moved from place to place, looking for a place to cross; at night we lay down on the ground for a little rest."[13] This soldier left out a great many details, but his account of the proceedings must have seemed a fairly accurate depiction for most of the men in Jackson's command.

Jackson was once more exhibiting a slowness of action that was inconsistent with his previous record, and it was almost noon when he finally reached White Oak Swamp. About a half mile across the swamp he could see the enemy: the last of the supply wagons, a few batteries of artillery, and several ranks of infantry. Jackson collected 28 cannon in a clearing on the right of the road and opened fire shortly before 2:00 P.M. Along with skirmishers from D.H. Hill's division, and a regiment of cavalry, Stonewall then forded the creek to size up the situation for himself. Four batteries of Federal artillery opened on Jackson and his party, forcing the general and the cavalry to beat a hasty retreat back across the stream. The skirmishers remained. Once back across, Jackson turned his attention to repairing the bridge that Franklin had burned. But Union fire concentrated on any soldiers employed in the bridge repair, making it an almost impossible task. Apparently, that was enough to cause Jackson to give up the chase. By 3:00 P.M., he had gone to sleep under a tree, and had given up all intention of pressing Franklin's rear guard. This, despite the fact that one of his cavalry officers informed him that he had found a cow crossing 400 yards upstream, and General Hampton had built a pole bridge a mile downstream, beyond the Federal right flank. When Hampton reported the completion of the bridge, Jackson "was seated on a log, his head down & cap over his eyes. When H(ampton) reported Gen. J(ackson) raised his head, looking under his hat brim, & said 'Hm-m?' General H. repeated about his having built the bridge, (and) Gen. J. said 'Um-h-m-m' and resumed his first position. Gen. Hampton waited for further remarks, until the situation seemed awkward, & then went back to his brigade."[14] Jackson was moving no further that day, and one more time during the Seven Days' he was proving to be a disappointment to Lee's plans.

A soldier in the 2nd Vermont Infantry had apparently thought that they had safely eluded Confederate pursuit when the bridge had been burned. Most of his comrades were enjoying the first real sleep they had gotten in days. Wilbur Fisk said that when the Confederate artillery opened fire "it was as if a nest of earthquakes had suddenly exploded under our feet.... A cannonball passed close by a friend's ear.... An inclination of his head ... to one side, of not more than two inches, would have secured to him an eternal discharge from all terrestrial warfare." Second Division Commander William F. Smith had been conferring with one of his brigade commanders in a nearby house when the bombardment commenced. The officers ran from the house just as it was shredded by enemy shells. Smith ordered the division withdrawn to the cover of some nearby woods to recompose themselves from the shock of the shelling, and to reorganize to meet an expected assault, but the anticipated attack never came. Jackson had sent his calling card, but he did not intend to come in person today.[15]

A few miles to the southwest of Jackson, on the Charles City Road, General Huger was also experiencing serious delays. Longstreet and A.P. Hill were to Huger's right, advancing down the Darbytown Road. When Huger got into position at Glendale, his artillery was to be the signal for both columns to attack. But when Huger reached a point two miles northwest of Glendale, he found that the Federals had obstructed the road by felling trees across it. General William Mahone commanded the lead brigade, and he decided to go around the obstruction by chopping a new route through the heavy woods on the side of the road. General Slocum's Federals saw what the Confederates were doing, and took steps to counteract it. Taking axes in hand, they felled more trees in front of Mahone's proposed route, and a sort of comical lumberjack contest ensued, with each side chopping down trees as quickly as they could. In the end, Mahone's men won this woodsmen's challenge, by creating a path one mile long that joined back into the Charles City Road, about a mile from Glendale. But when Huger's men emerged from the forest, they found Slocum's entire division in line of battle across the road. Huger wheeled up a battery of artillery and opened fire at about 2:30 P.M. Federal guns responded, and Huger was so unnerved by the whole situation that he had his men retire back to the woods without committing any of his 9,000 infantry to an attack.[16] Thus, by 3:00 P.M., Jackson's entire corps-sized column and Huger's division were both out of the fight, without contributing anything of consequence to the assault.

Magruder's Division would also take no active part in the fighting on June 30. Magruder had been ordered, by General Longstreet, to march his division to the support of Holmes, on the New Market Road. Longstreet had ordered Magruder to the right not so much to assist Holmes as to guard his own right flank in case Holmes should be pushed back. Magruder had difficulty reaching his assigned position, and when he got there, he could not find General Holmes to find out where his men were to be deployed. Finally, Colonel R.H. Chilton, Lee's chief of staff, informed Magruder that he wished his men to be placed to the right of Holmes's line. Magruder was in the process of carrying out these orders when he received instructions that he was to relieve Longstreet's command on the Charles City Road. This shift in position took until 3:00 A.M. to complete, and by that time Magruder and his men had marched 20 miles in 18 hours, and had not fired a shot against the enemy.[17]

In the meantime, General Holmes had been engaged with a portion of the Union army at Malvern Hill. Holmes had been in position at New Market Heights with 6,000 infantry and six batteries of artillery, when Major R.K. Meade, of the Engineers, rode up to Holmes's headquarters to announce that a column of Federals were retreating across Malvern Hill, approximately two and one half miles east of New Market Heights. Meade suggested that Holmes could move up his artillery on either side of the River Road and deploy it in covering woods. He could then shell the retreating enemy and possibly cause some panic among their ranks. Holmes ordered three two-gun sections to be sent to the place indicated by Major Meade, supported by a regiment of infantry. Holmes went off to scout the position himself, and ordered the rest of his division to be brought forward to supporting distance of the six guns and regiment of infantry. Along the way, Holmes ran into General Lee, who was conducting a scouting mission of his own. Lee had been informed by a young cavalryman, Colonel Thomas Rosser, that the Federals were moving south, and Lee had come to see if McClellan's rear guard was escaping his trap at Glendale. Lee approved of Holmes's movements, and told him to open with his artillery the moment his infantry was up. Holmes rushed his division forward, but the telltale cloud of dust raised by his marching men alerted the Federals to their approach, and a shell soon burst above the column. A member of the 50th Virginia wrote, "We could form no idea whence it came, but were not long kept in doubt, for in a few minutes there was a perfect shower of shells of tremendous proportion and hideous sound." The men in Holmes's division were all perfectly green, and the Union artillery was causing consternation in the ranks. Holmes's cavalry spooked and dashed toward a plank fence, crushing some of their infantry comrades who had taken refuge behind it. The 45th North Carolina was completely panicked and broke. Gunners in a reserve battery sent up to support the six advanced guns rushed for the rear, leaving two guns and three caissons behind. Holmes, who had been in a little house by the roadside, exited to find his division in a state of chaos. The general was partially deaf, and when he stepped out into the road he put a hand to his ear and remarked, "I thought I heard firing." Holmes got his guns up and entered into an artillery duel with the Federals on Malvern Hill for about an hour, during which time the Confederate gunners were taking the worst of it. The general concluded that it would be "perfect madness" to commit his infantry to an attack on the heights, as "it would have required a march of over three-quarters of a mile up a steep hill destitute of cover." As night fell, Holmes withdrew his batteries and broke off the action.[18]

The burden of attacking the Federals at Glendale would ultimately fall upon the shoulders of James Longstreet and A.P. Hill. When Longstreet heard Huger's artillery at 2:30, he assumed that this was the signal for the assault, and ordered his own cannon to open fire. Federal artillery responded from Long Bridge Road. General Lee and President Davis were with Longstreet at the time, watching the effects of the bombardment, when a Union shell "burst in the midst of us, killing two or three horses and wounding one or two men. Our little party speedily retired to safer quarters."[19]

McClellan was not personally on the field when events began to take form at Glendale. On the morning of June 30, after conferring with his corps commanders and arranging for the placement of the troops, he had ridden to the James River for a meeting with Commander John Rogers on the gunboat *Galena*. That afternoon, while things were heating up at Glendale, Rogers and McClellan decided the final location of the new Federal base. McClellan had proposed to make Haxell's Landing, near Turkey Bend, his final destination. The Willis Church Road (or Quaker Road) ran into this point after crossing Malvern Hill. Rogers stated that the most practical place was at Harrison's Landing, six miles downriver. The landing boasted a wharf and a three-mile river front, and was the site of the Berkeley Plantation, the ancestral home of the Harrison family. Among the noted lineage that had been born at Berkeley Plantation were Benjamin Harrison V, signer of the Declaration of Independence, and William Henry Harrison, the ninth president of the United States. McClellan seems to have become obsessed at this time with his own efforts to get the army safely to Harrison's Landing. From Turkey Bend he wired Stanton: "I fear I shall be forced to abandon my material to save my men under cover of the gunboats.... If none of us escape, we shall at least have saved the honor of the country.... Send more gunboats." He also wired the adjutant general, in Washington, to send 50,000 fresh men, stating, "That number sent at once will, I think, enable me to assume the offensive." To Fortress Monroe, he sent word to General Casey to come to that point with the 5,000 men he had evacuated from White House when the base was abandoned.[20] The commanding general was exerting maximum

Artist's depiction of the battle of Glendale (Military History Institute, United States Army War College).

effort toward concentrating all of his available forces at Harrison's Landing, but he was seemingly not showing any concern that the force at Glendale might never reach the objective.

Lee's well-planned offensive was coming unhinged. Other than Longstreet and A.P. Hill, none of his subordinate commanders were where they were supposed to be, or doing what they had been ordered to do. The Confederate commander was faced with a serious question: Should he admit the failure of his well-laid plans, or should he assail the Union army, and contest its further withdrawal with the limited force he had at hand? Knowing that the results would be minimal, Lee still could not allow the Federals to pass by his front unchallenged, so he ordered Longstreet and Hill forward.[21]

It would be a great deal to ask of two lone divisions. The Union forces in and around Glendale were made up of two full corps, Heintzelman's and Sumner's, with the addition of McCall's Pennsylvania Division, from Porter's corps. The Confederates would be outnumbered two-to-one, and would be assaulting a superior force fighting from behind hastily thrown up fieldworks.

Longstreet ordered Micah Jenkins to use his long-range guns to silence the Federal battery that had fired on President Davis, General Lee, and himself. Jenkins engaged the enemy, troops under the command of General McCall, and finally determined to make a frontal charge against the guns, in close proximity to Frayser's Farm, the name by which the Confederates would call the battle. Brigadier General James Kemper led his brigade forward on Jenkins's right, and soon the engagement became general. McCall's line was forced back in some places, and Longstreet committed his other four brigades to the assault, in an effort to deliver a knockout blow.[22] The Union location was a good one. As Private Alfred Bellard, of the 5th New Jersey, recalled, "The position was well chosen having a cross fire on the enemy from no matter what quarter they came from."[23] Despite the natural strength of the Union position, and despite the disparity in numbers between the contending forces, the spirited nature of Longstreet's attack was gaining ground and threatening to pierce the Union line. When McCall's division began to give ground, Hooker's division was ordered to restore the line. Martin Haynes, of the 2nd New Hampshire, remembered that the "battle was at its height" when his regiment was thrown into the fray. "Forty pieces of artillery, stationed in the field to our right, were showering their deadly missiles upon the woods through which the rebels were advancing, while the infantry were pouring in volley upon volley of musketry."[24]

Much of the fighting was done at close range, and Colonel Alexander Hays, of the 63rd Pennsylvania, reported that "it was muzzle to muzzle, and the powder actually burned the faces of the opposing men."[25] The fight for the Union guns degenerated into hand-to-hand combat, and saw some of the most severe struggles with bayonets and

General Benjamin Huger. His division had great difficulty getting into position for the fighting at Glendale (Military History Institute, United States Army War College).

clubbed muskets witnessed during the entire war. E.P. Alexander declared that the hand-to-hand fighting at Glendale surpassed anything he witnessed in any other battle. General Cadmus Wilcox's brigade was in the thick of this melee, and Wilcox reported how one of his lieutenants "had a hand-to-hand collision with an officer, and just dealt a severe blow upon his adversary he fell, cut over the head with a saber-bayonet from behind, and had afterward three bayonet wounds in the face and two in the breast." Wilcox pushed the Federals back, but they reformed and counterattacked, and a second round of close combat ensued. This time it was Wilcox who was forced to give ground. At the end of the day, the general counted six bullet holes in his clothing, but he had amazingly escaped the fighting unharmed.[26]

Longstreet's division had been carrying the fight for some time. Hill was being held in reserve, with the intention that he would follow up any breakthroughs that were made when Jackson and Huger added their weight to the attack. As the battle raged on and it became evident that Jackson and Huger were not coming, Longstreet ordered Hill in to support his own desperately outnumbered men. The Federals countered by bringing their own reserves into the fight, and the battle lines went back and forward throughout the late afternoon and evening. As darkness began to cover the field, the Union forces had been forced back in several places, but the line had not broken. The Confederates had captured 18 cannon and a few stand of colors, but the Willis Church Road was still open, and the final wagons of the supply train had safely passed by on their way to Harrison's Landing. By 9:00 P.M., the fighting was pretty much ended, except for some sporadic picket fire. A total of some 60,000 men had been involved in the engagement, and losses for both sides were approximately 6,500. Longstreet and A.P. Hill had displayed exceptional fighting spirit in their lopsided contest, and had dictated the action for most of the engagement, but there was little gained by their valiant efforts. McClellan's supply train had made its way to safety, unimpeded, and the Federal infantry would follow it during the night. Colonel E.P. Alexander thought that the golden opportunity for the Confederacy had been squandered at Glendale, where 50,000 Confederate troops were within hearing of the battle, but did not march to the sound of the guns. Porter summed it all up by stating, "Had all our troops been at Frayser's Farm, there would have been no Malvern Hill."[27]

One last episode was to transpire before the action at Glendale was officially concluded. General McCall, and several of his staff officers, had been searching the field for a separated portion of his division when they came across a group of soldiers. McCall asked what command the men belonged to, and was answered that they were part of General Field's brigade. "General Field! I don't know him," McCall said. "Perhaps not, as you are evidently in the wrong place," said Major W. Roy Mason, an officer on Field's staff. McCall and his comrades turned to flee, but a soldier from the 47th Virginia grabbed the bridle of McCall's horse and prevented him from doing so. Captain H.J. Biddle, McCall's adjutant-general, was shot and killed trying to make good his escape, but the rest of the general's party disappeared into the gathering darkness and made their way back to their own lines. When McCall was brought to headquarters, Longstreet recognized him at once. McCall and Longstreet had served together in the 4th United States infantry, 20 years before the war, and had been quite close friends. Longstreet approached his old comrade and extended his hand as McCall dismounted his horse. This was to be no joyful reunion, however. McCall's posture exhibited all of the dignified outrage he could muster, and he refused to take Longstreet's hand. "Excuse me, sir," he said, "I can stand defeat but not insult."[28]

Much had been expected from the operations around Glendale, and it really did seem as though the Confederates had caught McClellan's army in a vulnerable position from which it could be easily defeated. In the end, Lee's plans for a concentrated offensive thrust came to naught, and he had to be satisfied with holding a small portion of the field that had been in Federal hands at the opening of the engagement. D.H. Hill gave voice to his own disgust when he stated, "Escape seemed impossible for him [McClellan], but he *did* escape, at the same time inflicting heavy damage upon his pursuers." The Army of the Potomac had not been stopped, or even seriously hampered in its objective of shifting to its base on the James. By midnight, the last of McClellan's wagon train and his herd of beef cattle had reached the comparative safety of Haxell's Landing.[29] The last of his infantry would soon follow, and the concentration of his army would be complete.

Thus far, the Seven Days Battles had been fiercely fought, and costly to both sides. From the Confederate perspective, a failure to coordinate attacks had deprived General Lee of several possible opportunities to cripple or destroy the enemy. Lee's plans had been consistently miscarried, and the Confederates were never able to bring the full weight of the force that had been amassed to bear. One Rebel, Private Eugene Levy, thought that the campaign thus far had been "an enormous waste of human life," and that "McClellan's fine army was driven to Harrison's Landing, fighting at every available position with skill and intrepidity."[30] But the Army of the Potomac was marching away from Richmond. No one could know it at that time, but McClellan had already come as close to the Confederate capital as he would get in the Peninsula Campaign. The moment he began marching away from his positions in the vicinity of Seven Pines and Fair Oaks he had, for all appearances, given up the prospects of capturing Richmond. In the South, this was seen as a cause for

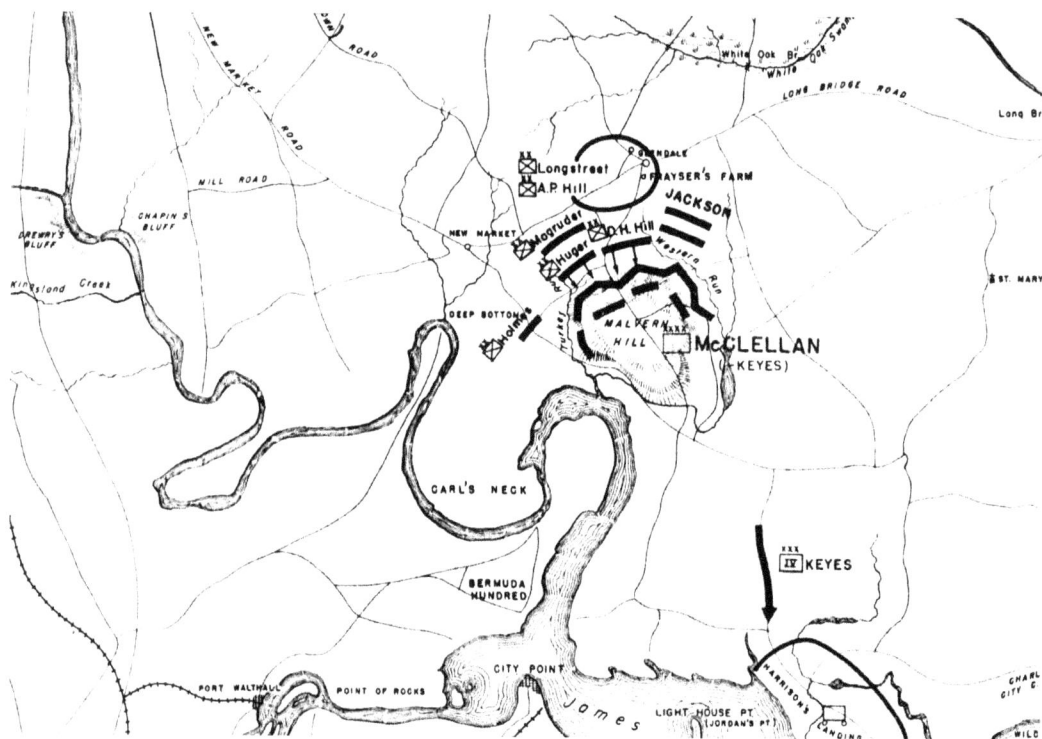

Map showing the relative positions of the opposing forces at Malvern Hill (Military History Institute, United States Army War College).

rejoicing. The immediate threat to Richmond had been averted, and the enemy was marching in the opposite direction. In the North, little notice was paid to the manner in which McClellan's army had blunted the designs of the enemy, and had managed to inflict many more casualties than it sustained in doing so. The retrograde movement was all that the government in Washington could see. McClellan had recently been heralded as the savior of the Union. Now, he was being branded as a failure, and his change of base was being labeled as a thinly veiled attempt to cover the tragic defeat of his campaign. The Peninsula Campaign would see one more pitched battle, however, and that would show how "defeated" his army really was, and would illuminate the illusion of final Confederate victory in the campaign.

July 1, 1862, dawned hot and clear. The Army of the Potomac had been collected together on Malvern Hill. It was a formidable position, indeed. The hill was approximately one and one-half miles long, and three-quarters of a mile wide. At its crest, it was over 100 feet high. To the south, there was a band of swampy ground that separated it from the James River, and to the east and west there were natural barriers formed by creeks and ravines. McClellan had placed his army in a semi-circle, along the northern rim of the hill. The Confederates would have to attack him from the north, over open ground, much of it planted in wheat, marching right into the maelstrom of Federal artillery and musketry fire. One late-coming Federal said that when he reached Malvern Hill "the sight that met our eyes was magnificent. From our position we had a good view of the grand Army of the Potomac.... The cavalry were encamped, while the infantry were drawn up in long lines of battle, one behind the other, waiting for the enemy. The sun flashing on the bayonettes and brass guns presented a beautiful sight."[31] With everything in readiness, McClellan waited for Lee's next move. In the meantime, he went to confer with Commander Rogers aboard his flagship. Though he was in close proximity to the army, he would not actually be on the field until the engagement was well under way.

Lee was still looking to salvage something of a decisive victory out of the Seven Days' Campaign, so he ordered his army to pursue McClellan, and try to bring the Federals to bay. He accordingly ordered his divisions forward. Private Joseph Kauffman, of the 10th Virginia Infantry, wrote in his diary, "This morning we were ordered up and marched out on the road to draw our crackers. We have been living on crackers and a little meat once in a while for the last two or three weeks and God knows how much longer we will have to live off them. We got our rations for one day and started on after the enemy, for they had fallen back during the night. We overtook them about ten o'clock and they began to shell us."[32] Private Bartlett Malone,

Commander John Rogers. McClellan coordinated his change of base to the James River with the naval ships under his command (Military History Institute, United States Army War College).

Center of the Union position at Malvern Hill (photograph taken by author).

of the 6th North Carolina Infantry, was more to the point in his description, merely reporting making contact with the Federals at "about 10 oclock [sic]," when "we overtaken the scamps again."[33]

When the Army of the Potomac was found, drawn up in line of battle, on Malvern Hill, Lee asked General Longstreet to make a reconnaissance of the position to find a good location to place his artillery.[34] At least a few of the high-ranking Confederate officers recognized that McClellan's army occupied a nearly impregnable spot, and an attack against it would be fruitless and bloody. General D.H. Hill examined the ground and expressed his opinion to Lee and Longstreet that "if General McClellan is there in force we had better let him alone." Longstreet laughed off Hill's warning by saying, "Don't get scared now that we have got him shipped." Hill felt that Lee and Longstreet thought the Federals to be demoralized by their recent withdrawals, and this incorrect assessment had caused Lee to order an attack against such a undeniably strong defensive position. General Wilcox also felt it was a mistake to fight at Malvern Hill. Wilcox made no reference to the spirit of the Federals, he simply thought that the Confederates were caught up in their own recent success and "the excuse ... was, we were hot on a trail."[35]

Lee intended to place his cannon so that his big guns would have the Union battle line in a crossfire, and while the Yankees were thus engaged, he would loose his infantry against their disorganized troops. The only problem was that the Confederate artillery was strung out far to the rear, and sufficient numbers could not be gotten up quickly enough to facilitate Lee's plan.[36] E.P. Alexander recalled, "A good many efforts were made to bring a heavy artillery fire to bear upon the enemy, but all were failures in the end, partly for lack of organized battalions of guns, & partly because of the enormous development of the enemy already in position, & with range of our few possible points of approach, & with heavier metal & better ammunition, could practically crush our isolated batteries as fast as we could get them on the field."[37]

General Hood, on the Confederate left, thought that the ground to the enemy's "right appeared to be open, and to afford an easy approach. I therefore dispatched some of my Texas scouts to reconnoitre in that direction. The report, shortly received, was of a favorable character, and General Hampton and I requested of General Whiting permission to turn and assail this exposed flank. Our application was not granted, however."[38] Lee's plan called for a frontal assault up the slope of Malvern Hill, once his artillery had silenced the enemy guns and created havoc among their infantry. The Confederate battle line, from left to right, was composed of the divisions of Whiting, D.H. Hill, Huger, and Magruder. Ewell and Jackson were held in reserve on the Confederate left, with Longstreet and A.P. Hill in reserve on the right. Magruder, whose division had been much fatigued by the 18 hours of marching it had done on the previous day, was not yet on the field at the time Lee assigned positions to his commanders. Lee had issued orders at approximately 1:30 P.M., directing all of his division commanders that they were to advance when they heard a signal given by Brigadier General Lewis Armistead. A part of Huger's division, Armistead's brigade was on the right of the Confederate line, in a position where it was thought he would have the best vantage point to observe the effect of the bombardment by the Southern guns. When, in his estimation, sufficient damage had been done to the Union line, he was to lead his brigade forward as a signal for a general assault. "Batteries have been established to rake the enemy's line. If it is broken, as is probable, Armistead, who can witness the effect of the fire, has been ordered to charge with a yell. Do the same."[39]

By 3:00 P.M., Lee realized that he was not going to be able to amass sufficient artillery support to break up the Union guns, or demoralize the lines of blue-clad infantry. He thus abandoned his plan for a frontal assault on the heights, but neglected to inform his division commanders that there was any change in orders. Riding to the left of his line, the commander searched for a way to flank the Federals, but his efforts came up empty. By this time, it was approximately 4:00 P.M. The day was rapidly progressing. Six hours had passed since contact had been made by the opposing armies, with no serious thrust made by the Confederates. Lee feared that McClellan was going to make good his withdrawal to Harrison's Landing without any significant challenge being mounted to stop him. It was at this time that Lee received reports from two of his subordinates that caused him to believe that an attack might yet be possible. On the left, General Whiting reported that the enemy seemed to be withdrawing from his front. What Whiting actually witnessed was General Sumner shifting his forces. It was not a withdrawal, as Whiting believed it to be. From the right came word from General Magruder that Armistead's brigade had attacked the enemy in its front, and had gained significant ground. In reality, Armistead had not launched an attack at all. Union skirmishers had taken position behind shocks of wheat at the bottom of the hill, and had been giving Armistead's troops a rough time. Without orders, a portion of the brigade surged forward to drive the skirmishers out of the field. This was accomplished, but it brought about a concentrated barrage from the Union artillery that forced the attackers to take refuge in a ravine on the edge of the wheatfield. Armistead had joined his men in the ravine just before Magruder arrived on the field, and this is what Magruder mistakenly reported as being an assault, in force, by his brigade. When Lee received this news, he directed Magruder to "press forward your whole line and follow up Armistead's success."[40]

Magruder's men were not yet in their assigned position, so he obeyed Lee's order by sending forward what units were readily at hand—the brigades of Ambrose Wright and William Mahone, of Huger's division. At approximately 4:45 P.M., Huger's men marched to the attack. When they reached the position held by Armistead, his men joined in the assault. That meant that a little more than 4,000 troops were being sent against the impregnable Union line. It was doomed to be a forlorn hope. The Confederates advanced gallantly, but their ranks were shredded by the combined fire from the Union artillery and infantry. Over on the left, D.H. Hill heard the sound of the firing and the cheering of Huger's men. Lee had not informed his commanders that his original plan had been changed, so Hill thought that this was the signal for a general advance. In accordance to his existing orders, he formed his division and led it up the hill toward the center of the Union line, sometime after 5:00 P.M. On the right, the field was broken by ravines and undulations of the ground, which afforded the attackers some little measure of concealment from the enemy guns. The field on the left offered no such protection for Hill's men. Hill formed his line on either side of the Willis Church Road. Garland's men were in the lead, followed by Hill's other four brigades. As the attack started up the slope, Union artillery erupted with a horrible display of firepower. Gunners switched from shot and shell to grape and cannister, tearing gaping holes in the advancing gray ranks with each forward step. The storm of lead was more than men could bear, and Garland's troops threw themselves on the ground to escape it, despite the entreaties of their commander to keep moving. Garland sent word back to Hill that his attacked had stalled, and urgently requested support.[41]

There was little Hill could do to relieve the pressure on Garland, however. His division was without artillery. The guns had previously been sent away for refitting, so Hill had no means of distracting the Federal gunners, leaving them free to concentrate their entire attention on his infantry. Hill's other brigades were in the same situation as Garland's, and were in need of support themselves. Where was Magruder? Where was Whiting? Hill realized that the general advance Lee had ordered was not taking place, and that his division was fighting virtually alone. As at Fair Oaks, Hill's men were shouldering the brunt of the battle. Hill sent a hasty message back to Jackson that he must have reinforcements. Jackson's men had been withdrawn to the rear, however, in an effort to put them out of range of the Union artillery. This move also placed them out of effective supporting range of Hill's hard-pressed troops. Stonewall's men could not reach Hill in time to provide any assistance. For the time being, Hill was on his own.[42]

Colonel John B. Gordon was on Hill's right flank, leading Robert Rodes's brigade. Gordon's men advanced to within 400 yards of the Union line, where 50 men were detailed as sharpshooters to harass an enemy battery to their front. This action brought Gordon's men to the full attention of the enemy guns, and "subjected us to a most terrific fire for some time." The only way to silence the guns was to take them, so Gordon ordered his men forward. Gordon asserted that "never was the courage of troops more severely tried and heroically exhibited than in this charge. They moved on under this terrible fire, breaking and driving off the first line of infantry, until within a little over 200 yards of the batteries. Here the canister and musketry mowed down my already thinned ranks so rapidly that it became impossible to advance without support; and had it been possible to reach the batteries, I have high authority to back my own judgment that it would have been at the sacrifice of the entire command. I therefore ordered the men to lie down and open fire." Major Robert M. Sands, commanding the 3rd Alabama Infantry, stated that at this time in the fighting "each man behaved and fought as though the issue of the battle depended on his own individual efforts. Men never fought more gallantly." The 3rd Alabama would lose over half their number, and six color bearers would be shot down during this fearful engagement. Hill's men hugged the ground and kept up what fire they could until darkness covered their withdrawal from the field. Gordon was probably correct in stating that his command would have been sacrificed if it had attempted to move any further forward. As it was, nearly half of his men had fallen in the charge, and the entire brigade mustered only about 600 men, slightly more than half the normal strength of a regiment, when they retired from the field.[43]

Alfred Roe, of the 10th Massachusetts, witnessed the charge of Hill's men, who attacked against the portion of the line held by General Darius Couch's division. Roe reported that the attack "had been handsomely repulsed." Much of the credit was due to the artillery, and the "excellent practice of Kingsbury's Battery with the steady fire of the Tenth Massachusetts and a charge of the 36th New York — the latter Regiment capturing the colors of the 14th North Carolina in a hand-to-hand conflict."[44] General Porter thought that the enemy acted "as if moved by a reckless disregard of life ... with a determination to capture our army, or destroy it by driving us into the river, regiment after regiment, and brigade after brigade, rushed at our batteries; but the artillery ... mowed them down with shrapnel, grape, and canister; while our infantry, withholding their fire until the enemy were within short range, scattered the remnants of their columns, sometimes following them up and capturing prisoners and colors." One Federal battery reported expending no fewer than 1,392 rounds into Hill's charging line.[45] Private Robert K. Sneden, of the 40th New York, recorded in his diary that the enemy had rushed upon them "at a run with terrifying yells, heard all above the crash of musketry and the roar of artillery," only to be crushed by the fire of artillery and musketry coming from the crest. Sneden said the Confederates would be pushed back, to reform in a patch of woods to charge again "only to be met with the same murderous volleys of shot, shell, and bullets.... The Rebel cavalry were seen driving the remnants of regiments out of the woods into the open ground, and were shooting those who did not keep in line and 'face the music.'" Sneden thought that Hill's men "fought like fiends," but felt that the fire from the Federal position made it "impossible for any troops to hold the line and live."[46]

Hill's men had done all that human flesh could. Those not pinned down by enemy fire had been forced to retire. The ground over which his men had fought "presented a shocking sight of dead, dying, and mangled corpses, while the numerous dead and wounded horses were crawling and kicking in death agony among them."[47] Assistance from Huger and Jackson was on the way, but it would not arrive in time to salvage the attack against the Union center. The action now shifted to the Confederate right, where Magruder's division was finally getting into its assigned positions. As dusk began to darken a sky already thick with the acrid haze of gunpowder smoke, Magruder sent his brigades forward. He committed his division piecemeal, as they got into place, not waiting until everyone was in position so that the weight of his entire division could be brought to bear. The result was much the same as Hill had experienced on the left, with Union artillery playing havoc on the attacking troops. Magruder took heavy casualties advancing across the wheatfield — more than half of them resulting from enemy artillery fire. D.H. Hill thought that the number of men felled by the Union guns was "an unprecedented thing in warfare," as headless and limbless torsos littered the field. Magruder's assault had little chance of success, as it was charging into an absolute hell on earth. Above that, the Army of the Potomac had seven full divisions in reserve, ready to plug any breakthrough that might occur. Even so, Magruder's men were

Ground over which the Confederates had to advance to attack the Union position on the crest of the ridge (photograph taken by author).

doggedly braving the storm of lead and making things hot for the Federals, and advancing to within 50 yards of the Federal batteries. General Porter called for reinforcements from Sumner and Heintzelman, and two brigades were sent to bolster the line. Porter led General Meagher's brigade into position himself, during which time he feared that he might be captured, so he destroyed the diary and dispatch book he was carrying. By the time the reinforcements reached the front, the issue had been decided, however, and Magruder's division had been repulsed with heavy losses.[48] It was now about 9:00 P.M., and the battle was, for all intents and purposes, ended, though Union artillery continued to serenade the discomfited Confederates for another hour. The fallen members of Hill's, Huger's and Magruder's commands lay thick on the slope leading to the Union position atop Malvern Hill. Colonel William Averell would write that "dead and wounded men were on the ground in every attitude of distress. A third of them were dead or dying, but enough were alive and moving to give the field a singular crawling effect." The battle of was ended. General Hill had been quite correct in advising Lee against attacking McClellan in this stronghold. Confederate losses totaled 5,355, as opposed to the 3,214 suffered by the Federals.[49] These losses were extreme, considering the short duration of the fighting, and the fact that only three of Lee's divisions had been under fire. Seven divisions of the Army of the Potomac had also not seen action. During the night, McClellan continued his withdrawal, and the army marched the eight miles to Harrison's Landing. Lee followed, but decided the Union position was too strong to risk an attack. Breaking off the pursuit, he ordered his army to retire back toward Richmond, where it could be supplied and reorganized in relative safety. The Peninsula Campaign was ended, and even as McClellan was sending messages to Washington requesting additional reinforcements to enable him to resume his offensive, events were transpiring that would move the seat of war away from the environs of Richmond. Private Joseph Kauffman lamented that over the past few weeks he had seen "hard times," and expected "harder times coming. Oh, God! Will this war never stop."[50] After two more years of bitter conflict, on fields made famous by the carnage they witnessed, the contending armies would once more find themselves fighting on this same ground. But for now, Richmond was safe, and McClellan's grand scheme to capture the Confederate capital and end the war had come to naught. Lee had emerged as the savior of the South, and he was poised to write his name in glory in the nation's history. McClellan's future held an entirely different outcome.

Epilogue

The battle of Fair Oaks proved to be the high-water mark of McClellan's ambitious plan to capture Richmond. The Army of the Potomac seemed on the verge of fulfilling its commander's promise to destroy the enemy army and bring a quick close to the war that had torn the nation asunder. McClellan had been the hero of the hour, and the success of the campaign had even made his political enemies hesitant to openly criticize him. The Peninsula Campaign had witnessed the largest concentration of military force that had ever been seen on the Western Hemisphere. More than 200,000 men had been gathered together to fight in what was thought to be the decisive operation of the war. On the Southern side, the Confederates amassed an army of more than 90,000 men, the greatest number that they would assemble in one place during the entire war. Casualties had been sustained on a scale commensurate with the number of men engaged. Over 15 major engagements and skirmishes had been fought, with over 57,000 men becoming casualties, approximately 25 percent of the aggregate total of both armies. The Confederates, being the attackers in most of the actions, suffered considerably heavier casualties than did the Union forces. During the Seven Days Battles, the Confederate loss in killed and wounded was 19,739, as opposed to the 9,796 suffered by the army of the Potomac. But the North lost more men as prisoners, owing to the fact that they were constantly retiring under pressure. During that same period of time, McClellan's army lost 6,053 men listed as captured or missing, compared to 875 for the Confederates.[1]

What was the end result of the vast expenditure of lives, money, and materiel that was the Peninsula Campaign? On the Confederate side, the anticipated fall of Richmond was averted, and the seat of war was eventually shifted back to Northern Virginia, and ultimately to Maryland. The wounding of General Joseph E. Johnston brought forth the emergence of Robert E. Lee, who would go on to become one of the greatest military leaders in American history, and his Army of Northern Virginia would gain world renown for their fighting élan. The South had gained time. Time to find a way to secure its independence through military or political victories. For a nation that was building everything from the ground up, time was as important as a victory on the battlefield.

General Johnston's plan of battle at Fair Oaks had been sound, and the result could possibly have been a resounding victory for the Confederates if his orders had been carried out, and the full weight of the attack he envisioned had been brought to bear. General Longstreet emerges as the figure most culpable in the mismanagement of Johnston's orders at Fair Oaks. He not only delayed getting his own division into place, but was directly responsible for causing the delay of Huger's men in reaching their assigned position. To add insult to injury, he later blamed Huger's tardiness as the reason why the attack was so late in getting underway. Once he had finally arrived at his designated location, Longstreet failed to commit his six brigades to the assault, sending several of them off to places where they were not needed, and retaining only two at the point of concentration. He allowed D.H. Hill to carry the fight almost single-handedly, with his four brigades, for the bulk of the engagement, before finally coming to his assistance during the final phases of the fighting on the first day. On the second day of the battle, Longstreet once more failed to follow his orders and commit his entire force to the assault. Only a small portion of his command was sent forward to attack the Union lines, and D.H. Hill once more got to do the heavy lifting. Longstreet had not supported either Johnston's or Smith's plans. Instead of acting in a manner befitting a trusted subordinate, the general sulked and hesitated, and refused to give his maximum effort to a battle plan he did not personally endorse. This character trait would surface again during the war, most notably on the hills and fields at Gettysburg.

General Lee's plan of campaign during the Seven Days Battles was also fundamentally sound, and could have produced results far above those that were actually achieved. As with Johnston, he experienced difficulty in having his orders and plans executed on the field by his subordinate commanders. While numerous breakdowns took place during the campaign, the most glaring example of lack of execution would have to be that of Stonewall Jackson. The general who had become world renowned for his lightning-quick movements and crushing attacks seemed repeatedly tardy and timid on the fields outside of Richmond. His actions during these battles is in stark contrast with his performance both before and after the campaign, and has become a topic of speculation for historians. Whatever the cause, it is certain that Jackson's lack of execution hindered Lee's plans, and prevented the Confederates from achieving maximum results in the campaign. Other generals, such as D.H. Hill, A.P. Hill, and John Bell Hood exhibited leadership abilities that would propel them in the command structure of Lee's reorganized army. Lee had found a number of "fighting" generals, and he would employ their talents to the utmost in the coming months.

For the North, the outcome on the Peninsula was entirely different. General McClellan, the architect of the campaign, was being labeled a failure by the administration and his enemies among the Radical Republicans. He would eventually be stripped of his command when it was siphoned off to augment John Pope's army in Northern Virginia. McClellan, along with his key supporters like Porter and Franklin, would be attacked by the Joint Committee, and would end their military careers either disgraced, or in a greatly diminished capacity. For other officers, like Hooker and Hancock, the Peninsula Campaign saw their stars begin to ascend, because of the leadership abilities they had exhibited on the battlefield.

Most traditional studies of the campaign blame its failure on McClellan. It is true that the general made many mistakes during his tenure as commander of the army, and he is in line for his share of the blame. His unquestioning acceptance of Pinkerton's estimates of the size of the Confederate army have served as a basis for contempt and derision from his detractors. The fact is that he consistently overestimated the size of the opposition, and planned his movements based on the supposition that he was always in command of the inferior force. There is no denying McClellan's propensity for inflating the odds against him, which brought about his almost continuous calls for more of everything: more men, more guns, more horses, and even more authority. But what of the other charges? Specifically, what of the charges made by McClellan himself that the administration failed to support its principal army, or its commanding general, during the most critical military operation in the history of the nation to that point? It would seem that there is ample evidence to support McClellan's claim. In fact, there is so much evidence that one could hardly blame McClellan if he indeed suffered from the paranoia that his critics have ascribed to him. Let us review the events leading up to the commencement of the campaign, and its earliest stages, before Yorktown.

- March 8, 1862. Lincoln confronts McClellan about his Urbanna Plan, charging him with "Traitorous intent" in exposing Washington to attack, because of the number of troops the general's plan left in the capital. An angry McClellan convinces Lincoln to back down from the charges.
- March 8, 1862. Lincoln and Stanton canvass twelve of McClellan's top generals about their opinion of the Urbanna Plan. Eight are in favor of it and four are opposed.
- March 8, 1862. Lincoln issues General War Order No. 2. Without consulting McClellan, the president forms the Army of the Potomac into four corps. Three of the four generals that were against McClellan's plan are appointed to corps command. All four are Republicans.
- March 11, 1862. Politician Edward Bates urges Lincoln to remove McClellan from the general-in-chief position and assume it himself. On that same day, Lincoln issues Special War Order No. 3, demoting McClellan to army commander. He also creates the Mountain Department, appointing Republican John Fremont as commander. McClellan is issued no orders regarding his demotion, and reads about it in the newspaper the following day.
- March 13, 1862. Lincoln appoints James Wadsworth to command the defenses of Washington. McClellan protests the appointment on the grounds that Wadsworth is a New York Republican politician with no previous military experience.
- March 14, 1862. Navy Secretary Gideon Welles refuses naval cooperation for McClellan's invasion, declining to send supporting ships above Yorktown.
- March 15, 1862. Stanton asks Ethan Allen Hitchcock, retired since 1855, to take command of the Army of the Potomac. Hitchcock declines.
- March 19, 1862. General John Barnard, Admiral Goldsborough, and General John Wool secretly divert resources away from McClellan's campaign to make an effort to capture Norfolk, Virginia.
- March 27, 1862. General Hitchcock, now senior military advisor to the administration, advises that men be taken from Fremont's force to augment McClellan's army. Stanton ignores his advice and instead takes two divisions from McClellan to reinforce Fremont.
- April 1, 1862. McClellan embarks for the Peninsula.
- April 3, 1862. Stanton issues War Order No. 33. This edict inexplicably closes all recruitment centers in the North. The Union is embarking on the most significant military operation of the war, but Stanton has closed down the pipeline through which replacements and reinforcements might be obtained.
- April 4, 1862. Lincoln removes McDowell's corps from McClellan's invasion force, reducing the size of his army by some 40,000 men. Most of McClellan's cavalry, which has not yet embarked, is also withheld by the president. McDowell is made department commander and placed under the direct orders of Lincoln and Stanton. McClellan has been stripped of control of Banks' and Fremont's forces, as well as McDowell's, the garrison at Fortress Monroe, and the men in the Washington defenses. He can neither coordinate their actions nor call on them for assistance.

- April 5, 1862. The navy commits a tiny four-ship flotilla to cooperate with the campaign. The naval commander refuses to approach Yorktown to conduct reconnaissance, or even to meet with McClellan.
- April 13, 1862. McClellan requests that the Navy shell positions below Gloucester to support an advance, but the request is refused.
- April 15, 1862. Napoleon Buford is summoned to Washington by Stanton. The secretary offers Buford command of the Army of the Potomac, to replace McClellan. Buford declines the offer.[2]

All of these events transpired before the Army of the Potomac had made any significant strides in the campaign. If they do not illustrate a desire to hamstring McClellan's efforts, they certainly exhibit a lack of active support, especially where the general was concerned. After the expedition was fairly underway, Stanton made yet another attempt to replace McClellan by offering command of the army to General Burnside. The administration also meddled in McClellan's tactical operations by ordering him to extend the right wing of his army for a promised junction with McDowell's corps, which never came to pass. It was this extension that gave General Johnston the opportunity he sought to strike a blow against the Federal army while it was separated, and brought about the battle of Fair Oaks. The administration also allowed itself to be duped into withholding reinforcements from McClellan because of Stonewall Jackson's antics in the Shenandoah Valley, despite the protests of senior officers like McDowell, Shields, and Hitchcock. Lincoln and Stanton dismissed the advice of these prominent military leaders, allowing the Confederates to achieve their objective: a concentration of all available Southern forces in front of Richmond, while preventing the Federal forces from being able to do the same.

It is a matter of conjecture what might have happened if the administration had given McClellan's campaign its wholehearted support. What is certain is that the Confederate high command desperately feared the very movements the Army of the Potomac was making, and the way in which McClellan was making war. Deficient in naval power, artillery, and engineering, the Confederacy could not hope to withstand the "war of posts" McClellan proposed to conduct against it. President Davis, and Generals Johnston and Lee, all concurred in this conclusion. In a war of siege and confinement, the death of the Confederacy was only a matter of time, as General Grant proved over the very same ground two years later.

General McClellan has often been criticized by contemporaries and historians for his perceived hesitancy to fight. He has been painted as a great little organizer and administrator, and he is grudgingly given credit for creating the Army of the Potomac as an efficient and well-trained military machine. But when it came to fighting, it has been alleged that the general loved the army he had created too much to see it bleed on the battlefield. The 57,000 casualties suffered during the Peninsula Campaign would tend to discredit these allegations. The battle of Antietam — the bloodiest single day of the war, which saw some 23,000 men fall — was also fought under McClellan's command. McClellan's personal bravery has never been questioned, and he commanded the army during some of the bloodiest conflicts of the war. So where do these allegations of his being afraid to fight come from?

The answer lies in the manner in which the general conducted his campaigns. His engineering training made him a master of organization and planning. Everything had to be accounted for, and actions were never taken rashly or without due consideration. Planning, training, and preparing for any eventuality were the hallmarks of his leadership style, a style exhibited by another Union officer who was sometimes derided by his critics, but who never lost a battle or failed to hold a position throughout the course of the war: George H. Thomas. But there is another factor that played into the manner in which McClellan conducted his campaign on the Peninsula that I have never before heard a historian address. Military necessity compelled McClellan to exercise as much economy as possible when it came to the lives of his men. As has been previously stated, the reinforcements he requested were denied, and the recruiting offices had been closed throughout the North, making it impossible for him to receive replacements for the losses he sustained. Many of the regiments who fought at Fair Oaks were at half strength or less, even though this was their first time in battle. The malarial swamps of the Peninsula combined with other diseases to decimate the ranks of the Army of the Potomac before many of the men had ever seen combat. Losses on the battlefield only intensified the diminishing numbers of soldiers who could be counted on to carry the fight to the enemy. It is interesting to compare and contrast the Peninsula Campaign of 1862 with Grant's Overland Campaign in 1864. Grant began his campaign with an army totaling 130,000 men. By the time he reached Richmond and Petersburg, he had lost 60,000 men as casualties—as many as Lee had in his command at the inception of the campaign. But when Grant arrived at Richmond and Petersburg he still had 130,000 men in his army. His losses were constantly replaced by the administration so that his effective force remained constant. McClellan enjoyed no such support from the government. Had he conducted a campaign of frontal assaults and battering-ram tactics (commonly called a war of attrition) as Grant did, the Army of the Potomac would have been destroyed in 1862, and the Confederacy might well have attained their independence. By contrast, if Grant had been hampered by the same conditions McClellan faced, he would likely have gone down in history as a butcher who destroyed the Federal army instead of the hero who won the war.

People who have been in the military will tell you that soldiers will not long suffer a fool in command. The soldiers in the Army of the Potomac were absolutely devoted to McClellan. He remains to this day one of the most popular leaders in American military history, and the devotion of his men rivals that shown toward Robert E. Lee and George Washington. Though it is rarely reported in modern histories, the soldiers of the Army of the Potomac fought like poet warriors on McPherson's Ridge at Gettysburg, on July 1, 1863, because the rumor had been intentionally spread through the ranks that McClellan had been reinstated to command, replacing Joe Hooker. The reaction of a large number of the troops to his being removed from command is even less reported or known.

On November 10, 1862, when McClellan was taking his leave of the army to board a train to begin his journey to his home in New Jersey, approximately 30,000 of his men were drawn up in line to see him off. A Union officer reported, "As General McClellan passed along its front, whole regiments broke and flocked around him, and with tears and entreaties besought him not to leave them, but to say the word and they would settle matters in Washington. Indeed, it was thought at one time there would be a mutiny, but by a word he calmed the tumult and ordered the men back to their colors and their duty. As he passed our regiment he was thronged by men of other commands, making a tumultuous scene beyond description. He was obliged to halt in front of us." The officer described a general "who was riding near McClellan, was forced by the crowd towards our line and I heard him say to another mounted officer close by that he wished to God McClellan would put himself at the head of the army and throw the infernal scoundrels at Washington into the Potomac.... What do you think of such a man? He had it in his power to be dictator—anything he chose to name—if he would but say the word, but he preferred retirement rather than ambition."[3]

Lee is known to have stated that he feared McClellan above all of the other Union commanders he had faced during the war. That's a pretty good testimonial. Here is the evaluation of another hero of the war, Ulysses S. Grant:

> All my impressions are in his favor.... The test which was applied to him would be terrible to any man, being made a major-general at the beginning of the war. It has always seemed to me that the critics of McClellan do not consider this cast and cruel responsibility — the war, a new thing to all of us, the army new, everything to do from the outset, with a restless people and Congress.... If he had gone into the war as Sherman, Thomas, or Meade, had fought his way along and up, I have no reason to suppose that he would not have won as high distinction as any of us.[4]

In 1864, Grant sought to have McClellan reinstated to command, along with Don Carlos Buell. The War Department declined to even answer his request.

In the final analysis, the battle of Fair Oaks and the entire Peninsula Campaign has been unjustly relegated to a second layer of importance in the study of the Civil War, as has McClellan himself. The author was notably impressed by the almost total lack of commemoration to be found at the battle sites that made up the Peninsula Campaign. Monuments and memorials are conspicuous by their absence. The battlefields at Fair Oaks and Seven Pines have been lost to the encroachment of civilization, covered by houses, businesses, and even an airport. Two simple iron slabs bear witness to the fact that one of the great battles of the Civil War was fought in these locations. It is much the same at the rest of the battlefields of the Peninsula Campaign. A solitary iron slab marks the location of Porter's victory at Mechanicsville. A couple miles away, at Cold Harbor, numerous monuments and memorials have been erected to the defeat Grant suffered there in 1864. The only important site of the Peninsula Campaign that even looks like a battlefield is at Malvern Hill. A few cannon, a sparse scattering of monuments, and an interpretive stand do provide the visitor with the feeling that some important piece of history took place there. As for the rest, it is almost as though the contempt the administration showed toward McClellan was also placed upon the fields where he and his army fought — as if commemorating the fields where so many brave men fell would be in some way offering redemption to McClellan. Fair Oaks is gone, and nothing can be done to change that. The rest are still there, in one state or another, bearing in silence, and without adornment, memories of the 57,000 Americans that became casualties in one of America's greatest military campaigns.

Appendix 1.
The Opposing Forces at Fair Oaks*

Union Army

    **Second Army Corps:
Brigadier General Edwin Vose Sumner**

First Division: Brigadier General Israel B. Richardson
  FIRST BRIGADE: Brigadier General Oliver O. Howard
    5th New Hampshire Infantry
    61st New York Infantry
    64th New York Infantry
    81st Pennsylvania Infantry
  SECOND BRIGADE: Brigadier General Thomas F. Meagher
    63rd New York Infantry
    69th New York Infantry
    88th New York Infantry
  THIRD BRIGADE: Brigadier General William H. French
    52nd New York Infantry
    57th New York Infantry
    66th New York Infantry
    53rd Pennsylvania Infantry
  ARTILLERY: Captain G.W. Hazzard
    Battery B, 1st New York Light Artillery
    Battery G, 1st New York Light Artillery
    Battery A, 4th U.S. Light Artillery
    Battery C, 4th U.S. Light Artillery

Second Division: Brigadier General John Sedgwick
  FIRST BRIGADE: Brigadier General Willis A. Gorman
    15th Massachusetts Infantry
    1st Minnesota Infantry
    34th New York Infantry
    82nd New York Infantry
    1st Company Massachusetts Sharpshooters
    2nd Company Minnesota Sharpshooters
  SECOND BRIGADE: Brigadier General William W. Burns
    69th Pennsylvania Infantry
    71st Pennsylvania Infantry
    72nd Pennsylvania Infantry
    106th Pennsylvania Infantry
  THIRD BRIGADE: Brigadier General N.J.T. Dana
    19th Massachusetts Infantry
    20th Massachusetts Infantry
    7th Michigan Infantry
    42nd New York Infantry
  ARTILLERY: Colonel Charles H. Tompkins
    Battery A, 1st Rhode Island Light Artillery
    Battery B, 1st Rhode Island Light Artillery
    Battery G, 1st Rhode Island Light Artillery
    Battery I, 1st U.S. Light Artillery
  CAVALRY:
    Company K, 6th New York Cavalry

    Third Army Corps: Brigadier General Samuel P. Heintzelman

Second Division: Brigadier General Joseph Hooker
  SECOND BRIGADE: Brigadier General Daniel E. Sickles
    70th New York Infantry
    71st New York Infantry
    72nd New York Infantry
    73rd New York Infantry
    74th New York Infantry
  THIRD BRIGADE: Brigadier General Francis E. Patterson

Battles and Leaders, volume 2, pages 313–317.

5th New Jersey Infantry
6th New Jersey Infantry
ARTILLERY: Major Charles S. Wainwright
Battery D, 1st New York Light Artillery
6th New York Battery

Third Division: Brigadier General Philip Kearny
FIRST BRIGADE: Brigadier General Charles D. Jameson
87th New York Infantry
57th Pennsylvania Infantry
63rd Pennsylvania Infantry
105th Pennsylvania Infantry
SECOND BRIGADE: Brigadier General David B. Birney
3rd Maine Infantry
4th Maine Infantry
5th Maine Infantry
40th New York Infantry
THIRD BRIGADE: Brigadier General Hiram G. Berry
2nd Michigan Infantry
3rd Michigan Infantry
5th Michigan Infantry
37th New York Infantry

Fourth Army Corps: Brigadier General Erasmus D. Keyes

First Division: Brigadier General Darius N. Couch
FIRST BRIGADE: Brigadier General John J. Peck
55th New York Infantry
62nd New York Infantry
93rd Pennsylvania Infantry
102nd Pennsylvania Infantry
SECOND BRIGADE: Brigadier General John J. Ambercrombie
65th New York Infantry
67th New York Infantry
23rd Pennsylvania Infantry
31st Pennsylvania Infantry
61st Pennsylvania Infantry
THIRD BRIGADE: Brigadier General Charles Devens Jr.
7th Massachusetts Infantry
10th Massachusetts Infantry
36th New York Infantry
ARTILLERY: Major Robert M. West
Battery C, 1st Pennsylvania Light Artillery
Battery D, 1st Pennsylvania Light Artillery
Battery E, 1st Pennsylvania Light Artillery
Battery H, 1st Pennsylvania Light Artillery

CAVALRY: Colonel David McM. Gregg
8th Pennsylvania Cavalry

Second Division: Brigadier General Silas Casey
FIRST BRIGADE: Brigadier General Henry M. Naglee
11th Maine Infantry
56th New York Infantry
100th New York Infantry
52nd Pennsylvania Infantry
104th Pennsylvania Infantry
SECOND BRIGADE: Brigadier General Henry W. Wessells
96th New York Infantry
85th Pennsylvania Infantry
101st Pennsylvania Infantry
103rd Pennsylvania Infantry
THIRD BRIGADE: Brigadier General Innis N. Palmer
81st New York Infantry
85th New York Infantry
92nd New York Infantry
98th New York Infantry
ARTILLERY: Colonel Guilford D. Bailey
Battery A, 1st New York Light Artillery
Battery H, 1st New York Light Artillery
7th New York Battery
8th New York Battery
UNATTACHED: Battery E, 1st U.S. Light Artillery

Confederate Army

Right Wing: Major General James P. Longstreet

Longstreet's Division: Brigadier General Richard H. Anderson
KEMPER'S BRIGADE: Colonel James L. Kemper
1st Virginia Infantry
7th Virginia Infantry
11th Virginia Infantry
17th Virginia Infantry
ANDERSON'S BRIGADE: Colonel Micah Jenkins
5th South Carolina Infantry
6th South Carolina Infantry
Palmetto Sharpshooters
Virginia Battery: Captain Robert Stribling
PICKETT'S BRIGADE: Brigadier General George E. Pickett
8th Virginia Infantry
18th Virginia Infantry
19th Virginia Infantry
28th Virginia Infantry
Virginia Battery: Captain James Dearing

Wilcox's Brigade: Brigadier General Cadmus M. Wilcox
  9th Alabama Infantry
  10th Alabama Infantry
  11th Alabama Infantry
  19th Mississippi Infantry
Colston's Brigade: Brigadier General Robert E. Colston
  13th North Carolina Infantry
  14th North Carolina Infantry
  3rd Virginia Infantry
Pryor's Brigade: Brigadier General Roger A. Pryor
  8th Alabama Infantry
  14th Alabama Infantry
  14th Louisiana Infantry

Hill's Division: Major General Daniel H. Hill
Garland's Brigade: Brigadier General Samuel Garland Jr.
  2nd Florida Infantry
  2nd Mississippi Infantry Battalion
  5th North Carolina Infantry
  24th Virginia Infantry
  38th Virginia Infantry
  Alabama Battery: Captain J.W. Bondurant
Rodes' Brigade: Brigadier General Robert E. Rodes
  5th Alabama Infantry
  6th Alabama Infantry
  12th Alabama Infantry
  12th Mississippi Infantry
  4th Virginia Infantry Battalion
  Virginia Battery: Captain Thomas H. Carter
Rains' Brigade: Brigadier General Gabriel J. Rains
  13th Alabama Infantry
  26th Alabama Infantry
  6th Georgia Infantry
  23rd Georgia Infantry
Featherston's Brigade: Colonel George B. Anderson
  27th Georgia Infantry
  28th Georgia Infantry
  4th North Carolina Infantry
  49th Virginia Infantry

Huger's Division: Brigadier General Benjamin Huger
Armistead's Brigade: Brigadier General Lewis A. Armistead
  5th Virginia Infantry
  9th Virginia Infantry
  14th Virginia Infantry
  53rd Virginia Infantry
Mahone's Brigade: Brigadier General William Mahone
  3rd Alabama Infantry
  12th Virginia Infantry
  41st Virginia Infantry
Blanchard's Brigade: Brigadier General A.G. Blanchard
  3rd Georgia Infantry
  4th Georgia Infantry
  22nd Georgia Infantry
  1st Louisiana Infantry
Artillery:
  Louisiana Battery: Captain Victor Maurin
  Virginia Battery: Captain David Watson

Left Wing: Major General Gustavus W. Smith

Smith's Division: Brigadier General William H.C. Whiting
Whiting's Brigade: Colonel Evander M. Law
  4th Alabama Infantry
  2nd Mississippi Infantry
  11th Mississippi Infantry
  6th North Carolina Infantry
Hood's Brigade: Brigadier General John B. Hood
  18th Georgia Infantry
  1st Texas Infantry
  4th Texas Infantry
  5th Texas Infantry
Hampton's Brigade: Brigadier General Wade Hampton
  14th Georgia Infantry
  19th Georgia Infantry
  16th North Carolina Infantry
  Hampton Legion
Hatton's Brigade: Brigadier General Robert Hatton
  1st Tennessee Infantry
  7th Tennessee Infantry
  14th Tennessee Infantry
Pettigrew's Brigade: Brigadier General James J. Pettigrew
  Arkansas Infantry Battalion
  35th Georgia Infantry
  22nd North Carolina Infantry
  47th Virginia Infantry

Appendix 2: Casualties at Fair Oaks*

Union Army

Second Corps
  FIRST DIVISION
    First Brigade: killed 95, wounded 398, missing 64
    Second Brigade: killed 7, wounded 31, missing 1
    Third Brigade: killed 32, wounded 188, missing 22
    Artillery: no casualties
  SECOND DIVISION
    First Brigade: killed 40, wounded 153, missing 3
    Second Brigade: killed 5, wounded 30
    Third Brigade: killed 16, wounded 95
    Artillery: killed 1, wounded 4
    Cavalry: no casualties
Corps Totals: killed 196, wounded 899, missing 90 = 1185

Third Corps
  SECOND DIVISION
    Second Brigade: killed 7, wounded 61, missing 6
    Third Brigade: killed 9, wounded 67, missing 3
  THIRD DIVISION
    First Brigade: killed 86, wounded 297, missing 36
    Second Brigade: killed 23, wounded 174, missing 10
    Third Brigade: killed 84, wounded 344, missing 36
    Headquarters: wounded 1
Corps Totals: killed 209, wounded 934, missing 91 = 1234

Fourth Corps
  Staff: wounded 1
  Cavalry: wounded 2
  FIRST DIVISION
    First Brigade: killed 47, wounded 236, missing 64
    Second Brigade: killed 124, wounded 433, missing 67
    Third Brigade: killed 34, wounded 136, missing 8
    Artillery: killed 2, wounded 12
  SECOND DIVISION
    First Brigade: killed 89, wounded 383, missing 167
    Second Brigade: killed 35, wounded 264, missing 59
    Third Brigade: killed 46, wounded 251, missing 95
    Artillery: killed 7, wounded 28, missing 2
    Unattached: killed 1, wounded 3
Corps Totals: killed 385, wounded 1750, missing 466 = 2601

Total Union Casualties: killed 790, wounded 3594, missing 647 = 5031

Confederate Army

Right Wing
  LONGSTREET'S DIVISION: Incomplete returns
  Hill's Division
    Garland's Brigade: killed 98, wounded 600, missing 42
    Rodes' Brigade: killed 241, wounded 853, missing 5
    Rains' Brigade: Incomplete returns
    Featherston's Brigade: killed 149, wounded 680, missing 37

Battles and Leaders, volume 2, pages 313–317.

HUGER'S DIVISION: Incomplete returns
Right Wing reported losses: killed 816, wounded 3739, missing 296 = 4851

Left Wing
SMITH'S DIVISION
Hood's Brigade: wounded 13
Hampton's Brigade: killed 45, wounded 284, missing 42
Hatton's Brigade: killed 44, wounded 187, missing 13
Pettigrew's Brigade: killed 47, wounded 240, missing 54

Left Wing reported losses: killed 164, wounded 1010, missing 109 = 1283

Total Confederate Casualties: killed 980, wounded 4749, missing 405 = 6134

Appendix 3.
The Opposing Forces in the Peninsula Campaign*

The Army of the Potomac: Major General George B. McClellan

General Headquarters
  PROVOST MARSHALL AND HEADQUARTERS GUARD:
    Brigadier General Andrew Porter
    2nd U.S. Cavalry (7 companies)
    93rd New York Infantry (4 companies)
    Sturges Illinois Rifles
    8th U.S. Infantry (2 companies)
    Oneida (New York) Cavalry
  ENGINEER BRIGADE: Brigadier General Daniel P. Woodbury
    15th New York Infantry
    50th New York Infantry
    U.S. Engineer Battalion
  CASEY'S BRIGADE: Brigadier General Silas Casey
    4th Pennsylvania Cavalry (squadron)
    11th Pennsylvania Cavalry (3 companies)
    Battery F, 1st New York Light Artillery
    93rd New York Infantry (6 companies)

Second Corps: Brigadier General Edwin V. Sumner
6th New York Cavalry (4 companies)
  FIRST DIVISION: Brigadier General Israel B. Richardson
    First Brigade: Brigadier General John C. Caldwell
      5th New Hampshire Infantry
      7th New York Infantry
      61st New York Infantry
      81st Pennsylvania Infantry
    Second Brigade: Brigadier General Thomas F. Meagher
      29th Massachusetts Infantry
      63rd New York Infantry
      69th New York Infantry
      88th New York Infantry
    Third Brigade: Brigadier General William H. French
      2nd Delaware Infantry
      52nd New York Infantry
      57th New York Infantry
      64th New York Infantry
      66th New York Infantry
      53rd Pennsylvania Infantry
    Artillery: Captain George W. Hazzard
      Battery B, 1st New York Light Artillery
      Battery A, 4th United States Light Artillery
      Battery D, 4th United States Light Artillery

  SECOND DIVISION: Brigadier General John Sedgwick
    First Brigade: Colonel Alfred Sully
      15th Massachusetts Infantry
      1st Minnesota Infantry
      1st Company Massachusetts Sharp shooters
      34th New York Infantry
      82nd New York Infantry
      2nd Company Minnesota Sharpshooters
    Second Brigade: Brigadier General William W. Burns
      69th Pennsylvania Infantry

*Battles and Leaders, volume 2, pages 313–317.

71st Pennsylvania Infantry
72nd Pennsylvania Infantry
106th Pennsylvania Infantry
Third Brigade: Brigadier General N.J.T. Dana
  19th Massachusetts Infantry
  20th Massachusetts Infantry
  7th Michigan Infantry
  42nd New York Infantry
Artillery: Colonel Charles H. Tompkins
  Battery A, 1st Rhode Island Light Artillery
  Battery I, 1st United States Light Artillery
Reserve Artillery:
  Battery G, 1st New York Light Artillery
  Battery B, 1st Rhode Island Light Artillery
  Battery G, 1st Rhode Island Light Artillery

Third Corps: Brigadier General Samuel P. Heintzelman
  SECOND DIVISION: Brigadier General Joseph Hooker
    First Brigade: Brigadier General Cuvier Grover
      1st Massachusetts Infantry
      11th Massachusetts Infantry
      16th Massachusetts Infantry
      2nd New Hampshire Infantry
      26th Pennsylvania Infantry
    Second Brigade: Brigadier General Daniel E. Sickles
      70th New York Infantry
      71st New York Infantry
      72nd New York Infantry
      73rd New York Infantry
      74th New York Infantry
    Third Brigade: Colonel Joseph B. Carr
      5th New Jersey Infantry
      6th New Jersey Infantry
      7th New Jersey Infantry
      8th New Jersey Infantry
      2nd New York Infantry
    Artillery:
      Battery D, 1st New York Light Artillery
      4th New York Light Artillery
      Battery H, 1st United States Light Artillery
  THIRD DIVISION: Brigadier General Philip Kearny
    First Brigade: Brigadier General John C. Robinson
      20th Indiana Infantry
      87th New York Infantry
      57th Pennsylvania Infantry
      63rd Pennsylvania Infantry
      105th Pennsylvania Infantry
    Second Brigade: Brigadier General David B. Birney
      3rd Maine Infantry
      4th Maine Infantry
      38th New York Infantry
      40th New York Infantry
      101st New York Infantry
    Third Brigade: Brigadier General Hiram G. Berry
      2nd Michigan Infantry
      3rd Michigan Infantry
      5th Michigan Infantry
      1st New York Infantry
      37th New York Infantry
    Artillery:
      Battery E. 1st Rhode Island Light Artillery
      Battery G, 1st United States Light Artillery
    Reserve Artillery:
      6th New York Light Artillery
      2nd New Jersey Light Artillery
      Battery K, 4th United States Light Artillery

Fourth Corps: Brigadier General Erasmus D. Keyes
8th Pennsylvania Cavalry
  FIRST DIVISION: Brigadier General Darius N. Couch
    First Brigade: Brigadier General Albion P. Howe
      55th New York Infantry
      62nd New York Infantry
      93rd Pennsylvania Infantry
      98th Pennsylvania Infantry
      102nd Pennsylvania Infantry
    Second Brigade: Brigadier General John J. Ambercrombie
      65th New York Infantry
      67th New York Infantry
      23rd Pennsylvania Infantry
      31st Pennsylvania Infantry
      61st Pennsylvania Infantry
    Third Brigade: Brigadier General Innis N. Palmer
      7th Massachusetts Infantry
      10th Massachusetts Infantry
      36th New York Infantry
      2nd Rhode Island Infantry
    Artillery:
      Battery C, 1st Pennsylvania Light Artillery

Battery D, 1st Pennsylvania Light Artillery

SECOND DIVISION: Brigadier General John J. Peck
  First Brigade: Brigadier General Henry M. Naglee
    11th Maine Infantry
    56th New York Infantry
    100th New York Infantry
    52nd Pennsylvania Infantry
    104th Pennsylvania Infantry
  Second Brigade: Brigadier General Henry W. Wessells
    81st New York Infantry
    85th New York Infantry
    92nd New York Infantry
    96th New York Infantry
    98th New York Infantry
    85th Pennsylvania Infantry
    101st Pennsylvania Infantry
  Artillery:
    Battery H, 1st New York Light Artillery
    2nd New York Light Artillery
  Reserve Artillery
    8th New York Light Artillery
    Battery E, 1st Pennsylvania Light Artillery
    Battery M, 5th United States Light Artillery

Fifth Corps: Brigadier General Fitz-John Porter
8th Illinois Cavalry
  First Division: Brigadier General George W. Morell
    First Brigade: Brigadier General John H. Martindale
      2nd Maine Infantry
      18th Massachusetts Infantry
      22nd Massachusetts Infantry
      1st Michigan Infantry
      13th New York Infantry
      25th New York Infantry
      2nd Company, Massachusetts Sharpshooters
    Second Brigade: Brigadier General Charles Griffin
      9th Massachusetts Infantry
      4th Michigan Infantry
      14th New York Infantry
      62nd Pennsylvania Infantry
    Third Brigade: Brigadier General Daniel Butterfield
      12th New York Infantry
      17th New York Infantry
      44th New York Infantry
      16th Michigan Infantry
      83rd Pennsylvania Infantry
      Brady's Company, Michigan Sharpshooters
    Artillery:
      3rd Massachusetts Light Artillery
      5th Massachusetts Light Artillery
      Battery C, 1st Rhode Island Light Artillery
      Battery D, 5th United States Light Artillery
    Sharpshooters: Colonel Hiram Berdan
      1st United States Sharpshooters

Second Division: Brigadier General George Sykes
  First Brigade: Colonel Robert C. Buchanan
    3rd United States Infantry
    4th United States Infantry
    12th United States Infantry
    14th United States Infantry
  Second Brigade: Lieutenant Colonel William Chapman
    2nd United States Infantry
    6th United States Infantry
    10th United States Infantry
    11th United States Infantry
    17th United States Infantry
  Third Brigade: Colonel Gouvernor K. Warren
    5th New York Infantry
    10th New York Infantry
  Artillery:
    Battery L, 3rd United States Light Artillery
    Battery M, 3rd United States Light Artillery
    Battery I, 5th United States Light Artillery

Third Division: Brigadier General George A. McCall
  First Brigade: Brigadier General John F. Reynolds
    1st Pennsylvania Reserve Infantry
    2nd Pennsylvania Reserve Infantry
    5th Pennsylvania Reserve Infantry
    8th Pennsylvania Reserve Infantry
    13th Pennsylvania Reserve Infantry
  Second Brigade: Brigadier General George G. Meade
    3rd Pennsylvania Reserve Infantry
    4th Pennsylvania Reserve Infantry
    7th Pennsylvania Reserve Infantry
    11th Pennsylvania Reserve Infantry
  Third Brigade: Brigadier General Truman Seymour

6th Pennsylvania Reserve Infantry
9th Pennsylvania Reserve Infantry
10th Pennsylvania Reserve Infantry
12th Pennsylvania Reserve Infantry
Artillery:
  Battery A, 1st Pennsylvania Light Artillery
  Battery B, 1st Pennsylvania Light Artillery
  Battery G, 1st Pennsylvania Light Artillery
  Battery C, 5th United States Light Artillery
Artillery Reserve: Colonel Henry Hunt
First Brigade: Horse Artillery: Lieutenant Colonel William Hays
  Battery A, 2nd United States Light Artillery
  Battery B, 2nd United States Light Artillery
  Battery L, 2nd United States Light Artillery
  Battery M, 2nd United States Light Artillery
  Battery C, 3rd United States Light Artillery
  Battery G, 3rd United States Light Artillery
Second Brigade: Lieutenant Colonel George W. Getty
  Battery E, 1st United States Light Artillery
  Battery G, 1st United States Light Artillery
  Battery K, 1st United States Light Artillery
  Battery G, 4th United States Light Artillery
  Battery A, 5th United States Light Artillery
  Battery K, 5th United States Light Artillery
Third Brigade: Major Albert Arndt
  Battery A, 1st Battalion New York Light Artillery
  Battery B, 1st Battalion New York Light Artillery
  Battery C, 1st Battalion New York Light Artillery
  Battery D, 1st Battalion New York Light Artillery
Fourth Brigade: Major Edward R. Petherbridge
  Battery A, Maryland Light Artillery
  Battery B, Maryland Light Artillery
Fifth Brigade: Captain J. Howard Carlisle
  5th New York Light Artillery
  Battery E, 2nd United States Light Artillery
  Battery F, 3rd United States Light Artillery
  Battery K, 3rd United States Light Artillery
Siege Train:
  1st Connecticut Heavy Artillery

Sixth Corps: Brigadier General William B. Franklin
1st New York Cavalry
  FIRST DIVISION: Brigadier General Henry W. Slocum
    First Brigade: Brigadier General George W. Taylor
      1st New Jersey Infantry
      2nd New Jersey Infantry
      3rd New Jersey Infantry
      4th New Jersey Infantry
    Second Brigade: Colonel Joseph J. Bartlett
      5th Maine Infantry
      16th New York Infantry
      27th New York Infantry
      96th Pennsylvania Infantry
    Third Brigade: Brigadier General John Newton
      18th New York Infantry
      31st New York Infantry
      32nd New York Infantry
      95th Pennsylvania Infantry
    Artillery:
      1st Massachusetts Light Artillery
      1st New Jersey Light Artillery
      Battery D, 2nd United States Light Artillery
  SECOND DIVISION: Brigadier General William F. Smith
    First Brigade: Brigadier General Winfield S. Hancock
      6th Maine Infantry
      43rd New York Infantry
      49th Pennsylvania Infantry
      5th Wisconsin Infantry
    Second Brigade: Brigadier General W.T.H. Brooks
      2nd Vermont Infantry
      3rd Vermont Infantry
      4th Vermont Infantry
      5th Vermont Infantry
      6th Vermont Infantry
    Third Brigade: Brigadier General John W. Davidson
      7th Maine Infantry

20th New York Infantry
33rd New York Infantry
49th New York Infantry
77th New York Infantry
Artillery:
  Battery E, 1st New York Light Artillery
  3rd New York Light Artillery
  Battery F, 5th United States Light Artillery
Cavalry:
  Companies I and K, 5th Pennsylvania Cavalry
  Reserve Cavalry: Brigadier General P. St. George Cooke
    6th Pennsylvania Cavalry
    5th United States Cavalry (3 companies)
    1st United States Cavalry (4 companies
    6th United States Cavalry

Note: Effective force for the Union army was 105,445 troops of all arms.

Army of Northern Virginia: General Joseph E. Johnston/ General Robert E. Lee

Jackson's Command: Major General Thomas J. Jackson
2nd Virginia Cavalry
  WHITING'S DIVISION: Brigadier General William H.C. Whiting
    First Brigade: Brigadier General John B. Hood
      18th Georgia Infantry
      1st Texas Infantry
      4th Texas Infantry
      5th Texas Infantry
    Third Brigade: Colonel Evander M. Law
      4th Alabama Infantry
      2nd Mississippi Infantry
      11th Mississippi Infantry
      6th North Carolina Infantry
    Artillery:
      Virginia Battery (Staunton Artillery)
      North Carolina Battery (Rowan Artillery)

  JACKSON'S DIVISION
    First Brigade: Brigadier General Charles S. Winder
      2nd Virginia Infantry
      4th Virginia Infantry
      5th Virginia Infantry
      27th Virginia Infantry
      33rd Virginia Infantry
    Artillery:
      Virginia Battery (Allegheny Artillery)
      Virginia Battery (Rockbridge Artillery)
    Second Brigade: Brigadier General J. R. Jones
      21st Virginia Infantry
      42nd Virginia Infantry
      48th Virginia Infantry
      1st Virginia Irish Battalion
    Artillery:
      Virginia Battery (Hampden Artillery)
    Third Brigade: Colonel S.V. Fulkerson
      10th Virginia Infantry
      23rd Virginia Infantry
      37th Virginia Infantry
    Artillery:
      Virginia Battery (Danville Artillery)
    Fourth Brigade: Brigadier General Alexander R. Lawton
      13th Georgia Infantry
      26th Georgia Infantry
      31st Georgia Infantry
      38th Georgia Infantry
      60th Georgia Infantry
      61st Georgia Infantry

EWELL'S DIVISION: Major General Richard S. Ewell
  Fourth Brigade: Brigadier General Arnold Elzey
    12th Georgia Infantry
    13th Virginia Infantry
    25th Virginia Infantry
    31st Virginia Infantry
    44th Virginia Infantry
    52nd Virginia Infantry
    58th Virginia Infantry
  Seventh Brigade: Brigadier General Isaac R. Trimble
    15th Alabama Infantry
    21st Georgia Infantry
    16th Mississippi Infantry
    21st North Carolina Infantry
    1st North Carolina Sharpshooter Battalion
  Artillery:
    Courtney's Virginia Battery
  Eighth Brigade: Brigadier General Richard Taylor
    6th Louisiana Infantry
    7th Louisiana Infantry
    8th Louisiana Infantry
    9th Louisiana Infantry
    1st Louisiana Special Battalion
  Artillery:
    Virginia Battery (Charlottesville Artillery
Maryland Line

1st Maryland Infantry
  Baltimore Battery, Maryland Light
    Artillery
HILL'S DIVISION: Major General Daniel H. Hill
  First Brigade: Brigadier General Robert
    E. Rhodes
    3rd Alabama Infantry
    5th Alabama Infantry
    6th Alabama Infantry
    12th Alabama Infantry
    26th Alabama Infantry
  Artillery:
    Virginia Battery (King William
      Artillery)
  Second Brigade: Brigadier General
    George B. Anderson
    2nd North Carolina Infantry
    4th North Carolina Infantry
    14th North Carolina Infantry
    30th North Carolina Infantry
  Artillery:
    Alabama Light Artillery (Hardaway's
      Battery)
  Third Brigade: Brigadier General Samuel
    Garland Jr.
    5th North Carolina
    12th North Carolina
    13th North Carolina Infantry
    20th North Carolina Infantry
    23rd North Carolina Infantry
  Artillery:
    Alabama Battery (Jeff Davis Artillery)
  Fourth Brigade: Colonel Alfred H.
    Colquitt
    13th Alabama Infantry
    6th Georgia Infantry
    23rd Georgia Infantry
    27th Georgia Infantry
    28th Georgia Infantry
  Fifth Brigade: Brigadier General Roswell
    S. Ripley
    44th Georgia Infantry
    48th Georgia Infantry
    1st North Carolina Infantry
    3rd North Carolina Infantry
  Artillery:
    Virginia Battery (Hanover Artillery)
    Jones' Battalion: Major Hillary P. Jones
      Clark's Virginia Battery
      Virginia Battery (Orange Artillery)
      Rhett's South Carolina Battery

Magruder's Command: Major General
  John B. Magruder
  JONES' DIVISION: Brigadier General David
    R. Jones

  First Brigade: Brigadier General Robert
    Toombs
    2nd Georgia Infantry
    15th Georgia Infantry
    17th Georgia Infantry
    20th Georgia Infantry
  Third Brigade: Colonel George T.
    Anderson
    1st Georgia Regulars
    7th Georgia Infantry
    8th Georgia Infantry
    9th Georgia Infantry
    11th Georgia Infantry
  Artillery:
    Virginia Battery (Wise Artillery)
    South Carolina Battery (Washington
      Artillery)
    Virginia Battery (Madison Artillery)
    Dabney's Virginia Battery
MCLAW DIVISION: Major General Lafayette
  McLaws
  First Brigade: Brigadier General Paul J.
    Semmes
    10th Georgia Infantry
    53rd Georgia Infantry
    5th Louisiana Infantry
    10th Louisiana Infantry
    15th Virginia Infantry
    32nd Virginia Infantry
  Artillery:
    Manly's North Carolina Battery
  Fourth Brigade: Brigadier General
    Joseph B. Kershaw
    2nd South Carolina Infantry
    3rd South Carolina Infantry
    7th South Carolina Infantry
    8th South Carolina Infantry
  Artillery:
    Virginia Battery (Alexandria Artillery)
MAGRUDER'S DIVISION
  Second Brigade: Brigadier General
    Howell Cobb
    16th Georgia Infantry
    24th Georgia Infantry
    Cobb's Georgia Legion
    2nd Louisiana Infantry
    15th North Carolina Infantry
  Artillery:
    Georgia Battery (Troup Artillery)
  Third Brigade: Brigadier General
    Richard Griffith
    13th Mississippi Infantry
    17th Mississippi Infantry
    18th Mississippi Infantry
    21st Mississippi Infantry

Artillery:
   Virginia Battery (1st Richmond Howitzers)
Artillery Reserve: Lieutenant Colonel Stephen D. Lee
   Georgia Battery (Pulaski Artillery)
   Virginia Battery (James City Artillery)
   Virginia Battery (Magruder Artillery)

LONGSTREET'S DIVISION: Major General James P. Longstreet
   First Brigade: Brigadier General James L. Kemper
      7th Virginia Infantry
      11th Virginia Infantry
      17th Virginia Infantry
      24th Virginia Infantry
   Artillery:
      Virginia Battery (Loudon Artillery)
   Second Brigade: Brigadier General Richard H. Anderson
      2nd South Carolina Rifles
      4th South Carolina Battalion
      5th South Carolina Infantry
      6th South Carolina Infantry
      Palmetto South Carolina Sharpshooters
   Third Brigade: Brigadier General George E. Pickett
      8th Virginia Infantry
      18th Virginia Infantry
      19th Virginia Infantry
      28th Virginia Infantry
      56th Virginia Infantry
   Fourth Brigade: Brigadier General Cadmus M. Wilcox
      8th Alabama Infantry
      9th Alabama Infantry
      10th Alabama Infantry
      11th Alabama Infantry
   Artillery:
      Virginia Battery (Thomas Artillery)
   Fifth Brigade: Brigadier General Roger A. Pryor
      14th Alabama Infantry
      2nd Florida Infantry
      14th Louisiana Infantry
      1st Louisiana Battalion
      3rd Virginia Infantry
   Artillery:
      Louisiana Battery (Donaldsonville Artillery)
   Sixth Brigade: Brigadier General Winfield S. Featherston
      12th Mississippi Infantry
      19th Mississippi Infantry
      2nd Mississippi Battalion

Artillery:
   Virginia Battery (3rd Richmond Howitzers)
Artillery Reserve:
   Louisiana Battery (Washington Artillery)
   Virginia Battery (Lynchburg Artillery)
   Virginia Battery (Dixie Artillery)

HUGER'S DIVISION: Major General Benjamin Huger
   Second Brigade: Brigadier General William Mahone
      6th Virginia Infantry
      12th Virginia Infantry
      16th Virginia Infantry
      41st Virginia Infantry
      49th Virginia Infantry
   Artillery:
      Virginia Battery (Portsmouth Artillery)
      Moorman's Virginia Battery
   Third Brigade: Brigadier General Ambrose R. Wright
      44th Alabama Infantry
      3rd Georgia Infantry
      22nd Georgia Infantry
      1st Louisiana Infantry
   Artillery:
      Huger's Virginia Battery
   Fourth Brigade: Brigadier General Lewis A. Armistead
      9th Virginia Infantry
      14th Virginia Infantry
      38th Virginia Infantry
      53rd Virginia Infantry
      57th Virginia Infantry
      5th Virginia Battalion
   Artillery:
      Virginia Battery (Fauquier Artillery)
      Turner's Virginia Battery

HILL'S DIVISION: Major General Ambrose P. Hill
   First Brigade: Brigadier General Charles W. Field
      40th Virginia Infantry
      47th Virginia Infantry
      55th Virginia Infantry
      60th Virginia Infantry
   Second Brigade: Brigadier General Maxey Gregg
      1st South Carolina Infantry
      1st South Carolina Rifles
      12th South Carolina Infantry
      13th South Carolina Infantry
      14th South Carolina Infantry
   Third Brigade: Brigadier General Joseph R. Anderson

14th Georgia Infantry
35th Georgia Infantry
45th Georgia Infantry
49th Georgia Infantry
3rd Louisiana Battalion
Fourth Brigade: Brigadier General L. O'B. Branch
7th North Carolina Infantry
18th North Carolina Infantry
28th North Carolina Infantry
33rd North Carolina Infantry
37th North Carolina Infantry
Fifth Brigade: Brigadier General James J. Archer
5th Alabama Infantry
19th Georgia Infantry
1st Tennessee Infantry
7th Tennessee Infantry
14th Tennessee Infantry
Sixth Brigade: Brigadier General William D. Pender
2nd Arkansas Infantry Battalion
16th North Carolina Infantry
22nd North Carolina Infantry
34th North Carolina Infantry
38th North Carolina Infantry
22nd Virginia Infantry Battalion
Artillery:
Snowden's Maryland Battery
South Carolina Battery (German Artillery)
Virginia Battery (Fredericksburg Artillery)
Crenshaw's Virginia Battery
Virginia Battery (Letcher Artillery)
Johnson's Virginia Battery
South Carolina Battery (Pee Dee Artillery)
Virginia Battery (Purcell Artillery)

HOLMES' DIVISION: Major General Theophilus H. Holmes
Second Brigade: Brigadier General Robert Ransom
24th North Carolina Infantry
25th North Carolina Infantry
26th North Carolina Infantry
35th North Carolina Infantry
48th North Carolina Infantry
49th North Carolina Infantry
Third Brigade: Brigadier General Junius Daniel
43rd North Carolina Infantry
45th North Carolina Infantry
50th North Carolina Infantry
Burroughs' Virginia Cavalry Battalion
Fourth Brigade: Brigadier General John G. Walker
3rd Arkansas Infantry
2nd Georgia Infantry Battalion
27th North Carolina Infantry
46th North Carolina Infantry
30th Virginia Infantry
Goodwyn's Virginia Cavalry Company
Artillery:
Branch's Virginia Battery
Brem's North Carolina Battery
French's Virginia Battery
Graham's Virginia Battery
Wise's Command (attached to Holmes Division): Brigadier General Henry A. Wise
26th Virginia Infantry
46th Virginia Infantry
Artillery:
Andrews' Virginia Battery
Rives' Virginia Battery

RESERVE ARTILLERY: Brigadier General William N. Pendleton
1st Virginia Artillery
Williamsburg Artillery
Richmond Fayette Artillery
1st Battalion Sumter Artillery
Blackshear's Georgia Battery
Lane's Georgia Battery
Price's Georgia Battery
Ross's Georgia Battery
Hamilton's Georgia Battery
Virginia Battery (Fluvanna Artillery)
Milledge's Georgia Battery
Virginia Battery (Ashland Artillery)
Virginia Battery (Amherst Artillery)
Virginia Battery (Morris Artillery)

CAVALRY: Brigadier General James E.B. Stuart
1st North Carolina Cavalry
1st Virginia Cavalry
3rd Virginia Cavalry
4th Virginia Cavalry
5th Virginia Cavalry
9th Virginia Cavalry
10th Virginia Cavalry
Cobb's Georgia Legion Cavalry
15th Virginia Cavalry Battalion
Hampton Legion (squadron)
Jeff Davis Legion Cavalry
Stuart Horse Artillery

Note: Official returns are not available, but the effective force of the Confederate army was probably between 80,000 and 90,000 men.[1]

Appendix 4: Casualties of the Opposing Armies in the Peninsula Campaign*

Union Army

Headquarters Engineer Brigade
2 wounded, 9 missing, total 11

Second Corps
FIRST DIVISION
First Brigade: 61 killed, 356 wounded, 137 missing, total 554
Second Brigade: 24 killed, 227 wounded, 232 missing, total 493
Third Brigade: 3 killed, 43 wounded, 162 missing, total 208
Artillery: 19 wounded, 10 missing, total 29
SECOND DIVISION
First Brigade: 12 killed, 32 wounded, 152 missing, total 246
Second Brigade: 40 killed, 193 wounded, 172 missing, total 405
Third Brigade: 51 killed, 262 wounded, 163 missing, total 466
Artillery: 12 wounded, 4 missing, total 16
Reserve Artillery: 6 wounded, 2 missing, total 8

Third Corps
SECOND DIVISION
First Brigade: 2 killed, 214 wounded, 116 missing, total 355
Second Brigade: 26 killed, 173 wounded, 103 missing, total 308
Third Brigade: 4 killed, 24 wounded, 31 missing, total 59
Artillery: 1 wounded, 7 missing, total 8
THIRD DIVISION
First Brigade: 56 killed, 310 wounded, 161 missing, total 527
Second Brigade: 10 killed, 53 wounded, 185 missing, total 248
Third Brigade: 28 killed, 225 wounded, 176 missing, total 429
Artillery: 2 killed, 16 wounded, 5 missing, total 23
Reserve Artillery: 1 killed, 3 wounded, 1 missing, total 5

Fourth Corps
FIRST DIVISION
First Brigade: 27 killed, 148 wounded, 33 missing, total 208
Second Brigade: 19 killed, 168 wounded, 16 missing, total 203
Third Brigade: 23 killed, 193 wounded, 48 missing, total 265
SECOND DIVISION
First Brigade: 0
Second Brigade: 1 killed, 2 wounded, 121 missing, total 124
Artillery: 0
Reserve Artillery: 0

Fifth Corps
Headquarters Cavalry: 3 killed, 9 wounded, 3 missing, total 15
FIRST DIVISION
First Brigade: 114 killed, 443 wounded, 329 missing, total 886
Second Brigade: 182 Killed, 772 wounded, 199 missing, total 1153
Third Brigade: 166 killed, 546 wounded, 269 missing, total 981

Battles and Leaders, volume 2, pages 313–317.

Artillery: 9 killed, 38 wounded, 9 missing, total 56
Sharpshooters: 8 killed, 35 wounded, 13 missing, total 56
SECOND DIVISION
First Brigade: 89 killed, 297 wounded, 181 missing, total 567
Second Brigade: 38 killed, 228 wounded, 93 missing, total 359
Third Brigade: 47 killed, 154 wounded, 85 missing, total 286
Artillery: 4 killed, 24 wounded, 4 missing, total 32
THIRD DIVISION
First Brigade: 109 killed, 497 wounded, 403 missing, total 1009
Second Brigade: 107 killed, 284 wounded, 1009 missing, total 1400
Third Brigade: 78 Killed, 339 wounded, 142 missing, total 559
Artillery: 21 killed, 42 wounded, 11 missing, total 74
Cavalry: 2 killed, 13 wounded, 7 missing, total 22
Artillery Reserve: 13 killed, 71 wounded, 42 missing, total 126

Sixth Corps
FIRST DIVISION
First Brigade: 116 killed, 380 wounded, 582 missing, total 1078
Second Brigade: 69 killed, 409 wounded, 68 missing, total 546
Third Brigade: 40 killed, 279 wounded, 114 missing, total 433
Artillery: 1 killed, 13 wounded, 4 missing, total 18
SECOND DIVISION
First Brigade: 9 killed, 93 wounded, 98 missing, total 200
Second Brigade: 45 killed, 271 wounded, 139 missing, total 455
Third Brigade: 12 killed, 23 wounded, 87 missing, total 122
Artillery: 3 killed, 4 wounded, 15 missing, total 22
Cavalry: 1 killed, total 1
CAVALRY RESERVE
First Brigade: no losses
Second Brigade: 14 killed, 55 wounded, 85 missing, total 154

Confederate Army

Jackson's Command
WHITING'S DIVISION
First Brigade: 92 killed, 526 wounded, 5 missing, total 623
Third Brigade: 66 killed, 482 wounded, 5 missing, total 553
Artillery: 16 wounded, total 16
JACKSON'S DIVISION
First Brigade: 30 killed 149 wounded, total 179
Second Brigade: 1 killed, 15 wounded, total 16
Third Brigade: 2 killed, 15 wounded, 1 missing, total 18
Fourth Brigade: 115 killed, 452 wounded, total 567
EWELL'S DIVISION
Fourth Brigade: 52 killed, 229 wounded, 3 missing, total 284
Seventh Brigade: 71 killed, 280 wounded, 49 missing, total 400
Eighth Brigade: 56 killed, 236 wounded, total 292
Maryland Line: 3 killed, 8 wounded, total 11
D.H. HILL'S DIVISION
First Brigade: 112 killed, 458 wounded, total 570
Second Brigade: 159 killed, 704 wounded, total 863
Third Brigade: 192 killed, 637 wounded, 15 missing, total 844
Fourth Brigade: 75 killed, 474 wounded, 5 missing, total 554
Fifth Brigade: 171 killed, 707 wounded, 30 missing, total 908

Magruder's Command
JONES' DIVISION
First Brigade: 44 killed, 380 wounded, 6 missing, total 430
Third Brigade: 64 killed, 327 wounded, 46 missing, total 437
Artillery: 3 killed, 11 wounded, total 14
MCLAW'S DIVISION
First Brigade: 31 killed, 121 wounded, 61 missing, total 215
Fourth Brigade: 70 killed, 349 wounded, 38 missing, total 457
MAGRUDER'S DIVISION
Second Brigade: 66 killed, 347 wounded, 2 missing, total 415
Third Brigade: 91 killed, 434 wounded, total 525
Artillery: no losses
LONGSTREET'S DIVISION
First Brigade: 44 killed, 205 wounded, 165 missing, total 414

Second Brigade: 136 killed, 638 wounded, 13 missing, total 787
Third Brigade: 72 killed, 563 wounded, 19 missing, total 654
Fourth Brigade: 229 killed, 806 wounded, 20 missing, total 1055
Fifth Brigade: 179 killed, 681 wounded, 11 missing, total 862
Sixth Brigade: 115 killed, 543 wounded, 9 missing, total 667

HUGER'S DIVISION
Second Brigade: 66 killed, 274 wounded, 124 missing, total 464
Third Brigade: 93 killed, 483 wounded, 90 missing, total 606
Fourth Brigade: 51 killed, 281 wounded, 69 missing, total 401

A.P. HILL'S DIVISION
First Brigade: 78 killed, 500 wounded, 2 missing, total 580
Second Brigade: 152 killed, 773 wounded, 4 missing, total 929
Third Brigade: 62 killed, 300 wounded, 2 missing, total 364
Fourth Brigade: 105 killed, 706 wounded, 28 missing, total 839
Fifth Brigade: 92 killed, 443 wounded, total 535
Sixth Brigade: 130 killed, 692 wounded, total 822
Artillery: 12 killed, 96 wounded, total 108

HOLMES' DIVISION
Second Brigade: 95 killed, 453 wounded, 76 missing, total 624
Third Brigade: 2 killed, 22 wounded, total 24
Fourth Brigade: 12 wounded, total 12
Artillery: 17 wounded, total 17

Wise's Command: no losses
Reserve Artillery: 1 wounded, total 1
Jones' Battalion: 10 killed, 35 wounded, total 45
Cavalry: 5 killed, 26 wounded, 40 missing, total 71

Appendix 5.
Medal of Honor Winners at Fair Oaks*

Thomas T. Fallon
Private in Company K, 37th New York Infantry. Though Fallon was disabled, and thus excused from duty, he shouldered his musket and took part in the battle.

Alexander A. Foreman
Corporal in Company E, 7th Michigan Infantry. Although severely wounded, Foreman maintained his place in the line and continued fighting until he collapsed from loss of blood and had to be carried from the field.

Samuel J. French
Private in Company E, 7th Michigan Infantry. Continued fighting after being severely wounded, until he fainted from loss of blood and had to be carried from the field.

Gabriel Grant
Surgeon, United States Volunteers. Displayed exceptional gallantry by going onto the field to rescue wounded officers and enlisted men, continually exposing himself to heavy fire from the enemy.

Frank W. Haskell
Sergeant Major of the 3rd Maine Infantry. When all of the company officers in the left wing of his regiment were killed or wounded, Sergeant Haskell assumed command of the wing and led it gallantly in attacking the Confederates.

Oliver O. Howard
Brigadier General, United States Volunteers. Led the 61st New York Infantry in a gallant charge that drove the enemy from that portion of the field. In the course of the charge, Howard received two wounds in the right arm, necessitating its amputation.

James R. O'Bierne
Captain of Company C, 37th New York Infantry. Displayed exceptional gallantry in holding his portion of the line against the Confederate attack, maintaining his position until ordered to retire.

Hiram W. Purcell
Sergeant in Company C, 104th Pennsylvania Infantry. Displayed conspicuous gallantry in saving the regimental colors from capture by the enemy during the retreat of the regiment.

William R. Shafter
First Lieutenant of Company I, 7th Michigan Infantry. While engaged in bridge construction, Shafter left the bridge to participate in the charge of his regiment against the enemy. In this charge, he was severely wounded. He concealed his wound so as not to be sent to the rear, and fought again on the following day. He continued to hide his wound for three more days, until the wounded had been evacuated, in order that he might remain with his company.

*Robert P. Broadwater, *Civil War Medal of Honor Recipients: A Complete Illustrated Record* (Jefferson, NC: McFarland, 2007).

Appendix 6.
"Kearney at Fair Oaks"*

So the soldierly legend is still on his journey—
   That story of Kearney who knew not to yield!
'Twas the day when Jameson, fierce Berry and Birney,
   Against twenty thousand he rallied the field.
When the red volleys poured, where the clamor rose highest,
   Where the dead lay in clumps through the dwarf oak and pine,
Where the aim from the thicket was surest and righest—
   No charge like Phil Kearney's along the whole line.

When the battle went ill, and the bravest were solemn,
   Near the dark Seven Pines, where we still held our ground,
He rode down the length of the withering column,
   And his heart at our war-cry leaped up with a bound.
He snuffed, like his charger, the wind of the powder,
   His sword waved us on and we answered the sign;
Loud our cheers as we rushed, but his laugh rang the louder;
   "There's the devil's own fun boys, along the whole line."

How he strode his brown steed! How we saw his blade brighten
   In the one hand still left, the reins in his teeth,
He laughed like a boy when the holidays heighten,
   But a soldier's glance shot from his visor beneath!
Up came the reserves to the melee infernal,
   Asking where to go in—through the clearing or pine?
"O, anywhere! Forward! Tis all the same Colonel;
   You'll find lovely fighting along the whole line."

O, evil the black shroud of night at Chantilly,
   That hid him from sight of his brave men and tried!
Foul, foul sped the bullet that clipped the white lily,
   The flower of our knighthood, the whole army's pride!
Yet we dream that he still: in the shadowy region
   Where the dead form their ranks at the wan drummer's sign—
Rides on, as of old, down the length of this legion,
   And the word is still FORWARD! along the whole line.

—Edmund Clarence Stedman

*Gilbert Adams Hays, *Under the Red Patch: Story of the Sixty Third Regiment Pennsylvania Volunteers 1861–1864* (Pittsburgh: Regimental Association, 1908), page 85. The misspelling of Kearny's name is in the original.

Chapter Notes

Introduction

1. Price, 67.
2. Luther Dickey, *History of the 103rd Regiment Veteran Volunteer Infantry, 1861–1865* (Chicago: Dickey, 1910).

Chapter One

1. Rafuse, 115.
2. Ezra J. Warner, *Generals in Blue*, 290–291.
3. Ibid., 291.
4. Donald H. Bailey, *Forward to Richmond*, 17.
5. *War of the Rebellion: Official Records of the Union and Confederate Armies*, Series 1, Vol. 5 (Washington, DC: Government Printing Office, 1882), 9–11.
6. Glazier, 290.
7. Cullen, 21.
8. Russell H. Beatie, *Army of the Potomac: McClellan Takes Command, September 1861–February 1862* (Cambridge, MA: Da Capo, 2004), 382.
9. George B. McClellan, *McClellan's Own Story*, 231–235.
10. *Washington Evening Star*, February 18, 1862.
11. *New York Tribune*, February 19, 1862.
12. Meade, vol. 1, 247.
13. Randall and Donald, 283–284.
14. Sandburg, 273; Perret, 328.
15. *The Congressional Globe*, 324–334.
16. Pease and Randall, vol. 1, 515–516.
17. Randall and Donald, 282–283.
18. *Report of the Joint Committee on the Conduct of the War*, vol. 2, 427–429; Beale, vol. 1, 229.

Chapter Two

1. David Herbert Donald, *Lincoln*, 340.
2. George B. McClellan, *McClellan's Own Story*, 195–196; Johnson and Buel, vol. 2, 166.
3. Journal entry of March 8, 1862, Samuel Peter Heintzelman Papers, Library of Congress, Washington, DC; Hassler, 61–62.
4. Keyes, 438; Richardson, vol. 6, 110; McClellan, *McClellan's Own Story*, 222.
5. Lt. Col. Robert N. Scott, series 1, vol. 14, 57–58.
6. Gilmore, 228.
7. Welles, vol. 1, 62–65.
8. John Sedgwick, vol. 1, 41; Meade, vol. 1, 259; Stephen W. Sears, *The Civil War Papers of George B. McClellan*, 202.
9. Beale, 239.
10. Basler, vol. 5, 155.
11. Marcy to McClellan, March 11, 1862, McClellan Papers, Scott Memorial Library, Thomas Jefferson University, Philadelphia, PA; Sears, *The Civil War Papers of George B. McClellan*, 201, 207.
12. Halleck to McClellan, February 24, 1862, McClellan Papers.
13. Thomas and Hyman, 175.
14. Ibid., 183.
15. Julian, 205.
16. Hassler, 70.
17. Stanton to McClellan, March 13, 1862, McClellan Papers.
18. Richardson, vol. 6, 111.
19. Hitchcock to Mary Mann, March 15, 1862, Ethan Allen Hitchcock Papers, Library of Congress, Washington, DC.
20. McClellan, *McClellan's Own Story*, 237–238.
21. William Swinton, 100.
22. Address dated March 14, 1862, McClellan Papers.
23. Acken, 56.
24. John G. Adams, 25.
25. McDermott, 10.
26. Brewer, 20.
27. Wert, *The Sword of Lincoln*, 66.
28. Hassler, 75.
29. Long, series 1, vol. 7, 210.
30. McClellan to Stanton, March 19, 1862, and McClellan to Stanton March 20, 1862, McClellan Papers.
31. Gibbs to McClellan, March 13, 1862, McClellan Papers.
32. Hassler, 78.
33. *Official Records*, series 1, vol. 12, 107.
34. Hassler, 83; *Official Records*, series 1, vol. 11, pt. 3, 60–61.
35. *Report of the Joint Committee on The Conduct of the War*, vol. 1, 305.
36. Franklin to McClellan, April 7, 1862, McClellan Papers.

37. Warner, *Generals in Blue*, 53–54; Thomas and Hyman, 185–186, 189.
38. Pease and Randall, vol. 1, 537–539.
39. Thayer, vol. 1, 39.
40. *Battles and Leaders*, vol. 2, 170–171.

Chapter Three

1. Sears, *Civil War Papers of George McClellan*, 218–219.
2. Johnston, 101–102.
3. *Official Records*, series 1, vol. 9, 41.
4. Johnston, 113.
5. William C. Davis, 412–413.
6. Sears, *Civil War Papers of George B. McClellan*, 228.
7. *Official Records*, series 1, vol. 5, 10.
8. McClellan, *McClellan's Own Story*, 262–263.
9. Sears, *Civil War Papers of George B. McClellan*, 230.
10. Hewitt, vol. 2, 30.
11. *Official Records*, series 1, vol. 11, pt. 1, 13–14.
12. Hassler, 89.
13. Cozzens and Girardi, 96.
14. Ronald H. Bailey, *Forward to Richmond*, 94.
15. Fisk and Blake, 23.
16. Johnston, 113.
17. Catton, *Terrible Swift Sword*, 75–76.
18. Johnston, 109.
19. Ibid., 110.
20. Ibid.
21. Bailey, 146–151.
22. Bailey, 102; Cozzens and Girardi, 98–99.
23. G.G. Benedict, *Vermont In The Civil War, A History of the Part Taken by the Vermont Soldiers and Sailors in the War for the Union, 1861–65* (Burlington, VT: The Free Press Association, 1886), 163.
24. Ervin L. Jordan Jr., *Black Confederates and Afro-Yankees in Civil War Virginia* (Charlottesville: University Press of Virginia, 1995), 222–223.
25. Fishel, 151.
26. *Official Records*, series 1, vol. 14, 477.
27. Lincoln to McClellan, May 1, 1862; McClellan to Lincoln, May 1, 1862, Abraham Lincoln Papers, Library of Congress, Washington, DC.
28. Forrest Little to "Father and Mother," May 2, 1862, Forrest Little collection, Rare Book and Manuscript Collection, Saint Mary's College Library, Moraga, CA.
29. Fishel, 152.
30. Ibid., 152; Willard Brown, *The Signal Corps, U.S.A. in the War of the Rebellion* (Boston: U.S. Veteran Signal Corps Association, 1896), 304.
31. Fisk and Blake, 23–24.
32. Hassler, 96.
33. Anker, 21–22, 50.
34. McDermott, 11.
35. Acken, 71.
36. J.J. Marks, 150–151.
37. Moxley Sorrell, *Recollections of a Confederate Staff Officer* (Jackson, TN: McCowat-Mercer, 1958), 60–61.
38. Burke Davis, *The Civil War: Strange & Fascinating Facts*, 56–59.
39. Randall, vol. 2, 79.
40. McClellan, *McClellan's Own Story*, 319–321.
41. Ibid., 320–321.

Chapter Four

1. McClellan, *McClellan's Own Story*, 321–322.
2. Paul D. Casdorph, *Prince John Magruder: His Life and Campaigns* (New York: John Wiley & Sons, 1996), 155.
3. Gordon, 53–54.
4. Johnston, 120, 124.
5. Hassler, 100.
6. Wert, 76.
7. Bailey, 109–110.
8. Donald, 66–67.
9. Bailey, 110–111.
10. Ibid., 111–113.
11. Tucker, 86.
12. Goodrich, 201.
13. Tucker, 87.
14. McClellan, *McClellan's Own Story*, 327–330.
15. Tucker, 89.
16. Livermore, 80–81.
17. Hays, 87–88.
18. Ibid., 89.
19. Bailey, 124–125.
20. Johnston, 126.
21. Hood, 21.
22. Dyer, 68.
23. J. Willard Brown, *The Signal Corps, U.S.A. in the War of the Rebellion* (Boston: U.S. Veteran Signal Corps Association, 1896), 306.
24. Richard W. Iobst, *The Bloody Sixth: The Sixth North Carolina Regiment Confederate States of America* (Raleigh: North Carolina Centennial Commission, 1965), 66.
25. *Battles and Leaders*, vol. 2, 276.
26. Bailey, 127.
27. Pollard, 33.
28. Gallagher, *The Richmond Campaign of 1862*, 124.
29. Howard, vol. 1, 228.
30. Sears, *The Civil War Papers of George B. McClellan*, 251.
31. Hassler, 107.
32. Cullen, 51.
33. *Official Records*, series 1, vol. 11, pt. 3, 473.
34. Dowdey and Manarin, 175.
35. Sears, *Civil War Papers of George B. McClellan*, 263.
36. *Official Records*, series 1, vol. 11, pt. 3, 164.
37. Bailey, 128.
38. Graham, 395.
39. Ibid., 396.
40. Barlow to McClellan, May 10, 1862, Samuel L. Barlow Papers, Henry E. Huntington Library, San Marino, CA.
41. Sears, *The Civil War Papers of George B. McClellan*, 262–263.
42. Heintzelman's Journal entry for May 13, 1862, Heintzelman Papers.

43. Tucker to Stanton, May 22, 1862, Edwin M. Stanton Papers, Library of Congress, Washington, DC.
44. Rafuse, 213.
45. McClellan to Ellen, May 16, 1862, McClellan Papers.
46. Hassler, 108.
47. *Report of the Joint Committee on the Conduct of the War*, part 1, 272.
48. *Official Records*, series 1, vol. 14, 176–177.
49. Stanton to McClellan, May 17, 1862, McClellan Papers.
50. *Report of the Joint Committee on the Conduct of the War 1863*, part 1, 327.
51. *Official Records*, series 1, vol. 11, pt. 3, 154–155.
52. Bailey, 133.
53. McClellan, *McClellan's Own Story*, 363.
54. *Report of the Joint Committee on the Conduct of the War 1863*, part 1, 274
55. Lincoln to McClellan, May 24, 1862, McClellan Papers.
56. McClellan to Lincoln, May 24, 1862, McClellan Papers.
57. McClellan, *McClellan's Own Story*, 375.
58. *Official Records*, series 1, vol. 18, 220–221.
59. McClellan, *McClellan's Own Story*, 367.
60. McClellan to Lincoln, May 25, 1862, Lincoln Papers.
61. Price, 67.
62. Hassler, 114.
63. *Battles and Leaders*, vol. 2, 319–320.
64. Ibid., 321–322.
65. McClellan to Stanton, May 27 and 30, 1862, McClellan Papers.
66. Hassler, 118.
67. Ibid.

Chapter Five

1. Johnston, 130–132.
2. Ibid., 133.
3. Mott, 45.
4. Hays, 94–95.
5. George Wise, *History of the Seventeenth Virginia Infantry, C.S.A.* (Baltimore, MD: Kelly, Piet, 1870), 65.
6. Webb, 102.
7. *The Story of One Regiment: The Eleventh Maine Infantry Volunteers in the War of the Rebellion* (New York: The Regimental Association, 1896), 38.
8. Bruce, 91.
9. Gary Schreckengost, "Brigadier General Silas Casey at the Battle of Seven Pines," *America's Civil War* (May 2002), 33–39.
10. Warner, *Generals in Blue*, 75.
11. Bailey, 136.
12. Konstam, 64.
13. *Official Records*, series 1, vol. 11, pt. 1, 914.
14. Ibid., 933–934.
15. Gustavus W. Smith, 164–165.
16. Ibid., 166–167.
17. *Official Records*, series 1, vol. 11, pt. 1, 933–934, 937, 942; *Battles and Leaders*, vol. 2, 228, 244; Douglas Southall Freeman, *Lee's Lieutenants*, vol. 1, 166, 235.
18. Longstreet, 93–94.
19. Bridges, 40–41.
20. *Official Records*, series 1, vol. 11, pt. 1, 961–962.
21. Howard, 322.
22. Webb, 103.
23. Hassler, 123–124.
24. Schreckengost, 33–39.
25. *Official Records*, series 1, vol. 11, pt. 1, 962–963.
26. Mott, 46.
27. *Official Records*, series 1, vol. 11, pt. 1, 921–922.
28. Broadwater, *Civil War Medal of Honor Recipients*, 162.
29. Bridges, 42–43.
30. *Official Records*, series 1, vol. 11, pt. a, 922.
31. Brock, vol. 13, 263.
32. *The Story of One Regiment*, 40.
33. Sorrell, 65.
34. Roe, 90.
35. Newell, 99; *The Berkshire Courier*.
36. Newell, 99.
37. Ibid., 100.
38. *The Berkshire Courier*, 5 June 1862.
39. *Official Records*, series 1, vol. 11, pt. 1, 888–889.
40. Mark, 143–144.
41. Bailey, 140–141; *Official Records*, series 1, vol. 11, pt. 1, 838–840, 843.
42. Gordon, 56–58; Bailey, 141.
43. Bailey, 141, 144.
44. Wise, 66.
45. Cozzens and Girardi, 67–69.
46. Ibid., 69–70.
47. Oliver Wilson Davis, 44–46.
48. Konstam, 69.
49. *History of the Twenty Third Pennsylvania Volunteer Infantry*, 47.
50. *Official Records*, series 1, vol. 11, pt. 1, 947–948.
51. Brewer, 24–25, 27–28.
52. Johnston, 136; Bailey, 145.
53. Dyer, 75.
54. *Battles and Leaders*, vol. 2, 245.
55. Iobst, 69–71; Bailey, 154.
56. Leonne M. Hudson, *The Odyssey of a Southerner: The Life and Times of Gustavus Woodson Smith* (Macon, GA: Mercer University Press, 1998), 106.
57. Konstam, 72; Bailey, 155.
58. *Official Records*, series 1, vol. 11, pt. 1, 791–792.
59. Ibid., 791.
60. Bailey, 155.
61. Johnston, 137.
62. *Battles and Leaders*, vol. 2, 246–247.
63. Henry T. Childs, "The Battle of Seven Pines," *Confederate Veteran*, vol. 20 (Jan. 1917): 20.
64. *Battles and Leaders*, vol. 2, 247.
65. D.B. Easley, "Experiences at Seven Pines," *Confederate Veteran*, vol. 37 (April 1929): 130–131.
66. Childs, 20.
67. Marks, 200.
68. McDermott, 12.
69. Cisco, 85.
70. Clement A. Evans, *Confederate Military History*,

vol. 5, *Virginia* (New York: The Blue and Grey Press, no date), 56.
 71. Wade Hampton to Mary Hampton, May 26, 1862, Hampton Family Papers, University of South Carolina, Columbia, SC.
 72. Cisco, 85.
 73. Johnston, 138–139; William C. Davis, 424.
 74. Hudson Strode, *Jefferson Davis: Confederate President* (New York: Harcourt, Brace, 1959), 254.
 75. Chinn, 42.

Chapter Six

 1. Hassler, 125.
 2. *The Story of One Regiment*, 44.
 3. Cozzens and Girardi, 71–72.
 4. Gordon, 58; the Rev. J. William Jones, vol. 1, 117–118.
 5. Howard, 242.
 6. Ibid., 240–241.
 7. Ibid., 241.
 8. Ibid.
 9. Newell, 111.
 10. Bailey, 158.
 11. Jordan, 223.
 12. Mary Chesnut, *A Diary from Dixie* (New York: Portland House, 1997), 173.
 13. Steven E. Woodworth, *Jefferson Davis and His Generals: The Failure of Confederate Command in the West* (Lawrence: University Press of Kansas, 1990), 178.
 14. Hudson, 111.
 15. Smith, *Confederate War Papers*, 182, 184–185.
 16. *Official Records*, series 1, vol. 11, pt. 1, 940.
 17. Smith, *Confederate War Papers*, 183–185.
 18. Burke Davis, *Gray Fox*, 75–76.
 19. Hill to Longstreet, Oct. 19, 1885, James Longstreet Papers, Duke University.
 20. Bailey, 158–159.
 21. Ibid., 159.
 22. Hilliard, 168.
 23. Bailey, 159.
 24. Bridges, 49.
 25. *Official Records*, series 1, vol. 11, pt. 1, 785–786.
 26. Howard, 243.
 27. *Official Records*, series 1, vol. 11, pt. 1, 782.
 28. Howard, 242.
 29. *Official Records*, series 1, col. 11, pt. 1, 782.
 30. Ibid., 982.
 31. Ibid., 782.
 32. Bailey, 159.
 33. Howard, 245.
 34. *Official Records*, series 1, vol. 11, pt. 1, 787.
 35. Ibid., 982–983.
 36. Bridges, 49.
 37. Ibid., 50.
 38. *Official Records*, series 1, vol. 11, pt. 1, 790.
 39. Howard, 246.
 40. William H. Spencer, "How I Felt in Battle and in Prison," *War Papers Read Before the Commandery of the State of Maine, Military Order of the Loyal Legion of the United States*, vol. 2 (Wilmington, NC: Broadfoot, 1992), 124–126.
 41. Ibid., 126–127.
 42. Howard, 246–247.
 43. *Official Records*, series 1, vol. 11, pt. 1, 773.
 44. Ibid.; Spencer, 129–130.
 45. Howard, 249–251.
 46. *Official Records*, series 1, vol. 11, pt. 1, 857, 863.
 47. Bailey, 165.
 48. *Official Records*, series 1, vol. 11, pt. 1, 858–859.
 49. Ibid., 856, 863.
 50. Bailey, 166.
 51. Patterson, 37.
 52. *Official Records*, series 1, vol. 11, pt. 1, 819.
 53. Swanberg, 125.
 54. Bridges, 51.
 55. Glatthaar, 123.
 56. Hudson, 115.
 57. Burke Davis, *Gray Fox*, 76–77.
 58. *History of the Nineteenth Regiment Massachusetts Volunteer Infantry 1861–1865*, 75.
 59. Haynes, *History of the Second Regiment New Hampshire Volunteers*, 66–67.
 60. Davis, William, 425.
 61. Strode, 257.
 62. Hassler, 127.

Chapter Seven

 1. *Philadelphia North American*, June 3, 1862.
 2. *New York Tribune*, June 6, 1862.
 3. Hassler, 129–130.
 4. *Official Records*, series 1, vol. 11, pt. 3, 210.
 5. Burke Davis, *Gray Fox*, 77.
 6. Newton and Simmons, 22–23.
 7. Ibid., 77–78.
 8. Ibid., 82.
 9. *Report of the Joint Committee on the Conduct of the War*, vol. 1, 633; *Official Records*, series , vol. 11, 998–1000.
 10. McClellan to Stanton, June 7, 1862, Lincoln Papers.
 11. Dowdey, 134.
 12. Ibid., 25.
 13. Robert E. Lee Jr., 416.
 14. Hassler, 132.
 15. Stanton to McClellan, June 11, 1862, McClellan Papers.
 16. Montgomery Meigs, "The Relations of President Lincoln and Secretary Stanton to the Military Commanders in the Civil War," *American Historical Review*, January, 1921, 291.
 17. McClellan, *McClellan's Own Story*, 403.
 18. Livermore, 86.
 19. Thomas, 113–125.
 20. McClellan to Stanton, June 12, 1862, Lincoln Papers.
 21. Hassler, 135.
 22. Dowdy, 159–160; Newton and Simmons, 31; Stephen W. Sears, *On Campaign with the Army of the Potomac*, 29.
 23. Dowdy, 160–161.
 24. Dowdy, 161; Newton and Simmons, 31, 33.
 25. Douglas, 102–105; Worsham, 97.
 26. Glatthaar, 136.
 27. Douglas, 105–106.

28. Joseph P. Cullen, "Mechanicsville," *Civil War Times Illustrated* 5, no. 6 (October, 1966): 9–10.
29. Ibid., 11, 46.
30. Henry I. Kurtz, "Berdan's Sharpshooters Most Effective Union Brigade?" *Civil War Times Illustrated* 1, no. 10 (February, 1963), 17.
31. *Battles and Leaders*, vol. 2, 330.
32. Newton and Simmons, 34–35.
33. Newton and Simmons, 35–36; *Battles and Leaders*, 331.
34. George B. McClellan, *Report on the Organization and Campaigns of the Army of the Potomac*, 238.
35. Newton and Simmons, 36.
36. Joseph P. Cullen, "Gaines's Mills," *Civil War Times Illustrated* 3, no. 1 (April 1964): 12.
37. Newton and Simmons, 37, 39.
38. Angus Konstam, *Seven Days Battles 1862: Lee's Defense of Richmond* (Westport, CT: Praeger, 2004), 45–46.
39. Frank E. Vandiver, *The Civil War Diary of General Josiah Gorgas* (Tuscaloosa: University of Alabama Press, 1947), 8.
40. Hyde, 67–68.
41. Cullen, "Gaines's Mill," 15.
42. Newton and Simmons, 41.
43. Worsham, 99.
44. Dayton, 62.
45. Konstam, *Seven Days Battles*, 47–48.
46. Hood, 28.
47. Konstam, *Seven Days Battles*, 49.
48. Dowdey, 240–241.
49. Evander M. Law, "The Fight for Richmond in 1862," *The Southern Bivouac* 2, no. 11 (April 1887): 659.
50. Livermore, 82–83.
51. Glover, 94.
52. Gallagher, *Fighting for the Confederacy*, 104.
53. John C. Oeffinger, *A Soldier's General: The Civil War Letters of Major General Lafayette McLaws* (Chapel Hill: University of North Carolina Press, 2002), 148.

Chapter Eight

1. Hassler, 151–152.
2. Newton and Simmons, 50.
3. Ibid.
4. *Battles and Leaders*, vol. 2, 371–372.
5. Ibid., 373.
6. Mac Wycoff. *A History of the 2nd South Carolina Infantry: 1861–65* (Fredericksburg, VA: Sergeant Kirkland's Museum and Historical Society, 1994), 102.
7. Sears, *To the Gates of Richmond*, 271–272; and Eicher, 291.
8. Wycoff, 103.
9. *Battles and Leaders*, vol. 2, 375.
10. McClellan, *Report*, 263.
11. Gary Gallagher, 110.
12. *Battles and Leaders*, vol. 2, 388.
13. Worsham, 103.
14. Newton and Simmons, 52–53; Gallagher, 108–109.
15. Mudgett, 11.
16. Newton and Simmons, 55.
17. Freeman, *Lee's Lieutenants*, vol. 2, 585–587.
18. Ibid., 582–584.
19. Newton and Simmons, 56
20. Dowdey, 286–288.
21. Freeman, *Lee's Lieutenants*, vol. 2, 587.
22. *Battles and Leaders*, vol. 2, 401.
23. Donald, 102.
24. Haynes, 77.
25. Newton and Simmons, 60.
26. Wert, *General James Longstreet*, 144; Patterson, 44.
27. Wert, 144–145.
28. *Battles and Leaders*, vol. 2, 401–402; Wert, 144.
29. Hassler, 164–165.
30. Eugene Levy, "The Donaldsonville Artillery," *Southern Bivouac* 3, no. 7 (March 1885): 303–304.
31. Donald, 103.
32. Joseph Fant Kauffman, *The Civil War Diary of Joseph Fant Kauffman* (Luray, VA: K.P. Stiles, 2001), 11.
33. William Whatley Pierson Jr., *Whipt 'Em Everytime: The Diary of Bartlett Yancey Malone, Co. H 6th N.C. Regiment* (Wilmington, NC: Broadfoot, 1987), 59.
34. *Battles and Leaders*, vol. 3, 403.
35. Bridges, 77.
36. Glatthaar, 139.
37. Ibid., 112.
38. Hood, 30–31.
39. Newton and Simmons, 65–67.
40. Ibid., 67–68.
41. Bridges, 81.
42. Ibid., 81.
43. Brandon H. Beck, *Third Alabama! The Civil War Memoir of Brigadier General Cullen Andrews Battle, C.S.A.* (Tuscaloosa: The University of Alabama Press, 2000), 31–33.
44. Roe, *The Tenth Regiment Massachusetts Volunteer Infantry 1861–1865: A Western Massachusetts Regiment* (Springfield, MA: Tenth Regiment Veteran Association, 1909), 117.
45. *Battles and Leaders*, vol. 3, 417; Newton and Simmons, 71.
46. Charles E. Bryan and Nelson D. Lankford, *The Eye of the Storm: A Civil War Odyssey—Written and Illustrated by Private Robert Knox Sneden* (New York: Simon & Schuster, 2000), 95.
47. Ibid., 96.
48. *Battles and Leaders*, vol. 3, 421.
49. Newton and Simmons, 73.
50. Kauffman, 22.

Epilogue

1. Livermore, 86.
2. Robert P. Broadwater, *Did Lincoln and the Republican Party Create the Civil War? An Argument* (Jefferson, NC: McFarland, 2008), 107–108.
3. John L. Smith, *History of the Corn Exchange Regiment, 118th Pennsylvania Volunteers from Their First Engagement at Antietam to Appomattox* (Philadelphia: J.L. Smith, 1905), 107–108.
4. Young, vol. 2, 216–217.

Bibliography

Primary Sources

Manuscript Collections

Abraham Lincoln Papers
Arthur Whitford Papers
Author's Collection
Benjamin Lyons Farinholt Papers
Boston Public Library, Rare Books and Manuscripts Dept.
Charles A. Rubright Diary
Duke University Library
Dwight Henry Cory Letters
East Carolina University Library
Edward E. Cross Papers
Edwin M. Stanton Papers
Ethan Allen Hitchcock Papers
Forrest Little Letters
The Fox Collection
George McClellan Papers
Gettysburg College Library
Giles Frederick Ward Papers
Hampton Family Papers
Henry E. Huntington Library
Lt. Henry Ropes Letters
James Longstreet Papers
John McCahan Letters
Library of Congress
Milton Hyman Boullenet Letters
National Archives
Ohio State University Library
St. Mary's College Library
Samuel L. Barlow Papers
Samuel Peter Heintzelman Papers
S.W. Branch Letters
Thomas Jefferson University
University of Michigan Library
University of New Hampshire Library
University of South Carolina Library
Virginia Historical Society

Books

Acken, J. Gregory. *Inside the Army of the Potomac: The Civil War Experience of Captain Francis Adams Donaldson.* Harrisburg, PA: Stackpole Books, 1998.

Adams, F. Colburn. *The Story of a Trooper, with Much of Interest Concerning the Campaign on the Peninsula, Not Before Written.* New York: Dick & Fitzgerald, 1865.

Adams, John G. *Reminiscences of the Nineteenth Massachusetts Regiment.* Boston: Wright & Potter, 1899.

Anderson, Jubal. *Lieutenant General Jubal Anderson Early C.S.A.: Autobiographical Sketch and Narrative of the War Between the States.* Philadelphia: J.B. Lippincott, 1912.

Baquet, Camille. *History of The First Brigade, New Jersey Volunteers from 1861 to 1865 Compiled Under the Authorization of Kearny's First New Jersey Brigade Society.* Trenton, NJ: MacCrelish & Quigley, 1910.

Barnard, J.G. *The Peninsular Campaign and Its Antecedents as Developed by the Report of Maj.-Gen. Geo. B. McClellan and Other Published Documents.* New York: D. Van Nostrand, 1865.

Basler, Roy P. *The Collected Works of Abraham Lincoln,* 9 vols. New Brunswick, NJ: Rutgers University Press, 1953–1955.

Beale, Howard K. *The Diary of Edward Bates 1859–1866.* New York: Da Capo Press, 1971.

Booth, George Wilson. *A Maryland Boy in Lee's Army: Personal Reminiscences of a Maryland Soldier in the War Between the States, 1861–1865.* Lincoln: University of Nebraska Press, 2000.

Brewer, A.T. *History of the Sixty-First Regiment Pennsylvania Volunteers 1861–1865.* Pittsburgh: The Regimental Association, 1911.

Brock, R.A. *Southern Historical Society Papers.* Richmond, VA: Southern Historical Society, 1876–1944.

Bruce, George A. *The Twentieth Regiment of Massachusetts Volunteer Infantry 1861–1865.* Boston: Houghton, Mifflin, 1906.

Child, William. *A History of the Fifth Regiment New Hampshire Volunteers in the American Civil War 1861–1865.* Bristol, NH: R.W. Musgrove Printer, 1893.

Coffin, Charles Charleton. *Following the Flag*. Boston: Estes and Lauriat, 1865.

The Congressional Globe, 1860–1861. Washington, DC: Government Printing Office, 1861.

Crotty, Daniel G. *Four Years Campaigning in the Army of the Potomac*. Grand Rapids, MI: Dygert Bros., 1874.

Cudworth, Warren H. *History of the First Regiment Massachusetts Infantry from the 25th of May, 1861, to the 25th of May, 1864, Including Brief References to the Operations of the Army of the Potomac*. Boston: Walker, Fuller, 1866.

Dayton, Ruth Woods. *The Diary of a Confederate Soldier: James E. Hall*. Charleston, WV: no publisher, 1961.

Dennis, Frank Allen. *Kemper County Rebels: The Civil War Diary of Robert Masten Holmes, C.S.A.* Jackson: University and College Press of Mississippi, 1973.

Dickey, Luther S. *History of the Eighty-fifth Regiment Pennsylvania Volunteer Infantry 1861–1865: Comprising an Authentic Narrative of Casey's Division at the Battle of Seven Pines*. New York: J.C. & W.E. Powers, 1915.

Dinkens, James. *1861–1865 By an Old Johnnie: Personal Recollections and Experiences in the Confederate Army*. Cincinnati, OH: Robert Clarke, 1897.

Donald, David Herbert. *Gone for a Soldier: The Civil War Memoirs of Private Alfred Bellard*. Boston: Little, Brown, 1975.

Douglas, Henry Kyd. *I Rode with Stonewall*. Covington, GA: Mockingbird Books, 1976.

Dowdey, Clifford, and Louis Manarin. *The Wartime Papers of R.E. Lee*. Boston: Little, Brown, 1961.

Dunaway, Wayland Fuller. *Reminiscences of a Rebel*. New York: Neale, 1913.

Early, Jubal Anderson. *Lieutenant General Jubal Anderson Early C.S.A.: Autobiographical Sketch and Narrative of the War Between the States*. Philadelphia: J.B. Lippincott, 1912.

Edge, Frederick Milne. *Major-General McClellan and the Campaign on the Yorktown Peninsula*. New York: New York Loyal Publication Society, 1865.

Evans, Clement A. *Confederate Military History*. Vol. 5, *Virginia*. New York: Blue & Grey Press, no date.

Fisk, Joel C., and William H.D. Blake. *A Condensed History of the 56th Regiment New York Veteran Volunteer Infantry Which Was Part of the Organization Known as the Tenth Legion in the Civil War 1861–1865*. Newburgh, IN: Newburgh Journal Printing House and Book Bindery, 1906.

Fleming, George Thornton. *Life and Letters of Alexander Hays Brevet Colonel United States Army, Brigadier General and Brevet Major General United States Volunteers*. Pittsburgh: [s.n.], 1919.

Fletcher, William A. *Rebel Private Front and Rear: Memoirs of a Confederate Soldier*. New York: Meridian Books, 1997.

Flower, Milton E. *Dear Folks at Home: The Civil War Letters of Leo W. and John I Faller with an Account of Andersonville*. Carlisle, PA: Cumberland County Historical Society, 1963.

Ford, Andrew E. *The Story of the Fifteenth Regiment Massachusetts Volunteer Infantry in the Civil War 1861–1864*. Clinton, MA: Press of W.J. Coulter, 1898.

Frederick, Gilbert. *The Story of a Regiment: Being a Record of the Military Service of the Fifty-Seventh New York State Volunteer Infantry in the War of the Rebellion 1861–1865*. Chicago: The Fifty-Seventh Veteran's Association, 1895.

Gallagher, Gary W. *Fighting for the Confederacy: The Personal Recollections of General Edward Porter Alexander*. Chapel Hill: The University of North Carolina Press, 1989.

Gilmore, James R. *Personal Recollections of Abraham Lincoln and the Civil War*. Boston: L.C. Page, 1898.

Glimpses of the Nation's Struggle: Papers Read Before the Minnesota Commandery of the Military Order of the Loyal Legion of the United States 1897–1902. St. Paul, MN: Review, 1903.

Gordon, General John B. *Reminiscences of the Civil War*. New York: Charles Scribner's, 1903.

Govan, Gilbert E., and James W. Livingood, *The Haskell Memoirs: John Cheves Haskell*. New York: G.P. Putnam's, 1960.

Graham, C.R. *Under Both Flags: A Panorama of the Great Civil War, as Represented in Story, Anecdote, Adventure, and the Romance of Reality*. Chicago: W.S. Reeve, 1896.

Harrison, Walter. *Pickett's Men: A Fragment of War History*. New York: D. Van Nostrand, 1870.

Haynes, Martin A. *A History of the Second Regiment, New Hampshire Volunteer Infantry in the War of the Rebellion*. Lakeport, NH: [s.n.], 1896.

_____. *History of the Second Regiment New Hampshire Volunteers: Its Camps, Marches and Battles*. Manchester, NH: Charles F. Livingston, 1865.

Hays, Gilbert Adams. *Under the Red Patch: Story of the Sixty Third Regiment Pennsylvania Volunteers 1861–1864*. Pittsburgh: Sixty-third Pennsylvania Volunteers Regimental Association, 1908.

Hewitt, Janet B. *Supplement to the Official Records of the Union and Confederate Armies*. 20 Vols. Wilmington, NC: Broadfoot, 1995.

History Committee of the Regiment. *History of the Nineteenth Regiment Massachusetts Volunteer Infantry 1861–1865*. Salem, MA: The Salem Press, 1906.

Hood, John B. *Advance and Retreat*. New York: Blue and Grey Press, 1985.

Howard, Oliver O. *Autobiography of Oliver Otis Howard: Major General United States Army*. New York: The Baker & Taylor Company, 1908.

Hyde, Thomas W. *Following the Greek Cross; Or Memories of the Sixth Corps.* Boston: Houghton, Mifflin, 1894.

Ingersoll, C.M. *Catalogue of Connecticut Volunteer Organizations (Infantry, Cavalry and Artillery) in the Service of the United States, 1861–1865, with Additional Enlistments, Casualties, Etc.* Hartford, CT: Brown & Gross, 1869.

Johnson, Robert Underwood, and Clarence Clough Buel. *Battles and Leaders of the Civil War.* 4 Vols. New York: Castle Books, 1956.

Johnston, Joseph E. *Narrative of Military Operations During the Late War Between the States.* New York: D. Appleton, 1874.

Jones, J. William. *Southern Historical Society Papers.* 55 Vols. Wilmington, NC: Broadfoot, 1980.

Jones, John B. *A Rebel War Clerk's Diary at the Confederate States Capital.* 2 Vols. Philadelphia: J.B. Lippincott, 1866.

Julian, George W. *Political Recollections, 1840–1872.* Chicago: Jansen, McClure, 1884.

Keyes, E.D. *Fifty Years' Observation of Men and Events Civil and Military.* New York: Charles Scribner's, 1885.

Keylin, Arleen, and Douglas John Bowen. *The New York Times Book of The Civil War.* New York: Arno, 1980.

Lee, Robert E., Jr. *Recollections and Letters of General Robert E. Lee.* Garden City, NY: Garden City, 1924.

Livermore, Thomas L. *Numbers and Losses in the Civil War in America, 1861–1865.* Boston: Houghton Mifflin, 1901.

Long, John D. *Official Records of the Union and Confederate Navies in the War of the Rebellion.* 31 Vols. Washington, DC: Government Printing Office, 1894–1927.

Longstreet, James. *From Manassas to Appomattox: Memoirs of the Civil War in America.* Philadelphia: J.B. Lippincott, 1896.

Mark, Penrose G. *Red, White, and Blue Badge: Pennsylvania Veteran Volunteers; A History of the 93rd Regiment Known and the Lebanon Infantry and One of the 300 Fighting Regiments from September 1861 to June 27th, 1865.* Harrisburg: The 93rd Pennsylvania Veteran Volunteers Association, Aughinbaugh Press, 1911.

Marks, the Rev. James J. *The Peninsular Campaign in Virginia or Incidents and Scenes on the Battle-Fields and in Richmond.* Philadelphia: J.B. Lippincott, 1864.

Martin, Isabella D., and Myrta Lockett Avary. *Mary Chesnut: A Diary from Dixie, the Civil War's Most Celebrated Journal, Written 1860–1865 by the Wife of James Chesnut, Jr., N Aide to Jefferson Davis and a Brigadier General in the Confederate Army.* New York: Random House, 1997.

Marvin, Edwin E. *The Fifth Regiment Connecticut Volunteers: A History.* Hartford, CT: Press of Wiley, Waterman & Eaton, 1889.

McClellan, George B. *McClellan's Own Story: The War for the Union, the Soldiers Who Fought It, the Civilians Who Directed It, and His Relations to It and to Them.* New York: Charles L. Webster, 1883.

_____. *Report on the Organization and Campaigns of the Army of the Potomac: To Which Is Added an Account of the Campaign in Western Virginia with Plans of Battle-Fields.* New York: Sheldon, 1864.

McDermott, Anthony W. *A Brief History of the 69th Regiment Pennsylvania Veteran Volunteers from Its Formation Until Final Muster Out of the United States Service.* Philadelphia: D.J. Gallagher, 1889.

Meade, George Gordon, Jr. *Life and Letters of George Gordon Meade, Major General United States Army.* 2 Vols. New York: Charles Scribner's, 1913.

Miller, Richard F., and Robert F. Mooney. *The Civil War: The Nantucket Experience.* Nantucket, MA: Wesco, 1994.

Mott, Smith B. *The Campaigns of the Fifty-Second Regiment Pennsylvania Volunteer Infantry First Known as the Luzerne Regiment Being the Record of Nearly Four Years' Continuous Service, from October 7, 1861, to July 12, 1865, in the War for the Suppression of the Rebellion.* Philadelphia: J.B. Lippincott, 1911.

Nevins, Allan. *A Diary of Battle: The Personal Journals of Colonel Charles S. Wainwright 1861–1865.* New York: Da Capo, 1998.

Newell, Captain Joseph K. *Ours: Annals of the 10th Regiment, Massachusetts Volunteers in the Rebellion.* Springfield, MA: Ceith A. Nichols, 1875.

Oeffinger, John C. *A Soldier's General: The Civil War Letters of Major General Lafayette McLaws.* Chapel Hill: The University of North Carolina Press, 2002.

Owens, John Algernon. *Sword and Pen: Ventures and Adventures of Willard Glazier, in War and Literature.* Philadelphia: Ziegler, 1883.

Pease, Theodore Calvin, and James G. Randall. *The Diary of Orville Hickman Browning 1850–1864.* 2 Vols. Springfield: Trustees of the Illinois State Historical Library, 1925.

Pollard, Edward A. *Southern History of the War: The Second Year of the War.* New York: Charles B. Richardson, 1864.

Quint, Alonzo, H. *The Record of the Second Massachusetts Infantry 1861–65.* Boston: James P. Walker, 1867.

Reid-Green, Marcia. *Letters Home: Henry Matrau of the Iron Brigade.* Lincoln: University of Nebraska Press, 1993.

Report on the Joint Committee on the Conduct of the War. Washington, DC: Government Printing Office, 1863.

Rhodes, James Ford. *History of the Civil War 1861–1865.* New York: Macmillan, 1917.

Rhodes, Robert Hunt. *All for the Union: A History of the 2nd Rhode Island Volunteer Infantry in the War of the Great Rebellion as Told by the Diary and Letters of Elisha Hunt Rhodes*. Lincoln, RI: Andrew Mowbray, 1985.

Richardson, James D. *A Compilation of the Messages and Papers of the Presidents*. 20 Vols. New York: Bureau of National Literature, 1917.

Robertson, John. *Michigan in the War*. Lansing, MI: W.S. George, 1882.

Roe, Alfred S. *The Tenth Regiment Massachusetts Volunteer Infantry: A Western Massachusetts Regiment*. Springfield, MA: Tenth Regiment Veterans Association, 1909.

Scott, Lt. Col. Robert. *The War of the Rebellion: A Compilation of the Official Records of the Union and Confederate Armies*. 128 Vols. Washington, DC: Government Printing Office, 1886.

Scott, Robert Garth. *Fallen Leaves: The Civil War Letters of Major Henry Livermore Abbott*. Kent, OH: Kent State University Press, 1991.

Sears, Stephen W. *The Civil War Papers of George B. McClellan: Selected Correspondence, 1860–1865*. New York: Ticknor & Fields, 1989.

Secretary of the Survivors Association Twenty Third Regiment Pennsylvania Volunteers, *History of the Twenty Third Pennsylvania Volunteer Infantry, Birney's Zouaves: Three Months and Three Years Service Civil War 1861–1865*. Philadelphia: Survivors Association, 1904.

Sedgwick, John. *Correspondence of John Sedgwick, Major-General*. 2 Vols. Baltimore, MD: Butternut and Blue, 1999.

Sketches of War History 1861–1865: A Compilation of Miscellaneous Papers Read Before the Ohio Commandery of the Loyal Legion April 1912–April 1916. Wilmington, NC: Broadfoot, 1993.

Smith, Gustavus W. *Confederate War Papers, Fairfax Court House, New Orleans, Seven Pines, Richmond and North Carolina*. New York: Atlantic Publishing and Engraving, 1884.

Smith, John L. *History of the Corn Exchange Regiment, 118th Pennsylvania Volunteers, from Their First Engagement at Antietam to Appomattox*. Philadelphia: J.L. Smith, 1905.

Sneden, Robert Knox. *Eye of the Storm*. New York: Touchstone Books, 2002.

Summers, Festus P. *A Borderland Confederate*. Pittsburgh: University of Pittsburgh Press, 1962.

Swinton, William. *Campaigns of the Army of the Potomac: A Critical History of Operations in Virginia, Maryland and Pennsylvania, from the Commencement to the Close of the War, 1861–1865*. New York: Charles Scribner, 1882.

Thayer, William R. *The Life and Letters of John Hay*. Boston: Houghton Mifflin, 1915.

Urban, John W. *Battle Field and Prison Pen or Through the War and Thrice a Prisoner in Rebel Dungeons*. Philadelphia: Edgewood, 1882.

War Papers Read Before the Commandery of the State of Maine, Military Order of the Loyal Legion of the United States. Portland, ME: Lefavor-Tower, 1902.

Webb, Alexander S. *The Peninsula: McClellan's Campaign of 1862*. Wilmington, NC: Broadfoot, 1989.

Welles, Gideon. *Diary of Gideon Wells Secretary of the Navy Under Lincoln and Johnson*. Boston: Houghton Mifflin, 1911.

Wiley, Bell Irvin. *Whipt 'Em Everytime: The Diary of Bartlett Yancey Malone, Co. H, 6th N.C. Regiment*. Wilmington, NC: Broadfoot, 1987.

Worsham, John H. *One of Jackson's Foot Cavalry*. New York: Neale, 1912.

Young, John Russell. *Around the World with General Grant: A Narrative of the Visit of General U.S. Grant, Ex-President of the United States, to Various Countries in Europe, Asia, and Africa, in 1877, 1878, 1879*. 2 Vols. New York: American News, 1879.

Magazines, Newspapers and Periodicals

American Historical Review, January 1921.
The Berkshire Courier, 5 June 1862
Confederate Veteran, January 1917; April 1929.
Harper's Weekly, June 21, 1862.
New York Tribune, 19 February 1862; 6 June 1862.
Northwest Georgia Historical and Genealogical Society Quarterly 28, no. 2.
Philadelphia North American, 3 June 1862.
Southern Bivouac, March 1885; May 1887; April 1887.
Washington Evening Star, 18 February 1862.

Secondary Sources

Books

Allardice, Bruce S. *More Generals in Gray*. Baton Rouge: Louisiana State University Press, 1995.

Anker, Robert. *Civil War Tales: True Life Stories Told by Soldiers After Actual Battles*. New Oxford, PA: published by the author, 1979.

Bailey, Chester P. *Tioga Mountaineers: Company B, 101st Regiment Pennsylvania Volunteer Infantry 1861–1865*. Mansfield, PA: Bailey, 1962.

Bailey, Ronald H. *Forward to Richmond: McClellan's Peninsula Campaign*. Alexandria, VA: Time Life Books, 1983.

Beyer, W.F., and G.F. Keydel, eds. *Deeds of Valor: How America's Civil War Heroes Won the Congressional Medal of Honor*. Stamford, CT: Longmeadow, 1994.

Bowen, Catherine Drinker. *Yankee From Olympus: Justice Holmes and His Family*. Boston: Little, Brown, 1944.

Bowers, John. *Stonewall Jackson: Portrait of a Soldier*. New York: William Morrow, 1989.

Bridges, Hal. *Lee's Maverick General: Daniel Harvey Hill.* Lincoln: University of Nebraska Press, 1991.
Broadwater, Robert P. *Civil War Medal of Honor Recipients: A Complete Illustrated Record.* Jefferson, NC: McFarland, 2007.
Catton, Bruce. *Terrible Swift Sword.* New York: Doubleday, 1963.
_____. *This Hallowed Ground.* New York: Pocket Books, 1961.
Chinn, George M. *The Machine Gun: History, Evolution, and Development of Manual, Automatic, and Airborne Repeating Weapons.* 5 Vols. Washington, DC: Government Printing Office, 1951.
Cisco, Walter Brian. *Wade Hampton: Confederate Warrior, Conservative, Statesman.* Washington, DC: Brassey's, 2004.
Cozzens, Peter, and Robert I. Girardi. *The News Annals of the Civil War.* Mechanicsburg, PA: Stackpole Books, 2004.
Cullen Joseph P. *The Peninsula Campaign 1862: McClellan & Lee Struggle for Richmond.* New York: Bonanza Books, 1973.
Dannett, Sylvia G.L. *Noble Women of the North.* New York: Thomas Yoseloff, 1959.
Davis, Burke. *The Civil War: Strange & Fascinating Facts.* New York: The Fairfax Press, 1960.
_____. *Gray Fox: Robert E. Lee and the Civil War.* New York: Holt, Rinehart and Winston, 1956.
_____. *They Called Him Stonewall: A Life of Lt. General T.J. Jackson.* New York: Wings Books, 1954.
Davis, Oliver Wilson. *Life of David Bell Birney, Major-General United States Volunteers.* Philadelphia: King & Baird, 1867.
Davis, William C. *Jefferson Davis: The Man and His Hour.* New York: Harper Collins, 1991.
Dennett, Tyler. *John Hay: From Poetry to Politics.* New York: Dodd, Mead, 1934.
Donald, David Herbert. *Lincoln.* New York: Simon & Schuster, 1995.
Dowdey, Clifford. *The Seven Days: The Emergence of Lee.* Boston: Little, Brown, 1964.
Dyer, John P. *The Gallant Hood.* New York: Bobbs-Merrill, 1950.
Eicher, David J. *The Longest Night: A Military History of the Civil War.* New York: Simon & Schuster, 2001.
Esposito, Major V.J. *Civil War Atlas to Accompany Steele's American Campaigns.* West Point, NY: United States Military Academy, 1941.
Fishel, Edwin C. *The Secret War for the Union: The Untold Story of Military Intelligence in the Civil War.* Boston: Houghton Mifflin, 1996.
Foster, G. Allen. *The Eyes and Ears of the Civil War.* New York: Criterion Books, 1963.
Freeman, Douglas Southall. *Lee's Lieutenants: A Study in Command.* 3 Vols. New York: Charles Scribner's, 1970.
_____. *R.E. Lee: A Biography.* New York: Charles Scribner's, 1934.
Gallagher, Gary W. *The Richmond Campaign of 1862: The Peninsula & The Seven Days.* Chapel Hill: University of North Carolina Press, 2000.
_____. *Stephen Dodson Ramseur: Lee's Gallant General.* Chapel Hill: University of North Carolina Press, 1985.
Garrison, Webb. *Friendly Fire in the Civil War: More Than 100 True Stories of Comrade Killing Comrade.* Nashville, TN: Rutledge Hill Press, 1999.
Glatthaar, Joseph T. *General Lee's Army: From Victory To Collapse.* New York: Free Press, 2008.
Glazier, Willard. *Heroes of Three Wars: Comprising A Series of Biographical Sketches of the Most Distinguished Soldiers of the War of the Revolution, the War with Mexico, and the War for the Union, Who Have Contributed by Their Valor to Establish and Perpetuate the Republic of the United States.* Philadelphia: Hubbard Brothers, 1880.
Glover, Edwin A. *Bucktailed Wildcats: A Regiment of Civil War Volunteers.* New York: Thomas Yoseloff, 1960.
Goodrich, Frederick E. *Life of Winfield Scott Hancock, Major-General, U.S.A.: His Childhood, Youth, Education, Military Career, Social and Domestic Life.* Boston: B.B. Russell, 1886.
Hassler, Warren. *General George McClellan: Shield of the Union.* Baton Rouge: Louisiana State University Press, 1957.
Haydon, F. Stansbury. *Military Ballooning During the Early Civil War.* Baltimore, MD: The Johns Hopkins Press, 2000.
Henderson, Lt. Col. G.F.B. *Stonewall Jackson and the American Civil War.* New York: Longman, Green, 1905.
Hilliard, George S. *The Life, Campaigns, and Public Services of General George McClellan.* Philadelphia: T.B. Peterson Brothers, 1864.
Katcher, Phillip. *Battle History of the Civil War 1861–1865.* New York: Barnes & Noble Books, 2000.
Kirkland, Frazar. *The Pictorial Book of Anecdotes of the Rebellion of the Funny and Patriotic Side of the War.* St. Louis, MO: F.H. Mason, 1889.
Longacre, Edward G. *Gentleman and Soldier: The Extraordinary Life of General Wade Hampton.* Nashville, TN: Rutledge Hill Press, 2003.
_____. *The Man Behind the Guns: A Military Biography of General Henry J. Hunt, Chief of Artillery, Army of the Potomac.* Cambridge, MA: Da Capo, 2003.
Lonn, Ella. *Desertion During the Civil War.* Lincoln: University of Nebraska Press, 1998.
Lowry, Thomas P. *Tarnished Eagles: The Courts-Martial of Fifty Union Colonels and Lieutenant Colonels.* Mechanicsburg, PA: Stackpole, 1997.
Madden, David. *Beyond the Battlefield: The Ordinary Life and Extraordinary Times of the Civil War Soldier.* New York: Simon & Schuster, 2000.
Maurice, Frederick. *Robert E. Lee the Soldier.* New York: Bonanza Books, 1925.

Meltzer, Milton. *Voices From the Civil War*. New York: Thomas Y. Crowell, 1989.

Miller, Francis Trevelyan. *The Opening Battles: The Photographic History of the Civil War*. New York: Castle Books, 1957.

Miller, Richard F., and Robert F. Mooney. *The Civil War: The Nantucket Experience*. Nantucket, MA: Wesco, 1994.

Mitchell, Lt. Col. Joseph B. *Decisive Battles of the Civil War*. New York: Fawcett Premier, 1989.

Mudgett, Timothy B. *Make the Fur Fly: A History of a Union Volunteer Division in the American Civil War*. Shippensburg, PA: Burd Street, 1997.

Newton, John, and Gerald Simmons. *Lee Takes Command: From Seven Days to Second Bull Run*. Alexandria, VA: Time Life Books, 1984.

Orrmont, Arthur. *Master Detective: Allan Pinkerton*. New York: Julian Messner, 1965.

Patterson, Gerard A. *From Blue to Gray: The Life of Confederate General Cadmus M. Wilcox*. Mechanicsburg, PA: Stackpole Books, 2001.

Perret, Geoffrey. *Lincoln's War: The Untold Story of America's Greatest President as Commander in Chief*. New York: Random House, 2004.

Price, William H. *The Civil War Handbook*. Fairfax, VA: Prince Lithograph, 1961.

Rafuse, Ethan S. *McClellan's War: The Failure of Moderation in the Struggle for the Union*. Bloomington: Indiana University Press, 2005.

Randall, J.G., and David Herbert Donald. *The Civil War and Reconstruction*. Lexington, MA: D.C. Heath, 1969.

Randall, James G. *Lincoln the President*. 4 Vols. New York: Dodd, Mead, 1945–1955.

Rowland, Thomas J. *George B. McClellan & Civil War History: In the Shadow of Grant and Sherman*. Kent, OH: The Kent State University Press, 1998.

Sandburg, Carl. *Abraham Lincoln: The Prairie Years and the War Years*. New York: Harcourt, Brace & World, 1954.

Sears, Stephen W. *On Campaign with the Army of the Potomac: The Civil War Journal of Theodore Ayrault Dodge*. New York: Cooper Square, 2003.

_____. *To The Gates of Richmond: The Peninsula Campaign*. New York: Mariner Books, 1992.

Spruill, Matt III, and Matt Spruill IV. *Echoes of Thunder: A Guide to the Seven Days Battles*. Knoxville: The University of Tennessee Press, 2006.

Swanberg, W.A. *Sickles the Incredible*. New York: Ace Books, 1956.

Tapert, Annette. *The Brothers' War: Civil War Letters to Their Loved Ones from the Blue and Gray*. New York: Vintage Books, 1988.

Thomas, Benjamin P., and Harold M. Hyman. *Stanton: The Life and Times of Lincoln's Secretary of War*. New York: Alfred A. Knopf, 1962.

Thomas, Emory M. *Bold Dragoon: The Life of J.E.B. Stuart*. Norman: University of Oklahoma Press, 1999.

Tucker, Glenn. *Hancock the Superb*. Dayton, OH: Morningside Bookshop, 1980.

Victor, Orville J. *The History, Civil, Political and Military of the Southern Rebellion from Its Incipient Stages to Its Close*. New York: James D. Torrey, 1861.

Walker, General Francis A. *General Hancock*. New York: D. Appleton, 1898.

Warner, Ezra J. *Generals in Blue: Lives of the Union Commanders*. Baton Rouge: Louisiana State University Press, 1964.

_____. *Generals in Gray: Lives of the Confederate Commanders*. Baton Rouge: Louisiana State University Press, 1981.

Wert, Jeffry D. *General James Longstreet: The Confederacy's Most Controversial Soldier*. New York: Touchstone Books, 1994.

_____. *The Sword of Lincoln: The Army of the Potomac*. New York: Simon & Schuster, 2006.

Wertz, Jay, and Edwin C. Bearss. *Smithsonian's Great Battles & Battlefields of the Civil War*. New York: William Morrow, 1997.

Wheat, Thomas Adrian. *A Guide to Civil War Yorktown*. Knoxville, TN: Bohemian Brigade Bookshop and Publishers, 1997.

Wiley, Bell Irvin. *The Life of Johnny Reb: The Common Soldier in the Confederacy*. Baton Rouge: Louisiana State University Press, 1993.

Wills, Mary Alice. *The Confederate Blockade of Washington, D.C., 1861–1862*. Shippensburg, PA: Burd Street Press, 1998.

Magazines, Newspapers and Periodicals

America's Civil War May 2002.

Civil War: The Magazine of the Civil War Society 13, no. 23.

Index

Ager, Wilson 59
Alexander, Col. Edward P., C.S.A. 135, 150, 156, 163, 166
Ambercrombie, Gen. John 102, 104, 105, 111, 180, 185
Anderson, Col. George B., C.S.A. 94, 97, 105, 181, 189
Anderson, Gen. Joseph R., C.S.A. 82, 143, 190
Anderson, Gen. Richard H., C.S.A. 105, 146, 180, 190
Antietam, Md., Battle of 1, 5, 7, 175
Archer, Gen. James, C.S.A. 143, 146, 191
Armistead, Gen. Lewis, C.S.A. 118, 120, 122, 123, 126, 167, 181, 190
Army of Northern Virginia 4, 5, 6, 41, 80, 85, 134, 137, 138
Army of the Potomac 1, 4, 6, 7, 10, 11, 12, 14, 15, 17, 18, 24, 25, 26, 29, 31, 32, 34, 36, 37, 38, 39, 41, 42, 46, 48, 54, 55, 57, 69, 76, 77, 80, 82, 84, 85, 86, 90, 114, 130, 135, 136, 137, 141, 156, 164, 165, 166, 169, 174
USS *Aroostook* 74
Ashland, Va. 142
Averell, Gen. William W. 139, 176

Bailey, Col. Guilford D. 89, 99
Baker, Col. Edward 21
Ball's Bluff 21
Baltimore & Ohio Railroad 7
Banks, Gen. Nathaniel P. 25, 29, 36, 80, 81, 138
Barker, Capt. Charles 60
Barnard, Gen. John G. 24, 37, 47, 74
Bates, Edward 28, 174
Beauregard, Gen. P.G.T., C.S.A. 51, 117, 144
Beaver Dam Creek 143, 145
Bellard, Pvt. Alfred 56, 65, 162
Benjamin, Judah P. 11
Berdan, Col. Hiram 82, 143

Berry, Gen. Hiram G. 102, 104, 180, 185
Birney, Gen. David B. 102, 104, 105, 119, 122, 180, 185
Blenker, Gen. Louis 36, 38, 40
Boatswain's Creek 145, 146, 148
Bondurant, Capt. J.W., C.S.A. 98
Brady, Capt. James 106, 109, 111
Branch, Gen. Lawrence O., C.S.A. 82, 85, 146, 191
Bratton, Col. John, C.S.A. 105, 128
Brentsville, Va. 13
Briggs, Col. Henry 101
Brooke, Colonel John 124, 125
Brooks, Gen. William T. 54, 154, 187
Browning, Orville 19, 38, 39
Buell, Gen. Don Carlos 12, 14, 15, 177
Buford, Gen. Napoleon B. 38, 137, 175
Burns, Gen. William W. 110, 111, 154, 179, 184
Burnside, Gen. Ambrose E. 5, 7, 12, 14, 16, 136, 137, 175
Burnt Chimneys, Va. 54
Butler, Gen. Benjamin J. 16
Butterfield, Gen. Daniel 146, 186

Camp Lloyd 90
Camp Scott 56
Carter, Capt. Thomas, C.S.A. 98
Carter, Lt. William, C.S.A. 98
Casey, Gen. Silas 60, 79, 84, 88, 90, 91, 92, 95, 96, 98, 99, 100, 102, 105, 108, 114, 118, 139, 161, 180, 184
Charlottesville, Va. 142
Colston, Gen. Raleigh E., C.S.A. 181
Cooper, Gen. Samuel, C.S.A. 51
Covode, John 21
Centreville, Va. 13, 14, 15, 27
Chandler, Zachariah 17, 21, 39
Charles City Road 90, 93, 94, 99, 101, 117, 118, 156, 159, 160

Chase, Salmon P. 70
Cheat Mountain, battle of 134
Chickahominy River 74
Chickamauga, Ga., Battle of 5
Chilton, Col. R.H., C.S.A. 160
Cobb, Gen. Howell, C.S.A. 54, 130, 189
Cobb Legion 54
USS *Commodore* 35, 36
Cooke, Gen. Philip St. George 149
Couch, Gen. Darius 60, 99, 100, 105, 106, 108, 114, 119, 169, 180, 185
Cross, Col. Edward E. 120, 121, 125
Cross Keys, Va. 81
Cullen, Joseph P. 73
USS *Cumberland* 26
Custer, Gen. George A. 4, 68

Dana, Gen. Napoleon 110, 119, 185
Davis, Jefferson 4, 11, 41, 51, 52, 73, 74, 85, 109, 112, 116, 130, 131, 134, 160, 162, 175
Deal, John 72
De Fontaine, Gregory 154
Dennison, William 8, 28
Department of the Mississippi 28
Department of the Potomac 28
Devens, Gen. Charles, Jr. 100, 127, 180
Dickey, Luther 5, 6
Diggs, Cpl. C.W. 104
Drewry's Bluff 74, 136
Dumfries, Va. 13, 14

Early, Gen. Jubal A., C.S.A. 52, 67
Easley, D.B. 112
18th Georgia Infantry Regiment 72, 181, 188
8th Illinois Cavalry Regiment 60
8th New Jersey Infantry Regiment 66, 185

81st Pennsylvania Infantry Regiment 122, 124, 126, 127, 179, 184
82nd New York Infantry Regiment 109, 179, 184
87th New York Infantry Regiment 102, 180, 185
11th Alabama Infantry Regiment 54, 190
11th Maine Infantry Regiment 89, 98, 114, 180, 186
Eltham's Landing, Va. 71, 72
Emory, Gen. William H. 82
Ericsson, John 27
Evansport, Va. 13
Ewell, Gen. Richard, C.S.A. 52, 53, 80, 188

Fair Oaks, Va., Battle of 1, 2, 5, 6, 80, 84, 86, 88, 91, 99, 100, 101, 102, 106, 108, 109, 118, 120, 131, 136, 150, 172, 176, 177
Fairfax Courthouse, Va. 24, 28
Fallon, Pvt. Thomas 195
Farragut, Admiral David G. 16
Featherston, Gen. Winfield S., C.S.A. 94, 190
Field, Gen. Charles W., C.S.A. 143, 146, 163, 190
15th Massachusetts Infantry Regiment 110, 116, 179, 184
15th Virginia Infantry Regiment 54, 145, 189
5th Michigan Infantry Regiment 102, 180, 185
5th Mississippi Infantry Regiment 115
5th New Hampshire Infantry Regiment 120, 121, 124, 179, 184
5th New Jersey Infantry Regiment 56, 65, 129, 162, 180, 185
5th New York Infantry Regiment (Zouave) 145, 186
5th North Carolina Infantry Regiment 67, 95, 181, 189
5th Texas Infantry Regiment 72, 181, 188
5th United States Cavalry Regiment 149, 188
5th Vermont Infantry Regiment 57, 154, 187
55th New York Infantry Regiment 100, 180, 185
52nd New York Infantry Regiment 120, 122, 179, 184
52nd Pennsylvania Infantry Regiment 86, 97, 180, 186
57th New York Infantry Regiment 122, 179, 184
56th New York Infantry Regiment 48, 58, 59, 180, 186
53rd Pennsylvania Infantry Regiment 122, 124, 125, 179, 184

1st Minnesota Infantry Regiment 110, 111, 154, 179, 184
1st New York Light Artillery (Battery A) 99, 179
1st Pennsylvania Light Artillery (Battery C) 100
1st South Carolina Rifles 145, 190
1st Texas Infantry Regiment 72, 181, 188
1st United States Cavalry Regiment 8, 60
1st United States Light Artillery (Battery I) 65, 111
1st United States Sharpshooter Regiment 143
Fisk, Wilbur 159
Floyd, Gen. John B., C.S.A. 133
Foreman, Cpl. Alexander 195
Fort Casey 91, 98, 99, 104
Fort Darling 74, 75
Fort Donelson, Tn. 16, 17, 108, 132
Fort Henry, Tn. 16, 17, 132
Fort Magruder 60, 62, 65, 66
Fort Wool 70
Fortress Monroe, Va. 27, 30, 34, 36, 41, 44, 46, 51, 70, 76, 161
40th New York Infantry Regiment 126, 128, 129, 169, 180, 185
45th North Carolina Infantry Regiment 160
44th Georgia Infantry Regiment 144, 189
49th Pennsylvania Infantry Regiment 143, 187
42nd New York Infantry Regiment 110, 179
47th Virginia Infantry Regiment 163, 181
14th Louisiana Infantry Battalion 143, 181
14th New York Infantry Regiment 143, 186
14th North Carolina Infantry Regiment 169, 181, 189
4th Maine Infantry Regiment 126, 127, 128, 129, 180, 185
4th Michigan Infantry Regiment 143, 186
4th North Carolina Infantry Regiment 99, 181, 189
4th Texas Infantry Regiment 72, 149, 181, 189
4th Vermont Infantry Regiment 54, 187
Frayser's Farm *see* Glendale
Fredericksburg, Va., Battle of 5, 7
Fremont, Gen. John C. 28, 36, 81, 138, 174
French, Pvt. Samuel 195
French, Gen. William 119, 120, 121, 122, 124, 149, 179, 184
Front Royal, Va. 80

Gaines's Mill, Va. 84, 150, 152
USS *Galena* 74, 75, 161
Galliard, E.S. 112
Garland, Gen. Samuel, Jr., C.S.A. 94, 95, 96, 97, 98, 105, 168, 181, 189
Gettysburg, Pa., Battle of 5, 108, 133, 150, 173, 176
Gibbs, George 35, 36
Gilles Creek 94
Glazier, William 11
Glendale, Va. 156, 159, 160, 161, 162, 163
Gloucester Point, Va. 34, 35, 36, 42, 44, 45, 48, 56, 61, 175
Goldsborough, Cmdr. Louis 35, 45, 56, 61, 74, 135, 136, 174
Gooch, D.W. 21
Gordon, Capt. Augustus, C.S.A. 103
Gordon, Gen. John B., C.S.A. 62, 103, 114, 168
Gordonsville, Va. 142
Gorgas, Gen. Josiah, C.S.A. 146
Gorman, Gen. Willis A. 110, 111, 179
Gove, Col. Jesse 58
Grant, Dr. Gabriel 195
Grant, Gen. Ulysses S. 7, 12, 16, 26, 175, 176, 177
Greeley, Horace 132
Gregg, Gen. Maxy, C.S.A. 143, 145, 146, 190
Griffin, Gen. Charles 143, 186
Griffith, Gen. Richard, C.S.A. 153, 189
Grimes, Maj. Bryan, C.S.A. 99

Halleck, Gen. Henry 12, 14, 28, 29
Hampton, Gen. Wade, C.S.A. 71, 72, 109, 111, 112, 119, 159, 167, 181
Hampton Roads, Va. 26
Hancock, Gen. Winfield S. 4, 56, 66, 67, 68, 69, 187
Hanover Court House, Va. 82, 89
Harris, Ira 46
Harrison, Benjamin, V 161
Harrison, William Henry 161
Harrison's Landing, Va. 139, 161, 162, 163, 164, 170
Haskell, Sgt. Frank 195
Hatteras, N.C. 16
Hatton, Gen. Robert, C.S.A. 108, 109, 111, 112, 119, 181
Haxell's Landing, Va. 164
Hay, John 40
Hays, Gilbert 87
Heintzelman, Gen. Samuel P. 24, 25, 30, 31, 34, 41, 77, 84, 86, 90, 95, 101, 102, 104, 105, 109, 113, 114, 119, 126, 129, 140, 141, 162, 170, 179, 185

Index

Herzog, Charles 57
Hill, Gen. Ambrose P., C.S.A. 4, 85, 117, 118, 142, 143, 144, 145, 146, 148, 153, 156, 160, 163, 173, 190
Hill, Gen. Daniel H., C.S.A. 52, 64, 67, 85, 90, 92, 94, 98, 99, 100, 102, 103, 108, 113, 114, 118, 119, 120, 122, 123, 124, 126, 142, 143, 144, 145, 146, 158, 164, 166, 167, 168, 169, 173, 189
Holmes, Gen. Theophilus, C.S.A. 52, 130, 159, 160, 191
Hood, Gen. John B., C.S.A. 4, 71, 72, 108, 109, 118, 148, 149, 167, 173, 181, 188
Hooker, Gen. Joseph 5, 36, 60, 65, 66, 67, 119, 128, 129, 133, 136, 140, 162, 179, 185
Howard, Lt. Charles 124
Howard, Gen. Oliver O. 73, 95, 115, 119, 121, 122, 125, 126, 179
Hundley's Corner, Va. 143
Huger, Gen. Benjamin, C.S.A. 71, 85, 90, 92, 93, 94, 117, 118, 140, 141, 153, 156, 159, 160, 163, 167, 168, 169, 170, 172, 181, 190
Hunter, Alexander 103, 114

Illinois Central Railroad 8
Ives, Col. Joseph, C.S.A. 135

Jackson, Gen. Thomas J., C.S.A. 25, 53, 80, 81, 82, 85, 135, 138, 142, 143, 144, 146, 149, 153, 158, 159, 163, 169, 173, 175, 188
James River 30, 35, 47, 72, 73, 135, 151, 152, 161, 165
Jameson, Gen. Charles D. 102, 180
Jenkins, Col. Micah, C.S.A. 105, 106, 109, 118, 162, 180
Jerome, Lt. A.B. 57
Johnson, Andrew 21
Johnston, Gen. Albert S., C.S.A. 16, 51, 52, 132
Johnston, Gen. Joseph E., C.S.A. 1, 3, 5, 7, 11, 15, 26, 41, 42, 44, 51, 52, 56, 58, 64, 65, 71, 74, 89, 90, 92, 94, 108, 109, 111, 114, 116, 117, 134, 172, 173, 175, 188
Joint Committee on the Conduct of the War 15, 17, 23, 38, 39, 55, 132, 136
Julian, G.W. 21

Kauffman, Pvt. Joseph F., C.S.A. 165, 171
Kearny, Gen. Philip 66, 67, 102, 103, 104, 105, 126, 128, 140, 180, 185

Kemper, Gen. James, C.S.A. 103, 104, 105, 106, 162, 180, 190
Kernstown, Va., battle of 36
Kershaw, Gen. Joseph B., C.S.A. 117, 154, 189
Kettle Bottom Shoals 27
Keyes, Gen. Erasmus D. 25, 30, 41, 47, 77, 84, 86, 88, 89, 90, 93, 95, 100, 101, 105, 108, 109, 113, 114, 118, 119, 156, 180, 185
King William Artillery 98
Kirby, Lt. Edmund 111

Lamar, Col. Lucius M., C.S.A. 54
Lamb, William W. 71
Law, Col. Evander M., C.S.A. 108, 111, 148, 149, 156, 181, 188
Lee, Gen. Fitzhugh, C.S.A. 76
Lee, Col. George Washington Custis, C.S.A. 74
Lee, Gen. Robert E., C.S.A. 1, 4, 5, 7, 51, 52, 57, 73, 74, 80, 85, 108, 112, 116, 118, 129, 130, 131, 134, 136, 137, 138, 139, 140, 141, 142, 143, 144, 150, 152, 153, 160, 152, 164, 166, 168, 172, 176, 188
Lee, Capt. Robert M., Jr. 122
Lee's Mill, Va. 46, 55, 57
Levy, Pvt. Eugene, C.S.A. 164
Lincoln, Abraham 8, 15, 16, 17, 18, 19, 23, 24, 25, 26, 28, 29, 36, 37, 39, 40, 42, 51, 57, 59, 77, 79, 80, 131, 174, 175
Little, Forrest 57
Longstreet, Gen. James P., C.S.A. 25, 51, 59, 64, 65, 67, 70, 85, 86, 90, 92, 93, 94, 99, 100, 103, 113, 114, 117, 118, 127, 130, 153, 156, 158, 159, 162, 163, 166, 167, 172, 173, 180, 190
Loring, Gen. William W., C.S.A. 133
Lowe, Thaddeus 2, 53, 58, 75
Lynchburg, Va. 14

Mackie, John 75
Magruder, Gen. John, C.S.A. 1, 15, 41, 44, 45, 47, 48, 53, 64, 67, 69, 111, 118, 141, 142, 152, 153, 158, 160, 167, 170, 189
Mahone, Gen. William, C.S.A. 118, 119, 123, 259, 168, 181, 190
Mallory, Stephen 42, 130
Malone, Pvt. Bartlett, C.S.A. 165
Manassas, Va. 3, 4, 7, 8, 10, 13, 14, 15, 27, 30, 37
Marcy, Ellen 8
Marcy, Gen. Randolph 8, 28
Mark, Penrose 102
Martindale, Gen. John H. 146, 186
Mason, Maj. W. Roy, C.S.A. 163
Mattapony River 15

McCall, Gen. George A. 137, 143, 145, 149, 162, 163, 186
McCarter, Col. J.M. 102
McCarthy, Capt. Jeremiah 100
McClellan, Gen. George B. 1, 2, 3, 4, 5, 7, 8, 9, 10, 11, 12, 16, 18, 19, 22, 24, 25, 26, 28, 29, 30, 31, 32, 35, 36, 37, 39, 40, 44, 45, 46, 47, 48, 51, 52, 54, 55, 56, 57, 58, 60, 61, 65, 68, 70, 71, 74, 75, 76, 77, 79, 80, 81, 82, 84, 85, 86, 89, 95, 97, 114, 119, 131, 132, 133, 134, 135, 136, 137, 138, 139, 141, 142, 145, 151, 152, 153, 156, 158, 160, 161, 164, 165, 166, 167, 170, 171, 174, 175, 176, 177, 184
McDowell, Gen. Irvin 3, 8, 10, 11, 24, 25, 30, 37, 38, 44, 45, 77, 80, 82, 84, 85, 135, 136, 137, 138, 142, 145, 174, 175
McFarland, Capt. John D. 128
McIntyre, Lt. William 125
McKinney, Col. Robert M., C.S.A. 54
McLaws, Gen. Lafayette, C.S.A. 54, 55, 117, 118, 145, 150, 189
Meade, Gen. George G. 4, 5, 17, 27, 186
Meade, Maj. R.K., C.S.A. 160
Meagher, Gen. Francis 119, 121, 126, 149, 170, 179, 184
Mechanicsville, Va. 79, 117, 140, 142, 143, 145, 150, 152, 177
USS *Merrimac* (see CSS *Virginia*)
Miles, Lt. Nelson A. 115, 122, 124
Mill Springs, Kentucky, Battle of 16, 133
Miller, Col. James 122, 124
Miller, Capt. Orzo 101
Mills, J.D. 59
USS *Minnesota* 26, 70
USS *Monitor* 27, 42, 70, 74, 75
Morell, Gen. George W. 82, 145, 146, 148, 186
Morrill, Sgt. W.T. 104
Mott, Smith B. 86
Mountain Department 28, 174

Naglee, Gen. Henry M. 60, 91, 96, 97, 98, 99, 105, 180, 186
USS *Naugatauck* 74
Neel, W.H.R. 57
New Bridge Road 140, 153
New Cold Harbor, Va. 84, 145
New Market Heights, Va. 139, 160
New Market Road 158
New Orleans, Louisiana 16, 133
Nicolay, John 40
Nine Mile Road 93, 94, 99, 105, 108, 109, 111, 119, 125, 129, 140
19th Massachusetts Infantry Regiment 110, 179

19th Mississippi Infantry Regiment 190
9th Alabama Infantry Regiment 181, 190
93rd Pennsylvania Infantry 100, 101, 102, 180, 185
Norfolk, Va. 14, 41, 51, 70, 73, 174
North Atlantic Blockading Squadron 44

O'Bierne, Capt. James 195
Occoquan River 13
Odell, Moses 21
Old Tavern, Va. 140
100th New York Infantry Regiment 92, 180, 186
102nd Pennsylvania Infantry Regiment 100, 101, 180, 185
Orr, Capt. Robert 106

Palfrey, John C. 90
Palmer, Gen. Innis M. 91, 180, 185
Palmetto Sharpshooters Infantry Regiment 105, 190
Pamunkey River 76, 77, 82
CSS *Patrick Henry* 74, 75
Peck, Gen. John G. 88, 100, 101, 102, 180, 186
Pegram, Capt. William R., C.S.A. 143
Pender, Col. Dorsey, C.S.A. 109, 119, 146, 191
Peninsula Campaign 2, 5, 6, 27, 47, 56, 65, 73, 165, 170, 172, 173, 175, 177
Pennsylvania Bucktails 143
Pettigrew, Gen. James J., C.S.A. 108, 109, 111, 112, 119, 181
Pinkerton, Allen 11, 12, 56, 76, 144, 173
Pollard, Edward 73
Port Republic, Va. 81, 82
Port Royal, S.C. 133
USS *Port Royal* 74
Porter, Gen. Fitz John 2, 46, 61, 71, 79, 82, 84, 85, 140, 141, 142, 143, 144, 146, 148, 149, 151, 152, 163, 164, 170, 177, 186
Powhite Creek 140
Pryor, Gen. Roger, C.S.A. 118, 122, 123, 128, 129, 181, 190
Purcell, Sgt. Hiram 98, 195

Rains, Gen. Gabriel J., C.S.A. 59, 67, 94, 98, 99, 102, 181
Randall, James G. 21
Randolph, George 130
Ransom, Gen. Robert, C.S.A. 140, 191
Rappahannock River 15, 27, 37, 52
Reagan, John 130
Regan, Jeremiah 75

Reynolds, Gen. John F. 143, 150, 186
Rich Mountain, battle of 7, 134
Rich Mountain Campaign 7
Richardson, Gen. Israel 61, 69, 71, 110, 115, 119, 120, 121, 124, 149, 184
Richmond, Va. 1, 7, 14, 23, 30, 36, 41, 42, 44, 51, 52, 56, 64, 71, 73, 77, 80, 84, 113, 134, 136, 138, 141, 142, 152, 171, 172, 179
Ripley, Gen. Roswell S., C.S.A. 144, 189
Rippey, Col. Oliver 106
USS *Roanoke* 26
Rodes, Gen. Robert, C.S.A. 13, 94, 98, 99, 102, 103, 105, 181, 189
Roe, Alfred 169
Rogers, Commander John 74, 75, 161, 165
Rosser, Col. Thomas, C.S.A. 160

Sands, Maj. Robert M., C.S.A. 168
Savage's Station, Va. 151, 154, 156
Scales, Col. Alfred, C.S.A. 123
Scott, Gen. Winfield 8, 18, 19
Scott, J. Traviso 59
2nd Florida Infantry Regiment 95, 96, 114, 181, 190
2nd Michigan Infantry Regiment 102, 180, 185
2nd New Hampshire Infantry Regiment 130, 185
2nd United States Cavalry Regiment 149
2nd Vermont Infantry Regiment 159, 187
Sedgwick, Gen. John 27, 61, 115, 119, 179, 184
Seven Pines, Va. *see* Fair Oaks
17th Mississippi Infantry Regiment 54, 189
17th Virginia Infantry Regiment 87, 103, 104, 114, 180, 190
7th Georgia Infantry Regiment 54, 189
7th Massachusetts Infantry Regiment 100, 106, 109, 127, 129, 180, 185
7th New Jersey Infantry Regiment 66, 185
72nd Pennsylvania Infantry Regiment 110, 179, 185
Seward, William H. 29, 77
Shafter, Lt. William 195
Shields, Gen. James 77, 81, 175
Shiloh, Tn., Battle of 1, 4, 7
6th Alabama Infantry Regiment 62, 103, 114, 181, 189
6th Georgia Infantry Regiment 59

6th New Jersey Infantry Regiment 66, 129, 180, 185
6th New York Light Artillery 65, 180
6th North Carolina Infantry Regiment 109, 111, 166, 181, 188
6th South Carolina Infantry Regiment 105, 128, 180, 190
6th United States Cavalry Regiment 60, 62
6th Vermont Infantry Regiment 54, 187
65th New York Infantry Regiment 106, 109, 180, 185
61st New York Infantry Regiment 124, 125, 126, 179, 184
61st Pennsylvania Infantry Regiment 106, 110, 180, 185
64th New York Infantry Regiment 124, 125, 179, 185
69th Pennsylvania Infantry Regiment 33, 110, 179, 184
62nd New York Infantry 101, 180, 185
67th New York Infantry Regiment 106, 185
66th New York Infantry Regiment 122, 179, 184
63rd Pennsylvania Infantry Regiment 87, 162, 180, 185
Smith, Maj. George 106
Smith, Gen. Gustavus W., C.S.A. 1, 52, 53, 64, 69, 85, 86, 90, 92, 93, 94, 100, 109, 111, 112, 116, 117, 118, 127, 130, 173, 181
Smith, Gen. William F. 54, 60, 65, 146, 159, 187
Sneden, Pvt. Robert K. 169
Spear, Lt. Col. George 106
Spencer, Maj. William 124, 125, 126
Stanton, Edwin 12, 17, 24, 26, 27, 29, 31, 35, 36, 37, 39, 42, 55, 70, 74, 77, 84, 131, 137, 138, 144, 151, 152, 161, 174, 175
Stevens, Thaddeus 17
Stone, Gen. Charles P. 21, 22
Stoneman, Gen. George 60, 61, 62, 82
Stoughton, Col. Edwin 55
Stuart, Gen. James E.B., C.S.A. 7, 60, 85, 117, 130, 138, 139, 142, 191
Sully, Col. Alfred 110, 111, 184
Sumner, Charles 60
Sumner, Gen. Edwin V. 24, 25, 30, 60, 61, 65, 66, 67, 77, 85, 95, 108, 109, 110, 112, 119, 154, 162, 179, 184
Sykes, Gen. George 61, 82, 145, 146, 148, 149, 186

10th Louisiana Infantry Regiment 187
10th Massachusetts Infantry Regiment 100, 101, 115, 169, 180, 185
10th Virginia Infantry Regiment 165
3rd Alabama Infantry Regiment 168, 169, 181, 189
3rd Louisiana Infantry Regiment 143
3rd Maine Infantry Regiment 128, 129, 180, 185
3rd Michigan Infantry Regiment 102, 180, 185
3rd Vermont Infantry Regiment 54, 187
13th North Carolina Infantry Regiment 123, 181
13th Pennsylvania Infantry Regiment 128
38th New York Infantry Regiment 126, 129
38th Virginia Infantry Regiment 67, 95, 97, 114, 181, 190
34th Georgia Infantry Regiment 143
34th New York Infantry Regiment 110, 179, 184
37th New York Infantry 102, 180, 185
36th New York Infantry 100, 169, 180, 185
Thomas, Gen. George H. 16, 133, 176, 177
Thomas, Gen. Lorenzo 36, 37, 38, 46
Toombs, Gen. Robert, C.S.A. 54, 55, 189
Tucker, John 31, 76
21st Virginia Infantry Regiment 188
24th Virginia Infantry Regiment 67, 95, 181, 190
22nd Massachusetts Infantry Regiment 58, 186
23rd North Carolina Infantry Regiment 189
23rd Pennsylvania Infantry Regiment 105, 106, 110, 180, 185
23rd Virginia Infantry Regiment 67

Union Mills, Va. 13
United States Military Academy, West Point 8, 18, 67, 90
United States Balloon Corps 53, 54, 58
Urbanna, Va. 15, 30
Urbanna Plan 12, 23, 174

Van Wyck, Col Charles H. 60
Vicksburg, Ms., Battle of 5
CSS *Virginia* 26, 27, 35, 36, 42, 70, 71, 72

Wade, Benjamin 17, 18, 21, 29, 39
Wadsworth, Gen. James G. 25, 37, 38, 81, 174
Walker, Gen. John G., C.S.A. 52, 191
Ward, Col. John H.H. 126, 128, 129
Warren, Gen. Gouverneur K. 82
Warwick River 45, 46, 47, 55, 60
Washington, George 17, 18, 24, 76, 174
Washington, Martha 76
Washington, D.C. 3, 7, 12, 13, 14, 17, 18, 27, 30, 31, 38, 52, 81, 84, 137, 138, 174, 176

Webb, Gen. Alexander S. 88, 95
Wessells, Gen. Henry W. 91, 180, 186
West Point, N.Y. 8, 18, 67, 90
White House on the Pamunkey 76, 77, 126, 135, 152, 161
White Oak Swamp 102, 117, 151, 153, 156, 158
Whiting, Maj. Jasper, C.S.A. 142
Whiting, Gen. William H.C., C.S.A. 71, 72, 90, 93, 108, 109, 111, 117, 127, 142, 148, 167, 188
Wilcox, Gen. Cadmus M., C.S.A. 52, 99, 118, 122, 128, 129, 148, 163, 166, 181, 190
Wilderness, Va., battle of 5, 103
Williamsburg, Va. 62, 64, 65, 66, 68, 69, 70, 132
Williamsburg Road 44, 79, 90, 91, 92, 94, 100, 101, 102, 106, 118, 119, 128, 140, 141, 154
Willis Church Road 156, 161, 163, 168
Wills, George 60
Wilson, Col. William T., C.S.A. 54
Wirz, Henry 1
Wise, George 103
Wool, Gen. John E. 30, 36, 70, 71, 174
Worsham, John 142

Yorktown, Va. 34, 35, 36, 42, 45, 47, 48, 51, 52, 56, 57, 65, 74, 132

Zook, Col. Samuel K. 122

www.ingramcontent.com/pod-product-compliance
Ingram Content Group UK Ltd.
Pitfield, Milton Keynes, MK11 3LW, UK
UKHW050527150426
5217IPUK00026B/1837